'Often, academic texts by writers from outs
struggle to engage with and bring the u ne other
into the predominantly white middle-class world of counselling and psychotherapy.

Yet, not often enough, we come across texts like this one, *Therapy in Colour*, where a plethora of writers of colour have come together to present what is a both a clarion call for their witnessing and a love letter to the profession we all work within. These are therapists of colour from across the generations, who have come together to present some of the most interesting and far-reaching thoughts and clinical ideas that counsellors of colour have had maybe for a generation.

This text therefore does much to challenge this stereotypical academic ideal. In the way it is constructed, in the way that it is written, with a definite feeling of accessibility and a marginalization of the academic jargon which can leave many counselling and psychotherapy students of colour cold and often rightly disengaged.

Honouring everything from the writings and the perspectives of some of our ancestors, to the words and feeling of those practitioners of colour who hold intersecting identities, this broad-reaching, yet still incredibly dense tome does much to plant our flag in the multicultural world within which psychotherapy resides.

A book like this is a bit like a rare event. It therefore deserves to be both witnessed and read and studied.'

—Dr Dwight Turner, Course Leader in Humanistic Psychotherapy, University of Brighton and author of Intersections of Privilege and Otherness in Counselling and Psychotherapy

'*Therapy in Colour* is an expansive and in-depth text exploring psychology from a variety of Africanist voices, for whom we have been waiting. Each chapter invites the reader to become vulnerable in seeing through the eyes of those who have been witness to/healers of deep suffering because of racism. Each clinician shares the wisdom of their lives from the first chapter to the end of the edited volume. *Therapy in Colour* is a brilliant teaching for practising clinicians, psychoanalytical students as well as members of the general public. The heart of the book is the intense and personable way each author writes about raciality, racism and the need for introspection into the patient as well as the therapeutic process. This is based on a constantly deepening view of the inclusion of Africanist ethnicity and principles as essential to the healing process.

The book is a work of creative art, blending ideas, ideals and a soft compassionate gaze for those engaged in the work as therapists and their Africanist patients. *Therapy in Colour* appears as an act of love in motion, giving language to all those places within our psyche that have been hungry for racial understanding of Afrocentrism culture, within the field of psychology. The writing within this book is a gift to inspire us all.'

—*Fanny Brewster, PhD, MFA, LP, author of* The Racial Complex: A Jungian Perspective on Culture and Race

'This new book deftly navigates readers through a path that deeply analyses Eurocentric "givens and perspectives" on issues relating to mental health and trauma. A core tenet is the reconfiguration of therapy by taking stock of Black communities' historical lived experience and drawing upon their cultural traditions to enrich therapeutic practice. If you are interested in anti-racist therapeutic practice, this book is a must-read.'

—*David Weaver, President of BACP*

Therapy in Colour

of related interest

Overcoming Everyday Racism
Building Resilience and Wellbeing in the Face of
Discrimination and Microaggressions
Susan Cousins
ISBN 978 1 78592 850 5
eISBN 978 1 78592 851 2

Cultural Perspectives on Mental Wellbeing
Spiritual Interpretations of Symptoms in Medical Practice
Natalie Tobert
Foreword by Michael Cornwall
ISBN 978 1 78592 084 4
eISBN 978 1 78450 345 1

Working with Ethnicity, Race and Culture in Mental Health
A Handbook for Practitioners
Hári Sewell
Foreword by Suman Fernando
ISBN 978 1 84310 621 0
eISBN 978 1 84642 855 5

Cultural Humility in Art Therapy
Applications for Practice, Research, Social Justice, Self-Care, and Pedagogy
Louvenia C. Jackson, PhD, MFT, ATR-BC
Foreword by Dr Melanie Tervalon
ISBN 978 1 78592 643 3
eISBN 978 1 78592 644 0

Therapy in Colour

Intersectional, Anti-Racist and Intercultural Approaches by Therapists of Colour

EDITED BY
Dr Isha Mckenzie-Mavinga, Kris Black,
Karen Carberry and Eugene Ellis

Jessica Kingsley Publishers
London and Philadelphia

First published in Great Britain in 2023 by Jessica Kingsley Publishers
An imprint of John Murray Press

3

Copyright © Dr Isha Mckenzie-Mavinga, Kris Black,
Karen Carberry and Eugene Ellis 2023

The right of Dr Isha Mckenzie-Mavinga, Kris Black, Karen Carberry and
Eugene Ellis to be identified as the Author of the Work has been asserted by
them in accordance with the Copyright, Designs and Patents Act 1988.

Chapter 3 'The Racist Gaze: Bearing Witness' was originally published
in *Racist States of Mind: Understanding the Perversion of Curiosity and
Concern* by Narendra Keval (published by Karnac Books in 2016),
and is reprinted with kind permission of Karnac Books.

All rights reserved. No part of this publication may be reproduced, stored
in a retrieval system, or transmitted, in any form or by any means without
the prior written permission of the publisher, nor be otherwise circulated
in any form of binding or cover other than that in which it is published and
without a similar condition being imposed on the subsequent purchaser.

A CIP catalogue record for this title is available from the
British Library and the Library of Congress

ISBN 978 1 83997 570 7
eISBN 978 1 83997 571 4

Printed and bound by CPI Group (UK) Ltd, Croydon, CR0 4YY

Jessica Kingsley Publishers' policy is to use papers that are natural,
renewable and recyclable products and made from wood grown in
sustainable forests. The logging and manufacturing processes are expected
to conform to the environmental regulations of the country of origin.

Jessica Kingsley Publishers
Carmelite House
50 Victoria Embankment
London EC4Y 0DZ

www.jkp.com

John Murray Press
Part of Hodder & Stoughton Limited
An Hachette UK Company

Contents

Acknowledgements 10

Preface. 11
Eugene Ellis

Introduction 14

Part I: Colour, Creativity and Anti-Racist Reflection

1. Adaptations to Psychotherapy for Effective Treatment of
   Black and Minority Ethnic People 37
   Lennox K. Thomas

2. The Racist Gaze: Bearing Witness 51
   Dr Narendra Keval

3. Can the Image Bridge Our Differences? 62
   Ann Boxill

4. An Encounter Between a White Patient and a Black
   Psychotherapist 75
   Wanderley M. Santos

5. Counsellor Training and Beyond: A Practical Application . . . 84
   Kiren Khosla

Part II: Training in Context of Pasts, Presents and Futures

6. Two Black Tutors! 107
   Patmarie Coleman & Paulette Gibson

7. Misery Loves Company, But There's No Need to Walk Alone . 119
Lydia Puricelli-Culverwell

8. Myself as Therapist, Trainee, and the Power of Creativity . . . 134
Symone Stephens-Morgan

Part III: CPD: Supervision and Self-Care – Our Mental, Spiritual, Physical and Emotional Health

9. Conversation About Co-Supervision with Two Senior African Heritage Therapists 147
Dr Isha Mckenzie-Mavinga & Arike Grant

10. Sitting With Discomfort or Embodying Joy? 160
Moriam Grillo

11. Embodied Ancestors 173
Roshmi S. Lovatt

Part IV: Therapeutic Needs and Psychological Wellbeing: In the Context of Identity, Culture and Belonging

12. Transracial Adoption 191
Anthea Benjamin

13. The Power of a Name. 206
Umaa Thampu

14. Belonging: Who Decides? 220
Karen Minikin

15. Embodied Experiencing – Relational Learning. 230
Carmen Joanne Ablack

16. The Impact of Racism and Culture on Identity. 244
Gita Patel

17. Character Work 256
Shirani Situnayake

Part V: Celebrating Our Intersectionality: Ancestral Constellations – African Healing Contexts, Traditions and Origins

18. A Queer Love Letter: 267
Joel Simpson

19. Ancestral Constellations 281
Sonya Welch-Moring

20. A Journey in Decolonizing Therapy 294
Oye Agoro

21. Effective Anti-Racist Practice in Counselling and Therapy
Training 312
Tonia Mihill

Epilogue 326
Kris Black

About the Co-Editors. 330

About the Authors 333

Subjerct Index. 341

Author Index 345

Acknowledgements

I am eternally grateful for the privilege of participating in a community of black people and people of colour. Thanks to the co-editors and therapists gathering their wisdom, insights, skills and experience for the wellbeing of our village and those who support healing from the trauma of racism.

Isha

Thanking all the clients and families I have had the opportunity to work with, who have added to and enhanced my reflective practice and interventions. I salute you for your courage to have those difficult conversations, explore generational stories and make a difference – that makes a difference.

Karen

I feel honoured to be part of the journey to bringing this publication to light and to work alongside my co-editors. Thank you to our beautiful community of black, brown and people of colour practitioners for your unceasing enthusiasm, dialogue and inspiration.

Eugene

I want to dedicate the labour of this work, with love and gratitude to our ancestors, and to our children past present and future.

Kris

Preface

EUGENE ELLIS

This important publication is a collaborative effort in every sense of the word. The project began with a series of discussions with my colleagues back in 2016 within the Black, African and Asian Therapy Network (BAATN), of which I am the founder and director. The discussions took place predominantly within the BAATN leadership team. BAATN is a network of Black and Asian therapists who practice in the UK and it is a place for the community to connect with ideas, information and people that support Black and Asian psychological health and mental fitness. BAATN is also seen as a 'thought leader' in the area of teaching, delivering programmes and networking with the largest group of therapists of colour in the UK. These therapists, and therapists in training, are at the cutting edge of honing established theoretical models and developing new ways of working that encapsulate the self of the therapist as an important construct in the therapeutic alliance.

The discussions within the BAATN leadership team reflected on the then-current crop of books related to the racialized experience in the context of therapy. This led us to aspire to create an anthology that we would have liked to have had available to us when we were students. We wanted a publication that inspired Black people and people of colour who are currently training as therapists or thinking of training; we wanted a focus on the next generation. It was also important that this publication articulated new theoretical perspectives useful for both white practitioners and practitioners of colour, which supported therapy with Black clients and people of colour clients through an intersectional lens, including the intersection of gender, sexuality and relationship diversity and colourism. We imagined that we could also offer lay Black people and people of colour a glimpse into the world of counselling for those interested in exploring their psychological lives.

Dr Isha Mckenzie-Mavinga, author of *The Challenge of Racism in*

Therapeutic Practice: Engaging with Oppression in Practice and Supervision, was initially tasked with reaching out to the BAATN membership and bringing the project to life. Integrative arts psychotherapist Kris Black soon followed. As the project gathered momentum, especially during the period of raised consciousness following the murder of George Floyd, Karen Carberry, family and systemic psychotherapist and myself, Eugene Ellis, joined the co-editing team.

Birthed out of the intensification of the Black Lives Matter (BLM) movement, this collection of works incorporates a global outlook and addresses the intersectional response required for organizations seeking an understanding of the myriad ways in which Black people and people of colour are internally affected. *Therapy in Colour* emphasizes the importance of addressing ways to support the mental wellbeing of these groups within the backdrop of the challenge of institutional racism within therapy training and therapeutic approaches. We were keen to cover the challenges within therapy practice from the perspective of therapy training, therapist supervision and being a client.

Of note is the posthumous opening work by Lennox Thomas. Thomas was a thought leader, a mentor to many and an inspirational Black man. He was the first senior probation officer of African Caribbean origin who went on to become a consultant psychoanalytical psychotherapist. His historical contributions to the field of psychotherapy and counselling since the 1970s advocated for the transformation of the discipline to account for the impact of colonization, war, ethnic cleansing, immigration and assimilation. Thomas's chapter presents the historical backdrop for the chapters that follow and is a call to arms for the integration of culturally sensitive counselling services into the mainstream.

Another posthumous contribution was made by my dear colleague Arike Grant, who co-authored a chapter with Dr Isha Mckenzie-Mavinga. This chapter is a discourse on co-supervision between two prominent psychotherapists from within the Black community. As an individual, Arike was a major inspiration to me, who kept me connected to the type of Black man I wanted to be – he still does. His ability to get to clear thinking within the midst of emotional storms was legendary, and for me, his contribution to the development of BAATN was invaluable.

We feel honoured to have put together a distinctive collection of voices, both young and old, which reinforce the importance of intersectional, anti-racist, and intercultural practice that meets the therapeutic needs of Black people and people of colour. Many of the authors in this collection are well known to me or are colleagues I have worked with over the years. Without exception, all of the authors have made significant contributions to bringing therapy and wellness to Black and people of colour communities in the UK. Each one is a pioneer in their own right.

This ground-breaking text elucidates content lacking in training manuals, educational programmes, supervision discussions and clinical team reflection. Readers will take away insights, experiences and examples of professional conduct that address training, supervision and ways of working with the complex and traumatic impact of racism with a balance of both academic rigour and personal reflection. I hope you will agree that collectively the authors have addressed the gaps in therapeutic practice inherent in Eurocentric perspectives and brought together diverse perspectives and therapeutic approaches based on the various needs of students, therapists and clients that have not been previously shared in a single volume.

Introduction

The Colour of Power uniquely gives our society a framework for that discussion and potential change...[and] helps keep this renewed positive momentum for change on the right track. If we're getting the top right, it's more likely we are changing the organization's culture, and with that transformation throughout. (Woollsey & Patel, 2021, p.1)

Often books of this ilk will begin with the impact of colonial history globally and its impact on the subjugated, with a literary of racism, misdiagnosis in service, and professionalization of clinicians in training from a narrow white Eurocentric view (Newnes, 2021; Majors, Carberry & Ransaw, 2020; Daneshpour, 2017). This is of course important, and yet on this occasion, we will dilute the strengths of the global majority by initially giving so much narrative in the opening paragraphs of introduction to a book that brings the appropriate challenges and the strengths covered extensively within the chapters. In addition, our stories do not need to be diluted, in fact our lived experience also brings an *overcoming* strategy and technique, together with 'aha' moments, where we begin to understand how our everyday racialized struggles, and the effects of these, have embodied our trauma (Guzzetti, 2022).

Our black and brown histories often illustrate how our elders benevolently shared their excellence in succent timing, and commitment to develop astonishing tactics and techniques through clinical and educative transformation for generational community equity. Elders such as Florence Zengeni, who graduated with a master's degree at 79, illustrate perseverance through a lifetime of adversity, while encouraging the younger generations through their lived experience to continue to succeed (Sigodo, 2022). Transformation and change require the development and application of knowledge production that is fresh, and unusual from that which is taught in our institutions. It is birthed out of the lived experiences of the individual, couple, family and collective who have engaged in the journey out of the prism of the othering of their perspectives. In the defining of knowledge production, we can draw on many conversations through cultural lenses in our clinical and research fields that inform us of our globalized majority experience across the life cycle (Daneshpour, 2017; Arnold, 2012; Boyd-Franklin, 1989). This can include drawing on theories developed by our elders and clinical peers on the impact of migration and attachment (Arnold, 2012) to augment existing theoretical knowledge of popular theorists who have honed their own theories by observing the indigenous interactions of families in Uganda and applying a reflective construct to clients in so-called western culture.

Linda Tuhiwai Smith, in her book, *Decolonizing Methodologies. Research and Indigenous Peoples* (2012, p.68), cites that:

> most of our disciplines and fields of knowledge, and our cultural world view is grounded in western ideology...anthropology is one of the closest associated with the study of the Other...taking the primitive society as their specialist subject, but in practice (so called) primitive society proved to be their own society (as they understood it) seen in a distorting mirror.

Thus, in producing knowledge our voice of colour is no longer silenced. Rather, the lived experience is evidenced by how transformation takes place, while utilizing one's narrative. This then illustrates 'that practice research in this situation can play an important role in a knowledge production scaffolding a new understanding of professionalism and expertise' (Russman, 2011, p.28).

Often, there is a dilemma in practising therapy about sharing one's story without taking advantage of one's own anonymity. Themes of secrecy and shame abound (Imber-Black, 1993). There is an ethical risk to one's reputation, and yet sharing the process of knowledge production is couched in openness, vulnerability, strength and action, recognition, identity and collective transformation. Often, we as therapists are asked, 'How has your life story led you to a profession in psychotherapy?' As someone from the black majority, I experience that we often recoil from sharing something so personal with our peers, clinicians or supervisors. We do not want to be stigmatized and put into a basket with others who look like us, whom we, or our white colleagues might treat as statistically suffering from a specific condition, or as 'hard to reach'. Such is the trauma of not exploring reflectively the impact of systems of racism (Moreland-Capuia, 2021). In the counselling room, self-disclosure by the therapist is often frowned upon in training, and yet, in session, parents may often ask, 'Do you have children?' to ascertain whether we can indeed empathize and understand their unique parenting positioning of a child with emotional, physical or mental health difficulties. What do we do with the strong black woman trope, when our own lived experience may have mirrored aspects of our clients? In reflecting on this dilemma, I deduced that we could use these lived experiences to extend our reach into knowledge production for sharing across the collective communities of the global majority, and with our allies to meet past the middle of our reflections and formulations from a position of strength, rather than 'permission seeking', to show that we are more than statistics. Otherwise 'We miss the opportunity to see Black families from a lens of intellect, resilience, wisdom' (Carberry, 2021, p.47).

We are more than our statistics

Self-advocacy is an important tool, and my journey into therapeutic training originated with a career in organizational change, which gently made a segue into a clinical career, following a traumatic car accident some 30 years ago, in which my then five-year-old daughter fell into a coma, after sustaining a traumatic brain injury. For my own self-care, I underwent six months of therapy for post-traumatic stress disorder (PTSD).

Although she is much recovered, the journey to healing, from a parental perspective, was further aided by commissioning an independent team of individual practitioners, clinicians and teachers to deliver an ambitious programme of recovery, contrary to the suggestion of other professionals to reduce my aspirations for her to a lower level of expectation. It is from this lens that I can understand the frustrations of black families who employ a 'healthy cultural suspicion' (Boyd-Franklin, 1989) when attempting to access mental health services to reduce distress. Blighted by racism, and misdiagnosis in healthcare, inappropriate service provision has been comprehensively documented (Majors *et al.*, 2020). Conversely, it is also this tenacity that drove me as a black person – and other black and brown people too – to forge a path of achievement and confidence for our communities to succeed in life.

After 'assessment', a neuropsychologist suggested that my daughter should be enrolled in a special school, and situated not near a window, but in the centre of the class to avoid distraction. I suggested my daughter would be back in private school within two years. I was informed that I 'needed to be realistic'. Offended, by the 'the tone', and inference, I decided further discussion would be futile. My own experience of being educated, both at primary and high school within the same region, led me to believe that black children were viewed as educationally subnormal (Coard, 2021) and therefore I could not offer up the next generation to this didactic approach. My daughter needed to be given a chance to regain her excellence. We can see the importance of parental and community advocacy nationally exacted in the recent incident of a young black girl racially profiled and disgracefully strip-searched at school (Thomas, 2022). We must be vigilant and aware, and share our tools of advocacy.

Equipped with my three-year psychology training, and after 18 months of rehabilitation for my daughter, there were many signs of confidence and improvement. We then applied for the next opening of occasional places at an excellent preparatory school for assessment and entry in a year's time. Out of five applicants for three places, she was offered a place, and moved schools when she was eight; she has now completed her education, has a degree and is successful in her career. As parents, our role is to continue to strengthen the little person for adulthood and provide a template for safe supportive networks.

We are more than statistics; we are more than conquers
I have previously discussed Carberry's statement that:

> Black clients and families are often portrayed in literature, film, and clinical papers with deficit models, and reported as hard to reach. As practitioners, educated through a western lens we may miss the opportunity to see our clinicians, or black families from a lens of intellect, resilience, wisdom, and lose the opportunity quickly to connect and build hope. (Carberry, 2021, p.47)

Yet despite the recent flurry of books on racialized experiences of people of colour, the depth of nuanced experiences of trainees and experienced therapists is not often contained in a single volume. Herein is the setting of the stage for our book, *Therapy in Colour*, addressing ways to support the mental wellbeing of our community, in a post-pandemic period of review and challenge to institutional racism, therapy training and therapeutic approaches. The structure of this book provides insights, experiences and examples of professional conduct that address training, supervision, and ways of working with the complex and traumatic impact of racism, and gaps in training that have previously been based exclusively on Eurocentric perspectives.

It will introduce and explore perspectives and approaches based on the diverse needs of students, therapists and clients, that have not previously been shared. This book will enhance psychology, psychiatry, psychotherapy, social work, occupational therapy, counsellor training and thinking in the field of social care and humanities. It will also encompass and include descriptive terms that may be familiar or unfamiliar to the reader regarding people of colour, such as 'black'. 'Black', either with a small or capital letter, and the term 'coloured' are included in the authors' texts. Not only does this inclusion present itself as an expression of how and why we work as black, African, Caribbean and South Asian therapists, it also supports the development of critical thinking about black, African, Caribbean and Asian training and therapeutic needs, and demonstrates the importance of exploring, acknowledging and celebrating our inter-sectionality as people who are impacted by colonialism and white racism. Therefore, in keeping with Lord Woollsey and Rita Patel's highly regarded rhetoric at the beginning of this text, the intentional and transformational power of knowledge production should permeate throughout all areas, including training organizations, developmental models of therapeutic and supervisory practice, and research.

Structure of the book

Therapy in Colour has 26 contributors, and 21 chapters, followed by an Epilogue. There are five parts in total:

Part I: Colour, Creativity and Anti-Racist Reflection

Part II: Training in Context of Pasts, Presents and Futures

Part III: CPD: Supervision and Self-Care – Our Mental, Spiritual, Physical and Emotional Health

Part IV: Therapeutic Needs and Psychological Wellbeing: In the Context of Identity, Culture and Belonging

Part V: Celebrating Our Intersectionality: Ancestral Constellations – African Healing Contexts, Traditions and Origins

Part I: Colour, Creativity and Anti-Racist Reflection

How we are encountered, and what we encounter in our journey for healing through the mental health system and training courses is well documented in our first section. It comprises five chapters, beginning with an esteemed author who is giant in our clinical field, with 'Chapter 1: Adaptations to Psychotherapy for Effective Treatment of Black and Minority Ethnic People' by *Lennox K. Thomas*. In this chapter, the author's discussion arises from questions such as: What are the issues that lead those who might be termed Black and Minority Ethnic (BME) to not seek support for their mental health? What changes to mental health practice might lead BME individuals to use therapy and other forms of mental health support? The author states that societal racism and prejudice in the UK mental health system has historically led professionals to regard BME people as incapable of using talking therapy. This ran alongside the fact that a disproportionate number of BME people were in the mental health system. These assumptions were challenged by research funded by the Department of Health in 1992 that found that BME individuals did, in fact, use therapy when the service had them in mind and when the service was provided with sensitivity.

Issues of shame and secretiveness in Caribbean populations – an attitude born out of historical enslavement – has led Caribbean people to not 'tell their business' to white people and white institutions. In addition to the lack of trust between black and white people complicating the access to support, the legacy of historical enslavement has also disrupted trust between black people through an internalization of racism, which significantly complicates the transference between black therapists and black clients.

When negotiating the route to becoming an enabling therapist, shame and envy need to be worked with between black therapists and black clients. In the transference, there are very likely to be notions of black solidarity along with the nagging fear that, as a black person, you might have 'sold out'. To release internal change and desire within the black client, these critical and challenging issues must first be resolved within the black therapist.

As a post-slavery population, black people have many things to unlearn alongside shame, secretiveness and internalized racism. These include patterns of separation and loss and broken attachments passed down through generations. Therapy then can support the process of unlearning and healing. Case vignettes are used to illustrate working with negative psychological constructs and helping to restore healthy functioning. The chapter concludes with an exploration of the education and training of therapists and the importance of making adjustments to the delivery of training and integrating cultural ideas into therapeutic theory.

Our following text delves further into self-reflection in 'Chapter 2: The Racist Gaze: Bearing Witness' by *Narendra Keval.* The author skilfully begins an exploration of the psychological trauma of being at the receiving end of racism. He describes how the racist gaze impinges silently on the psyche, affecting feelings of self-worth. When the racist gaze of another has colonized the sense of self, the conditions are set for profound confusion in thinking, feeling and identity. The psychological trauma of racism is a malignancy that has many faces, both overt and covert. To be told relentlessly that you are inferior or not good enough is to experience a daily assault on the self that involves not only what is unwittingly said in words and gestures, but what is not said. These types of assault on the capacity for freedom of thought are often caught up with feelings of weakness, shame and humiliation.

Three cases are presented where racist states of mind have permeated into the psyche resulting in a lack of capacity for creative thought, self-reflection or empathy. Through the author's self-reflection, we are invited into the therapist's challenge of creating a space that allows freedom of movement in thinking and feeling and the type of therapeutic engagement that can witness, empathise, and articulate an inner agony that had previously gone unvoiced. Through the author's struggle with his own internal freedom and his attempts to reach his patients, we get a glimpse of what enables victims of racism to face the unnameable, develop their own sense of inner freedom and expand on their abilities to protect themselves.

'Chapter 3: Can the Image Bridge Our Differences?' by *Ann Boxill* expands this theme and draws on the use of creativity. This chapter sets out to explore the impression this author formed about art psychotherapy while training and how important it is that practitioners recognize and process their own ingrained bias through the creative and/or psychoanalytic process. Experiences of microaggression, discrimination and being negatively labelled while training or in work placements highlight that racism continues to endure in spaces that should be safe. For example, BME NHS staff are at least twice as likely to be disciplined than their white counterparts (Archibong & Darr, 2010). Personal accounts and vignettes from practice are used to consider theories of social constructivism and psychodynamic phenomena that help to explain why racism and other inequalities persist, despite being socially unacceptable.

Working with racism in the consulting room, together with the acknowledgement of difference in colour between client and patient is documented in 'Chapter 4: An Encounter Between a White Patient and a Black Psychotherapist' by *Wanderley M. Santos*. The author posits that part of the experience of being a black psychotherapist is dealing with racial power dynamics in the consulting room, and discusses the challenge of addressing their first-ever patient's unconscious racist state of mind. The patient, an upper-middle-class, white, English woman, had learned to transfer her unwanted feelings onto people with dark skin. When the patient was feeling stuck in her treatment, a racial attack would occur. The patient made some initial attempts to shut the therapist out, isolating them in the sessions by seeing herself as superior. Because of this, the therapist felt inadequate in their role as a psychotherapist in training.

At first, the therapist found it hard to understand this split, typical of the paranoid schizoid position with racial elements. After understanding this dynamic, however, the therapist could sustain the position as her psychotherapist, containing and conveying to the patient the aggression she was expressing. The patient moved towards a depressive position where the splits took place less frequently, and where therapist and patient could co-exist in the room. The therapist's capacity to deal with the patient's distress and aggression was fundamental to building a therapeutic alliance. It gave the therapist the confidence to use their countertransference to guide the clinical interventions. Through the treatment, the patient experienced having a space to explore her uncomfortable feelings, including those related to the therapist, with someone who could cope with her distress and aggression. Towards the end of her treatment, the patient could hold the therapist as an ambivalent figure in her mind, different from one who could not help her before. This challenging clinical encounter helped the therapist tune in to what was arising in the work with patients in the long run. Upskilling in working with racist interactions within the therapeutic relationship is difficult enough for the experienced practitioner and trainee with specialist supervision. However, the training experience is sensitively explored in 'Chapter 5: Counsellor Training and Beyond: A Practical Application' by *Kiren Khosla* as a reflection on the author's personal experience of racism on their training course. The author explicitly names the issues as 'We're sick of hearing about your differences', 'You've changed from white to black', 'Friendly not professional', 'You're dangerous', 'You're playing the race card', 'Black bitch' and 'You're related to the 9/11 bombers.' The author shares her experience as a mixed-race child growing up in a white and black household, and narrates a personal overview, weighing up the white and black perspectives of the loss of both parents during and after counselling training followed by the reflective insights arising out of research, and the capacity to be equipped with tools to provide practical applications for healing. These experiences posed many challenges in training and highlighted the importance of taking an intersectional approach to include the whole person's identity in the counselling relationship and to deliver a training model that minimizes discrimination. The chapter explores collectivist and individualist cultures, the Helms Model and power misuses in counselling, looking at both the explicit and implicit ways that these issues may not be acknowledged or taught in counselling courses. The chapter also explores the healing and understanding that follows through art and drawings with clients and mentees. These include a simple drawing of a volcano, the adult–child–persecutor triangle, the perfectionist bars and the nice and horrible list.

The first section of this book clearly frames the historical impact and experience of practitioners and the necessity for anti-racist alliances and coalitions to work towards a national anti-racist framework. In addressing this narrative, we are required to embed within our training organizations the lived experiences of the personally lived, professional expertise and powerful experience of therapists of colour, in their role as clinical leads, in order to consider the importance and relevance of the client, therapist and supervisee's relationship to the past, present and future of the clinical material reflexively worked with at the different stages of their personal and professional identity.

Part II: Training in Context of Pasts, Presents and Futures

This section consists of three chapters, commencing with 'Chapter 6: Two Black Tutors!' by *Patmarie Coleman* and *Paulette Gibson*. This chapter outlines two black therapists' journey in becoming counselling tutors and reflects on their experience of working together to train a diverse group of counselling students. The authors include their reflections on how they themselves were trained and how this has influenced them as trainers. They also reflect on working with their diverse group of counselling students and how race and culture impacted the group's dynamic. The issues experienced along the way at times were challenging, but the triumphs have been very rewarding and have given them a sense of empowerment.

The questions posed reflect on issues such as: How do we make theory written by dead middle-class white men more relevant to us? What do we need to support the work we do with our students? How do we manage the responsibility of mapping this journey? How do the students feel working with us? How would the other people in the department react to us? What are the implications for the wider teaching team? How do we ensure the safety of black students? Can we conquer the world?

The strength of colleagues is imperative on this journey in teaching, as is the supportive networks trainees need to develop, which naturally brings us to 'Chapter 7: Misery Loves Company, But There's No Need to Walk Alone' by *Lydia Puricelli-Culverwell*. This chapter is a reflection, recollection, retelling and response to the journey a student therapist has had so far in their training as an integrative transpersonal psychotherapist while co-chairing a student of colour network. The author explores what drives them to do this work and hopes to inspire other trainees to better cope with the intense experiences of isolation and frustration while working alongside white trainees and training staff. Additionally, the author shows how building and/or seeking affinity networks can provide support through training and beyond.

Sourcing alternative and comfortable methods of strengthening the psyche is found in 'Chapter 8: Myself as Therapist, Trainee, and the Power of Creativity' *by Symone Stephens-Morgan*. This chapter aims to explore the benefits of art therapy and how emotional, psychological and overall wellbeing can be facilitated through this medium. The author draws attention to the use of creativity as an important tool to communicate something about identity and culture from a black and other ethnic minority perspective through clinical work and by sharing personal experiences. What is highlighted is the need for diversity to be better represented within the arts therapeutic field on a practitioner level.

Throughout the chapter, the terms 'black' and 'other ethnic minority' are used to refer to people who identify as non-white. However, this may not reflect everyone's experiences of how they view themselves. Some people may be inclined to use the term 'person of colour' or feel that these terms overly define or categorize them. The author uses the word black as a celebration of skin colour and the cultural aspects it encapsulates, of music, food and embracing black in a positive way, rather than viewing the term through the negative stereotypes that can so commonly be attached.

This section encompasses the way in which lead tutors and lead trainees on therapy courses have positioned themselves to succeed through the choppy waters of institutional racism, and mitigated using collaboration, creative methods and networking to dialogue appropriately and create appropriate formulations for all students which incorporate culturally relevant texts, practice and networks. In this way, transformation can take place systemically.

As one can presume, well-established and experienced lecturers, teachers and supervisors who work in a racialized academic institution require access to different methods of wellbeing to provide a high level of care to their students and supervisors. We discuss this further in the next section.

Part III: CPD: Supervision and Self-Care: Our Mental, Spiritual, Physical and Emotional Health

This section consists of three chapters. The first chapter provides an opportunity to observe the narrative of two global and distinguished supervisors with a ground-breaking approach, in 'Chapter 9: Conversation About Co-Supervision with Two Senior African Heritage Therapists' by *Dr Isha Mckenzie-Mavinga* and *Arike Grant*. This chapter is presented as a dialogue and highlights the advantages of supervision with someone who can think outside dominant Eurocentric therapeutic perspectives. Having experienced a lack of understanding about the significance of racism and its impact during their training, the authors explore co-supervision with a fellow African heritage therapist and share the advantages of not having to justify, rationalize or educate the supervisor about the dynamics of race in the therapeutic dyad. In doing so, they discuss their own diversity and its impact on their clinical work and supervisory relationship.

Arike was born in a mining community in the north of England; Isha was born in the Midlands and raised in south London. Both were born just after the Second World War. They discuss their connections, and the cultural significance of working together.

In their discussion, they consider the psychology of black and Asian peoples and engaging with white people and black therapists. This approach bridges the divide between the traditional Eurocentric therapy approaches of their training and the here and now of multi-dimensional oppressions. They openly discuss their difficulties in a holistic way which fosters cultural empathy.

These two therapists share many historical points in their journey. They both experienced working at Broadmoor Hospital, the African

Caribbean Mental Health Association and teaching in south-east London. Some of these key points in their learning and development created a foundation for their connection as therapists and supervisors.

The authors describe how co-creating their own version of co-supervision and bonding as African heritage co-supervisors enabled them to develop a level of safety against the oppression of racism, and maintain space to engage in anti-oppressive practice. Their main challenge in this approach was to maintain integrity when supporting each other's therapeutic work.

The authors highlight the importance of having someone who shows an understanding of the impact of race and culture in the process. This keeps the therapist/supervisee focused on the work with the client and assists them not to get distracted by their own material (countertransference). Aware of possible collusion, Arike and Isha indicate to each other where they need to work in their own therapy and the challenges of addressing their intersecting gender and racial diversity. By interviewing each other, they show the challenges and rewards of being male and female black British therapists. Their own journeys through life and the education system have been key in shaping their shared perspectives.

Exploring and reflecting on challenges can often reveal that distress is situated within the body, exhibited by palpitations, faulty breathing patterns and lack of sleep. In 'Chapter 10: Sitting With Discomfort or Embodying Joy?', *Moriam Grillo* draws on her profession as an art psychotherapist to explores what it means to live in a black body. What is the impact of racial trauma and the resulting learned helplessness we may experience in a dominant culture that appears to profit from our psychological distress? We are invited to consider other ways of being that go beyond the influences of a hostile environment which constantly leaves people of colour in a state of homelessness. The author considers the question: As therapists, have we worked enough on our own racial trauma so that we can effectively begin helping others? Healing must be sought through introspection and self-care. For the work with clients to be done with integrity, we must first heal ourselves, and it is through this dynamic healing that we can begin to move our clients from a state of discomfort to one of joy.

Understanding the embodied and experiential belief and healing systems within familial and professional networks is important to explore reflectively through 'Chapter 11: Embodied Ancestors' by *Roshmi S. Lovatt*. This chapter focuses on the affects, dynamics and behaviours which re-emerge through our bodies as ancestral memories provoked within psychotherapy and supervision training. Taking the key areas of UK-based trainings – taught lectures, experiential process groups, auto-biographical/arts performances, skills/facilitation practice and academic writing, personal therapy and supervision – this chapter looks at how each area activates the colonizer-colonized dynamics of our ancestors. Vignettes focus primarily on how we re-member (i.e. through our bodies) and re-create (through artwork) these painful dynamics in the inter and intra psychic dimensions. The author brings these inter and intra psychic dimensions to life by describing textures, nuances and sensory material from their own experience. Personal experiences of how these dynamics have been addressed or facilitated are explored, and the impact of these dynamics on therapy and supervision trainees and trainers. The author posits that these unnamed and unacknowledged processes result in the lack of trainees of colour within the profession. With a view to encouraging potential trainees of colour to navigate these areas of their trainings, the author offers their take on what supports them in continuing to pursue their professional ambitions in the presence of their colonized self.

Holding the past, present and future through a spiritual narrative of wellbeing and positioning takes the reader to the here and now, making a commitment to find a space for looking after themselves and finding like-minded comrades to journey with while developing their professional and personal identity.

Part IV: Therapeutic Needs and Psychological Wellbeing: In the Context of Identity, Culture and Belonging

This section consists of five chapters which illustrate that there are many ways to belong, whether this is via a professional network, friendships system, witnessing traumatic events, or being brought into a family through formal or informal adoption. 'Chapter 12: Transracial Adoption' by *Anthea Benjamin* starts by describing the events of 25 May 2020, when African American George Floyd was killed in America in a modern-day lynching by police officers. This violent act was captured on video and circulated via social media, causing a worldwide outcry for justice. This event has highlighted once again the racism and inequality that exists here in the UK. The white majority were then confronted with the reality of people of colour's experiences of living within a structural and institutionalized racist society. This was further reflected within the growing evidence that the communities most impacted by Covid-19 and its devastating effects were those of people of colour. This has led to a response from most organizations to reflect on and reinvestigate how historical and racial bias within a social context, built on imperialism and colonialism, still informs all organizational cultures in Britain.

It is this social context that continues to put people of colour at a disadvantage and often perpetuates oppressive practices. This is particularly true within transracial and intercountry adoption. These issues are rarely addressed within therapy trainings even though, for the most part, these are the communities we are often offering services to. The author is located within this context as an integrative arts psychotherapist who has worked within adoption for over 15 years, first as a staff member within a child and family team in one of the UK's biggest post-adoption services and then as a freelance in private practice. Throughout the integrative arts psychotherapy training, these important issues relating to identity were never addressed. It was only due to the author's interest in transracial identity that further training was sought after the main training had been completed. In light of race becoming a central issue in society, how are these issues addressed within transracial and intercountry adoption?

It is known that through transracial and intercountry adoption, a child's name is changed to allegedly make it easier for other children. The child's first name is often moved to a middle name, in order to preserve some form of cultural identity. In 'Chapter 13: The Power of a Name' *Umaa Thampu*, a Gestalt therapist, reflects on her personal experience of being othered while working as a therapist in London. Issues relating to the author's ancestral baggage and unfinished business are explored, along with insights from her therapeutic work. Gestalt theory and intercultural theory perspectives are used to explore the nuances surrounding a name, including Zinker's Cycle of Awareness, Dr Isha Mckenzie-Mavinga's concepts and the Johari Window. These explorations highlight the evocative themes regarding the initial meeting between therapist and client that strike the transferential relationship and establish a pattern around power. Jennifer Mackewn's Interruption to Contact table is used as a model to demonstrate the implications for therapists working with difference and how to heighten awareness around the initial meeting and ongoing working alliance. Pop culture references are used to highlight societal pressure to speak and present as English that exposes internalized racism and the oppressive energy of living in two or more cultures.

Continuing the themes of association and connection, 'Chapter 14: Belonging: Who Decides?' by *Karen Minikin*, is a personal and reflective exploration from a transactional analyst, that tracks the connections between personal life experience, intergenerational legacy and the longings and ruptures around a desire to belong and feel 'at home'. The author brings together the political and the personal with links and connections made between the social culture and environment and the impact on the family. In considering racial identity, the author remembers and reflects on early childhood experiences that are both conscious and unconscious. She reveals her exposure to life in Nigeria as dual heritage Indian and English during the 1960s and life in England during the 1960s and 1970s. These international life experiences reflect a post-colonial identity that she has struggled with, leaving a sense of ongoing labour in finding and retaining a sense of 'home'.

Following from the last chapter is the notion of different types of attunement within the therapy session in 'Chapter 15: Embodied Experiencing – Relational Learning' by *Carmen Joanne Ablack*. The author is a body therapist with many decades of experience running groups and consultations. Over that time, she has developed a deepening awareness of the processes that create fatigue for black, African, Asian and people of colour communities as they are exposed to the ongoing toxicity of hidden/sub-textual racism in the therapy room, training organization and wider society.

The author begins with an exploration of her personal journey towards understanding the importance of embodied relationality. An exploration of heritage, race and identity in the context of embodied relating in therapeutic practice then follows. The painful act of deconstructing one's racism alongside an understanding of collective delusions around race and their impact is explored. In the very act of being racially organized and doing the work of therapy and teaching, there is an embodiment of stress, and this embodiment needs to be met therapeutically through the facilitator's embodied process.

The vignette offered highlights the possibilities for non-verbal invitations from the therapist that support the client to stay with their embodied experience of movement, language, gesture and voice when working through race stress so that clients feel fully met and seen in their experience. This is an important chapter from which to launch further into the self of the therapist in the next chapter.

'Chapter 16: The Impact of Racism and Culture on Identity' by *Gita Patel* explores several concepts within intercultural therapy, including the 'concept of the self', which is assumed to be a universal concept in the western world. Most therapeutic interventions in the West are based around this idea of the self. The 'category fallacy' argues that all models of healing are embedded in the culture in which they are practised and helps us to see that the concept of identity only really exists in its own cultural framework. Living in a minority culture and experiencing racism will inevitably affect the internal world and identity. Negotiating identities while living between two or more cultures can lead to an internalization of the cultural norms, which identify a dominant and subdominant identity and lead to emotional distress, including depression, guilt and anxiety. The author explores how they have used their own personal and professional experiences to develop intercultural work that addresses issues around identity, race, racism and culture, and the resulting internalized assumptions. The author also explores how the intercultural model can support therapists and organizations in the consulting room to deliver a more accessible and inclusive therapy.

Once we have settled on a sense of self, it is often a springboard to explore and work through character traits. In 'Chapter 17: Character Work' author *Shirani Situnayake* explores the idea of 'character work' in the therapeutic process. Character work is the idea that certain characters often dominate our world, who may be born out of conditioning or degrees of trauma. These characters may obscure other aspects of our identity and often distort and limit our self-expression, communication and relationships – both with others and ourselves. This is particularly destructive if we belong to a black or minoritized group, reinforcing the belief or experience that only certain parts of us or our behaviours are acceptable or belong. Where an intersection of malign identities determines our footsteps in the world, this can be an annihilating experience, denying us a place to live in flow or connection. Character work helps us to reclaim the parts of ourselves that have been shut down, buried or even forgotten. Now in the UK, being ourselves can be a painful, rage-filled and frustrating experience for black and minoritized people. Through creating images of our dominating characters, we can begin to see and understand their origins and honour how some of them may have protected us in the past. These dominating characters then become three-dimensional, and we can change our relationship with them.

This section provides essential grounding ideas in which to holistically explore a sense of self, both embodied and non-verbal, with tools to develop self-acceptance, internal and external belonging, together with strategies for owning or rejecting aspects of our character to embed our wellbeing. With this work in place, it beautifully sets up the place for honouring.

Part V: Celebrating Our Intersectionality: Ancestral Constellations – African Healing Contexts, Traditions and Origins

This section has four chapters, and begins with 'Chapter 18: A Queer Love Letter: The Severing and Redeeming Power of Eros in Psychotherapy' by *Joel Simpson*. This queer love letter contemplates the redeeming power and connectivity of Eros (love) to mutually heal, re-awaken, stimulate and inspire psychotherapists, counsellors and trainees' practice and queer African Diasporan people's therapeutic experiences. The author's lived experience as an African Diasporan client, working with a white Italian psychoanalyst, is included. Drawing on the author's integrative approach, these encounters examine how Eros may be severed through a focus on race, intersecting identities, and relationships in psychotherapy. In contrast, working with an African Diasporan psychoanalyst, the author considers how Eros may redeem 'kinship libido' owing to loss and transgenerational grief suffered from the African holocaust's colonial legacies. Client vignettes, where both client and psychotherapist are queer and of African Diasporan heritage, explore a wounded healer archetype and Eros as a messenger. Acknowledging the discourse around boundaries, what is foregrounded is love's potential as a conduit to promote the psychological wellbeing of African Diasporan queer people who have been displaced and disconnected.

The impact of generations of traditional and emotional displacement is discussed in 'Chapter 19: Ancestral Constellations' by *Sonya Welch-Moring*. Ancestral constellations are short-term therapeutic interventions that can be regarded as a form of brief therapy. They integrate western systemic thinking and African ancestral family traditions. They are a visual, embodied 'storying' process that explores unresolved past transgenerational relationships. This chapter explores how these transgenerational patterns reappear in the current generation, impacting the psychological wellbeing of black family life, and how this past transgenerational material can be worked with.

The constellations process can help to surface these repeating, often hidden family patterns. When they are revealed, steps can be taken to resolve the conflicts in relationships or find healing solutions for other family dilemmas. In the author's therapeutic practice, they are researching how this approach can be used as a support and resource to strengthen black family relationships.

The author's systemic practice has highlighted the connection between a historical legacy of enslavement and colonialism and collective ancestral trauma. The impact of this resulted in social inequality and family fragmentation that has recycled down the generational line. The killing of George Floyd and rise of the Black Lives Matters movement has reinforced this inequality. Together with the Covid-19 pandemic, societal conversations around inequality and race are becoming more mainstream.

In contributing to this book, the author wants to initiate a social justice conversation around black transgenerational lives. Ancestral constellations as a therapeutic intervention includes and foregrounds the 'African ancestral' aspects embedded in the constellation's method, something that is often missing in therapy conversations.

Bringing the 'African ancestral' constellations model into the wider systemic field will open up existing western methodologies to much-needed scrutiny. How this process might be initiated is recounted in 'Chapter 20: A Journey in Decolonizing Therapy' by *Oye Agoro*, who outlines a personal journey through a process of decolonizing from the perspective of a female therapist of Yoruba ancestry. The author draws on their background in sociology and anthropology and over 30 years' experience of working in community therapy and mental health services as a therapist, supervisor and manager. A model of social justice applied therapy is outlined, based on a multi-dimensional liberation framework that promotes wellbeing and healing. Also described is an approach to therapeutic work that incorporates a critical analysis of the following theories and ideas and their significance to decolonizing therapy: the impact of neoliberal hegemony on wellbeing, intersectionality, trauma legacies, internalized oppression, together with the problem of talking therapies, and cultural imperialism, which is decolonized therapy.

Coupled with decolonized therapy is the requirement for situating an anti-racist practice approach. 'Chapter 21: Effective Anti-Racist Practice in Counselling and Therapy Training' by *Tonia Mihill* begins by framing the context within which the need for anti-racist practice sits. After this, it situates its author in the landscape of racial identity, describing her heritage and formative experiences. It goes on to survey issues of race and racism generally and the recent specific responses from professional therapy bodies before putting forward ten practical and 'easy' ways that training courses can incorporate anti-racist practice.

At the end of each of these ten sections, there are personal reflection and discussion points to actively engage the reader in examining and auditing their own thinking and experiences and encourage them to extend and share this enquiry with others. In conclusion, the chapter places the work of anti-racist practice on the age-old and continuing path of advancing justice and enhancing the quality of human existence, with a call to see this as a task that requires and generates inspiration and visioning.

Epilogue: Kris Black

This book is completed by an inspiring Epilogue, written by co-editor Kris Black. Kris's commitment to this work, alongside Dr Isha McKenzie-Mavinga, Eugene Ellis and myself, instils immense pride in working alongside our contributors in the production of this tome. *Therapy in Colour* supports the development of critical thinking about black, African, Caribbean, and Asian training and therapeutic needs. It is an expression of our experiences of working with and exploring the psychological wellbeing of black, African, Caribbean, and South Asian peoples. It demonstrates the importance of exploring, acknowledging, and celebrating our intersectionality as black, African, Caribbean, and South Asian peoples, who are impacted by colonialism and white racism, and we are proud of the scholarship and contribution made to the clinical field.

References

Ainsworth, M. (1967). *Infancy in Uganda. Infant Care and the Growth of Love*. Baltimore, MD: The John Hopkins Press.

Archibong, U., D. & A, Darr (2010) *The involvement of Black and Minority Ethnic Staff in NHS disciplinary proceedings*. Retrieved from http://www.nhsemployers.org/SiteCollection-Documents/Disciplinary%20Reports%20Final%20with%20ISBN.pdf

Arnold, E. (2012). *Working with Families of African Caribbean Origin. Understanding Issues Around Immigration and Attachment*. London: Jessica Kingsley Publishing.

Carberry, K. (2021). Member accounts. Inclusion in Psychotherapy. Listening and Learning. The conversation to boost diversity in the profession. *New Psychotherapist*, 77, 47.

Coard, B. (2021). *How the West Indian Child is Made Educationally Sub-Normal in the British School System*, fifth edition. Independently published.

Boyd-Franklin, N. (1989). *Black Families in Therapy: A Multi-Systems Approach*. New York, NY: Guilford Press.

Daneshpour, M. (2017). *Family Therapy with Muslims*. New York, NY: Routledge.

Guzzetti J. (2022). *Genders, Cultures, and Literacies. Understanding Intersecting Identities*. New York, NY: Routledge.

Imber-Black, E. (1993). Secrets in Families and Family Therapy: An Overview. In E. Imber-Black (ed.), *Secrets in Families and Family Therapy* (pp.3–28). New York, NY: W.W. Norton & Company.

Majors, R., Carberry, K. & Ransaw, T. (2020). *The International Handbook of Black Community Mental Health*. Bingley, West Yorkshire: Emerald Press Publishing.

Moreland-Capuia, A. (2021). *The Trauma of Racism. Exploring the Systems and People Fear Built*. Cham, Switzerland: Springer.

Newnes, C. (2021). *Racism in Psychology. Challenging Theory, Practice and Institutions*. Abingdon: Routledge.

Russman, T. (2011). Knowledge production and social work: Forming knowledge production. *Social Work & Social Sciences Review* 15(1), 28–48. doi: 10.1921/095352211X604309.

Sigodo, M. (2022, 21 May). Great-grandmother told she was 'too old' for a student loan graduates from university at 79. *My London*. www.mylondon.news/news/uk-world-news/great-grandmother-told-too-old-23934487.

Smith, L.T. (2012) *Decolonizing Methodologies. Research and Indigenous Peoples*, second edition. London: Zed Books.

Thomas, T. (2022). Two Met officers who strip-searched school girl removed from frontline duties. *The Guardian*, 23 March. www.theguardian.com/uk-news/2022/mar/23/two-met-officers-who-strip-searched-school-girl-removed-from-frontline-duties.

Woollsey, S. & Patel, R. (2021). The Colour of Power 2021. Operation Black Vote. Retrieved from www.obv.org.uk/colour-power-2021.

Part I

Colour, Creativity and Anti-Racist Reflection

Chapter 1

Adaptations to Psychotherapy for Effective Treatment of Black and Minority Ethnic People

LENNOX K. THOMAS

Abstract

Societal racism and prejudice in the health service, historically, had led to professionals regarding Black and minority ethnic (BME) people as not capable of using talk therapy. This ran alongside the fact that a disproportionate number of BME people were in the mental health system. The capacity of BME people to make use of therapy was challenged by research funded by the Department of Health in 1992 (Roach, 1992), which found that BME individuals did use therapy when the service had them in mind and when the service was provided with sensitivity. This chapter explores issues of shame and secretiveness in Caribbean populations, an attitude born out of historical enslavement, which has led to Caribbean people not wanting white people to know their business. To add to this, there is the complication of internalized racism disrupting trust between Black people. As a Black, post-slavery population, there are many things to unlearn with the support of therapy, including internalized racism and patterns of separation and broken attachments passed down through generations. Case vignettes are used to illustrate working with negative psychological constructs and to demonstrate help that restores healthy functioning. Finally, I turn my attention to the education and training of therapists.

Keywords

Racism, oppression, shame, inequalities, training, identities, intercultural, envy, self-hatred, bias

Introduction

Poor mental health in the UK is unevenly distributed in Black and minority ethnic groups compared with the general population. For some, therapy has too closely been associated with mental illness, and they have not been able to see the value of problem-solving talk. There is no tradition of talking to professionals about problems in Caribbean people, other than talking to the pastor. Seeking psychotherapy means risking others 'knowing mi biz-niz', and this is very closely guarded. Wariness towards therapy, however, might be marginally reduced if the therapist is of a similar cultural background (Carter, 1995; Guzder & Krishna, 2005).

Resistance to seeking therapy is also a response to a historical suspicion of the mental health service in the Black and Asian community. There were no good experiences from mental health professionals who were agents of the oppressors during the Raj. Also, since the 19th century, Blacks running away from plantation slavery was classified as a mental illness 'Drapetomania' (Cartwright 1851).

Drapetomania was the type of mental illness that only enslaved Africans could develop. This diagnosis implied that an enslaved person was mad to want to run away from captivity to be free. All these experiences have led Black and Asian communities to become organized around shame-related issues associated with generations of colonization and subjugation.

Health professionals, and GPs in particular, have for many years not referred Asian and African Caribbean people for therapy, believing that they lacked the conceptual skills to understand it. Unfortunately, this complex picture of wariness towards therapy services and not being referred to therapy by health professionals has led to BME people being more likely to be admitted to psychiatric hospitals.

Within the complex picture outlined above, Nafsiyat Intercultural Therapy Centre was the first therapy organization in the UK to solely offer services for BME people. This service was often oversubscribed, with long waiting lists.

History of BME and mental health issues in the UK

There is the question of why Black and Asian people don't make use of therapy more often. Well, there is history to this. Like all the institutions where power and authority have been wielded against minorities, psychotherapy has been subsumed under the heading of psychiatry, and there is no doubt that this institution has been viewed as dangerous and untrustworthy. Like policing, psychiatry has been one of the services that nobody wants to have to use, in short, another form of policing. In addition to the shamefulness associated with mental ill-health, mental health services have a poor track record as far as racism and prejudice are concerned. We don't need to dig too far to recall the compulsory detentions (section 136 of the 1983 Mental Health Act) and the view openly held by referrers in primary healthcare that therapy was not appropriate for Black, Asian and working-class people. Many white practitioners in primary healthcare considered these groups too intellectually challenged to cope with the complex concepts and nondirective process of a talking therapy. Also, these groups needed to be told what to do or were unable to cope with the 'as if' nature of therapy due to their concrete thinking or somatization. In the main, it required Black and Asian professionals to challenge this view. Professionally, much is owed to Aggrey Burke, Jafar Kareem, Roland Littlewood, Maurice Lipsedge and Sourangshu Acharyya. Over the past 35 years, it has been clear that there is an overrepresentation of BME patients in acute psychiatric hospitals.

The explanation given at the time was the ubiquitous 'cannabis psychosis', later formalized in the *Diagnostic and Statistical Manual of Mental Disorders* (DSM) IV (2013) as cannabis-induced psychosis. This explanation only served to blame the ill for their illness and did not consider the underlying factors. It seemed, at the time, to be a culturally specific diagnosis like Drapetomania, and it is only in recent times that the total picture has been publicly talked about. Dr Kwame Mckenzie's letter in *The Guardian* (2007) cited the day-to-day experiences of racism and the struggles of oppression as stressors contributing to mental ill-health. The experiences of racism, he said, can injure mental health. The cumulative effect of daily racism needs to be considered as a factor that is injurious to mental health. Ailene Alleyne (2004), refers to this as the daily micro acts of racism. The immigrants from the Empire, namely the Windrush generation and those who came to the UK after the partitioning of India in 1948, were getting on with survival and helping to rebuild their mother country. It would take many years for Black people to stand up to the systemic racism that existed in many areas of their lives. Arriving here with the colonial mentality, it took time to self-define and feel a sense of rights and entitlement in the UK. After the struggles with racial attacks, poor housing, unequal employment practices and the 'Sus' laws, debate moved on to inequalities in mental health and psychotherapy.

Community counselling was not too well known when the first dedicated community service was set up by community relations officer Gloria Cameron JP at the Brixton Abeng community centre in 1977. This family counselling service was set up for Black parents and teens who were going through difficulties and were not getting good enough social worker, education or child guidance services. Nafsiyat was established in 1981 and, after a few years, received NHS funding to research the services that were offered. Similarly, in the 1980s, projects were being set up in Bradford, Brixton, Manchester and Southall. They had no shortage of clients using their services, and Asian - and African - descended people had no problem accessing therapy and counselling. Having not referred BME populations for talking therapy in the past, GPs and hospital psychiatric services were falling over themselves to make referrals. Psychopharmacology and electroconvulsive therapy (ECT) had been the preferred form of treatment for Black and minority ethnic people until these voluntary groups took up against this trend. Therapy had been seen as a white intellectual activity and for many years established an exclusionary zone around the profession that could not think about training BME people or offering therapy. In recent years, there has been an impact on mainstream psychotherapy by minority psychotherapy organizations. Women's therapy, disability, and LGBT (lesbian, gay, sexual and transgender) therapy organizations have made their voices heard. The Thinking Space project at the Tavistock Clinic published its first book on diversity issues in psychotherapy in 2013 (Lowe, 2013).

Keeping things quiet and the connection to the colonizing experience

New immigrants struggled to survive in a new country and had a traditional deference to white authority yet at the same time had a suspicion of their power and how this could be used against them. People from the Indian sub-continent also had shameful experiences, particularly around partition when India became independent and many atrocities were committed, including mass murder and rape when communities turned against each other. The cultural system within these communities of family honour has ensured that this harm has been rarely talked about (Guzder & Krishna, 2005). In plantation society, the enslaved learned to keep their own counsel, and resistance has been an important part of Black history. Hiding what one might feel or believe from the slave master or the sahib was important for survival and self-protection.

This affected the degree of authenticity BME populations experienced with persons in positions of power even when they claimed to want to help. There were many injunctions to the young in Caribbean and Asian communities not to let people know about their business. This is a particular dynamic tension in intercultural relationships that white majority society appears to be oblivious of. It is only from close personal relationships with minorities that white majority people learn about the historical need for minorities to harbour mistrust. There is still a thread of protection or secrecy that runs through African and Asian communities. The shock of arriving in the UK, living in cramped conditions, eating so-called 'funny spicy food' and having extended kinship made it difficult to explain to white friends who 'uncles and aunties' were.

In some cases, young Blacks and Asians developed self-protective 'proxy identities' (Thomas, 1995), enabling them to fit in or protect themselves from ridicule or unwanted curiosity. These masks of psychological survival could become problematic and detrimental to the young person's mental health (Uwahemu, 2004; Sawyerr, 2007). Despite public declarations of Black pride, being hidden had its own companions of shame, inferiority and internalized racism which is still residual in dealings with white authority. In her paper, 'Daring to talk about internalised racism', Rose (1997) broaches this complex topic around how Black and Asian people have accommodated to centuries of racism and how this affects their psychological wellbeing. While this internal mental process contributes to self-regulation, it is also a considerable stressor to mental functioning. This issue is hardly touched on in the training of professionals. This is probably due to its complexity as a concept or denial of the internal damage of racism. One of the arguments has been that these issues are too difficult to teach in counselling and psychotherapy training and that white trainees would not understand them. If professionals are not taught, are we not failing students and perpetuating the exclusion of Black and Asian people from access to appropriate services? Intercultural therapy exposed students to a traditional curriculum alongside ideas of difference including theories from Black and Asian academics in the field. The training also sought to equip students with LGBT lectures and writings so that LGBT clients did not remain unseen minorities among BME communities. The Nafsiyat/University College London training laid to rest the notion that these ideas might be difficult for white trainees to understand because the Intercultural Psychotherapy course had Black Asian and white trainees who grasped the ideas and worked appropriately with BME patients and clients. Isha Mckenzie-Mavinga (2005) cogently argues that therapy training needs to address Black issues that are important to Black people's lives. Trainings that are not geared to the needs of a multicultural society leave gaps in treatment for ethnic minorities (Bhugra & Bhui, 1998).

If Black and Asian therapists can sit through a lecture and feel that none of the content speaks to them as people, how can we expect Black and Asian clients to sit through therapy with therapists who have training that excludes BME issues? This situation will only change if minority therapists change it. Dr Mckenzie-Mavinga researched the training of therapists in the 1980s and more recently the ability of institutions to include Black issues in their training. Frankly, most of the training bodies lack the skill and understanding to do this by themselves. While most Black and Asian people are in therapy with white therapists, effective therapy is often going to be a hit or miss situation for minorities.

An example of this is an Asian woman who went to therapy because she was experiencing racism at work. Presented with a white male therapist, she wondered if he would ever understand her issues but decided to wait and see. She decided to leave the therapy when she realized he had no understanding of or sensitivity even to gender issues, so how could he be sensitive to race.

Shame envy and the therapeutic process

Being in some form of therapeutic treatment will continue to be seen by some people as something to be ashamed of. The idea of transforming shame is very important in working with patients who are from minority communities. Shame and envy are evident in colonized people (Fanon, 1967) and are explored in Fanon's book, *Black Skins White Masks*. Tied up with material issues like lack of opportunity, poverty and discrimination, shame and envy need sensitive disentangling by the therapist. Envy has always been a powerful dynamic between Black people, who have been dealing with this issue since enslavement when Africans and Creoles were pitted against each other on the plantations in order to divide and rule. It is a fact that Black people were denied opportunities in the educational system for a variety of reasons (Coard, 1971). Many carry around a sense of disappointment, since the role of the migrant child is to make social and economic leaps above the achievements of their parents. In a land of new opportunities, doing less well than one's parents attracted accusations of shame by family, particularly those left behind in the old country.

People in many parts of Africa and the diaspora are still in the process of recovering their pride in the wake of this brainwashing of white superiority enforced by the whip. In an interesting paper, 'You're a white therapist: have you noticed?' Lago (2005), a white therapist, questions whether white therapists know that they are white because it is so easy for some white therapists to not think about their own ethnicity and view themselves as normal, making the other a something else. While there is white shame resulting from this, it sometimes cohabits with rage that some white people feel at 'being made to feel guilty'. This interesting dynamic is explored in a paper by Morgan (1998). Shame can also be experienced in the face of the rigid social class structure in the UK. Far from feeling a sense of having survived against the odds, many people harbour feelings of being misfits not because of anything they have done wrong but because they have moved from humble backgrounds into the professional classes.

Consequently, many in the UK cling to their parents' working-class roots even when this no longer seems realistic or appropriate to their values or socio-economic status. Patients in the past have talked of feeling alien in their families of origin, and not quite at ease in their professional group, yet feeling insulted if mistaken for middle class (Thomas, 1995, p.184). Self-improvement is not always seen as something positive, given that social class conventions despise those who come up through the ranks.

A prevalent view is that Black people are strong and able to survive anything, a view perpetuated by Black people themselves. This has not been helpful, as demonstrated by the mental health statistics of Black people in the UK. There are similar statistical trends in North America. Black invincibility is not borne out by the research of Glyn Harrison and colleagues (1999) and Kwame Mckenzie (2006). Large numbers of Black people are disproportionately ending up in mental hospitals. Belief in the enduring resilience in the face of struggle caused by racism, the mistrust of therapy and the shame and stigma of madness, pave the way to acute psychiatric services. There are many issues of culture that need to be thought about by the therapy professions. There is no shortage of minority professionals writing about this: Salma Khalid (2006) on the value of Islamic concepts in counselling, Barbara Fletchman-Smith (2000) on psychoanalysis of Caribbean people and Professor Freddy Hickling (2011), of the University of the West Indies, on psychoanalysis and post-slavery societies.

Negotiating the route to becoming an enabling psychotherapist

Meeting with another Black person, a psychotherapist in the consulting room, someone who, on the face of it, is successful, can provoke intense feelings in the transference. While there might be some feelings of pleasure and pride that someone of one's own colour has done well, perhaps demonstrating that not all Blacks are useless, there is likely to also be accompanying feelings of shame and envy for not having achieved similar status or success oneself. This shame operates at a variety of levels. Being able to get access to it is extremely difficult and requires great technical skill and delicacy on the part of the therapist. The notions of Black solidarity and the nagging fear that one might indeed have sold out make it difficult for the Black therapist to explore envy and shame where it might exist. Difficulties that might be unresolved for the therapist can become obstacles to the patient's development because the issue has become 'an unmentionable'. Until some negotiation is achieved, there will be no internal change and ambition or desire, and potential, will not be released in the patient. It should be said that some Black therapists might not consider themselves as having anything that might be envied. Often, success implies standing out and being different, possibly smug or superior. I discuss shame in relation to envy in an early paper on race and transference (Thomas, 1992). In that paper, I discussed the transference between the Black therapist and the Black patient where the therapist is mocked for having sold out to white values and beliefs.

> While envy covers up the rejection and the ridicule, bringing this to the patient's awareness requires a great deal of care. The patient might vigorously deny envious feelings since the shame of exposure is linked, not just with failed achievement but also with the patient's total experience of oppression and lack of opportunity. Hidden envy that is not brought out in the therapy will only perpetuate the patient's low self-image and impede development not only within the consulting room but also outside it. Protecting the patient from acknowledging their feelings of hatred or envy will be doing them a disservice. (Thomas, 1992, pp.143–144 in Kareem & Littlewood)

Taking pleasure in one's hard work and making use of one's talent is a double-edged sword. Black success confounds the white racist stereotype and at the same time offers a cogent challenge to the internalized racism of Black people, that of self-doubt, self-hatred, and belief in their Inferiority. The balance of Black self-hatred, the fear of success and actual racial discrimination can be an obstacle to participation. In therapy, envy and shame can be transformed into aspiration and pride. The person who is the therapist, the way they appear, their perceived social class and attitudes will influence how the patient can expose their feelings and their histories in therapy. Carter (1995) discusses the Black patient who has some social awareness subjecting the Black therapist to a 'Blackness test' before feeling able to disclose their story. Unburdening the shameful parts of ourselves will only occur when we feel safe and accepted by our therapists. Those who do not achieve this in therapy will carry a sense of dissatisfaction and low potential with them into relationships. If they are fortunate, there might be a life event that provides a breakthrough that will help them unravel their experiences. Others might have constructed false or proxy selves and are left unchanged in this regard. If they are themselves psychotherapists, then they are likely to be left unable to help their own patients with the issues of working with shame and the finding of an authentic self. Their own countertransference will not be attuned to the material that their patients present, and the therapist will not hear or feel what is brought.

Louise, 37, a Black psychotherapist, was a member of an ethnically mixed supervision group. She was working with a Black woman Sue, 26, who had come to therapy as part of a reduced fee scheme. Her family had ostracized her at the age of 17 for having a relationship with a married white man of 34. This relationship fell apart two years after they moved away to a different part of the country. Sue had managed to get her life together for a few years and worked in a hair salon. On Christmas Day, three years before she saw Louise, she made a serious suicide attempt. She was put on anti-depressants and was later referred for some therapy. Sue told her therapist that she would like to have her family back and that she had tried to be reconciled with them, but her mother would not have anything to do with her. She said that she always got depressed at Christmas and felt ashamed that she had no family to go to. Although she had had invitations from colleagues, she would feel worse seeing them together enjoying themselves. Sue experienced intense feelings of shame for missing out on the old family Christmases that she remembered.

In the discussion, Louise was very concerned for her client and told the supervision group that she would not be able to enjoy her Christmas break because of her patient's plight. She added that Sue talked of many friends and could easily take up an invitation rather than worry over her parents, who were so hard and unfeeling that they would not welcome her at Christmas when it is a time for families. After some weeks, it transpired that Louise, at 17, had left her family home to become a nurse after her mother's death and the hasty remarriage of her father. She felt that although her parents had a difficult and sometimes violent marriage, her father could have waited longer to remarry.

While Louise talked in romantic terms about Christmas, she had buried her own feelings of being away from her own family as a teenager and, probably as a result of this, found it difficult to understand the situation that Sue was now in. Louise's unworked personal history was getting in the way of her client's desire to talk longingly about missing her family. It seemed implicit from what was unsaid by Louise that Sue should give up worrying about her family, who were a waste of time. Genuine concern masked the guilt that Louise was feeling, as well as not noticing any envy that Sue might be experiencing.

Dedicated services for BME communities

To work effectively with BME patients and clients, the BME therapist will need to work beyond the curriculum standards of their training organization. This is a reminder of what was said to them while at school by their parents, aware of racial bias, 'You will have to work twice as hard to be considered good enough in this country.' The Black, African and Asian Therapy Network (BAATN) has existed as a training agency that enhances the learning and skills of BME therapists. In the 1980s, Black and Asian social workers and psychologists set up similar organizations because of their concerns about the poor service delivered to BME clients in the care system, criminal justice system and the mental health service. That people of Asian and African descent can use therapy has been a fact known to the Department of Health for many years. The Nafsiyat Intercultural Therapy Centre's research in the mid-1980s also came up with similar conclusions:

> What do these results mean? I would suggest that they show that the view that Black and ethnic minority people cannot benefit from formal therapy is wrong. The research also suggests, albeit with small numbers, that people who show severe symptoms as determined by conventional rating scales may benefit from psychotherapy. (Moorhouse, 1992, p.98, in Kareem and Littlewood)

The idea that BME patients do not use therapy is also not borne out by the fact that Nafsiyat was always oversubscribed, and people were literally queuing around the block waiting for therapy. As a therapeutic service, it was unusual in that it offered therapy in several languages. At the best times, it was possible for Nafsiyat to offer therapy in 21 languages as well as British Sign Language. Similar services existed in Birmingham, Manchester and Bradford in the voluntary sector or the National Health Service. Before their psychotherapy training, the Nafsiyat psychotherapists had previous mental health experience, having qualified in clinical social work, psychology, medicine and nursing. Most of the referrals came from GPs and hospital psychiatric departments as a result of funding from the local health authority. Children and family referrals came from the local authority on a block grant, and a quarter of clients were self-referrals. Against the trend in other white English-speaking therapy services, the number of Black and minority ethnic men referring themselves was almost equal to the number of women. In most general therapy services, women usually outnumbered men by more than two to one. At a conference some 30 years ago, a white professional asked whether or not there might be a risk of collusion if BME therapists were treating BME patients. The conference chair was a bit puzzled by the question, which raised a host of issues. Before the chair's response, a member of the audience asked whether or not there was a risk of bias if white therapists were treating white patients because this was the majority situation in therapy.

Why adaptations will make for a more appropriate therapy

In the early 1970s in New York, African American clinical social workers and psychoanalysts were working in drugs projects with poor Black children and parents in a Brooklyn neighbourhood. Their work had quite an impression on me. Until that time, I considered that psychotherapy was a dilettante exercise for the idle rich. I began to see psychotherapy as a force for liberation and change (Altman, 2000). To counter the deprivation and rise in crime in poor Black areas, African American family therapists Boyd-Franklyn (1989) and Reid, Mimms and Higginbottom (1995) felt that Black families and individuals needed to address unhelpful generational patterns acquired during slavery. The concept of Post-Traumatic Slave Syndrome (DeGruy, 2005), the idea that slavery in the United States that was followed by continued discrimination and oppression leading to intergenerational psychological trauma, has relevance for most minorities in therapy. Beginning from the classic Clark and Clark (1947) doll studies on children's racial identity, there has been a steady tradition of

Black academics researching and annotating orthodox ideas about Black psychological development. African American psychotherapists have been able to use their skills for reversing the Black self-hatred accrued by young children and how this is connected to the rising tide of Black-on-Black violence in young Black men (Wilson, 1978). These therapists made therapy relevant to the populations they served, which also needs to happen on this side of the Atlantic. It was the intention of the Department of Health to use the therapeutic methods described by Nafsiyat to introduce intercultural practice in state-run centres. However, this did not come about, and state access to this type of therapy is limited and dependent on the quality of training offered to individual practitioners. For Black and minority ethnic people, finding good therapy in the public and private sector is like taking a series of calculated risks. For many British Asian and African therapists, their professional training is often just the beginning of their overall training because little or nothing is taught about the complex issues around race and difference in the therapeutic work. Sudhir Kakar (1981) and Hopson & Hopson (1992) have commented on the issues of psychological development for Black and Asian children, yet this is unknown in mainstream therapy trainings.

Conclusion

It has been demonstrated that when offered culturally sensitive rigorous therapy, BME patients are happy to access it. For some people, getting over the unease of disclosing will prevent them from accessing a service, and some will wait until their symptoms and distress are at an advanced state. The control that some people think that they can exercise gets out of hand, and they are often swamped with their problems. Having grown too accustomed to struggle, minority patients take for granted the degree of stress they live with as a normal part of their daily lives. Unsurprisingly, Asian - and African - descended people suffer disproportionately from gastrointestinal complaints, hypertension, diabetes and chronic degenerative conditions like lupus and sarcoidosis, as well as anxiety and depression. If a small voluntary organization like Nafsiyat could successfully run a clinical service and train therapists to a high level to work interculturally, then it is possible for the regulatory bodies of psychotherapy to integrate intercultural ideas into training. There is obviously a political dynamic operating at all levels in the established psychotherapy services. They find it difficult to hear when BME services and research tell them that they might need to make adjustments to their delivery of training. The figures around the mental health problems in minority communities are well known. Equally well known is the reticence of those same populations to be pro-active with their psychological wellbeing. While therapy does not always have to be practised in the Eurocentric way that it is taught, the professional bodies regulating the therapy profession should take note of who gets excluded from therapy and how this happens. It is perhaps a matter of professional ethics that the figures and training standards are examined so that BME populations receive a fair and appropriate service from psychotherapists.

(Eugene Ellis has posthumously edited this chapter with the kind permission of Mr Lennox's family.)

References

Alleyne, A. (2004). Black identity and workplace oppression. *Counselling and Psychotherapy Research*, 4(1), 4–8.

Altman, N. (2000). *Psychoanalysis and the Inner City*. New York, NY: Analytic Press.

American Psychiatric Association (2013) *Diagnostic and Statistical Manual of Mental Disorders* (DSM) IV. Washington, DC: APA.

Bhugra, D. & Bhui, K. (1998). The psychotherapy for ethnic minorities: Issues, context and practice. *British Journal of Psychotherapy*, 14(3), 310–326.

Boyd-Franklyn, N. (1989). *Black Families in Therapy: A Multi Systems Approach*. New York, NY: Guilford Press.

Carter, R.T. (1995). *The Influence of Race and Racial Identity in Psychotherapy*. New York, NY: John Wiley & Sons.

Cartwright, S.A. (1851). Report on the diseases and physical peculiarities of the Negro Race. *New Orleans Medical and Surgical Journal*, 691–715.

Clark, K.B. & Clark, M.P. (1947). Racial Identification and Preference in Negro Children. In T.M. Newcomb & E.L. Hartley (eds), *Readings in Social Psychology* (pp.169–178). New York, NY: Holt, Rinehart & Winston.

Coard, B. (1971). *How the West Indian Child is Made Educationally Sub-Normal in the British School System*. London: New Beacon Books.

DeGruy, Joy. (2005). *Post Traumatic Slave Syndrome: America's Legacy of Enduring Injury and Healing*. Portland, OR: Joy DeGruy Publications.

Fanon, F. (1967). *Black Skin White Masks*. London: Penguin.

Fletchman-Smith, B. (2000). *Mental Slavery, Psychoanalytic Studies of Caribbean People*. London: Karnac.

Guzder, J. & Krishna, M. (2005). Sita Shakti @ Cultural Collision: Issues in the Psychotherapy of Diaspora Indian Women. In Akhtar, S. (ed.), *Freud Along the Ganges: Psychoanalytic Reflections on the People and Culture of India* (pp.205–234). New York, NY: Other Press.

Harrison, G., Holton, A., Neilson, D., Owens, D., Boot, D. & Cooper, J. (1999). Severe mental disorder in Afro-Caribbean patients: Some social, demographic and service factors. *Psychological Medicine*, 19, 683–696.

Hickling, F. (2011). *Psychohistoriography: A Post-Colonial Psychoanalytic and Psychotherapeutic Model*. Carimensa, Mona: University of the West Indies.

Hopson, D. & Hopson, D. (1992). *Different and Wonderful: Raising Black Children in a Race Conscious Society*. New York, NY: Simon & Schuster.

Kakar, S. (1981). *The Inner World, A Psychoanalytic Study of Childhood and Society in India*. New Delhi: Oxford University Press, India.

Kareem, J. & Littlewood, R. (1992). *Intercultural Therapy: Themes, Interpretations and Practice.* Oxford: Blackwell.

Khalid, S. (2006). Counselling from an Islamic perspective. *Counselling and Psychotherapy Journal,* (6)3, 7–12.

Lago, C. (2005). You're a white therapist: Have you noticed? *Counselling and Psychotherapy Journal,* 16(2), 35–37.

Lowe, F. (2013). *Thinking Space, Promoting Thinking about Race, Culture and Diversity in Psychotherapy and Beyond.* London: Karnac.

Mckenzie, K. (2006). Mind Your Head, Improving the Mental Wellbeing of Men and Boys. Wembley Conference presentation, UK.

Mckenzie, K. (2007). Being black in Britain is bad for your mental health. *The Guardian,* 1 April.

Mckenzie-Mavinga, I. (2005). Understanding black issues in postgraduate counsellor training. *Counselling and Psychotherapy Research,* 5(4), 295–300.

Moorhouse, S. (1992). Quantative Research in Intercultural Therapy: Some Methodological Considerations. In J. Kareem & R. Littlewood (eds), *Intercultural Therapy: Themes, Interpretations and Practice.* Oxford: Blackwood Scientific.

Morgan, H. (1998). Between fear and blindness: The White therapist and the Black patient. *Journal of the British Association of Psychotherapists,* 5(1), 48–61.

Reid, O.G., Mims, S. & Higginbottom, L. (2005). *Post Traumatic Slavery Disorder.* Charlotte, NC: Conquering Books.

Fred Roach (1992) Community mental health services for black and ethnic minorities, *Counselling Psychology Quarterly,* 5(3), 277–290

Rose, E. (1997). Daring to talk about internalised racism. British Association of Counselling.

Sawyerr, A. (2007). *Identity and Black Young People. Theoretical and Practice Considerations.* In M. Sallah & C. Howson (ed.), *Working with Black Young People.* Lyme Regis: Russell House Publishing.

Thomas, L.K. (1992). Racism and Psychotherapy: Working with Race in The Consulting Room, An Analytic View. In J. Kareem & R. Littlewood (eds), *Intercultural Therapy: Themes, Interpretations and Practice.* Oxford: Blackwood Scientific.

Thomas, L.K. (1995). Psychotherapy in the Context of Race and Culture: An Intercultural Therapeutic Approach. In S Fernando (ed.), *Mental Health in a Multi-Ethnic Society.* London: Routledge.

Uwahemu, A. (2004). The proxy self, a more acceptable version of me. *Counselling and Psychotherapy Journal,* 14(1), 44–45.

Wilson, A.N. (1978). *The Developmental Psychology of the Black Child.* New York, NY: Africana Research Publications.

Further Reading

Acharyya, S., Moorhouse, S., Kareem, J. & Littlewood, R. (1989). Nafsiyat: A psychotherapy centre for Ethnic minorities. *Psychiatric Bulletin,* 13, 358–360.

Akhtar, S. (1995). A third individuation: Immigration, identity, and the psychoanalytic process. *Journal of the American Psychoanalytic Association,* 43, 4.

Akhtar, S. (2005). (ed.) *Freud Along the Ganges: Psychoanalytic Reflections on the People and Culture of India.* New York, NY: Other Press.

Burke, A. (1984). Is racism a causatory factor in mental illness? *The International Journal of Social Psychiatry,* 30(1&2), 1–3.

Leary, K. (1997). Race self- disclosure and 'forbidden talk': Race and ethnicity in contemporary clinical practice. *Psychoanalytic Quarterly,* 66,163–189.

Littlewood, R. & Lipsedge, M. (1997). *Aliens and Alienists, Ethnic Minorities and Psychiatry,* third edition. London: Routledge.

Thomas L.K (2013). Empires of mind: Colonial history and its implications for counselling and psychotherapy. *Psychodynamic Practice,* 19(2), 117–128.

Chapter 2

The Racist Gaze: Bearing Witness

DR NARENDRA KEVAL

Abstract

This chapter[1] explores the psychological trauma of being at the receiving end of racism. It is a malignancy that has many faces, both overt and covert. To be told relentlessly that you are inferior or not good enough is to experience a daily assault on the self that involves not only what is unwittingly said in words and gestures but what is not said. Unconscious racism in everyday living impinges silently on the psyche, affecting feelings of self-worth, and the cumulative impact can even create feelings of profound confusion in what you think, feel and who you are when the sense of self has been colonized by the racist gaze of another. This type of assault on the capacity for freedom of thought is often caught up with feelings of weakness, shame and humiliation. This invites and necessitates a type of therapeutic engagement that can bear witness, empathize and articulate an inner agony that cannot be voiced, in the hope that this will enable the victim of racism to face the unnameable and protect the self from the subtle and overt ravages of the racism of everyday life.

Keywords

Racist gaze, racism, cumulative trauma, mental colonization, assault on thinking, bearing witness, psychotherapeutic engagement

---

1   This is based on the chapter, The Racist Gaze: Bearing Witness in Keval (2016).

Naming the unnameable

A black Nigerian man came to see me for his anxiety following a car accident. When he arrived at my consulting room he looked cautious as he spoke to me about the accident. I was particularly struck by the tone of his voice, which was somewhat hesitant, as if he was treading carefully with me. He said a car suddenly accelerated in his workplace car park and hit his car while he was waiting for a space. He got out of the car shocked and annoyed asking the other driver for his insurance details, but he said the driver refused to do this which left him feeling angry and frustrated. His anger turned to outrage when the white staff at the reception desk wanted to see his insurance details and other bits of paperwork but would not reciprocate his request concerning the other driver.

He said the staff were behaving as if he was at fault. He had a feeling something was going on. He hesitated for a while and looked at me saying: 'I am not being funny but something was going on here... I try not to think like this but it's happened to me before... I know something was going on here.' He repeated this several times, which made me think that he was trying to make a plea that something awful had been happening to him, which both he and I needed convincing about. He felt he would not be believed. He went on to tell me that the driver who crashed into him was a white man who worked as a senior official in the same organization as himself.

There are different levels on which this communication can be understood about who was not hearing him properly, but for the present purpose, I want to focus on the way this patient's immediate predicament was shaped by his experience of the white world at large, in which people going about their ordinary lives can experience a moment of madness in which racist thinking and feeling confronts them or ambushes their ordinary sensibilities. This man felt something awful was happening to him when he was asked for his papers, which he felt had to do with him being black, but he could not be sure, despite a feeling that he was being misused in a way that could not be made sense of or articulated in any other way. He tried to explain it away to make his life less conflicted and painful but he felt that doing so would also be a betrayal of a truth that was demanding recognition. I believe his plea had to do with wanting me to be a witness and assist him in naming an unnameable experience.

I would liked to have nudged him towards a recognition that was beginning to take shape in his mind, but I think I may have become a little impatient and named what he may have been feeling, perhaps because I found his agony difficult to bear. I said to him that he was trying to tell me that he felt he was being misused because he was black.

He looked visibly relieved and somewhat surprised at what he heard. I put it to him that he seemed a little taken aback that this type of painful experience could be thought about with me. He said he would not be able to say this to everybody, but who was going to believe an angry black man? He said he tried so hard not to fall into the typical stereotype of an angry black man but he could not get it right because the way he was being treated made him feel angry.

Listening to this patient's account brought the image of Kafka's trial (1925) to my mind as if black people often find themselves trapped in a Kafkaesque world from which there is no escape. Any reasonable plea for fairness made in his defence is used as evidence against him by the 'prosecution' because to argue his case at all is to unleash the spectre of the aggressive black man trying to intimidate you and 'get away with it'. He starts from the position of assumed guilt, and from there it is an uphill, if not an impossible struggle to establish his innocence. Because it is left for him alone to disentangle his convoluted and agonizing experience, this desperate scenario is what first needs recognition before further understanding can follow. This was perhaps what I picked up in his plea for empathy, which required a willingness to name the painful experience before he could mobilize his capacity to think freely again.

After this moment of recognition, he gave himself the space to think about other episodes that also pained and baffled him, describing an incident at his son's nursery when a white member of staff had taken his son's soiled pants and put them into a bag with his clean clothes so that all the clothes were covered in faeces. The patient was furious that something so thoughtless had occurred, especially as it was a member of staff whom he had a suspicion was not taking kindly to his boisterous son. He said he had a feeling that his son was being ill-treated.

The staff member's ordinary capacity to think was ambushed by equating the little boy's black skin with his faeces, resulting in all his clothes being smeared, otherwise it would have been a normal occurrence in a nursery for the clothes to be placed in separate bags. Was this a racist moment in the staff member that turned the patient's child into faeces to be got rid of? My patient felt something was very wrong here, but it was something which he could not fully recognize nor articulate. In the car park, he was not only trying to manage the emotional impact of physical trauma from the collision but another type of assault that involved his mistreatment at the reception desk. At the nursery, he was confronted with a faecal assault on his son's identity which also affected his capacity to think. This may explain why he needed a third person to first witness his predicament to pave the way towards more joined-up thinking that could help him articulate and make sense of his experience. I suggest that space where triangulation can occur in the therapist's mind is a starting point for the traumatized patient to repair the fractures in his thinking that become temporarily damaged by racism.

The furniture delivery man

When I was living in South Africa, a conversation with a furniture delivery man made me think further about the attacks on thinking that take place on those at the receiving end of racism. This man rang me to say he had my address but did not know how to find me geographically. I asked him whether he was as new to this place as I was, to which the reply came he knew where I was on the map but the area I was living in was historically white and he never ventured into that part of town. This was even though we were now in the new South Africa, 12 years after the end of official apartheid. He was inviting me to understand that he was faced with an internal situation that neither he nor I fully understood at the time. I directed him to where I was staying, but also found myself feeling slightly perplexed at the significance of what he had just told me and enquiring about this with him. This conversation has stayed with me.

I thought it was not the external world he wanted help in navigating but the internal geography of his mind, an area that perhaps mirrored a split that was state-imposed in a country that had partitioned-off races and social spaces so that venturing across the divide would have been potentially calamitous. I wondered what had become paralyzed inside his mind that made it so difficult to think, in a man who otherwise seemed capable of doing his job. What did he want me to do for him, psychically, that he seemed unable to do for himself? As this man was not a patient of mine, my hypothesis about his inner functioning has to remain tentative but may help in building up a picture of what might take place in a racist assault.

I wondered if his phobic reaction reflected a traumatized self that was pocketed away or partitioned-off in his mind, creating an internal apartheid that was effectively sealed off from conscious awareness or access. Perhaps this had become an encapsulated space within which the traumatic experience and the associated pain and defences were repeatedly re-enacted (Hopper, 1991). This may have become triggered when he had to exercise new freedom of movement that he was not accustomed to, such as travelling to a so-called white area. In this internal apartheid, he was caught up in what was effectively a state-sanctioned gang in his mind, that attacked his capacity to think about and separate past from present, despite being intellectually aware of the fact that official apartheid no longer existed.

On reflection, the furniture delivery man had unconsciously invited me to bear witness to a phenomenon of a racist past living in the present by bringing me the 'furniture' of his mind that had become temporarily scrambled when faced with a new challenge. My guidance required an inquiry about how things had come to be this way for him, which I had not purposefully set out to do when I began giving him directions to my address. It was clear that he was temporarily unable to think about navigating this particular task because the problem lay elsewhere in the deeper recesses of his mind. His capacity to think was either weak, damaged or temporarily unavailable to him when he was faced with the task of reintegrating an area of his mind that had been held at ransom by the murderousness of racism he experienced, that was frozen in time, like a psychic time-capsule that was oblivious to the changing realities. However, because it was an area outside the process of thinking and metabolizing the painful feelings associated with his experience of apartheid, this necessitated an attitude of curious inquiry that formed a backdrop of the content of our conversation. Perhaps this was a catalyst for an experience of a third object that could begin to mediate a space that was hitherto too difficult to think about.

When he arrived at my address it was clear that he was overcome with much feeling at having found my place. He stared out of the window of the apartment for a few minutes and said, 'You know, there was a time when people like you and I would not have been able to walk out there.' This comment, and the implicit feeling of both relief and sadness, conveyed to me that he was experiencing an important moment of separating in his mind what once took place in recent history but was no longer the case. It was another time and place. I thought it was the beginning of a process inside him that had yet to be made sense of in the fullness of time.

While the two men in these vignettes did not pose particular difficulties or challenges in reaching them emotionally, the situation is markedly different when trying to think with a person who needs to enact his or her inner disturbance in a more volatile way. Here, only two possibilities exist in the patient's mind – victim or perpetrator – which pose particular types of challenges in thinking and understanding humanely. This is difficult for both patient and therapist as the murderousness of racism that emerges in the consulting room can not only sabotage the healthy, functioning aspects of the individual but also attack the therapist's mind and work.

Re-animation of ghosts in the consulting room

A black African man whom I will call Mr B[2] (Keval, 2001) experienced an early life of physical and verbal racist assaults at the hands of his black father who became floridly psychotic from time to time, believing that he could wash his son's black skin colour to make him white. This was witnessed by his mother, who was unable to intervene directly as she too was a victim of his violence. Attempts to mitigate a family tragedy were met with another twist of fate when his mother, to protect him from his father, sent him to a boarding school where he suffered further racism. Not only was his psychological integrity attacked by the racist assault from his father, but his mother's relative passivity from being traumatized herself represented another type of failure of containment. It also compelled him to bear witness to his mother's experience as an impotent observer.

This laid the foundations for identifications with different states of mind – being a victim of assault, a witness vicariously terrorized but too impotent to act and a third identification with a racist object. Fortunately for him, there was a more positive intervention, albeit a mixed blessing, when he was sent to the boarding school, which at least prevented a potential homicide by his father. The patient triumphed over his terror of helplessness by getting others to feel vulnerable and terrorized when he was involved in a world of criminality. He was an observer as well as a participant, one might say an impotent observer, being swept along by fast-moving events that often landed him in prison. There were elements of high drama in situations involving the police that echoed some of the experiences in his early years when the police had to be called when his father was out of control. For the patient, however, the police were seen as both enemy and ally, a crucial third object whom he wished to involve as a potent and potentially sane figure

---

2   This case study was described in Keval (2016).

of authority that could intervene when he started to become volatile like his father. Perhaps this is why he told me he was often relieved when he was placed in prison. However, once there, his fate often took a turn for the worse as he experienced further brutality inside prison, mirroring his early experiences of being beaten by his father and being bullied at boarding school.

Some of the dynamics of his experience were often enacted with me in the consulting room when, under the grip of a racist object, based on his father, his murderous thinking took hold in his wish to peel off his black skin. He said he wanted to make his pain more tolerable by removing his black skin from the gaze of white people, which he felt had brought him nothing but trouble, both in his early life and later from racist projections in the world outside. He sought refuge in what he considered to be a safe place, the desire to have white skin, which took on suicidal overtones when it echoed his father's murderous attitude during his psychotic episodes.

These situations would be enacted with me in various ways that indicated a very troubled relationship to his sense of self, expressed concretely through the racist meanings he attached to his skin colour. He tested whether he could trust me to help him by becoming provocative about my colour, searching for ways to gauge how I felt about my brown skin. He often looked me up and down and perceived my suit as indicative of having 'sold out' to the white establishment. His doubts about my capacity to help him concealed his feelings of anger and guilt about what he had done to his good feelings about being black. By projecting the negative feelings and the guilt, he could look at me accusingly as the one who had 'sold out' and betrayed his black self. This was sometimes done through a 'tit-for-tat' strategy in reverse, by trying to devalue my help on the grounds of my not being black enough, with his wish to have a 'proper' black therapist.

Here his perception of being 'proper' repeated a racist dynamic with me, that is to say, my brown skin not being good enough just as he experienced at the hands of his father, in not being white enough. He was re-animating the ghost of his racist father who tried to beat all the blackness out of him. Some of his behaviours were attempts to take me back to that place of terror in his childhood.

In moments like these, it was important to listen to the different layers in his communication in the word 'proper' so that he could glean for himself that I could be responsive enough to explore his concerns without becoming defensive; for example, he was also trying to convey his understandable mistrust of any professional regardless of their skin colour, given his previous experience in different types of institutions.

On one occasion, he was furious about what he felt were the subtle gestures of some white people who looked nervous in his proximity. There was little doubt that this was also a reference to his perception of me, a situation that created a curious split in how this was experienced in and out of the consulting room. Some of my colleagues outside the consulting room felt more alarmed than I was when they heard him shouting, and thought maybe they should intervene for my safety. On reflection, we thought that this may have been an enactment of splitting and possibly even a dissociative process that reflected the patient's early experience of what could not be allowed to be emotionally acknowledged under a racist assault of his mind. This was in contrast to those on the outside, perhaps like his mother and siblings, helpless themselves and bearing witness to helplessness through the beatings taking place on the other side of the door. Because this experience could not be processed by him, the only means available to communicate his terror was through repetition, via a process whereby the 'audience' and participants experienced contrasting feelings inside and outside.

When patients are compelled to do to others what has been done to them they are experiencing a moment in which only two possibilities seem to exist in their mind: victim and perpetrator. Perhaps his search for mastery, to inflict what was passively endured, was in the service of being heard, seen or witnessed. In these circumstances, the therapist would be challenged to experience an element of the psychic impotence that the patient suffered and be able to recover enough to exercise his potency to continue thinking with the patient, unlike his earlier experience. This reflective space involves being both a participant and an observer – an experience that traumatized patients cannot access or one that is weak and absent in their functioning.

This difficulty is linked to the capacity for symbolic thinking, which becomes the main casualty in trauma (Garland, 1998). Symbolization acts like a bridge between the event and the person experiencing it so that overwhelming events can be thought about and processed, enabling them to be integrated into the rest of the personality rather than remain sequestered away. This is in sharp contrast to Mr B's internal situation, where feelings were either evacuated or reacted to passively. A third possibility lay in the potential to create a symbolic space to think and process rather than remaining a passive witness or observer. This possibility also paved the way for fostering the patient's growing curiosity about himself, which was expressed through his attempts to provoke me. For example, he could become patronizing by lecturing me about black history, trying to convince me that he was proud of being black, which I felt also concealed his anxieties about his precarious identity. Here it was not so much his wish to tell me something important about black history and his identity that was the issue but the particular use to which he put it – his patronizing tone of voice was aimed at trying to reverse the power dynamic so he felt less vulnerable with me.

Yet, I felt there was also something very important to listen to here about a young man trying to search and look for a good father to help him safely explore his own identity by 'poking and prodding' at my Asian identity, not unlike a parent watching their child discover and assert their sense of personal agency. I felt his annoying cockiness was designed to provoke a response that could facilitate his healthy rivalry with me, another man, in contrast to the way his masculine potency had been tragically crushed by his father but was now surfacing again in various ways.

I thought that he needed the safety of a space to flex his muscles and experiment with his aggression in healthy ways that were different from his brutal experience with racism. This involved searching for and discovering good aspects of his black self that were buried but given fresh life through his curiosity about me. He started to discover different aspects of his cultural history and good black role models to identify with. The therapeutic challenge was to enable different aspects of himself, identified with blackness and whiteness, to co-exist rather than be drawn into the murderousness of a racist solution to his difficulties.

From the conflicts he was struggling with in his psychic life it was important for him to test how comfortable I was in my skin, in all its symbolic meanings – whether I would easily shatter or retaliate and render his sense of trust and safety at risk, or whether I was permeable but robust enough to continue thinking with him. Most crucially, would I continue to value him as a person worthy of help in the face of his attacks on me? This is particularly poignant for a man whose experience was not only of being chronically devalued by the racism of his father, and many of his experiences in the white world at large, but also the experience of some of his earliest relations with his mother, despite what seemed to be her good intentions.

For this patient, the racist object within had ambushed his whole personality. Early psychic disasters (of which I have focused only on one: his relationship to his racist father) created profound failures in containment that became repeated most painfully and dramatically. This involved the use of skin and skin colour as a stage on which to enact painful conflicts to do with his struggle to acquire a more authentic sense of himself. When he used his black skin as a target for his aggression, as his father had done to him, he was left with all the self-hatred staring him in the face, which he wanted to eliminate by peeling off his skin. However, the graver problem was how his skin surface and colour had become not only the stage on which to enact his grievances and desire for revenge on the people who had failed him, but also the site of his most powerful identification. Any attempt to seek revenge on them using the medium of his skin then became a suicidal gesture.

Conclusion

Survivors of racist hatred, violence, and trauma in general, have experienced either a psychic assault on their mind through sheer force or something more silent, cumulative and insidious, which often renders them helpless and unable to think about the experience. This violent rupture in the continuity of self and experience inevitably affects the person's basic trust and sense of safety, throwing profound doubt on the reliability of both their internal and external objects. The problem of linkage to other potentially fragile areas of the mind that the racist assault can trigger also gives these doubts particular poignancy.

One of the therapeutic challenges is to be able to create a space for ourselves as therapists, allowing a freedom of movement in thinking and feeling under the watchful eyes of our patients, who need to observe, emotionally 'poke and prod' us, and experience our struggle to reach them. I believe our capacity to remain curious and empathic in the face of their attempts to both use and misuse us, is ultimately what gives them a felt sense of safety – that there is enough emotional robustness in us which can enable them to bring all aspects of themselves to be understood and managed better. This in turn can mobilize their hope and courage to exercise their own freedom of movement. This type of freedom is anathema to the racist state of mind (Keval, 2016), which is impermeable – lacking a capacity for truly creative thought, self-reflection or empathy. Its malignancy can manifest in indifference or a wish to devalue, debase, humiliate and shame the self and all its links to a good and fruitful inner and outer object world whose very fabric or protective skin is attacked.

The naming of an experience that is caught up with feelings of weakness, shame and humiliation often invites, overtly or covertly, another mind to bear witness, imagine, empathize and articulate an inner struggle that cannot be voiced. This brings to the fore painful issues of what has been lost through aggression by others and responsibility for one's collusion with the destructiveness of racism. The painstaking process of psychotherapy or analysis can enable possibilities for the traumatic event to be integrated into the rest of the self or personality. The self is then no longer defined solely by the trauma but is separated from it and more able to exercise a new kind of freedom and rhythm of movement in thinking and feeling. This involves a healthy vigilance (in contrast to the hypervigilance in trauma) that also gives the black victim the courage to bear witness to, name and protect the self from the subtle and overt ravages of the racism of everyday life, rather than turning a blind eye to it in a vain attempt to deny its existence.

References

Garland, C. (ed.) (1998). *Understanding Trauma: A Psychoanalytic Approach* (Tavistock Clinic series). London: Duckworth.

Hopper, E. (1991) Encapsulation as a defence against the fear of annihilation. *International Journal of Psychoanalysis*, 72, 607–624.

Kafka, F. (1925). The Trial. In *Franz Kafka* (pp.13–128). London: Secker & Warburg/Octopus Books.

Keval, N. (2001) Understanding the trauma of racial violence in a black patient. *British Journal of Psychotherapy*, 18(1), 34–51.

Keval, N. (2016) *Racist States of Mind: Understanding the Perversion of Curiosity and Concern.* London: Karnac Books.

Chapter 3

Can the Image Bridge Our Differences?

ANN BOXILL

Abstract
This piece sets out to explore the impression I formed about art psycho-therapy while training; that practitioners recognize and process their own ingrained bias through the creative and/or psychoanalytic process. Experiences of microaggressions, discrimination and being negatively labelled while training and in work placements indicate that racism is nevertheless acted out in spaces that should be safe. For example, BME NHS staff are at least twice as likely to be disciplined over their white counterparts (Archibong & Darr, 2010).

Personal accounts and vignettes from practice are used to consider theories of social constructivism and psychodynamic phenomena that help to explain why racism and other inequalities persist, despite being socially unacceptable.

Key words
Racism, prejudice, bias, social construct, difference, image, transference, projection, scapegoat, art psychotherapy

Racism as a two-way process

> *A normal Negro child, having grown up within a normal family, will become abnormal on the slightest contact with the white world. (Fanon, 1952/1967 translation, p.143)*

Frantz Fanon was writing in 1952 about his experience as a black person in a white world. He writes as a black man and as a psychoanalyst. He identifies the struggle a person of colour might have to be seen as the person they think they are, rather than as others, white and black, want or need them to be.

He describes how the pathology of mental illness, specifically the behaviours and mental ill-health associated with oppression in black people, have been attributed to individuals, but should in fact, be seen as universally inevitable given 'projections in our world that are utterly relentless' (Fakhry Davids, 2011, p.142).

Fanon and Fakhry Davids explore racism as a two-way process; racism is alive in both the aggressor and the victim. Its expression and effects, of course, are polar opposites but, it could be argued, create imbalance in the psyche at either side.

Identifying the 'other'

In critiquing bias in western psychiatry, Sampson (1993) summarizes the concept of 'the serviceable other'. This concept, constructed by the ruling class, refers to anyone outside their group who could be of use. The 'ruling class' consisted of white, upper-middle-class, educated males; anyone female, non-white, of openly minority sexual orientation and lower economic class is automatically 'the other' (Sampson, 1993, p.4).

Power – the structures and agencies of change – is controlled by a single, exclusive group to whom everyone else is the 'other'; society offers the illusions of self-determination and order, perpetuated by religions which help maintain the status quo. Referring again to public sector procedures to illustrate this, senior-level positions of strategy and management tend to be populated predominantly by white males (Archibong & Darr, 2010).

The insidious result is that the 'other' have no agency to operate beyond this constructed version of themselves. The 'other' exist to serve the needs of the dominant class. The ruling class own the means of production and are the manufacturers of popular culture – their constructs of 'the other' are intensely and repeatedly projected out, normalized and accepted as real so that people of this group are unable to behave like themselves; shattering the illusion is almost impossible, if everyone you meet believes it. The effect this can have on the developing personality is to grow with a sense that the very essence of what or who you are is wrong, unacceptable and undeserving.

Cixous and Clement (1975) sum this up, while illustrating the transactional nature of 'the other' construct:

> ...society trots along before my eyes reproducing to perfection the mechanisms of the death struggle: the reduction of a 'person' to a 'nobody' to the position of 'other' – the inexorable plot of racism. There has to be some 'other' – no master without a slave, no economico-political power without exploitation, no dominant class without cattle under the yoke, no 'Frenchmen' without wogs, no Nazis without Jews, no property without exclusion...if there were no other, one would invent it. (Cixous & Clement, 1975/1986, p.71 cited in Sampson, 1993, p.5)

I had always wondered, since being very young, why? Why are people racist? It was particularly confusing in my Catholic school, as we were taught God loves us all equally.

I struggled to accept my mixed Caribbean/Jewish background living in a white, working-class, Catholic community in the 1970s. There was no representation for me at the time; black and Asian people were mocked and vilified in the media, 'skin'ead' culture menaced us on the streets and sometimes at home, and beauty was blonde and blue eyed.

Why racism?

The roots of prejudiced behaviour may be found in struggles at the beginning of an individual's development. Freud proposed that humans are driven by inner conflicts and desires we are barely conscious of, the unconscious. His model of the unconscious mind consisted of the id, ego and the superego, with each part having its own agenda and priorities. The id holds our basic biological drives for survival. Psychic energy or cathexis is driven by the 'life instinct', opposed by the death instinct (Freud, 1926; 1915). The psychological dynamism created by this opposition locks us, from birth, in an inner struggle between the urge to survive and the urge to escape the tension: death.

The death instinct could prompt aggression and self-harm if not for this dynamic balance; aggressive impulses, however, are directed outwards into the world.

In seeking to relieve the tension outwards, the ego cannot always safely attack those closest and most needed; for example, the social group the individual identifies with. By directing aggression at members of other groups, whose difference is obvious and already associated with negativity, the tension is relieved.

In addition, the further apart one can make oneself from those viewed as inferior, dangerous or unknown, the stronger one can make one's own sense of self – one can feel superior.

What happens when you are one of those seen as inferior?

I remember, as a child the feelings of hot shame and discomfort issues of race aroused, whether it was teasing, entertainment or abuse, witnessed or experienced. Part of me wondered if the things that classmates and graffiti said about black people were somehow true: were we like monkeys, stupid, dangerous or lazy? I had no evidence any of this was true and yet it was apparently known.

Jean Paul Sartre (Sartre, 1946) further illustrates this point, identifying the fact that oppression of this kind is not just based on colour:

> Some children, at the age of five or six, have already had fights with schoolmates who call them 'Yids'. Others may remain in ignorance for a long time... But however it comes about, someday they must know the truth... The later the discovery, the more violent the shock. Suddenly they perceive that others know something about them that they do not know, that people apply to them an ugly and upsetting term that is not used in their own families. (Sartre, 1946 cited in Fanon, 1967)

From childhood to my early teens, I tried to disassociate myself from those aspects of blackness that appeared to be unacceptable to wider society, conflated with and reinforced by my mother's fearful admonishments: 'If you mess around, they'll say it's because you are black', 'If you do badly at school, they'll say all black people are stupid.' For me, the message was that being black was not desirable, and implied deserving less, but somehow, I had also to 'be proud, do my best and love myself' too.

In a chapter describing work done with children and young people exploring their own agency, identity and belonging through art, Caroline Case (Case, 1999) observes the effect of being 'othered' on a child's self-identity and body image: the effect of racism as projective identification:

> The social construction of 'race' obviously is not simply a matter of the perception of phenotypical differences. Perception itself does not constitute the ground on which the 'race' construction is built. The construction will have no power unless there are strong forces at work which coerce the construction. This is what we mean when we talk about the body as an object of coercion. A person who is treated and classified as a 'race' object comes to define his or her body as 'racialized'. Racism is successful when it forces its victims to define themselves in terms of phenotypical characteristics...lived experience of the body is

subverted by objective forces. (Brittain & Maynard 1984, cited in Case, 1999, p.82)

What is racism?

Racism is 'the belief that all members of each race possess characteristics, abilities or qualities specific to that race, especially so as distinguish it as inferior or superior to another race or races...prejudice, discrimination or antagonism directed against someone of a different race based on such a belief...' (The New Oxford Dictionary of English, 1998, p.1526).

What is prejudice?

Prejudice is 'preconceived opinion that is not based on reason or actual experience...dislike, hostility or unjust behaviour formed on such a basis' (The New Oxford Dictionary of English, 1998, p.1462).

These definitions demonstrate that embodied notions of superiority are based on perception and belief, not fact. Before the 16th century, nationhood took priority over skin colour. European colonialism and the attendant need to justify enslavement for cheap labour inspired the convenient belief that some humans were better than others, according to their 'race', with no scientific or biological basis.

Attempts by the establishment to overcome the effects of racism for a more equitable society have often further entrenched racist beliefs in their approach. The contemporary British version of the concept of race is found in legislation of the 1970s, which prohibited 'derogatory and aggressive discrimination against an individual on the basis of their "race" or ethnicity' (Race Relations Act 1976). A serious attempt to achieve social equity might focus on the right of all humans to live safely and equitably, regardless of skin colour, gender, sexual preference or wealth.

Farhad Dalal, speaking at the 2010 Black, African and Asian Therapy Network (BAATN) Men's Conference describes how processes put in place to overcome racism, perpetuate it, by removing people's freedom to think and exchange opinions; the negative associations of bias and prejudice are so taboo there is 'a paralysis of thought' (Dalal, 2012).

Having been forced to confront my own hidden racism through my profession I believe it is important to encourage clients to address the differences they see in us, as soon as possible. With persistence, humour and kindness, these issues can sometimes be confronted without insulting or hurting each other. I believe that recognizing our demons as our own does not have to diminish us. The following vignette illustrates how difference and clumsy cultural tropes were navigated in an art therapy group with white British teens, predominantly male.

Another Black History Month activity

A first art therapy session was held with a small group of pupils, considered to have learning disabilities and/or social and emotional behavioural difficulties. The school had offered a prize for the best decorated African mask during Black History Month. It was a typically ill-considered and kind of demeaning activity offered by non-black staff for Black History Month. I was new, a little nervous and we would be joined by an 'aggressive' pupil, for the first time.

We all stood around the table looking at these long, slim, black, stylized objects – 'African Masks': they began calling each other out as racist and questioned aloud the validity of the objects as racist. Why? Because they had been given deeply symbolic objects with no context, and the presence of a black person in a position of power made them uncomfortable and they didn't know how to behave. I decided not to rush to reassure, or to lead with an expectation. I acknowledged their difficulties and helped them work out how to negotiate this tricky territory. One person chose to paint theirs white, causing more confusion. We considered whether it is racist to turn a black face white; perhaps they wanted to whitewash me, or Black History Month. After a trawl through images of African body art, looking at people from the Omo Valley in Ethiopia for example, they stuck to their choice. I resisted the urge to rescue the situation and focused on supporting and scaffolding the interactions: they needed to remember who was human in the room. The activity turned out to be very powerful in establishing us as a group; it introduced and cemented the respectful and productive way we worked in those open art therapy sessions.

In an article about the non-disclosing black client, Charles Ridley (1984) offers explanations for and solutions to the problem of difference in the therapeutic relationship. Despite locating the pathology in the black client, Ridley (1984, p.1236) employs a model called the Johari Window (Luft, 1969) to illustrate the starting point and the ideal outcome of therapy for any client. He describes the power dynamic and forming of alliance in relationships where the therapist and client bring both offered and hidden information about themselves, and how that might impact the validity of the therapy.

> Cell one represents the ...'open' or fully 'discovered' self...Cell 2 represents the 'private' self...Cell 3 represents the 'blind' self...Cell 4 represents the 'undiscovered' self... Repressed feelings and denied experiences are embedded in this domain...

Ridley uses this model to explain what is happening in unsuccessful black client/white therapist relationships. He goes on to stress that successful therapy relies on the therapist's skill in responding to their client's needs, black or white; despite this, black clients have significantly fewer successful outcomes with white therapists than with black, because of their pathology. What may be added to this description is that the 'pathology' located in the 'blind self'– what is known about a person by others, but unknown to themselves – is present in the black client *and* white therapist.

Some more thoughts on projection

Melanie Klein (1946) developed Freud's theory which identified and conceptualized the subconscious as dynamic and full of conflict. All that is good and desirable is taken in or introjected; all that is bad, undesirable, threatening is pushed out or projected. The concept of projective identification (Klein 1946) seems almost mystical until you consider the experiences of people who have been 'othered'. For Fakhry Davids (2011), when a group of people have been identified as being different and unworthy, they become the natural bearers of unwanted projections.

He provides a personal illustration of the racist workings of prejudice in a talk for the 2012 BAATN conference, about the concepts presented in his book, *Internal Racism: A Psychoanalytic Approach to Race and Difference* (Fakhry Davids, 2011). He describes his small son asking one night for his dirty skin to be cleaned. He had also started to replace the brown crayon which he had used to draw himself, indicating some very real inner conflict. Fakhry Davids and his wife were disturbed; their son had shown no previous dislike of his skin colour. However, they concluded that this stemmed from separation anxiety, as their son was due to leave his beloved nursery teacher and move to the big class. They understood that developmentally their son would link this separation anxiety to the anxiety of separation from his mother. Although the school prepared the children to move, they ignored the pain and upheaval of separation.

His skin was what made him different from the other children, but like the other (white) children, he'd learned that his skin colour was wrong. He had therefore split off all the emotion connected with separation trauma and attached it to his own skin. The analogy illustrates that internal racism (Fakhry Davids, 2011) works the same way no matter what your skin colour, because the structure and system that make it possible already exist. Therefore, unwanted, uncomfortable feelings are projected onto black skin by both black and white people.

Scapegoat transference – using the image

'Scapegoat' is a word describing the conscious embodiment of all that is unwanted and hated by groups, which Joy Schaverien (1992) traces the first mention of to the Bible. Her exploration of the idea and uses of scapegoats throughout human history provides an explanation of how projective identification can be put to ritualized and almost explicit use: a scapegoat has been used in many ceremonies to bear all the 'badness' of a group; it could then be cast out and the community could feel cleansed and 'good' again. Scapegoats might also rid someone of pain or illness, either passing it on to someone else through ritual or held in an object which is imbued with the maleficent properties and can then be reused or destroyed. The ritual of scapegoating, for a village for example, would need to be repeated every year. This constant renewal and removal of toxic psychic build-up is also discussed in a piece about transference and projection in therapy by Grant and Crawley (2002):

> Critical comments about Aboriginals, sexist jokes about women and derogatory remarks about Asians are relatively common experiences in Australia. These experiences allow individuals to avoid awareness of possessing the characteristics that are projected. The 'otherness' that is created can then be used to help the person establish a sense of distance between self and the disowned parts. The difficulty with this process is that, like all other splitting off processes, it is only partially successful at keeping the anxiety-provoking material at bay...often such views, remarks and actions need to grow increasingly extreme to contain the repressed anxiety. (Grant & Crawley, 2002, p.23)

The implication in this is at some point the expression of anxiety will move from unconscious thought and processes to some kind of action or embodiment, such as a scapegoat. Schaverien (1992) places the scapegoat within the context of art therapy. She explains how the image can sometimes hold not only the affect, but clues to the underlying trauma, more effectively and eloquently than the use of the therapist for the same purpose. The image is not a person; it is an aspect of or an expression of some part of a person's inner world. Once the image is externalized, the person may enter into a relationship with it as its messages and symbolism are explored and re-internalized safely; contact between the individual and their shadow self is established and tolerated. The image is the scapegoat; the projection embodied. The person may relate to the image very closely and keep returning to it until the different parts are recognized, understood and assimilated.

Just as a scapegoat is disposed of in ritual, either by casting out into the wilderness as in the Bible or burial, the disposal of the image is the final act of assimilation. It may be kept, given away or stored in the art room, but its fate rests on the feelings and use its creator hold for it (Schaverien, 1992).

In art psychotherapy, this concept is embraced and used in the ritual and role-play aspects of image making, destroying, keeping and changing.

'But I have black friends!'

A long-term piece of work with a white British teen, began with them in a dissociative state, unable to relate to me or the materials. Eventually, they responded to the framework I provided and began to produce messy, spontaneous images involving primitive projections and violent destruction; it was difficult to contain. This happened repeatedly, until gradually as they became more verbal and curious, shapes and forms emerged. There was a period of creativity, play and delight. As our alliance deepened, however, they began to challenge me. The more vulnerable they became as their trust increased, the more they tried to wound me with racist and derogatory comments. They hated me and needed me. They projected their shame in their own vulnerability on to me. We worked with this carefully and slowly. If I made a direct challenge or alluded to the dilemma arising from our alliance, there was embarrassment, incredulity – someone with black and Asian friends could not be racist. They seemed genuinely puzzled.

However, when core issues of pain, loss and fear of abandonment came to the fore, it was unbearable to speak of or represent anything:

in a series of sessions they would produce, tight-lipped, formless and uncontainable images that gouged, dripped and drained paint bottles. Some were thrown away and some were left behind. At the apex of these sessions, they chose a brown very close to my own skin colour. Witnessing the pain and then literally being poured into that rawness left me feeling a little soiled; there was the tumultuous transference and then there was the sight of my own skin colour used as a container for their projections, which seemed to enact the concept of 'serviceable other' (Sampson, 1993). The dilemma was how to respond to being used without shaming them. I thought the best way to transmute this material symbolically was to ensure that they helped to clean up before leaving each session. The ritual seemed to support a significant moment when, as they stood at the sink, I offered some gentle words of acknowledgement and compassion for what had passed, and instead of shrugging or mocking, like usual, they thanked me.

Final thoughts and a plea

While studying for the MA Art Psychotherapy in Practice qualification, I worked as a therapeutic art tutor for a small group of white middle-class people living with a chronic illness. One day, the escalating tension between myself and one member of this group erupted: during an activity exploring colour and mixing paint, they had asked for help. I was unable to go to them straight away but called over to say I'd be there very soon. After a minute, they said loudly, 'I just need some help mixing brown,' so I answered, 'Try mixing the red, yellow and blue together, but I'll be there in a sec.' 'I have but I can't get the right shade of nigger brown, you know, it's a bit like the colour of poo!' When these words rang out across the room, the atmosphere sort of sucked inwards: everyone else went quiet, and then a couple of people challenged their comment. I joined in with the dissenting voices, but the person remained guiltless, saying, that it had only been meant as a joke; they were being descriptive.

What really stood out for me was the sense of guilt and shame that I felt following what had ostensibly been an attack. It was deeply embarrassing and hurtful and I felt exposed. However, this feeling of shame and exposure was what I couldn't understand: for a long time after I questioned why should I have felt guilty having been the victim of a racist projection.

Discomfort engendered by discussions about race is described by Dr Mckenzie-Mavinga as 'recognition trauma' (Mckenzie-Mavinga,

2009, p.30). She noted that these conversations among diverse groups of students could create feelings of shame in black students or silence among the white students.

When addressed on my own course, race stood alone briefly among other strands, without reflection, further reading or response attached to it; we didn't seem to know how to open discussion about difference, identity and bias. I was conscious that none of the tutors were black and of the fact that few of my cohort were black. Yet I found myself feeling uncomfortable or impatient when peers challenged lecturers on issues of difference. Eventually, with support and curiosity I came to recognize the conditioning that made me want to avoid these situations.

I graduated with a confusion of ideas around art psychotherapy related to race, identity and difference, which amounted to a couple of fundamental unspoken beliefs:

1. We, as art psychotherapists will naturally explore our identity, implicit biases, and vulnerabilities through our own artistic practice and personal therapy.

2. This process is sufficient to allow us to cope with any issues of identity and difference we may encounter during our work with clients.

The art-making process allows for an embodiment of identity beyond words. (Campbell *et al.*, 1999, p.32)

It was almost as if we didn't 'need' to examine our own biases, as we would have dealt with them through our creative work.

Except, if these biases are in our 'blind spot', we cannot recognize them at work, and are then left to act out or suffer the consequences of a rude awakening.

I wrote this long before the events of 2020 in the USA. After George Floyd was murdered on television no one could ignore what we all knew had been happening for so long. Like any abusive relationship there had been complicity and silence; a desire to start fresh rather than examine what had gone so badly wrong before. The responses to that tragedy have been huge; the body of work about the nature of the black/white relationship continues to emerge, casting light on the uneasy shadows of our co-existence and on the dissonance that allows racialized inequity and violence to exist alongside the belief that we are civilized, and that opportunity is universal.

In this chapter, I have attempted to understand my very personal response to a professional situation. This brought me to understand how difference has been weaponized by a relatively small social group by violently and universally projected influential ideas about other social groups, successfully keeping themselves in positions of privilege and power. This has required pervasive racism – prejudice engendering hate and violence against 'othered' groups – and has led us to the brink of ecocide.

The organization and location of power means that all our systems are built on these fictional beliefs, including our education system.

In psychotherapy training, the cause and effect of racism is largely dismissed as a pathology of the black condition. However, I have tried to demonstrate this is not a 'black' problem but a black/white problem; our shared history for more than 400 years has led us to this moment when, through collectively witnessing the reality of racial violence, we can no longer pretend; we have to bring all the secrets out in the open and acknowledge what is ours.

If, as therapists we cannot personally undertake this process, then we may not be fully equipped to help others heal.

The question posed at the beginning of this piece asked: Can the image serve as both container and bridge in therapeutic relationships where there is difference?'

In art psychotherapy, the transference contained in the image is not sufficient if the therapist is unable to recognize racism and bias in themselves.

Therefore, greater emphasis, exploration and focus on bias and difference should be fundamental to training courses as the model and catalyst for authentic, sweeping change.

References

Archibong, U. & Darr, A. (2010). The Involvement of Black and Minority Ethnic Staff in NHS Disciplinary Proceedings. In: E. Udake *et al.* (2019) *Black and Minority Ethnic: Disproportionality in disciplinary proceedings - Recommendations.* https://dspace.stir. ac.uk/retrieve/d7950fb3-b4a6-4654-8b94-2183147c8a7f/bjhc.2018.0063_R1.pdf

Brittain, A. & Maynard, M. (1984). Sexism, Racism and Oppression. Cited in C. Case. (1999) Foreign Images: Images of Race and Culture in Therapy with Children (1999) in J. Campbell *et al.* (eds), *Art Therapy, Race and Culture.* London and Philadelphia, PA: Jessica Kingsley Publishers.

Campbell, J., Liebmann, M., Brooks, F., Jones, J. & Ward, C. (eds) (1999). *Art Therapy, Race and Culture.* London and Philadelphia, PA: Jessica Kingsley Publishers.

Case. C. (1999). Foreign Images: Images of Race and Culture in Therapy with Children. In J. Campbell *et al.* (eds), pp. 67-84 *Art Therapy, Race and Culture.* London and Philadelphia, PA: Jessica Kingsley Publishers.

Cixous, H. & Clement, C. (1975/1986). *The Newly Born Woman.* Minneapolis, MN: University of Minnesota Press, cited in E.E. Sampson. (1993) (p.5), *Celebrating the Other: A Dialogic Account of Human Nature.* London: Harvester Wheatsheaf

Dalal, F. (2012). 'A critique of the Diversity Movement.' Episode 1: http://baatn.podomatic.com/player/web/2012-05-07T06_49_25-07_00.

Fakhry Davids, M. (2011). *Internal Racism: A Psychoanalytic Approach to Race and Difference.* London: Palgrave Macmillan.

Fanon, F. (1967). *Black Skin, White Masks.* Editions de Seuil, 1952 translation. New York, NY: Grove Press.

Freud, S. (1915) "Instincts and Their Visscitudes" in The Essentials of Psycho-Analysis, 197, Vintage 2005.

Grant, J. & Crawley, J. (2002). *Transference and Projection: Mirrors to the Self.* Maidenhead, Berkshire: Open University Press.

Klein, M. (1946). Notes on some schizoid mechanisms. *The International Journal of Psycho-analysis,* 27, 99–110.

Luft & Ingram (1955) "The Johari Window", *Classics of Organisational Behaviour* 2nd edition, Natmeyer, W.E & Gilberg, J.S eds The Interstate Printers and Publishers Inc. 1989.

Mckenzie-Mavinga, I. (2009). *Black Issues in the Therapeutic Process.* London: Palgrave.

The New Oxford Dictionary of English. (1998). United Kingdom: Oxford University Press.

The Race Relations Act (1976). www.legislation.gov.uk/ukpga/1976/74.

'Racism' and 'Prejudice' (1998). *The New Oxford Dictionary of English.* Oxford: Oxford University Press

Ridley, C.R. (1984). Clinical treatment of the no disclosing Black client: A therapeutic paradox. *American Psychologist,* 39(11), 1234–1244.

Sampson, E.E. (1993). *Celebrating the Other: A Dialogic Account of Human Nature.* London: Harvester Wheatsheaf.

Sartre, J.P. (1967). 'Anti-Semite and Jew' first French edition, Paris 1946 cited in F. Fanon, *Black Skin, White Masks,* p.116- Fanon, F, "Black Skin, White Masks" Pluto Books 1986. Editions de Seuil, 1952 translation. New York, NY: Grove Press.

Schaverien, J. (1992). *The Revealing Image, Analytical Art Therapy in Theory and Practice.* London: Jessica Kingsley Publishers.

Further Reading

DiAngelo, R. (2018). *White Fragility: Why It's So Hard for White People to Talk About Racism.* Boston, MA: Beacon Press.

Freud, S. (2007). 'The Ego and the Mechanisms of Defence.' London: Karnac 1936, referenced in A. Lemma, Psychodynamic Therapy: The Freudian Approach, Chapter 2 in W. Dryden (ed.) *Dryden's Handbook of Individual Therapy,* fifth edition. London: Sage Publications.

Fakhry Davids, M. (2012). 'A psychoanalytic Approach to Race and Difference: How Internal Racism Works'. http://baatn.podomatic.com/entry/2012-06-07t00_45_32-07_00_2 Episode 3 accessed 05/12/12.

Larrison, C. & Schoppelrey, S. (2011). Therapist effects on disparities experienced by minorities receiving services for mental illness. *Research on Social Work Practice,* 21(6), 727–736. http://rsw.sagepub.com/content/21/6/727.

Lemma, A. (2007). Psychodynamic Therapy: The Freudian Approach, pp 21-48. In W. Dryden (ed.), *Dryden's Handbook of Individual Therapy,* fifth edition. London: Sage Publications.

Chapter 4

An Encounter Between a White Patient and a Black Psychotherapist

WANDERLEY M. SANTOS

Abstract

This text will discuss my encounter with a white patient and the challenge of managing my countertransference in response to her unconscious racist state of mind. At first, when I sensed unconscious racism from the patient, I found it hard to grasp and felt my therapeutic capacity was being compromised, and I was inadequate to be her therapist. Later, I understood that her attack was related to how she experienced depression and anxiety. The racism was linked to the paranoid schizoid position, where the ego is split into good and bad, with the bad being projected into an external object, in this case, my racial characteristics. Subsequently, I could sustain my position as her psychotherapist, containing and conveying to her what she was feeling and expressing in the room. My capacity to deal with her distress and aggression was fundamental in building a therapeutic alliance. Towards the end of her treatment, she was able to hold me as an ambivalent figure in her mind, different from the one who could not help her before.

Keywords

Racial attack, defence mechanism, countertransference, transference, internal object, paranoid-schizoid position

An encounter between a white patient and a black psychotherapist

The clinical encounter in psychoanalysis is understood to be mediated by transference and countertransference. These two phenomena have the potential to help us understand what is going on *here and now* in the room. In this sense, a specific clinical encounter takes us from our comfort zone by challenging us while we are in contact with the client's emotional difficulties during a course of treatment.

In this context, as psychotherapists, we become an object for any source of transference and projection, which is fundamental for working on the client's internal world, for which they are seeking help. To be a container is fundamental to this process, but professionally, we need to investigate how we are also affected by being in touch emotionally with a client via countertransference. In doing this, we should be able to find a way to transfer back to the patient without retaliation to help them to learn from this clinical experience and perhaps extend it to other parts of their lives (Winnicott, 1969).

The case presented is my encounter as a trainee psychodynamic psychotherapist with my first client, a well-educated, upper-middle-class, white, English woman and myself, a black male and foreigner from the global south. The text will mainly present a case in which the challenge was to address my patient's unconscious racist state of mind. When she felt stuck in her treatment, a racial attack would take place in the therapy session. She made some attempts to shut me out, isolating me in the session and presenting herself as superior. Because of this, I could not find my internal resources, and I felt inadequate in my role as a psychotherapist in training. At first, I found it hard to understand this split, typical of the paranoid-schizoid position with racial elements.

The concept of the paranoid-schizoid position was coined by Klein (1946), a state of mind in which a different type of anxiety is built up when the ego feels in danger. In this moment, a strong defence mechanism takes place to split the unwanted part from the wanted part of the ego. This then gets projected out onto the external object. In this process, another phenomenon occurs called projection identification, in which the projection finds elements and conditions in the external object to justify it. Klein based this concept on infancy initially, but she also saw it through adulthood. In this case, Ms K unconsciously projected onto me the otherness (black, foreigner and male) of her feeling of being stuck, which she could not bear.

When I was able to understand this dynamic, it helped me to sustain my position as her psychotherapist and to contain and convey to her the aggression she was expressing. In her treatment, she moved towards a depressive position where the splits took place less frequently, and we could co-exist in the room. The depressive position created by Klein (1946) tends to follow the paranoid-schizoid position. It is a different state of mind where the person can keep the good and bad inside them as the whole self and similarly see others. The person can tolerate feeling more frustrated by others but also find that they are being helpful. This shift in relation to the paranoid-schizoid position goes towards the integration of the ego. In this position, there is a tendency to fantasize that some damage has been done, so a guilty feeling may arise along with a necessity to repair it.

Allport (1979) points out that an encounter is always mediated by our phantasies, preconceptions and prejudices concerning the other. Davids (2011) believes that when the other is from a different race, especially being white or black, a complex historical process tends to play into the imaginary to justify the phantasy. In this context, elements present in this encounter can, in a particular moment, be traced back historically to colonization and the conditions of slavery. According to Wilderson III (2020), the scholar who coined the concept Afro-pessimism, this idea allows us to analyse the conditions of contemporary life and the imaginary related to black people, which can be traced back to colonization and enslavement. In this line of thought, racism can be used as ammunition when someone feels the need to protect themselves or take advantage of someone else. In this sense, 'racism is not created solely out of external societal structures, nor is it a purely psychic phenomenon, but rather both shape and call upon each other in the service of different functions' (Keval, 2016, p.3).

Racism in the clinic is understood in Kleinian terms as a child-type defence mechanism. This mechanism can be used to attack the analyst based on the colour of his or her skin, as has been advocated by authors such as Clarke (2003) and Altman (2000). The attack has been understood as a form of communication, as well as an attempt to control the analyst's mind at the moment when the ego feels in danger, as Tan (1993) states.

Bion (1962) understands projective identification as a form of communication that requires the analyst or therapist to contain such feelings and be able to return such raw/primitive content as something more elaborate/palatable, and over time the patient may be able to make content of this kind less threatening. When the patient can do this, we call it the depressive position. A therapeutic alliance can be formed at this stage, allowing the patient to work together with the therapist. Reaching the depressive position is not the goal of a therapeutic process because these two positions are temporary, and therefore, we cannot think of them as an idea of progress or growth, because when the ego feels fragile and in danger again, the elements of the paranoid-schizoid position can be reactivated.

CLINICAL MATERIAL: MS K

Ms K is white, upper class, with degrees from the most prestigious universities in the UK. She was referred to one of the NHS clinics due to her depression and anxiety.

In our first session, Ms K expressed her gratitude to the NHS for the 18 months of treatment that she immediately accepted. She verbalized that she was open-minded about having therapy. After a month of her treatment, she admitted that she had prepared a script about what she would like to say during her session, as she used to do for her academic supervisors. In her anxiety to be a good patient, she wanted to deliver what she had decided I would like to hear from her to be cured by me, as she motioned a couple of times. In these moments, sometimes I would get lost in her eloquent labyrinth of thoughts. She did not listen to my interventions, the common phrase from her being, 'Yes, maybe', as she continued her narrative. I felt that I was interrupting her.

After eight months of treatment, Ms K expressed great difficulty with her therapy. In one session, she asked me if what she was doing in our session was 'right' or 'not'. My intervention that we should explore the meaning of that question was understood by her as me being unkind to her and uncaring about her suffering. She felt stuck by my refusal to answer her questions in the session. As a consequence, a defence mechanism was raised, and attacks started taking place. In this moment of fragility, she used the racial aspect and my position as a foreigner against me to get rid of her feelings of being stuck and to manifest her anxiety and depression. She never used any offensive words towards me. I felt as if I was being attacked in a diplomatic, English manner. The attack came in the form of her withdrawing from me and acting in a superior way, having doubts about my intellectual capacity, attempting to stop me from thinking in the session by not letting me speak or ignoring my comments and interpretations.

Hinshelwood (2006) points out that a common feature of the racist mind is superiority. This combination can lead to racist behaviours, understood as part of the paranoid-schizoid position, and anti-racist attitudes, showing features of the depressive position, which can lead to attempts at reparation and prevention.

At this challenging time, I tried to get closer to her anxiety and depression. She saw me as her attacker and could not see anything good or valuable in what I said. This situation is not uncommon with melancholy patients. Freud (1917) states that the archetype of these patients tends to torture their object while keeping it alive, refusing the beginning of a new relationship. For Brenman (1982), a melancholic patient cannot see something good in them, so it is projected onto others with the ability to make the other person correspond to this fantasy. Ms K said that she did not believe that I could help her with depression or anxiety. Such disbelief can be aggravated when a white patient faces a black therapist, as they tend to believe that such therapist does not have the 'linguistic or intellectual competence to help them' (Yi, 1998, p.245).

Ms K's attempts to control me by keeping me in this place had a significant effect on my countertransference. I felt an immense difficulty in thinking, to the point of not knowing what to say during the session. It was as if I had no control over my thoughts; it was as if I were rehearsing something to say, but it all got mixed up in my head and did not materialize in words. At times, I felt incompetent in my role as a trainee therapist, even a charlatan.

Despite her being a person with excellent qualifications, it must be said that this did not prevent her from using projection with racial elements as a form of attack. For Miller and Josephs (2009), whites, liberals and educated people commonly think that they have overcome any type of prejudice and discrimination related to race. In this situation, according to the authors, racist feelings are strongly inhibited and silenced. They tend to police themselves so that they do not express themselves in a racist manner, which according to the authors, already shows that they are racist. Ms K said that her family was liberal, and because of that, presented herself as someone who had no racial prejudice. Consciously, she never expressed any racism, on the contrary, she always presented herself as a person favouring anti-racist actions. For Miller and Josephs (2009), white, liberal, educated people regularly think that they have overcome any prejudices related to race, so racism is no longer an issue in their intolerance. In this situation, racism is heavily suppressed and silenced because liberal people tend to identify themselves as anti-racist. The challenge of discussing racism is that liberal people tend to police their language to avoid making a racist slip.

The effect of this on my countertransference was that I found it challenging to think in her presence; the feeling of having a blank, empty mind frequently occurred to me during the session. At these moments, I needed to pull myself together and re-engage in her conversation. This was a terrible experience – I felt inadequate, and I felt that she believed that I was not a good enough therapist for her. For my part, the emotions and the real difficulties of being a black foreign trainee in a white institution made it hard for me to believe in my potential to do this work and not give up the training.

My feelings at that time were that Ms K was blocking my intellectual capacity through her superior use of the English language and her doubts concerning my intellectual competence. Unconsciously she was acting in a way that stopped me from thinking independently. This situation can be related to her difficulties in bearing the fact that I was trying to interact with my thoughts and myself. Britton (1989) speaks of the experience of parental intercourse understood through the phrase of a female patient who said, 'stop that fucking thinking' (p.88), thus showing her difficulty in coping with him having his thoughts. When she found it very difficult to express herself or said she was very confused about her feelings and thoughts, I said to Ms K, 'Perhaps you have some criticisms about me as your therapist. We can work on this together.' Then she asked, 'What do you mean we can work on this together?' 'We can think about your difficulties here together', I commented. This seems to have been the crucial moment in which our therapeutic relationship had a brief but significant change and Ms K started to trust me a little more, and our therapeutic alliance began. At this moment, I wondered if such a move could be an attempt at redress in the light of what had happened before, which now seemed to take the shape of the depressive position.

Her feelings were associated with complaints and criticisms that she had towards me as her therapist. According to her, I should ask her questions and make her speak more and more. She felt my attitude of waiting and saying little in the sessions as my disinterest in her feelings, similar to what she felt from her parents. Here, this disappointment was minimally worked on. Ms K was also able to work a little on her anxieties and insecurities, for example feeling like a charlatan in her research field for not being able to publish articles, which made it difficult, according to her, to get a permanent job, and that sooner or later, everyone would discover this. She believed that she no longer had time to do anything to change this situation. Ms K also worked a little on how complex her relationship with her mother was, in particular the fact that she felt that her mother did not support her in her decisions and how it affected her ability to make her own decisions to the point of being extremely dependent on the approval of others.

At this stage of therapy, she projected her anxieties less and lessened her attacks. Perhaps Ms K's posture changed, enabling her to work on the feelings described because I managed to survive her attacks without retaliation, which is, as suggested by Winnicott (1969), one of the skills of a therapist or analyst. Ms K's statements seemed to take this direction when she said, 'I think you are happy with your work, and I am probably not a terrible person.' Ms K may have started a process of internalizing me as a therapist as a good object, or at least an object a little more ambivalent than the one experienced before. This stage of the therapy was a short but significant one when she could project her fear and attack me less, face her painful feelings and the difficulties of talking about them, and accept me as her therapist.

In this final stage, Ms K commented that she recognized that she was now listening more to what I was saying, even though she recognized that she had a long way to go. The phrase 'we can work on this together' was remembered by her, and she acknowledged that this had happened in the treatment and that she could see things a little differently. Very close to the end of her treatment, she mentioned that she found a picture of a distant member of her family from the days of slavery, and this person was black. This was understood as a sign that she internalized me also as a good object who would be part of her internal family world. Perhaps I became an ambivalent figure in her mind, different from one who could not help her before. Towards the end of the treatment, Ms K was again superior to me, but now the quality was different, her sessions were coming to an end. Now she was protecting herself from the end of the treatment.

Conclusion

In this text, I have examined the importance of racial difference as a tool in the therapeutic process when a patient encounters a therapist from a different racial background. Through the phenomenon of transference, the patient in the case outlined in this text projected onto the therapist (who is black and foreign) intolerable feelings and anxieties, as a defence mechanism, which is typical of the paranoid-schizoid position.

In this context, the therapist must have the capacity to handle these projections without taking revenge and finding ways to explore feelings and work on them to the extent that the patient can. I learned that when these feelings are conveyed in therapy, it is an attempt to open up a conversation about how the patient has perceived the therapist's presence in the room. In terms of intercultural psychodynamic therapy, the therapist's external appearance and other things such as posture and gesture are essential elements onto which the patient can project and introject unwanted parts of themselves. I learned from this clinical experience that I was not what my patient was transferring onto me. For me, the most essential aspect of this process was seeking the truth, not only on the patient's side but also on my side as a therapist in training. As Betty Josef[1] suggests, we will see what is going on in other people only when we can face what is going on in ourselves. However, the 18 months of treatment described in this text are only the beginning of her process in therapy as a patient, and mine as a therapist. This demonstrates the extent of what we could do during this time. Finally, this is only a single case study, and it would be important to have more investigation into how racial elements can become tools in the psychodynamic relationship, especially in the British context.

References

Allport, G. (1979). *The Nature of Prejudice.* Cambridge, MA: Addison-Wesley.

Altman, N. (2000). Black and white thinking: A psychoanalyst reconsiders race. *Psychoanalytic Dialogues,* 10(4), 589–606.

Bion, W.R. (1962). *Learning from Experience.* London: Heinemann.

Brenman, E. (1982). Separation: A clinical problem. *International Journal of Psychoanalysis,* 63(3), 303–308.

Britton, R. (1989). The Missing Link: Parental Sexuality in the Oedipus Complex. In J. Steiner (ed.), *The Oedipus Complex Today: Clinical Implications* (pp.83–101). London: Karnac.

Clarke, S. (2003). *Social Theory, Psychoanalysis and Racism.* London: Karnac.

Davids, F. (2011). *Internal Racism: A Psychoanalytic Approach to Race and Difference.* London: Palgrave Macmillan.

---

1 Available at: www.youtube.com/watch?v=dtxytpdO3JM (accessed: 10 April 2021).

Freud, S. (1917). *Mourning and Melancholia. Standard Edition, 14*. London: Hogarth Press.

Hinshelwood, R. (2006). Racism: Being ideal. *Psychoanalytic Psychotherapy*, 20(2), 84–96.

Keval, N. (2016). *The Racist States of Mind: Understanding the Perversion of Curiosity and Concern*. London: Taylor & Francis.

Klein, M. (1946). *Envy and Gratitude and Other Works 1946–1963*. London: Hogarth Press and Institute of Psychoanalysis.

Miller, A. & Josephs, L. (2009). Whiteness as pathological narcissism. *Contemporary Psychoanalysis*, 45(1), 93–119.

Tan, R. (1993). Racism and similarity: Paranoid-schizoid structures. *British Journal of Psychotherapy*, 10(1), 33–43.

Wilderson III, F. (2020). *Afropessimism*. New York, NY: Liveright.

Winnicott, D.W. (1969). The use of an object. *International Journal of Psychoanalysis*, 50(4), 711–716.

Yi, Y. (1998). Transference and race: An intersubjective conceptualisation. *Psychoanalytic Psychology*, 15(2), 245–261.

Chapter 5

Counsellor Training and Beyond: A Practical Application

KIREN KHOSLA

Dedicated to all of those who believed in me.

Abstract

This chapter is a reflection on my personal experience of racism on my training course. I explicitly name the issues: 'We're sick of hearing about your differences', 'You've changed from White to Black', 'Friendly not professional', 'You're dangerous', 'You're playing the race card', 'Black bitch' and 'You're related to the 9/11 bombers'.

As a mixed-race child growing up in a White and Black household, I narrate a personal overview, weighing up the White and Black perspectives of the loss of both parents during and after counselling training and the insights that followed through research and an application to heal. These experiences posed many challenges in training and highlighted the importance of taking an intersectional approach to include the whole person's identity in the counselling relationship and to deliver a training model that minimizes discrimination. The chapter explores collectivist and individualist cultures, the Helms model and power misuses in counselling, looking at both the explicit and implicit ways that these issues may not be acknowledged or taught in counselling courses. The chapter also explores the healing and understanding that follows through art and drawings with clients and mentees. These include simple drawings under Activities2Heal.

Keywords

Trauma, discrimination, racial issues, grief, bereavement, Black issues, Activities2Heal

Counsellor training and beyond – a practical application

Looking back over the years to write this chapter of my life, my journey to becoming a therapist and all that I have learned along the way seems so long ago, yet felt every day in my mind, body and spirit. I wonder if some experiences will ever truly leave me.

Having just finished my Health and Social Care degree, I wanted to have a change from studying before enrolling on a Counselling Diploma course. I took up a support role, working with mentally and physically impaired adults and went on to become an advocate.

As an advocate, I saw many clients who did not seem to have a voice and were left feeling powerless. They had their experiences, which had led to their mental health issues being ignored or brushed under the carpet by the very systems that were supposed to be supporting them. I wanted to change these clients' experiences and help them to find their voice. I wanted to encourage them to be heard and to feel valued, and I wanted to address the power imbalances that I saw. I just did not know how.

I asked each client what they felt would help me to understand them and to explain their story in a way that felt comfortable for them, so that I could try and explain it to others. I wanted to help mediate the huge gap between parties.

Some clients drew pictures, took photos or cut meaningful pictures or words from magazines, as they were not able to express themselves well through language. Somehow, they had become muted, and I did not know why. Other's wrote journals, letters or used a dictaphone to record their thoughts and express their deep trauma.

Many expressed themselves within the garden by nurturing plants or creating something beautiful out of a tiny seed. Some cooked a meal that they had experienced in happier times. As time went by, one thing became clear to me: clients felt empowered and I started to see confidence shine through as their spirits and voices were heard. I did not know at this point how powerful this foundation would be for me in my future practice.

My journey as a therapist began five years after my partner died by suicide and I became a single mum to our three boys. My partner had said, that I would 'make a good counsellor'. I did not know what he saw in me that I did not see in myself, but I knew that I had to find out.

A year into my Diploma training, my parents' health deteriorated. My duty of caring for my parents as an only daughter and for my three children became more apparent to those around me. I juggled everyday life along with studying and racial abuse from within our community. The 'superwoman effect' (Beauboeuf-Lafontant, 2007) had come into play for me. I became relentless in hitting goal after goal, in forcing myself to do everything. I had no choice, as there was only me.

Suddenly, during the final year of my Diploma training, my mum died unexpectedly. My dad, a Black, Hindu Asian, decided to apply Hindu last rituals to my mum, a White, Christian, for her funeral. I tried to explain to my Diploma group my thoughts around the complex issues of bereavement coming from a mixed-race and mixed-heritage background and the difficulties around satisfying both sides of my family, who had different expectations from me. When I looked up, I noticed that something had shifted in the room.

Sadly, the Diploma group did not understand what I was trying to say and as I had not experienced such turmoil before, I did not know how to explain it further. Having grown up accepting my mixed-heritage values and beliefs, which had fitted in seamlessly previously, it came as a shock to hear what followed.

During my Diploma group, I talked about a neighbour calling me a 'Black bitch' and the community thinking that my family and I were 'related to the 9/11 bombers' as we are Asian. Our property was damaged, my family stoned and 'gollywogs' danced in the windows held by a neighbour, to mimic my family. I was told that I was 'dangerous, friendly, not professional' and that I was 'playing the race card'. I did not even know what the race card was, let alone how to play it. I felt intimidated for being honest about my experiences of discrimination, especially when I was told that I had 'vented my spleen and disembowelled the tutor with a teaspoon', a form of torture in days gone by.

The Diploma group said that they were sick of hearing about my differences, and that I had changed from a White Asian to a Black woman. Group members used the encounter group to take it in turns to tell me how useless I was and that I should be more like them, 'looking at our similarities, not differences'. For me, it was not the similarities that were causing me distress, but our differences, as I slept with a cricket bat and my three children in one room, fearful of what we would experience next.

The Diploma group said that they were giving me the 'Core Conditions' (Rogers, 1957). I said that 'I did not feel them, and that I only heard congruence' (Rogers, 1957). The tutor said that this 'just showed how unaware' I was.

In time, I received three pages of 'failed coursework', having never failed any in the previous years. I also failed a bereavement course that was co-run by one of the tutors during the weekends. The counsellor supplied by the college was a business partner to one of the tutors. I was told that I was 'not self-aware enough to pass'. I had just graduated with a BSc(Hons) and a distinction in reflective practice. Sadly, the conflict of interests was only obvious to me.

I was left devastated and confused. I filed a complaint, as I did not understand what had happened. I thought that counselling was about exploring loss and grief, and so it did not make sense. I lied to my dad about how my career was going to protect the shame that I felt, shielding him from the shame that I would have brought on my family. Thirteen months later my dad died, and I sat in my car watching my class graduate with tears of despair rolling down my face. I felt suicidal, as I was told by the counselling provider, college and tutors that I would 'never have worked with people of difference anyway, as they never came into counselling'.

In time, my professional body applied sanctions to the college. However, I was left with huge debts and post-traumatic stress disorder (PTSD). I sought a year of free counselling and started to research into the issues that I faced. I needed to understand, to be validated. My counsellor encouraged me to apply for another counselling course, the Postgraduate Diploma (PG Dip,) after I got distinctions in neuro-linguistic programming (NLP), counselling and life coaching. But I had lost my way – my confidence – and nearly my life. I withdrew from the outside world. Now it was me who had become muted. Now I understood my clients from my time as a support worker.

I decided to try and express myself in the ways that I had offered as a support worker and advocate years before. I wondered if it worked for them, could it also help me to empower, heal and find myself again?

I started with painting a picture of how I felt before I started the Diploma course. I had such an amazing life, full of love, wonderful people, and activities to look forward to every day. During the course I saw myself and friends as dolphins playing away from the crabs (tutors and Diploma group), who I felt were unaccepting of me and my differences. Then I painted how I felt after the course, a tiny fish in the tidal wave, lost and suicidal. The pictures captured how much of myself I had lost. I did not have words to express my feelings. I put the pictures away. It was too painful, the scars deeply etched within.

Therapy in Colour

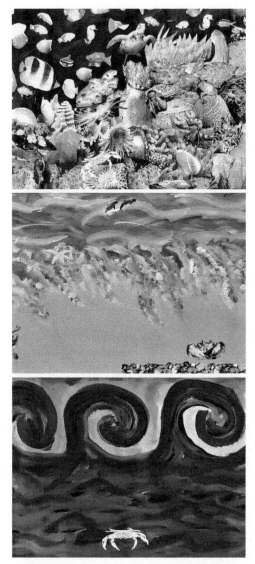

Figure 5.1: (Top) *At the start of counsellor training – free, vibrant, and dynamic.* (Middle) *Halfway through counsellor training – tutors, Diploma group and in-house counsellor – conflicts of interests, crabs about to attack. The dolphins represent me and my friends playing away from danger.* (Bottom) *At the end of the Diploma training – me the fish, in the tidal wave, suicidal and drowning*

In time, I began to assemble my life story, including life events and what I've learned, naming every change that I had experienced. I wanted to detail all my life to see if I really was 'unaware and incongruent' as I had been told in the Diploma group. I left no stone unturned, as I could not fail again. Once completed, I was finally ready to apply for a postgraduate course in person-centred counselling (PG Dip). Fortunately, I was accepted. They saw something in me that I did not see in myself.

As the course went on, I got an opportunity to explore and research what happened in the Diploma group, as part of my PG Dip. As my confidence grew, I realized that I could apply this research on 'Black issues' (Mckenzie-Mavinga, 2007) to help inform my PG Dip class, who were all White, to change the outcome for other students and future clients. I wondered if something good could come out of my experiences, as I was often told that 'through adversity comes creativity' (Open University, 1998). Now it was my opportunity to apply this in action.

My White supervisor and tutors were anxious, worried that I would be traumatized further if it did not go down well with my all-White class. I was anxious too; I was not sure if I had the courage to explain a second time. When the research module presentations came up, I decided to try. I placed a sign on the door saying, 'Political correctness is to be left here.' It felt important to put all judgement aside if we were truly going to talk about the crux of the issues, to create a safe space.

First, we looked at what Black issues (Mckenzie-Mavinga, 2007) were, as it had raised turmoil within my Diploma group. They comprise the following:

- the superwoman effect
- history and cultural trauma
- sexism
- racism
- politics, political correctness and ethical standards
- power – implicit and explicit
- spirituality and faith
- lacking Black and ethnic minority group (BEMG) role models
- ethnicity.

Next, I discussed my personal experiences of grieving and loss from when I lost both of my parents, from both a White and Black perspective, to highlight the gaps and confusion that tormented me.

Table 5.1: White and Black issues and the differences in loss and grief that I experienced

White issues	Black issues
Outwardly grieve in public and with the professionals involved.	Grieve in private – the paramedic was suspicious of my family not crying at Mum's sudden death.
My counsellor was shocked that I had called her to cancel our session.	Phoning my counsellor to let her know that I could not attend our session, while Dad's body was still on the floor in the kitchen. It is an elder's expectation that I will continue to follow traditional rules passed down of duty and respect, whatever the circumstances.
Disrespectful to pass Dad's body over the trampoline to get into the house.	Duty – practical role of a daughter after parent's death. Grooming the body of my elder with love and respect to honour Mum and Dad's final wishes to rest at home before the funeral.
Blinds shut showing respect.	Manoeuvring Dad's coffin into the sunshine. He liked it in life and so was not treated differently in death.
Friends and family felt uncomfortable eating with Dad's body in view, as it was not what would normally happen in a Chapel of Rest. 'This feels surreal' (friend).	'Do you want a bacon roll?' Life carrying on as normal. The kitchen is the heart of our family, where food is central.
Horror at pushing the body into the furnace and watching the body burn at the crematorium.	The soul has gone and only the case of the body remains, as the family push the coffin into the furnace. The final duty of the family and so a sign of love and respect for the elder and loved one.
Om symbol is seen as 30 – misunderstood but is the equivalent to a Cross. Lord's Prayer recited 'To be closer to God.' (White Christian family member)	Om – a knowing of peace and oneness with the universe above and beyond. Aarti prayer – a prayer to the Gods in gratitude for the elder and loved one's life (Black Hindu family member).

Humour… Mum's make up did not suit her in death.	Humour… Nearly cremating myself and my dad with candles from the alter.
Trying to explain traditions to friends and family in a way they could identify with, participate in and to help to understand, to feel included.	Trying to explain traditions to friends and family in a way they can identify with, participate in and help to understand, to feel included.
Giving Dad's ashes away to make a memorial by buying a plant and being close to the loved one. I felt torn, as I was trying to help the living to cope.	My dad's family were upset with me for giving away his ashes as his body was no longer complete, which could prevent his reincarnation.
	Offering the last Rakhi bracelet as a keepsake, where offence was taken.

I explained to the PG Dip group how in hindsight I could see that the Diploma group saw my White skin, but not my whole being, as my upbringing was important as a mixed-race woman. This created a split in my identity and trauma (Alleyne, 2021), as I had to ignore the intersectionalities of my race and heritage, status as a single mum, and my disabilities (Crenshaw, 1989), as none of these issues were validated within the Diploma counselling course, creating multiple discriminations.

The Diploma group had an expectation that I would behave in one way, and yet I had done the opposite. This made me unaware in their eyes. Ignorant and 'dangerous'…another stereotype was fulfilled.

I have always valued both my Whiteness and Blackness, but now, this took on a new meaning for me. My White skin meant that part of my identity was ignored, devalued and meaningless to others. This did not feel like a privilege to me, given the treatment from my Diploma group and community, which consisted of misunderstandings, misinterpretations and assumptions. All of these were made on the basis that they believed I was 'White'. This created further discrimination and cultural insensitivity and showed a lack of racial awareness. The intersectional identities (Crenshaw, 1989) that I valued were systematically blown apart.

I realized that all my differences had got in the way, as the Diploma group could not step into my shoes, as their experiences were so different. We were from different worlds; I had just learned to merge both worlds to survive and so had never questioned this before.

In time, I discovered that my frame of reference as a collectivist individual is seen as an 'external frame of reference' (Rogers, 1957) in person-centred training. This is the 'lacking awareness' that was alluded to by the Diploma group.

I also learned that the individualist and the collectivist cultures (Lago & Thompson, 1996) are triggered by loss and change. Now things were making sense, it felt easier to explain.

Table 5.2: Individualist versus collectivist (Lago & Thompson, 1996)

Collectivist culture	Individualist culture
'We'	'I'
Everyone is born into extended families. Communities protect each other in exchange for loyalty.	Everyone takes care of self and immediate family.
Identity is based in social systems, which could be interpreted as not looking after your own needs, as others needs are seen as more important.	Identity is based in the individual – self-regard and self-care, which could be interpreted as selfish, from the collectivist frame. Counselling is based in this frame, as it is a Eurocentric model.
Values and beliefs are drawn from within the group's discussions.	Values and beliefs are placed within the individual, and so are applicable to everyone, as a standard.
'External frame of reference' (Rogers, 1957).	'Internal frame of reference' (Rogers, 1957).

I discussed how power – both implicit and explicit – could be used and misused in counselling, especially working with people of colour (POC) who may have a distrust of services and professionals.

Implicit examples of power within counselling and training include:

- Note-taking after sessions.

- Confidentiality breaches without consent.

- Unidentified conflicts of interest and dual relationships.

- Unclear instructions, or boundaries changing, which may create uncertainty and anxiety.

- Prolonged eye contact and touching without consent.

- One person doing most of the talking.

- Silence, where the counsellor knows what the silence is for, but clients and students do not.

- Supervision – the uncertainty of information sharing, and the purpose.

- Not returning calls, texts and emails, which can knock confidence and create anxiety.

- Cost of courses, books, supervision, travelling to courses and placements and continuing professional development (CPD).

- Accessibility to information, offices and translation services. These can be expensive and so may limit choices for clients and students, and prevent the opportunity to access counselling, and training. Toilet facilities and Covid-safe environments are important for those who have been shielding.

- Time limits. These may need to be explored if someone is using translators, or is struggling to understand language, and so the 50-minute or one-hour session may need to be extended.

- Shorter sessions – could be offered for those with disabilities, or longer spaces for those with money issues, or on benefits, who may not be able to afford to travel as often.

- Appointments and accessibility issues – could be an issue if there is little or no public transport. Potential childcare issues, affordability in costs of the sessions or courses could be discussed, and evening and weekend appointments offered to allow flexibility.

- A variety of ways to deliver counselling, training and CPD – this will ensure a wider reach and diversity of people able to attend.

- Use of email, text, Instant Message (IM), online video, and Face to Face (F2F) and phone. Sadly, this was only reviewed when Covid struck in 2020 and counsellors and providers needed to change how they worked to meet the growing needs of the population. But this is imperative to address social justice issues.

- Power dressing – this is associated with authority figures and may not evoke a positive reaction for many people of colour.

- Age – older people may be seen as more experienced, younger people less experienced and so assumptions, which make an ASS/U/ME, may affect the participation of the parties, as the assumption may not be accurate.

- Gender and sexuality and whether the person is accepted as they are, as a client. If they cannot be genuine within the counselling relationship, or training, then the person will not feel able to show their complete identity and all their parts, and so identity splitting, and shame may occur (Alleyne, 2021) as it did for me.

Explicit examples of power within counselling include:

- Qualifications and certificates – these show professional status and success, but can undermine and intimidate those who are uneducated to a similar level, creating the 'expert'.

- The environment – this normally belongs to the counsellor and so the desk, chair, decor is to their taste and ability, or disability.

- Jargon, language, and words – these mean different things to different people and so the interpretation can vary.

- Knowledge, theory and practice – these are familiar to counsellors, but may not be for clients.

Next, I discussed the Helms Racial models (Helms, 1995), showing the Dip PG group how we each fitted into different categories so that we could connect our identities to each layer and see where the work needed to be done around CPD. It is vital to become aware of our own racial identity and that of others who may cross our paths. Sadly, this is an ethical issue that has not been addressed previously in counsellor training courses or CPD.

Table 5.3: Helms Racial models (Tatum, 1997, p.94)

White	Person of colour (POC)
Contact – oblivious to racism. If racism influences life decisions, it is viewed in a simplistic fashion. 'The white way is the right way.' (Tatum, 1997, p.94)	**Conformity** – devalues own cultural group allegiance to White standards. Oblivious to history or racial groups.
Disintegration – disorientation and anxiety by own dilemmas, forcing choice between racial group and humanism. 'Crisis.' (Tatum, 1997, p.94)	**Dissonance** – ambivalence and confusion, relates to own social group. May be ambivalent about life decisions.

Reintegration – idealization of own racial group and intolerance for others. Racial factors influence life decisions. Resolves the issue by going back to contact. (Tatum, 1997, p.94)	**Immersion/emersion** – idealization of own racial group. Puts down the White race. Uses own external standards to self-define, and loyalty is valued. Makes life choices for the benefit of the group.
Pseudo independence – an intellectualized commitment to own racial group. May make life decisions to help other racial groups. 'Paternalizing and tolerance of other racial group.' (Tatum, 1997, p.94)	**Internalization** – a positive commitment to own racial group which is internally defined and so more able to assess and respond objectively to dominant group. Makes life assessments and decisions by knowing groups' requirements and self-assessing.
Immersion/emersion – idealization of own racial group. Uses own external standards to self-define and re-evaluate own White identity, where loyalty is valued. Makes life choices for the benefit of the group.	**Integrative awareness** – values and empathizes with own culture and collective identities. Collaborates with oppressed racial groups. Makes life decisions based on self-expression.
Autonomy – informed positive socioracial group commitment. Uses internal standards and has the capacity to relinquish privileges of racism. More likely to avoid racial oppression.	

This exploration showed me that my Diploma group did not understand what I was saying, because we were in different racial groups. I realized that by trying to merge both the individualist and collectivist cultures within me, alongside the Helms models sometimes, it was not easy to get it right.

My Diploma class saw me as White and so assumed that I would think in the same linear way as they did. But I am a circular thinker and so I may start at the end, or the middle of a story, which can be hard to follow for some. Clients and students always apologize when they do the same. For me, it is my comfort zone. When I am stressed, I will revert to what is natural for me, as it is part of my upbringing, being closer to my dad and spending more time with him.

When I am in a good place, I notice that it is easier to think in a linear way, to fit into the individualist, or Eurocentric, framework, which is used as the basis of counselling, applying a beginning, middle and an end. It was a mind-blowing discovery!

For accreditation, I noticed again that my circular thinking was working against me when I was asked to resubmit. The Diploma course comments had knocked my confidence and I was not sure that I was good enough, as the three pages of failed coursework flashed through my mind, tormenting me further. I threw the work back into the cupboard and came back to it just before the accreditation deadline. This time I bullet-pointed each criterion and put my thoughts into a chart, to link my application together. It is easy when you understand.

Finally, we looked at what helps within a transcultural relationship, the counselling process and on courses, to give hope to my Dip PG group that they too could create a positive outcome by following a basic framework:

- Remember that all parties are humans and have a need for trust and rapport to establish a positive 'working alliance' (Barrett Lennard, 1998).

- Remember that both have a chosen to be there. If a Black, ethnic minority group (BEMG) client or student is presenting, then they may have a crisis and need support from someone outwith their network.

- Ensure clear contracting, to readdress the power imbalance within the relationship.

- Ensure that they have current knowledge around social justice issues and are racially aware of themselves and others, to increase the chance of being effective. The clients and students must 'feel' the core conditions (Rogers, 1957).

- Stay positive, as each party is likely to live in the same locality, and so stand a better chance of hearing about the competing perspectives that exist. Think from a bottom-up approach, otherwise issues could be missed and the relationship may fracture.

- Ask, if you do not know. Be honest, genuine and transparent with your clients and students. It is okay not to know.

- Validate the clients' and students' experiences, even if your own views differ.

- Use the Cultural Iceberg (Hall, 1976) to help you identify issues for supervision.

- Ensure that you use clear communication with basic vocabulary to prevent misunderstandings.

- Have BEMG literature available and strategies in place if BEMG clients or students present, as most counselling literature is from a Eurocentric perspective and so may not account for Black issues (Mckenzie-Mavinga, 2007) and equality, cultural diversity, and inclusion (EDI) issues.

- Monitor your service by using ethnicity and EDI sheets. Do you have a diverse number of clients from all backgrounds, able bodied and disabled, gender and age diverse? If not, ask yourself what you could change to become more inclusive.

- Ensure that you know where the barriers are for participation of BEMG clients and students, so that they do not fall through the gaps.

- Be power aware. You are more likely to attain a positive outcome for all parties by using an equal standpoint.

Once I qualified, I started work in services specifically designed to support disabled people and their families, using email and phone counselling. Again, I saw how hard it was for clients to understand their worlds, as words seemed to be a stumbling block and barrier for many, just as I had experienced years before. I felt that I had to find a way that helped to bridge this gap.

I started drawing a basic triangle which evolved into a Volcano metaphor, with a simple explanation of how things build up and what can fill the Volcano over time, starting from when we are young children then growing older and gaining more responsibilities at work and home, when the pressure increases. Then when clients least expect it, suddenly it explodes, affecting our mind, body and spirit. I explained that by talking about their worries in sessions, or in between sessions writing journals or letters, the client could offload the negatives which create pressure, and many patterns may surface to create self-awareness and an opportunity for change. However, by also acknowledging what has gone well every day and having some self-care time – as it is the positives that help to rebuild confidence and create balance – the client's wellbeing could start to improve.

As clients began to feel empowered by creating choices for themselves whether it was a good or a bad day, there was a sense of achievement. Every day there was something to get up for and acknowledge. As clients and students were inspired, so was I.

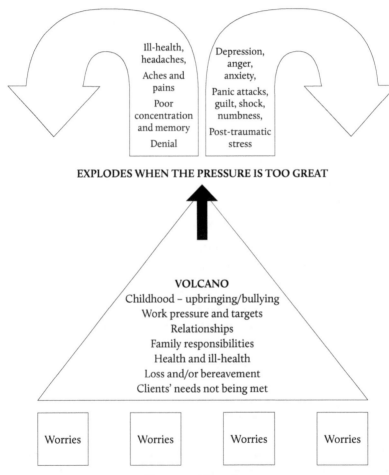

Figure 5.2: The volcano

I wanted to keep working on the Volcano, but giving it a different outcome, while not changing too much, so that it did not overwhelm clients. I looked at the Drama Triangle (Karpman, 1961) but found it too complicated to follow. So, I adapted it, to represent the adult–child–persecutor, as none of my clients reacted well to 'victim', so I needed to change the language to keep them listening.

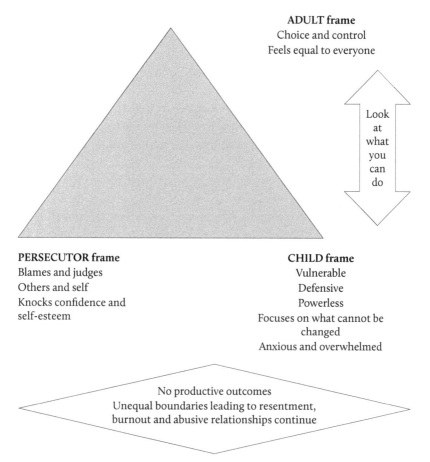

Figure 5.3: Cycle of human behaviour

I discussed the three positions – one for each corner of the Volcano. If the client was in the Adult frame and there was space between the middle and top, they would feel present, were able to concentrate, recall memories, enjoy life and be able to laugh again. All of this disappears with responsibility and pressure. If the Volcano was full, then they would shift positions to the bottom of the Volcano, as they may have lots going on, and feel burdened and resentful. Some clients were perfectionists and so would move to the Persecutor frame on the left-hand side and start beating themselves up, feeling guilty or arguing and judging others. For the Child frame, clients could feel vulnerable, sometimes defensive, and so might be more sensitive to what was being said, which could leave them feeling powerless, as they focused on all that they could not do and they became anxious and overwhelmed. I noticed some clients would feel muted – like a child who could not say anything. Others became rebellious, shouting and slamming doors like a teenager, and so either could be applicable.

I also noticed that both bottom positions knocked clients' confidence. Both positions experienced unequal boundaries, and this is also where abusive relationships seemed to begin and carry on. I encouraged clients to recognize where they were on the triangle and ask themselves just one question – what can I do right now? This enabled clients to take action to empower themselves at that moment in time, to look after their needs whatever they were.

Next, I drew an energy diagram, of what I felt I heard within the session, for students and clients to help them to see how their energy was being distributed from my perspective and where the possibilities might lie to create change. The aim was to make the arrow heads match in size to reflect energy going into the person and coming out. If they do not match, this can affect the mental and physical health of the client or student, as they show imbalance.

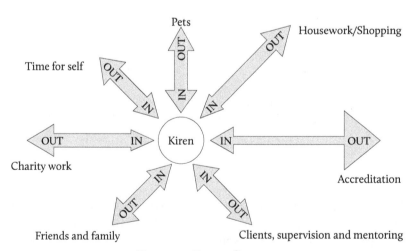

Figure 5.4: Energy diagram

While clients and students understood where their energy was going, I noticed that they felt confused as to why cycles kept continuing throughout their lives and the feeling of being stuck in a rut or on a hamster wheel continued, so I developed a self-sabotaging cycle diagram to help, based on Rosner and Hermes's (2006) theory.

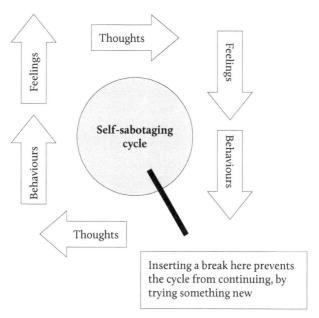

Figure 5.5: Self-sabotaging cycle

The arrow heads represent thoughts, feelings and behaviours which repeat as the circle goes round. So, if you think the same, you will feel the same, you will do the same and therefore the outcome must be the same, as nothing has changed. This is the stuck in a rut feeling that occurs. So now when the client or student captures themselves thinking the same as they have previously, then their self-awareness grows around their triggers within their Volcano, and from each of the different positions that they may sit in within the cycle of behaviour triangle. This becomes an opportunity for changing their behaviour, trying something new and creating a break. As self-sabotaging is a learned behaviour, it can be unlearned with practice and trial and error.

I asked clients and students to look at their 'What ifs', so that they had a plan of action in mind for when it may be triggered. I suggested making plans for time off by using a written diary, as it takes a smaller amount of space, making it more realistic and achievable, unlike online dairies which just grow. This helped the client and student to stay focused and appreciative of their time to recharge.

I noticed how perfectionists seemed to have an invisible bar that they must achieve, which for some clients and students created anxiety and panic attacks, as they dreaded what lay ahead, this and left them feeling exhausted before their day had begun.

To help clients and students to become aware of their expectations, I drew a bar on the ceiling and said that every morning when they woke up, they had to jump for this bar and whatever they had set themselves in their minds. However, what we are aiming for in counselling is to move the bar to above their heads, so that everything that they set for themselves is realistic. Between the top bar on the ceiling and the one above their heads is their confidence, self-esteem, energy and happiness. Having a priority list to tick off what they had to do in the day kept them focused on one day at a time. Other deadlines went into their diary to prevent procrastination, or distraction.

As clients and students became aware of where they had set their bar, the pressure dropped in their Volcanos, as they started to listen to their intuition and be kinder to themselves.

PERFECTIONIST BAR (on the ceiling)
Expectations create pressure, which adds to the Volcano
This then leads to incongruence and vulnerability, which brings clients into counselling
For the doubting practitioner, this is where imposter syndrome occurs

---

Between these two bars are the client's:
Confidence
Self-esteem
Happiness
Energy

This is the bar we aim for in counselling which is just above the client's head
Here, everything is achievable that the client wants for themselves, but without the pressure

---

Figure 5.6: The perfectionist bars

Finally, I noticed that some of my male clients and students, especially those with severe post-traumatic stress disorder (PTSD), did not seem to connect with the perfectionist bars and so I decided to try something else.

I drew a road from A to B and said that 'Perfectionists run from A to B as quickly as they can, get to the end of the day shattered and start all over again, and that this can go on for many years. But now if we put the client, or student on the road as a car and run it from A to B without looking after it...what happens to the car?' The client says it 'breaks down' and so that's my cue to say, 'That is what brings you into counselling. So now let us try to do something *nice* to recharge your batteries, a nice breakfast, five minutes outside with a drink focusing on your five senses, watch a TV series, or podcast before work. Then do one thing off your priority list – this is the *horrible* that uses energy, whether you are at home or work. We need a balance. Then go into a parking space, take time to recharge, have something nice to eat and drink away from your desk and get back onto the road.'

The Nice and Horrible list works on roughly an eight-hour day with parking spaces – breaks, lunch and leaving on time. If the client or student stays later, then more parking spaces are needed to create a balance of energy coming in and being used. If they do not match, then we get an imbalance of the mind, body and spirit.

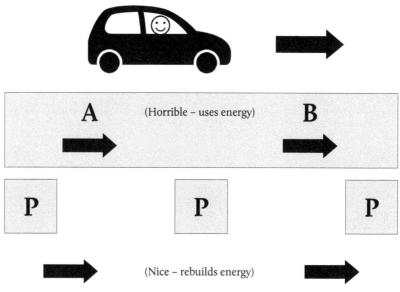

Figure 5.7: The Nice and Horrible list

In conclusion over the years, I have learned to express my own experiences and trauma in pictures and help clients and students to do the same – to view their trauma and lives in a different way, to validate and create understanding, as drawings really are universal to all humans, of all races. A picture can capture a thousand words, where even in the storm the smallest breath will still be heard.

References and Bibliography

Alleyne, A. (2021). Shame, Race and Identity, online course. Attended 3 July 2021.

Barrett Lennard, G.T. (1998). *Carl Rogers' Helping System: Journey and Substance*. London: Sage Publications. https://sk.sagepub.com/books/carl-rogers-helping-system.

Beauboeuf-Lafontant, T. (2007). You have to show strength: An exploration of gender, race, and depression. *Gender & Society*, 21(1), 28–51.

Hall, E.T. (1976). Cultural Iceberg Model. In Beyond culture. www.spps.org/cms/lib/MN01910242/Centricity/Domain/125/iceberg_model_3.pdf.

Helms, J.E. (1995). Racial Models. Cited in L. Puchner & Z. Szabo (2011) The short-term effect of a race-related course on racial identity of White students. *Teaching in Higher Education*, 16(4), 399–410. www.tandfonline.com/doi/abs/10.1080/13562517.2011.641003.

Karpman, S. (1961). *Drama Triangle*. https://themindsjournal.com/karpman-drama-triangle.

Lago, C. & Thompson. J. (1996). *Individualist v Collectivist. Race, Culture and Counselling*. Maidenhead, Berkshire: Open University Press.

Mckenzie-Mavinga, I. (2007). Understanding black issues in postgraduate counsellor training. https://onlinelibrary.wiley.com/doi/abs/10.1080/14733140500492581.

Open University (1998) Health and Social Care Certificate lecture. Cambridge.

Rogers, C. (1957). Cited in S.A. McLeod (2014, 5 February). Carl Rogers. *Simply Psychology*. www.simplypsychology.org/carl-rogers.html.

Rosner, S. & Hermes, P. (2006). *The Self-Sabotage Cycle: Why We Repeat Behaviors that Create Hardships and Ruin Relationships*. Westport, CT: Praeger. Annotated edition.

Tatum, B. (1997). Helms Racial Models. Cited in Identity Development (p.94). https://slidetodoc.com/identity-development-tatum-1997-p-94-n-according.

Further Reading

Beagle, A. (2016). Crashing into the Cultural Iceberg. LTC Language Solutions. https://ltclanguagesolutions.com/resources/blog/crashing-into-the-cultural-iceberg.

Crenshaw, K. (1989). Cited in The Intersectionality Wars. Vox. www.vox.com/the-highlight/2019/5/20/18542843/intersectionality-conservatism-law-race-gender-discrimination.

Dennison, M., Benschop, Y. & Van den Brink, M. (2020). Rethinking diversity management: An intersectional analysis of diversity networks. *Organization Studies*, 41(2), 219–240. https://journals.sagepub.com/doi/pdf/10.1177/0170840618800103.

Hays, D.G. & Enford, B.T. (2009). Helms People of Color Identity Model. *Developing Multicultural Counseling Competence*, second edition (pp.2–9). Boston, MA: Pearson Education.

Robson & Jerome (2016). 'I Believe' lyrics. Drake E., Graham. I., Shirl, J. & Stillman, A. (1953). www.youtube.com/watch?v=ybaC-VHN1MA.

Spalding B., Grove, J. & Rolfe, A. (2019). An exploration of Black, Asian and minority ethnic counsellors' experiences of working with White clients. *Counselling & Psychotherapy Research*, 19(1), 75–82. https://onlinelibrary.wiley.com/doi/epdf/10.1002/capr.12194.

Woods-Giscombé, C. (2010). Superwoman schema: African American women's views on stress, strength, and health. *Qualitative Health Research*, 20(5), 668–683. www.ncbi.nlm.nih.gov/pmc/articles/PMC3072704.

Part II

Training in Context of Pasts, Presents and Futures

Chapter 6

Two Black Tutors!

PATMARIE COLEMAN & PAULETTE GIBSON

Abstract
We describe our journeys to becoming counselling tutors, including our experiences of our own training and how it has influenced us as trainers. We reflect on some of the challenges and triumphs we experienced along the way. We share our thoughts about working with a diverse group of counselling students and how race and culture affected the dynamic of the training groups.

Keywords
Black tutors, race, culture, achievement, unspoken, risk, opportunities, support, training

Introduction
We will reflect on how we as two Black women of African and Asian Caribbean descent found our way into teaching and then to teaching together; how our heritage affected others and ourselves both during our own training and as trainers. We will also explore the challenge that just being ourselves presented to others and how the internalization of being strong Black women affected each of us.

Our work and training history
Paulette
In the early 1990s, I worked for a local authority as a housing manager. Over a period of time the work changed, I felt the need to move on and thought about a change of career. I became aware of an introduction to counselling course offered to staff in our department. I applied, joined

the short course and instinctively knew this training was something I wanted to pursue. I thought about what practical support would need to be in place before progressing onto the certificate level, and this involved having a conversation with my line manager at that time, who supported my decision to continue with my training. By then I had three young children, and a trusted family friend helped with the childcare and all the demands that come with having a family. Without her support, I could not have done my training.

The Diploma course: After completing my certificate in counselling, in 1998 I applied for a place on a Diploma in Counselling course (person-centred). I was accepted and was excited and anxious about gaining new personal insights and the possibility of changing my career.

Although the group was culturally diverse, I was aware of my 'difference' in this setting and that I was part of a small group that described themselves as Black. The majority of students were white female; this was also a reflection of the tutor group who were all white and female, apart from one male personal development (PD) group facilitator. The irony of this environment was that the college was located in an area that had a large African/Caribbean population. Outside the college I was from an ethnic group that formed the majority of the landscape; however, in the classroom my race, ethnicity and sense of belonging mirrored that of the 'otherness' I felt in the wider society.

I found the course consuming. I was learning about values that matter to me and about my relationships with others (Tudor *et al.*, 2004). An aspect of the course that stood out for me was that the topics of race and culture had been timetabled in the second year of my Diploma course for one-and-a-half hours. There was no teaching or discussion about cultural differences in the first year, although thankfully our PD facilitator was open to hearing the group's experience of race and issues associated with race and Black issues (Mckenzie-Mavinga, 2009). The allocated time frame seemed inadequate and I thought it would prevent the group from exploring these areas in any meaningful depth. On reflection, I imagine the tutor's decision to have a narrow window for discussion was a way of limiting what might 'spill out' from the group discussion. I wondered was keeping control of the time frame a way of managing their own anxiety in regards to race in particular?

The discussion on race was left to the students to take the lead on. In retrospect, I can now see that the Black students were deemed the experts in regards to what it means to be Black and with an eagerness for the discussion to take place I jumped right into the empty space left by the tutors. Frederica Brooks (1999, p.281) a Black trainee art therapist captures my experience when she writes '...on matters of colour I am no longer a trainee, but an honorary tutor...' Tutors have power and authority and in choosing not to facilitate the outlined discussion or to move the topic away from race to other areas of difference such as gender or sexuality, they can block exploration into the subject and can send a message that there are other areas that are more important to talk about, placing a hierarchy on lived experienced of oppression.

I did, however, develop safe relationships with peers, some tutors and supervisors. In these relationships, I began to take risks and my confidence grew. Two years after qualifying, my private practice was growing fast and I began to think about the possibility of teaching.

Patmarie

I trained as a counsellor in the early 1990s after working as an advice and support worker for a number of years. While I was employed in a further education (FE) college as a guidance and support officer, I decided to train as a counsellor. The decision felt right and I was determined that I would find a way to do it; Rogers (1959) would describe this as the actualizing tendency. At the time, I had no idea how I would pay for it or about the time and commitment required, or the way in which it would change my life. I had a young family, was working full time and had little to no excess income. A number of things supported my ability to complete this training: listening to myself and responding to my organismic valuing process (Mearns & Thorne with McLeod, 2013), a tenacity and determination that I would find a way, and belief that I could.

The course: I attended my first training in a South East London College. The tutors made a conscious effort to recruit a diverse student group; they made an effort to acknowledge difference and facilitated an environment of openness and exploration. They, a female white South African and a white British male had made efforts to provide the group with Black role models in the form of visiting tutors. One, a woman who facilitated sessions on race awareness, the other, a man who facilitated sessions on Gestalt therapy. Looking back, I view this as radical, a Black man who was employed to present sessions on something other than race! There were a number of sessions specifically dedicated to exploring race and racism, very different from something inadequate added on at the end of a course, as I came to hear about and experience on other courses and was confirmed by Watson (2011). I am aware now that this ethos of difference and diversity that I experienced was not the norm, and that the majority of trainees and qualified counsellors were ill-equipped to deal with these issues (Mckenzie-Mavinga, 2016). My training established a foundation on which my expectations were built. The Black trainers were people who were a reflection of me, they looked like people I knew and grew up with, they were not 'other' to me and they provided a 'Black empathic approach' as described by Mckenzie-Mavinga (2009, p.58). The core tutors encouraged rather than ignored issues of difference and facilitated an environment that stimulated discussion, reflection and challenge. This course encouraged and supported my growing self-awareness and provided an environment where risks could be taken (Watson 2011). My final essay, which was open to choice, focused on the emerging awareness of my identity.

Paulette: My introduction to teaching

In 2003, I was encouraged by a friend and colleague to apply for a position at an FE college to teach on their Introduction to Counselling Skills course, and although I questioned whether I was ready, my colleague arranged for me to observe her teach a few sessions and then I applied and got the job. Throughout the development of my teaching practice, I have learned the importance of having support.

I really enjoyed working with the students. I appreciated their enthusiasm for learning; it was a joy building relationships with them, and a privilege being a witness to their growth. I received a great deal of satisfaction from being a tutor. Being a small part of the students' journey towards becoming a counsellor excited me.

I taught on the Introduction to Counselling courses for a while, and as my confidence grew I began to consider what it might be like to teach on some of the other counselling courses. Around that time there was an opening on the certificate course at the same college; I applied but didn't get the job. I was told I needed more teaching experience, only to discover that the applicant who got the job had less counselling and teaching experience than I did. I questioned their decision, but also felt there were still other opportunities in the department to develop my teaching practice.

Some months later another opportunity arose in the same college to teach on another counselling course for one academic term. I made my interest in the position clear, but was again told it was better for me to stay on the Introduction to Counselling Course. It felt like I was being told 'you need to know your place'. I challenged their decision; I kept trying to find words that would articulate my distress but Eddo-Lodge (2017, p.223) reminds us that, 'Attacking racist frame, form, functions and codes with no words to describe them can make you feel like you are the only one who sees the problem.' I found myself arguing with them a lot, and often I felt hurt and alone.

That was a very difficult time for me, and I learned from that experience that support is crucial. I was part of a peer support group that supported me throughout this time. They helped me to understand the dynamics between me, a Black woman and some of the white female tutors in my team. Part of the process of my recovery involved forgiving myself for staying in what I experienced as a racist, unsupportive and stressful environment for so long. And being the 'strong Black woman' was not helpful.

> We are Black women, defined as never-good-enough... I will become strong, the best, excel in everything, become the very best because I don't dare to be anything else. It is my only chance to become good-enough to become human. (Lorde, 1984, p.170)

It became clear there were too many barriers for me to progress in the environment I have described. I continued to build my practice with my supervisor and use therapy to process my experience of racism, and both those relationships helped to restore and replenish some of what had been lost in my battle to be heard and seen. It was time for me to move on.

Patmarie

A year after graduating from the diploma, I was encouraged and supported into teaching by a politically aware white woman who had been a member of RACE. RACE was a branch of the British Association for Counselling and Psychotherapy (BACP) specifically set up to look at issues of race and working on anti-racism. Our supervisor had also been a member of RACE and had been involved in making a training video looking at how to deal with racism and sexism. In this supportive environment working with two allies, I was able to explore, develop and process the relationships and the issues that were emerging in our teaching groups.

I enjoy learning, and my grandmother instilled the importance and power of education in me from a young age. After taking my initial steps into teaching, I completed a Certificate in Teaching qualification, which provided confidence and a framework to support my developing teaching style. I continued to expose myself to training that challenged and stimulated my self-awareness and natural curiosity. Since then I have expanded my teaching qualifications and been a core tutor on a number of courses.

Paulette: Meeting Patmarie

In 2004, I joined a group work course that was facilitated by a white middle-class counsellor, which was of course a familiar experience. What was different, however, was the ease with which the facilitator talked about race and culture on the first day of the training and throughout the duration of the course. She acknowledged her whiteness and the power and privilege that came with that. This was very new for me; I had never experienced that level of self-awareness with any tutor in relation to race and power. I felt safe enough to challenge myself and other members of the group. At the end of the course I still had questions about my ability to be a facilitator (I was still recovering from my experience at the FE college). She encouraged me to apply for the position of PD group facilitator for their Counselling Certificate students. I was offered the job and that's when I first met Patmarie, who was the co-tutor on the certificate course.

I remember meeting Patmarie for the first time and being taken by surprise that she was Black. It was exciting, and I remember telling a few friends and colleagues that I was working with a Black tutor. It was bit like the times when you would call up friends to tell them there was a Black person on the TV! A year after joining the counselling tutor team, Patmarie's co-tutor resigned from their certificate course, I applied for the position, was accepted and never looked back.

Paulette: Working with Patmarie

Our training partnership worked. Although our friendship and professional relationship was still in its early stages there was an immediate feeling of trust, and this meant I could be vulnerable, I didn't need to 'know it all'. It also meant we could challenge each other – we are both opinionated. This relationship was important to me for so many reasons, but fundamentally it allowed me to be who I was at that time and gave space to who I would become. Experiencing a safe relationship and working in an environment that placed difference and diversity at the core of its courses helped us in creating a safe space for the students on our course.

Patmarie: Working with Paulette

I met Paulette while I was teaching with a white woman who spoke in an aware way about difference and diversity, but over time, my experience of her became increasingly at odds with what she said. During the period that we worked together I started doubting myself, I became more and more deskilled and started to feel anxious. I noticed that I dreaded the frequent communication that she initiated and I started limiting contact with her, my gut or organismic valuing process alerting me to my distress (Mearns & Thorne with McLeod, 2013). Paulette was part of the wider all-white teaching team and had noticed that something was wrong; she reached out to me and helped me make sense of what was happening. Having that space with her where I felt validated and supported enabled me to breathe and reground myself. My personal power started to return and I was able to set boundaries and take action. After a period of time and some changes in staff, Paulette and I became a teaching team and that was the start of an amazing working relationship.

Paulette: Teaching together

Five years after qualifying as a counsellor and encountering multiple experiences of racism I was finally in a position where I could co-design and deliver a counselling certificate course. More importantly, I was teaching with another Black female therapist, in an environment where we were supported. When we progressed to running the Counselling in Practitioner Diploma course we realized this was another significant achievement and I felt it was a special moment within British counselling training.

We felt excited about what two Black tutors would bring to our profession but I also had some anxiety about how we would deliver a course through a Black perspective, particularly as there was no evidence of this having been taught within a further education college setting. Some of our thoughts were as follows:

- As Black women, we were aware that aspects of ourselves were invisible in society and we wondered how this would translate to the classroom.

- How could we make theory written by dead middle-class white men more relevant to us? 'As with most therapies in the UK today, person-centred counselling/psychotherapy evolved from within a white, western paradigm' (Haugh & Paul, 2008, p.42).

- What support did we need to support the work we were doing with our students? I felt the responsibility of us mapping this journey.

Patmarie: Teaching together

We taught together on a one-year certificate-level course for a number of years and then later progressed to the Practitioner in Counselling Diploma. Our working relationship was compared to a successful marriage; we bounced off of each other, brought different strengths and qualities and received regular positive feedback from our students. This was a period in my teaching where I felt I had a solid foundation, I was confident in my abilities, I felt able to take risks and to allow the learning to unfold and emerge in the moment, facilitating encounter and working in the moment. I knew that I could take risks because trust was built in our teaching relationship; this foundation enabled us to support and provide opportunities to students who traditionally struggled more and perhaps would not have succeeded in other settings.

Before the commencement of teaching together on the diploma we had a period of reflection and introspection which included the implications of being a Black teaching team, *the* core team, carrying out the majority of the teaching and holding the course and students together. We recognized that this was an unprecedented occurrence and pondered on the impact on ourselves, our colleagues and our students.

Here are some of our reflections from that time:

- How might the students feel?

- How would other people in the department react?

- What were the implications for the wider teaching team?

- What did this mean for our future?

- How might we develop?

- Could we conquer the world?

At the outset, a Black colleague reacted with apprehension; the response startled and disappointed me. I felt hurt and unsupported and felt this deeply. I experienced it as a lack of positive regard and lack of confidence in our ability and visions for the future. Now I can reflect that I had expected support and encouragement because we had shared histories and both a spoken and unspoken understanding of the inequality of being Black in this environment. Mckenzie-Mavinga (2009) writes about the dynamics of racism and the impact that it has on all of us. I wonder whether this was such an unprecedented situation that it was impossible to imagine that it could work well – after all, why was it not already a regular occurrence? A memory from my education informs this last sentence: the only Black teacher in my secondary school was form tutor to the class in the lowest stream (i.e., the least academically able students). There were five classes in my year, and even at my tender and unaware age, I was aware of this dynamic.

Two white colleagues embarking on teaching together for the first time on this course would have been likely to have had some concerns, but due to their 'knapsack of privilege' would have been unlikely to have been reflecting on the impact of the colour of their skin (McIntosh, 1988).

Paulette and Patmarie: Working with students

The ethos in the department, consciously cultivated by the department head and her deputy, involved recruiting ethnically and culturally diverse teaching groups (Celia Levy's podcast, BAATN website). Putting this process into action required careful planning and clear decision-making. Students who met the entry requirements were processed in a way that ensured diversity and difference were represented in the group where possible. This meant that we were actively combatting the tide that perpetuates inequality based on academic qualifications (Lago & Smith, 2010).

It could be argued from a person-centred perspective that awareness and recognition of difference would take place through trusting the application and sufficiency of Rogers' (1959) conditions. However, we chose to make a conscious decision to explicitly include this throughout the training. Students, from the start of the course, were required through small and large group discussion and assessed written work, to examine who they were, in relation to class, race, gender and so on, and to begin to think about how their identity might impact on their client work. Some of these exercises tended to bring an unspoken resentment from some white students who felt, for example, that 'they didn't have a culture' and that we were somehow trying to 'put a label on them'. We witnessed a notable difference in the white students in the group: silences, lack of shared implicit understanding and confusion over terms that were being used and understood by the other students. We understood the importance of being aware of the 'unspoken relationship' (Mearns, 2003, p.64) and the dynamic this created in the group. Holding a facilitated space each week for the whole group to process what had impacted them enabled students to take a risk in exploring their assumptions about each other and us. As tutors, it was also inspiring to witness 'a gradual laying down of unvoiced reactions' (Mearns, 2003, p.65) in the group.

Smaller personal development groups were constructed in such a way that, where possible, a Black or ethnic minority student was not the solitary person of colour in the group. Our experience was that they would be perceived as the expert in Black issues and would have to contend with the white fragility (DiAngelo, 2018) that was evoked. An example of this we witnessed was a student of colour feeling the need to comfort the group by saying, 'It's okay, it's okay, nothing's changed we are all okay...' during a discussion on difference and racism. This additional stress and responsibility impacts their learning in a way that their white peers do not have to deal with. One of the previous teaching practices that we challenged was separating out students of colour so that their white peers could experience being in relationship with a Black peer. This strategy was not in support of the Black student and did not provide an opportunity to have their experiences recognized and resonated with from a Black perspective.

On a course where over a third of students were Black African, Caribbean or Asian, and with the addition of the two of us, two Black tutors, increasing this two almost half, the usual status quo was different. The students of colour experienced a level of safety that started implicitly and then through our facilitation was nurtured and evolved into being explicitly expressed through shared experiences which were acknowledged and understood. This environment provided a foundation which enabled the students to move beyond the need to explain, look after others or justify the inequalities they experienced, to having them acknowledged and feeling 'received' (Rogers, 1959). Discussions evolved to live struggles and naming issues like shadism, religion, culture, the white Eurocentric theory and training, making them feel like an outsider in their family and community, noticing and acknowledging their differences as Black people, intersectionality, dealing with racism in placement organizations, dealing with implicit racism from clients, disagreeing with peers, awareness or safety to explore, having to negotiate a world full of micro- and macroaggressions. Previously there had been little space to explore these issues, it being taken up by the need to explain and justify or placate white peers – a common phenomena acknowledged by Mckenzie-Mavinga (2009).

As tutors, it was *painful to hear and witness Black students' experiences of racism* – not wanting to be stereotyped as angry, aggressive, loud-mouthed or as holding all the answers when things got difficult talking about race. It was also extremely rewarding and life-enhancing to witness the change and growth in our students and know that our facilitation was contributing to the field of excellent counsellors.

Challenge, support and self-care

There have been many challenges along the way where we have needed support. We have found that having a supportive and experienced supervisor who has also been a trainer with experience of working with transcultural issues is a key cornerstone to this work. Having allies who can relate and support rather than deny, pathologize or ignore our experiences has been crucial. We have experienced the difference of being trained by and working with others who have theoretical knowledge in comparison to someone who is an ally. Watson (2011) highlights, and we have experienced, that trainers who are employed on academic merit have not necessarily worked on and processed their own cultural identity issues and consequently do not see them as an ongoing issue, as a result this obstructs their ability to support colleagues and of course students.

Conclusion

Our experience evidences that we achieved a developmentally supportive teaching and learning environment based on critical learning from our own training experiences. Along with making long overdue changes to counselling training (Lago & Thompson, 2002; McLeod, 2003; Mckenzie-Mavinga, 2009, 2016; Watson, 2011), the curriculum, materials and process of training have not embraced decolonization, which has hindered rather than supported our work.

We hope that the phenomenon of two Black trainers becomes a norm, a regular occurrence just like it is when there are two white trainers!

References

BAATN podcast, *Beyond silence – Black Issues in the therapeutic process*, Part 1, Episode 14.

Brooks, F. (1999). A Black Perspective on Art Therapy Training. In J. Campbell, M. Liebmann, F. Brooks, J. Jones & C. Ward, *Art Therapy, Race and Culture*, 281. London: Jessica Kingsley Publishers. Levy, Celia.

DiAngelo, R. (2019). *White Fragility: Why It's So Hard for White People to Talk About Racism.* London: Penguin, Random House.

Eddo-Lodge, R. (2017). *Why I'm No Longer Talking to White People About Race*. London: Bloomsbury Circus.

Haugh, S. & Paul, S. (2008). *The Therapeutic Relationship Perspectives and Themes*. Wyastone, Monmouthshire: PCCS Books.

Lago, C. & Smith, B. (2010). *Anti-Discriminatory Practice in Counselling & Psychotherapy*, second edition. London: Routledge.

Lorde, A. (1984). *Sister Outsider, Essays & Speeches*. Trumansberg, NY: The Crossing Press/ Freedom.

McIntosh, P. (1988). Working Paper 189. *White Privilege and Male Privilege: A Personal Account of Coming to See Correspondences through Work in Women's Studies*. Wellesley, MA: Wellesley College Center for Research on Women.

Mckenzie-Mavinga, I. (2009). *Black Issues in the Therapeutic Process*. Basingstoke: Palgrave Macmillan.

McKenzie-Mavinga, I. (2016). *The Challenge of Racism in Therapeutic Practice*. Basingstoke: Palgrave Macmillan.

Mearns, D. (2003). *Developing Person-Centred Counselling*, second edition. London: Sage Publications.

Mearns, D. & Thorne, B. with McLeod, J. (2013). *Person-Centred Counselling in Action*, fourth edition. London: Sage Publications.

Rogers, C.R. (1959). A Theory of Therapy, Personality, and Interpersonal Relationships, As Developed in the Client-Centered Framework. In S. Koch, (ed.), *Psychology: A Study of a Science. Vol. 3. Formulations of the Person and the Social Context* (pp.184–256). New York, NY: McGraw-Hill.

Tudor, L.E., Keemar, K., Tudor, K., Valentine, J. & Worrall, M. (2004). *The Person-Centred Approach: A Contemporary Introduction*. Basingstoke: Palgrave Macmillan.

Watson, V. (2011). Training for Multicultural Therapy: The Challenge and the Experience. In C. Lago (ed.), *The Handbook of Transcultural Counselling & Psychotherapy* (pp.17–29). Maidenhead, Berkshire: Open University Press.

Chapter 7

Misery Loves Company, But There's No Need to Walk Alone

Creating Supportive Networks and Coping with Isolation in Training for Students of Colour

LYDIA PURICELLI-CULVERWELL

Abstract

This is a reflection, recollection, retelling and response to the journey I've had so far in my training as an integrative transpersonal psychotherapist, while also co-chairing a student of colour network. I will explore what drives me to do this work. I hope to inspire other trainees to better cope with intense experiences of isolation and frustration, while working alongside white trainees and training staff. Additionally, I will show how building and/or seeking out networks can provide support through training and beyond.

Keywords

Race, racism, transcultural, transpersonal, therapy, counselling, students, networks, studying, coping, safety, allies, isolation, frustration

About me

I am of Indian, English and Italian heritage with Creole Mauritian influence from my step-mum. I grew up in south-east London where I was exposed to many different cultures. Being mixed-race, it was safer for me to be in black spaces than white. As a youth, I experienced racial abuse and I was made to feel inferior, 'othered', by middle-class white girls in my class at a convent school in Blackheath, an affluent part of

London. Culturally, I had more in common with my black, Asian and mixed-race friends.

As soon as I started my psychotherapy training, I felt triggered by some of the responses I got from middle-class white women. I hadn't been in similar company in an educational setting for nearly 20 years, since secondary school where they belittled me and my friends of colour. However, I wasn't concerned about making friends, and certainly not friends for whom I would have to shape-shift or dull my sparkle in order to fit in.

I worked for investment companies in the City for over 15 years, so I was all too familiar with the classist, racist and prejudiced views of white privileged middle- and upper-class people. At college, I made friends with smokers during breaks, breathing out the intensely emotional exercises where we explored our own and our peers' material. We shared a common denominator; we were all working class. So, I felt somewhat at home.

Sadly, these friends fell away because they couldn't afford the course fees and the cost of therapy, and they weren't able to stop working full-time to fit in the training and placement hours. Often, as students of colour, we are from lower socio-economic backgrounds and don't have the resources, time and money to train as counsellors and therapists. This is a barrier to training, which institutions and accrediting bodies still need to break down.

Connecting with other students of colour

I became aware of the Black, African and Asian Therapy Network (BAATN) at the end of my second year of training when race and transcultural therapy were discussed at our placement Christmas party. The discussion highlighted the lack of training on diversity and transcultural issues on our course. A white student said he had raised this issue with the college, which said there was no capacity in the curriculum for additional training; however, they would extend the reading list. Over a year later, we saw no sign of an extended reading list.

I joined BAATN in summer 2020 after setting up the Black, Asian and Minority Ethnic (BAME) student group. Instantly, I was struck by the number of available resources and groups and found only one transpersonal therapist of colour in the BAATN directory.

BAATN enabled me to gain valuable training when I attended its workshop 'The Challenge of Racism in Therapeutic Practice', hosted by leading transcultural psychotherapist Dr Isha Mckenzie-Mavinga. It was ideal because I wanted to fill knowledge gaps that my college wasn't covering regarding race, culture and racism in therapy. I felt admiration for Dr Mckenzie-Mavinga, seeing an inspiring and experienced woman of colour teach and hold the space. It occurred to me that, bar having one black tutor, Dr Dwight Turner, all my tutors and supervisors were white, which wasn't right in my eyes.

I was content being in a room, albeit virtual, with others like me, people from my community. That's the feeling white trainees walk into on entering college; they're at home with their peers, lecturers and supervisors. So, you cannot underestimate the impact this has on trainees of colour, which is why it's paramount to seek out black or brown lecturers and educators, and, most importantly, safe spaces with other therapists of colour in training.

Extracurricular activities

If you are studying psychotherapy and counselling, your course is likely to have limited training and support in transcultural issues. Reading publications by Dr Mckenzie-Mavinga has grounded so much of my lived experience and journey through training, as have other writers such as Colin Lago, Judy Ryde, Fanny Brewster and Dr Dwight Turner. These transcultural writers challenge racism in therapy, helping to fill the gaps in learning and supplement the generic Eurocentric/colonized training. Their material provides essential theories and concepts, which people of colour need present in discussions on race. Attending their talks and participating in groups like 'Sitting with Discomfort' and networks like 'Black Therapy Matters' reassures me that some of the therapeutic community is moving in the right direction, and therapists of colour are growing in numbers. I meet other students of colour from other colleges in these spaces and it has helped me build my network and friends in the industry.

Advice to students of colour

Join groups that will help you to deal with and process your experiences. Connect with students or therapists who are going through or have similar experiences to yours. These groups are healing, enriching and inspiring. More of these spaces are opening up but they're limited, so you should try to access what you can, when you can.

Once, I had to choose between attending a placement supervision session or a monthly student support group at BAATN (the previous one was oversubscribed). Apprehensive, I told my supervisor it was one of the only safe spaces I had to process my issues with racism on the course. He understood, and that was affirming. It's still a challenge for students of colour to find these spaces and access the support they desperately need, but things are improving. Black Therapy Matters is a student-led initiative that addresses this directly. It's building an online community, has WhatsApp groups, drop-in sessions, study groups and a book club to connect students of colour. These spaces are such a contrast to college because you are surrounded by other students of colour going through the same challenges of isolation and discomfort.

Time for action, starting the network

I began 2020 discussing the lack of transcultural and diversity issues with the six other students of colour in my year. We started a WhatsApp group to connect and share articles, resources and information about training events, but we didn't plan to approach the college at that stage. Suddenly, the Covid-19 pandemic hit, the murder of George Floyd happened, and the whole world woke up to racism!

Black people in America, like black people in the UK, are discriminated against, harassed, profiled, unjustly criminalized and disproportionately incarcerated. I often wondered why the world couldn't see this – the white world, that is. It had to take a pandemic for everyone to have an existential crisis and realize that we are no different as humans. The virus does not discriminate, so why should we?

Capacity and experience

When white students in my year began asking questions about the Black Lives Matter (BLM) protests and racism, I invited them to join our WhatsApp group. I scheduled a kick-off meeting, did some contracting to create a safe space for everyone and set out the following core aims:

- Establish contracting at the start of each meeting.

- Create a safe space for all members, especially for students of colour.

- Have open and honest dialogue around issues of race, racism and culture.

- Maintain confidentiality – information shared in meetings is not for onward distribution
- members should not use the group like a psychodynamic process group process.
- Show respect for each other's perspective and experience.
- Allow opinions and views to be shared in the 'I' space with non-judgemental acceptance from peers.

I gave each student time to share their thoughts on BLM and George Floyd's murder. The white students realized they had been oblivious to racism, and everyone expressed their sadness and grief. I captured key words and the frequency with which they were shared. I've illustrated these in the word cloud below (Figure 7.1).

Figure 7.1: The Centre for Counselling and Psychotherapy Education's student of colour and allies kick off meeting: 'What has come up for you?'[1]

We discussed the group's needs and the college's indifference towards the BLM protests. It was very clear that more training and support were critical, especially for the students of colour. We needed to recruit members from other years, so our year representatives reached out to

---

1   All rights reserved for Dearwhitetherapists.

those students. I asked the students who responded how they identified themselves racially, added white students to the WhatsApp group and set up calls with students of colour to enquire about their concerns, experiences of the training, how negative or positive it had been and their immediate needs.

My experiences with racism

As I set up calls with the students of colour, I reflected on my training experiences. I recalled when we had to select groups to identify which transpersonal element-type we most associated with. The Centre for Counselling and Psychotherapy Education's (CCPE) transpersonal model utilizes these types as personality or character traits. I was definitely *water*: compassionate, flexible, sensitive and so on. I sat with other element groups identified as *air* and *fire*. I didn't join *earth* because it didn't seem to reflect any aspect of my personality at the time.

When I joined the fire group, a white student exclaimed, 'You shouldn't have even sat anywhere else.' He said he only saw me as fire (anger). He didn't know me and he couldn't see past his projection that black and brown people are angry and aggressive. It hurt at the time, as it had hurt countless times before at work and school in white English groups.

I recalled another incident where we were talking about a lecturer on how the elements model worked. Suddenly, a white female student lunged at me, 'You take all the air out of the room. You're like a volcano ready to erupt. Why do we have to listen to what you think?' I tried to explain I was complementing, not raising my voice or insisting anyone agree with my point of view. She started yelling that I was just too much for her. I remained calm and said I didn't need to take this.

I said I'd leave if she didn't stop, but she continued her tirade. I left in tears. The facilitator didn't intervene. My friend Helen came to my aid and I asked her, 'Why do white English people treat me like this? It never happens with black or Italian people, I'm not too loud or too much for them.' I returned to the room and explained that this is what I was having to endure again from white English people. She protested she wasn't racist, but I said if she persisted, I would report her as this wasn't fair and safe for me. She cried (white tears), trying to gain the sympathy of the group and the facilitator, who couldn't see my pain or vulnerability as the only person of colour in the group being attacked.

The facilitator explained how projections worked, that the white student was projecting her unconscious anger onto me as an object, that as I was in touch with 'my anger' or 'fire' (truth and light) and this scared her. But I wasn't angry. I was simply talking. Conversely, while talking with the only black student in my year, she said, 'Lydia, you're a breath of fresh air.' The paradox was striking. The white woman said I took the air away and the black woman said I brought it into the space!

The third major incident that took place at college was when I submitted my first-year theory essay late due to extenuating circumstances. It was rushed and wasn't edited or proofed sufficiently prior to submission. When the mark came back capped at 50, I was just relieved I'd passed. The feedback included a remark, an assumption, about why my grammar and spelling may have fallen below expectations: 'This was understandable as English isn't your first language', wrote the marker. Based purely on my Italian name, she assumed I wasn't English and 'othered' me. Her sympathy was just patronizing.

I raised the issue with my tutor who said she didn't understand why I was so offended (gaslighting). She explained she knew the marker, and she was 'a lovely lady'. The actions of the marker and apathetic response of my tutor are a sad indictment of racism in our education system. This harvests the conditions that make it challenging to complain or call out racism.

Connecting your material to others

When I shared my experiences, the students of colour confirmed they too had experienced isolation, frustration and trauma. They had encountered many episodes of covert and overt racism by students and staff. I listened intently to their traumatic stories and made notes but kept anonymity, only pressing for names in cases involving staff. They hoped the network could make changes that would help students of colour. They informed their years and the numbers grew.

Building the steering committee

I had previous experience setting up and chairing networks at work, so knew what was required to drive it forward. We had to share responsibilities. Luckily, Namalee Bolle, a student in the year above me was also trying to make changes. She felt compelled to expose racism in the therapeutic profession after incidents involving her year head, the college and peers. She read a powerful poem she had written at her end-of-year lecture:

Dear White Therapists...
You are the healers, the holders of
'safe space'
It's therefore your duty to acknowledge race
To honour black clients and people of colour
Who pay you to see them for just under an hour
'I don't see colour'
You say it's 'well meaning'
I guarantee your client has...
Very.
Different.
Feelings.
So, do you see them clearly? Or is it through a lens?
A conditioned racial bias makes you THINK you comprehend?
Can you hold the client projection, if you 'become' the enemy?
Are you willing to dive deep and be honest about 'therapy'?
Are you doing shadow work on what your ancestors, maybe, did?
Or are you too afraid to look in case it challenges your 'id'?
Have you looked into your family tree to see, if racism shows up?
Can you summon up the courage to clear the generational muck?
When their family systems are 'enmeshed' and more 'collective'...
Are you 'helping' by enforcing an individualistic westernised
    perspective?
Are you aware of what slavery created? Of the trauma that remains
    unhealed ...?
Because naming it isn't instigated; talk of race unwelcome in our field
As a holocaust survivor's child, you validate my existence
With my epigenetic lineage, there's no need for my insistence
But 400 years of genocide is treated with distrust
Am I missing something here or is the 'mental health' system
    concussed?
Diagnosing black pain with white analysis feels like supremacy to me
In the age-old cultural tradition of controlling colony.
Monumentally narcissistic
Grandiosity is historic
Diagnosis for the 'other' is hysteric
Great Britain's owned everything, except its shadow – How ironic.
Stolen identity, whitewashed in their own nation, no depth examina-
    tion, only classification
YOU try psychologically existing freely in a system that systemically
    controls even therapeutic individuation

What of my brown mother's sense of self whose heritage was replaced
with someone else?

What of my black client's endless list of diagnoses?

Did any doctor who assessed them check the effect of being perma-
nently gaslit – did they even care to notice?

'Drapetomania', the disease of running away from your slave master
was once a respected pathology in psychiatry

Dear white therapists, the mental health system cannot take its racist
history lightly.

By Namalee Bolle, @dearwhitetherapists[2]

Namalee had offered to work with the faculty to address the issue, but
she was sadly ignored. I suggested we work jointly and co-chaired the
network to drive the changes we both desired. We asked representatives from each year to manage their year's requirements and requests
and succeeded in recruiting two first-year students of colour. No one
volunteered from the second, third or fourth years.

I approached Daniel, a white student who was already a very active
ally. He had energy and passion and understood the needs of the white
students in the group, expressing their views and needs. Another student
of colour in my year was reluctant to be a representative because she
wanted to heal her trauma during the protests without feeling the need
to educate white students in the group. However, she stayed on to help
us, and her contributions were invaluable. We had our team, our squad.

Balancing views and ideas is crucial and being diplomatic as chair
is paramount. You need to give everyone space to debate a topic or
idea. Having this sounding board allows for a diversity of thought. We
care about our work and want to get it right. We're realistic about the
changes we can make, and we have the momentum to achieve them.
We challenge and correct each other along the way, so we develop and
grow together rather than butt heads; humility is key. There is little to
no 'ego' in our squad.

Strength in numbers: people have extraordinary skills

If you're alone and marginalized, you can find allies and friends by connecting with other students of colour in other years. You'll be galvanized
into sharing ideas and working collaboratively. Everyone is endowed

---

2   All rights reserved for Dearwhitetherapists.

with different skills and experience. My skills are in marketing, writing presentations and refining messages. I was able to pitch my thoughts and ideas at the steering committee and catch valuable insights and points of view on the rebound.

What's in a name?

When building or creating your network you'll need to decide on a name. We started with the BAME acronym. At the time, I didn't realize the full extent of the unease around the term until a student of colour raised the issue. I was willing to accept alternative suggestions and we decided to go with Students of Colour and Allies (SOCA). I consulted the steering committee and took the decision to change it.

Be greedy, ask for help

We approached Dr Dwight Turner, a faculty member at the time, who secured a meeting with the college's management committee, where we presented an extensive proposal, highlighting easily actionable points to address the key issues. I spent time gathering suggestions for improvements from network members and the steering committee and collated the key issues that both students of colour and white students faced around safety, the lack of support, and receiving additional training on transcultural and racial diversity issues.

I sought advice about the proposal from friends who ran networks in other organizations. They advised me to include verbatim quotes and ensure I didn't allow anyone to talk over me. Most importantly, they told me to get the management committee to agree to follow-up. Don't be afraid to seek outside help or advice (something that people of colour often struggle with), and knowing when and how to ask for help is crucial.

Our proposal was clear and left no room for doubt about the issue of racism and the lack of transcultural training. This was now a matter the college couldn't ignore, it had to be addressed. Subsequently, I convinced the heads of supervision and academia to agree to follow up.

Working together

In preparation for the meeting with the heads of supervision, I devised 'workshops for working with race in supervision', which uncovered the issues both white and students of colour faced. I created two groups to provide a safe space for open discussions to uncover the main issues. It caused tension, but I was ready, thanks to the training I received from Dr Mckenzie-Mavinga.

One white student was very keen to participate. However, a mixed-race student questioned our motives for separating into two groups by race, so I explained the relevancy of this controlled research method. The previously eager white student then began to struggle with denial about her whiteness, guilt and shame and didn't want to be in the 'white' group. The aforementioned mixed-race student became very disruptive and revealed a lot of confusion around her identity and internalized racism. The mixed-race student had already caused a lot of upset to the students of colour when they questioned the need for a directory of transpersonal therapists of colour – and not wanting to be included on it either.

When those students asked for a mixed group, I realized they might compromise what we were trying to achieve and prove to the college. The resulting confusion and disruption threatened to jeopardize everything, so I had to intervene. Although I remained professional and diplomatic, careful not to exclude anyone, the mixed-race student backed down and I did an individual interview with them, and the white student then left the group.

Empowering workshops

The workshops were phenomenal. We asked students to prepare and process their thoughts to be in the right frame of mind to speak openly about their experiences of being isolated, ignored and facing racism from staff and students at college and during their placements and supervision.

The students of colour felt they were over-identifying with clients of colour and not having the space to process their pain and trauma, being left unsupported during the BLM protests by the college. There were tears and heads were nodding and shaking in disbelief as we shared our stories.

Overall, the students of colour were grateful for the space to be seen and heard. The white students acknowledged they were 'treading on eggshells' around the issue of race and culture. They felt there was a lack of training and support from the supervisors at the college. They struggled to find the correct language and terminology to use and wanted supervisors to get extra training. We took these findings to the college, and it has implemented compulsory anti-racist training for all staff. It has since updated the transcultural lecture to be more explicit about racial differences and added a weekend workshop for the first- and third-year students.

Continue to shine

We shouldn't be ashamed of feeling anger and resentment, but rather try to redirect that energy into bettering ourselves. We must take advantage of the knowledge and skills we acquire as we live out our lives in a white world. Don't dull your sparkle to appease others; continue to shine. Be unapologetic. Remaining silent isn't going to help you in the long run. You may get some backlash and resistance, but the option is there. If you don't, it will only allow others to dominate you and potentially cause more harm in the longer term. When you have a crew, a network, friends, associates and allies, you have a safety net to turn to and fall back on.

You don't have to speak out all the time

One of our biggest struggles is knowing when to speak up and when to remain silent. Timing is everything. Can you time it and leave room for a response or make your point and leave intact? Are there others who will support you? Can you incorporate the theory you have learned into your response?

Not speaking out doesn't mean you should tolerate racism. Deploy your therapeutic skills. Paraphrase or reflect on what is said and try to use 'I' statements so people understand that what they've said is offensive to 'you'.

Process your own trauma and experiences with racism

It's crucial to be aware of your own material to reduce instances of being triggered or re-traumatized. If you feel it's safe to do so, consult your therapist, even if the therapist is white. I did it. It wasn't without its challenges for both of us, but I made up my mind, I no longer wanted to endure this on my own.

Why can we bring every other issue to therapy, except for this one, racism? Because we're afraid of what the white person will think – will they get it? Will they gaslight us? If it feels safe to do, then at least try to honour your therapy for being able to be a place where you can be vulnerable.

Speak, write, draw, paint, dance, blog, podcast, start a journal, do whatever you need to express yourself creatively. Creativity is so important to the process of healing. Often, we struggle to find words or someone to talk to, so these outlets are essential.

Whether you talk to others in groups or one-on-one, when you feel able and safe to do so, please try. Bearing witness to the suffering and experiences of others can help you connect with your own material and experiences.

Find a mentor

One of the most critical elements of support, which I added to my artillery, is a mentor. I applied for a mentor via BAATN's Each One Teach One Programme. I spend an hour a month with my mentor who, like me, is mixed-race. She understands my blended family and background, which many white people struggle to comprehend.

I can bring anything to my mentor, who is always on hand to listen, guide and motivate me to go further. I want to appeal to qualified therapists to mentor others like me and help the next generation of students. You'll help to grow our community and touch so many others.

Build allies

Allyship has been pivotal to building support for students of colour. White students wanted to learn about our struggles and get involved in our fight against racism, so we brought them into our network. When I was subjected to a verbal racist attack by a white student, it meant I had support.

Our white allies stood by students of colour like me and spoke out in our defence. They confronted a group of hostile white students who wanted to lambast the victim of racism (me) for complaining, rather than confront the perpetrator. Although terrifying for me, it was a momentous occasion, which shows the need for white people to understand the nuances in racism and how they work. As a result, some white students changed their position while others unveiled more of their racism.

Allyship is vital within a network. It can come in the form of students of colour and white students who want to change. Allies can learn how to speak up for students of colour and help their transcultural client work. There is a place to support each other and deepen compassion and empathy for all races.

Don't be afraid to put your needs first

Self-care more than you've ever cared for yourself before – set boundaries for others and yourself. As a trainee therapist of colour, you must endure more than your white counterparts, work ten times harder and deal with a complex life that's demanding. That's just how it is.

Being in white spaces and suppressing so much of our personalities, experiences and material is damaging to our mental health. You'll need stamina to get through it, so take breaks at a manageable pace, for you. Prioritize your self-care.

Things to consider

Not all therapists are empathetic

This is a caring profession. We would like to believe that everyone has it in their heart to see the pain that we, as people of colour, experience. Some will, but for those who don't, all I can say is take time to contemplate and reflect and come to your own resolution. Otherwise, your struggle to convince them of your reality may wear you down. Your energy is better spent on healing yourself; it is not your job to educate them – that is the training institution's responsibility.

Develop patience and high level of tolerance

You need patience and tolerance to build compassion for white people, and people of colour who are in denial who can't see the harm they're doing to themselves and even their community. This is difficult work. At times, I've felt like I'm only three steps ahead and other times I see I'm ten steps ahead in developing my awareness and processing my recognition trauma (Mckenzie-Mavinga, 2009). However, I'm learning about myself. Concurrently, others are teaching me about their process and their journeys into their deep and complex material to uncover their racial prejudices or internalized racism.

Colour blindness

Some students don't want to see their own colour, whether white or brown. Rarely for black people do they have this option. This is an unlikely option for black people because they've had more time to identify with it. We don't live in a post-racial utopia, which many liberal white westerners would want you to believe. So, it's essential to identify with your colour and what it means to you. Don't be disheartened by students of colour who don't want to be part of your network. Respect their journey and level of self-enquiry.

Talk in their modality and their language
I'm studying integrative transpersonal psychotherapy, analysing the collective unconscious shadow where racism lies, so white therapists know why we're raising this issue. It's an existential problem we must work through to reach our true soul nature and self-actualize.

Transpersonal psychotherapists often bypass race and culture for the soul and spiritually. If you understand the therapeutic modality they are coming from, it can help you have the reflexive dialogue that needs to happen in a language that will make sense to them.

And finally...
We belong to a 'caring profession' struggling to come to terms with racism among its members. Yes, racism in therapy exists, and it creates barriers leaving students of colour feeling hurt, isolated, frustrated and traumatized. Let's challenge the status quo by creating networks that enable us to empower each other. We can tap into resources provided by BAATN and join support groups like Sitting with Discomfort and Black Therapy Matters. We must do whatever we can to succeed in our profession.

Starting the SOCA network led to changes at my college. It gave us a unified voice that the college's management committee could not ignore. Our requests for transcultural training for students and staff, and support for students of colour, were finally acknowledged. The college has implemented new policies, updated the reading list, introduced new transcultural lectures and weekend workshops and funded a therapeutic support group for students of colour. Notwithstanding, our work isn't complete. There's much more work to be done. With the support of organizations like BAATN, qualified therapists and influencers like Eugene Ellis, Dr Dwight Turner and Dr Mckenzie-Mavinga, there's no holding back for us students of colour (and maybe even some allies).

Dedicated to all the students of colour who tried but didn't make it to the end!

Reference
Mckenzie-Mavinga, I. (2009). *Black Issues in Therapeutic Process*. London: Palgrave Macmillan.

Chapter 8

Myself as Therapist, Trainee, and the Power of Creativity

SYMONE STEPHENS-MORGAN

Abstract

My chapter aims to explore the benefits of art therapy and how through this medium, emotional, psychological and overall wellbeing can be facilitated. I will draw attention to the use of creativity as an important tool to communicate something about identity and culture from a black and other ethnic minority perspective by sharing my own personal experiences in addition to clinical work. Through this, I hope to highlight the need for diversity to be better represented within the arts therapeutic field on a practitioner level.

Throughout my chapter I use the term 'black' and 'other ethnic minority' when referring to myself or people who identify as non-white. I am aware that this may not reflect everyone's experiences of how they come to view themselves. Some people may be inclined to use 'a person of colour' or may feel that these terms can define or categorize them. The word black for me is a celebration of the colour of my skin and the cultural aspects it encapsulates – that of my heritage, of music, food and embracing this word in a positive way, rather than the negative stereotypes that can so commonly be attached.

Keywords

Art therapy, creativity, culture, difference, awareness, race, change, healing

Myself as therapist, trainee and the power of creativity

When I was initially approached with the opportunity to contribute to a book entitled: *Therapy in Colour*, I felt honoured. This was due to being able to share my experiences as a black practitioner and to provide insight into the benefits of art therapy and how this can be particularly helpful when exploring the cultural needs of black and other ethnic minority groups. In addition, it has been useful for me to reflect on the role that this medium has played on a personal level and a practical level – which are both so often intertwined.

Within my chapter, I also aim to encourage further thinking surrounding the training and therapeutic needs of black and other ethnic minority groups, provide first-hand experiences of delivering art therapy to these groups and highlight the importance of why I am working as a black art psychotherapist. In doing so, I hope that a greater awareness surrounding unconscious bias and the need for difference to be recognized as an integral part of training can be established – with the view of contributing to change.

I will begin by providing an overview of art therapy – a form of psychotherapy that does not require words, yet can embody experiences, feelings, emotions and thoughts through the use of imagery or objects. There needn't be any artistic skills involved. Through this medium, the focus is on the process of the art-making, rather than the end result. As an evidenced-based intervention for a range of needs, including trauma, anxiety, depression and loss, improvements to emotional and psychological wellbeing are recognized.

I came across art psychotherapy as a profession in 2013, and I recall feelings of excitement and relief. This was largely to do with being content and satisfied that I had found a career that I felt represented both myself and my skill set. What I had not acknowledged, however, was that therapy at the time felt very much embedded into a white, middle-class profession; something of a privilege to both have and study. In hindsight, I am pleased I had not given too much thought surrounding this as it may have deterred me from applying to the course in itself and not have provided me with the opportunity to share some of my experiences.

Throughout my journey as a trainee on the MA Art Psychotherapy course, I was one of very few black people and other ethnic minority groups. This was in stark contrast to the tutors on the course who were all white. In response to this, I used art-making early on to consciously communicate something about my own blackness. I would say that, on reflection, this was done on a non-verbal level as I couldn't physically find the words to describe the urgent need to be able to relate to somebody of an authoritative stance who looked like me. Who spoke my language. Who understood me. Morris (2020) writes: 'But for people from ethnic minority groups, there is a distinct lack of professionals who are able to relate to their specific life experiences – including issues of race, religion and culture – because the overwhelming majority of therapists are white.'

Through my imagery, particularly in the early stages, I was perhaps preparing myself for the reality of feeling somewhat uncomfortable and used creativity as a way to not only express this unease, but also remind myself to not lose sight of my own identity.

I dedicated a series of images to this (see Figure 8.1).

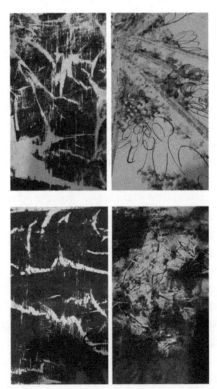

Figure 8.1: An expression of my blackness in art form

By exploring the colour black through mixed media, I wanted to create something aesthetically pleasing, something powerful and captivating. This was mainly due to challenging the description of what the word 'black' can represent and the negative connotations surrounding it. Art-making therefore provided me with a gradual platform, one which helped me to process my initial feelings and experiences and convey something about my identity in a more positive light.

In thinking about the fact that black and other ethnic minority groups make up a significant number of clients for art therapists (Barber & Campbell, 1999), I have found it useful to reflect on the way that difference (in relation to race) was addressed on the course itself. There was one day a year for 'Identity and Difference Day'. This was something which felt very much like a token gesture because although it existed for one day a year, in reality it felt very separate. It wasn't embedded within the training as part of the core lectures or literature. It also felt like a tick-box system rather than an honest approach to understanding difference. What it did provide, however, in addition to the experiential groups that I was in, was an opportunity to be aware of the language that art-making can echo about different cultures.

There were other ethnic minority groups, including international students, on the course, whose artwork at times spoke something about their heritage. Perhaps there was a sense of paralysis, particularly for me, in relation to naming the disproportionate representation of ethnic minority versus white students, and some of the imagery of this from black and other ethnic minority groups provided insight and captured something about their culture that could be recognized. For example, I became more aware of Asian and African influences surrounding tribal patterns, the vibrancy of colour, intricacies of design and even how things can become lost in translation through language differences and meaning.

It wasn't until I left university that I began to carry out my own research and came across BAATN (Black, African and Asian Therapy Network) for the first time. I recognized that there was a whole network of therapists and counsellors that represented diversity. This felt very fulfilling and may have informed my thinking when considering some of my own therapeutic needs at the time of my training surrounding race, identity and culture.

I recognized that as the years progressed, there were more students of black and other ethnic minority groups who were on the course. This felt very uplifting and perhaps made me aware that some change was happening.

When considering what my therapeutic needs were as a trainee, it would have been useful to have had a space to feel safe enough to address difference in relation to all the protected characteristics on the course. I believe that having this embedded within the training and literature would have encouraged important conversations to take place, between tutors and trainees alike, thus helping to prepare future practitioners for open and honest discussions between themselves and clients within and beyond the therapeutic space, where difference is represented in its entirety.

The language that art-making can convey is also open to interpretation and contains different meaning for different people from varied backgrounds. It would have been useful to have explored this while considering the cultural aspects that can be attached to imagery. Barber and Campbell (1999) suggest that: 'Fundamental questions (Were there cultural differences in imaging? How did differences in the race and colour of therapist and client affect the therapeutic relationship?) were not addressed.' Written over 20 years ago, it is saddening to acknowledge that little change has been made since.

Providing a therapeutic intervention within organizational settings plays a pivotal role when considering the overall wellbeing of those accessing their services. Through the medium of art therapy, I have worked with people from varied backgrounds and life experiences, each bringing their own individuality to the therapy space. There can, however, be shared themes and commonalities when thinking about the emotional and psychological wellbeing of some black and other ethnic minority groups. I will explain what this can look like when referring to my clinical work with adults and young people.

I have had the opportunity to work in the area of moderate to acute adult mental health and with children and young people who have a range of needs. This has been within a variety of settings, including education, the community and the National Health Service, and in complex and specialist areas including trauma, life-threatening conditions and behavioural needs.

I approached my clinical experience of working on adult inpatient wards with some apprehension and reservation. This was largely due to the stigma that can be attached to people who are acutely unwell – namely that recovery is deemed impossible. I therefore questioned how beneficial art therapy could be and if it would have any impact at all.

What was also apparent was the disproportionate representation of black and other ethnic minority patients on the wards, in comparison to white patients. It felt painful to see many people who looked like me but seeming so dazed, lethargic and, at times, out of touch with external reality; they were caught up in a state of their own internalized reality that manifested itself through behaviours, language and communication that was sometimes feared, regarded as being inappropriate or was difficult to engage with.

Gradually, I learned to acknowledge and appreciate that behind the medication, the overwhelming thoughts, visions and voices, there were many stories to be shared and listened to. I ran weekly art therapy open groups which helped to facilitate a well-needed space for this. Although there were always uncertainties as to how many people, if any, would attend the sessions, it became apparent how useful it was for some and how it seemed to provide others with a sense of hope and something to look forward to.

Engaging in art therapy allowed some people to process their experiences. Through the images, stories were shared about the reason(s) that brought them to the ward and, at times, why discharge and re-admittance felt like a repeated cycle. Some of the images spoke of distress, trauma and hopelessness. Although each person's experiences differed, there were parallels when thinking about the psychological wellbeing specific to some black and other ethnic minority people. There was a sense of being misunderstood, not listened to, people not caring, feeling unsupported, within the institutional setting itself and beyond, when discharged into the community. Although saddened to listen to this, I also felt fortunate for such experiences to be shared, not only with me but within the safety of the group. This encouraged others to tell their own stories and, in turn, helped to address some of those unmet needs by being heard. A sense of group cohesion was therefore formed through this, which, at times, helped to provide a space for empathy, relatedness and empowerment to be elevated, thus contributing to release and healing.

The groups also embodied difference. On the ward, people were from varying ethnicities, backgrounds, ages, religion and life experiences. At times, the weekly groups therefore represented a sense of togetherness, learning about others, and acceptance, where colour did not matter. I'm unsure of what the experiences were of every person who attended one of the art therapy open groups, but through feedback at the time I did manage to capture some thoughts:

'Every week it gave me something expressive to do, that is relaxing and creative.'

'I found the class very relaxing...and it made me get a clearer picture of my life.'

(Received through qualitative feedback forms: 2018–2019.)

In my work with black and other ethnic minority young people, there were similarities with the work I did with adults, including feelings of being unheard, silenced, stigmatized, and often misunderstood. In addition to the difficulties experienced surrounding race and inequality, it was also important to consider some of the other factors that may have exacerbated these feelings, such as trauma or where the emotional and psychological needs had previously gone unmet.

I have had the opportunity to work within community and educational settings with children and young people. Presenting needs differ and can include emotional, developmental or behavioural needs and attachment needs, often resulting from traumatic experiences and significant life changes, including loss. Art therapy has provided a useful space for these difficulties to be explored, which has helped to encourage important conversations around difference from the viewpoint of some black and other ethnic minority young people – which has come to contribute to some of these needs.

As with adults, the psychological and emotional needs of young people can vary and are dependent on individual circumstances. Some of the contributing factors can include upbringing, environment, socio-economic status or not having access to early help. While each of these plays an important role in the wellbeing of young people, I will share some of my experiences of working with those whose needs have felt unmet, namely due to the lack of cultural awareness and understanding of those working with and around them.

With the recent increased global awakening of some of the injustices surrounding racism and inequality, I have found the therapy space a helpful platform to reflect on some young people's experiences prior to this shift. My work with 7–18-year-olds has involved both one-to-one and group work. Shared feelings of being singled out, scapegoated, judged, diagnosed, or feeling misdiagnosed, unheard, and only seen if linked to negative situations, have all been expressed by young people when thinking about what being black or of another ethnic minority looks like.

It has been essential to keep the conversations going around identity, particularly from the perspective of how some young people come to view themselves. Exploring this within the therapy space through creativity, poetry and verbal interactions has helped to encourage this. At times, this has been very empowering and a useful tool to re-imagine, re-envisage or reaffirm a positive sense of self or a different type of self to that associated with not only being black or of another ethnic minority, but with young people in general. The therapy space can contribute to recognizing capabilities, strengths, vision and hope. Sometimes, this has been played out by acknowledging one another's qualities within a group setting or through self-reflection. In turn, this has helped with increased self-belief and a greater sense of identity and belonging.

When accessing early help and intervention, some young people feel that a broad range of existing mental health services are not culturally adapted or suitable to their needs, thus making engagement difficult. I believe it is therefore vital for further choice and options surrounding the type of therapy, approach and a good understanding of difference to be at the centre of practitioners' training and ongoing learning so that they can be effective in delivering the type of support appropriate to the varying needs of young people.

If the psychological and emotional needs of young people, particularly young black and other ethnic minority young people, go unmet, the impact that this can have on their sense of identity and belonging may worsen through their transition into adolescence and adulthood, and when faced with adversity. Therefore, working with young people to help build resilience, confidence, empathy and togetherness can help bring about increased positive changes and may reduce the statistics which demonstrate that black and other ethnic minority people are overrepresented within mental health services in comparison to their white counterparts.

The Mental Health Foundation provides some useful information and suggestions surrounding this:

- The impact of the higher rates of mental illness is that people from these [Black/African/Caribbean/Black British] groups are more likely than average to encounter mental health services.

- Detention rates under the Mental Health Act during 2017/18 were four times higher for people in the 'Black' or 'Black British' group than those in the 'White' group.

- Findings from the last Count Me In census found that the number of people in the Asian or Asian British groups who spent time compulsorily detained in hospital rose by approximately 9% from 2005 to 2010.

(Mental Health Foundation, 2019)

Conclusion

When I embarked on my journey of becoming an art therapist, the image that this evoked surrounding it was of a white, middle-class role. It has been both insightful and significant to be able to change this way of thinking and to establish a different type of perception, one which involves the awareness that therapists are from varying ethnicities and backgrounds and bring a breadth of expertise to the field. This is something which I am now proud to be part of.

Having worked in a variety of settings, I often find I am the only black practitioner on the therapeutic or counselling team. On one hand, this can be empowering. It has encouraged important conversations around culture, difference and white privilege. However, I am aware that these conversations have often been limited or have taken place on a one-to-one basis. This makes me question why race is not being spoken about more among professionals and who is responsible for igniting these conversations. Does it rely on the person of ethnic minority, or the other person, or a combination of both, for notice to be taken and better understanding to be made about difference? Barber and Campbell (1999) write: '...we, as black women, cannot ignore our race, colour and culture in our work as art therapists. Our colour matters both to the people of colour and to the white people with whom we work'.

I conclude that speaking about these issues can and should be everyone's responsibility, otherwise they continue to be ignored. The subject of race is often deemed a sensitive issue, something feared for perhaps saying the wrong thing. This does not take away from the inherent racism that exists within institutionalized settings at a systemic and hierarchical level. In my personal experience, when attempting to raise such conversations about difference with my white peers, it has often been met with silence – a response which silenced me and made me reconsider when and where to bring up such conversations. In this sense, being the only or one of very few black or other ethnic minority practitioners can be very isolating.

By sharing some of my own experiences, I am mindful that I cannot provide insight on behalf of all black and other ethnic minority groups because we are all different. Even my blackness may not be the same as other people's blackness, and that in itself is something that should be celebrated as part of our intersectionality that can be brought within and beyond the therapeutic setting.

In acknowledging that black and other ethnic minority groups are the minority race, yet are overrepresented in mental health services as clients, there does need to be fair representation of diversity among the professionals who are delivering support, to help address some of the needs around oppression, racism, difference, culture and identity. These are issues that can be understood through their own lenses and personal lived experiences.

I am working as a black, female art psychotherapist to contribute to bringing about positive change, on a personal, individual and systemic level. My experiences have taught me that I, and the use of creativity, can be relatable to people of all races, who may otherwise find it difficult to share their stories. It is therefore important that all therapists deliver the appropriate service to all clients on an individual basis, while considering the cultural and racial aspects that can present within the therapy space and form part of their presenting needs. This in turn, can bring about improved overall wellbeing and healing – something which is particularly significant within black and other ethnic minority communities.

References

Barber, V. and Campbell, J. (1999). Living Colour in Art Therapy. In Campbell, J., Brooks, F., Jones, J., Liebmann, M., & Ward, C. (editors) *Art Therapy, Race and Culture*. London, United Kingdom: Jessica Kingsley Publishers. 21–37.

Mental Health Foundation. (2019). Other factors – Different BAME groups and particular mental health concerns. *Black, Asian and Minority Ethnic (BAME) Communities.* www. mentalhealth.org.uk/a-to-z/b/black-asian-and-minority-ethnic-bame-communities (correct as of 14 April 2021).

Morris, N. (2020, 10 November). Why it's so important for Black and Asian people to access therapists of colour. *Metro.* https://metro.co.uk/2020/11/10/why-its-so-important-for-bame-groups-to-access-therapists-of-colour-13549642.

Part III

CPD: Supervision and Self-Care – Our Mental, Spiritual, Physical and Emotional Health

Chapter 9

Conversation About Co-Supervision with Two Senior African Heritage Therapists

DR ISHA MCKENZIE-MAVINGA & ARIKE GRANT

Abstract

This chapter highlights the advantage of supervising with someone who can think outside dominant Eurocentric therapeutic perspectives. We explore co-supervision as fellow African heritage supervisors and share the advantages of not having to justify, rationalize or educate each other about the dynamics of race in the therapy. We discuss our diversity. Arike, born in a mining community in the north of England. Isha, born in the Midlands, raised in south London. Both born just after the Second World War. We dialogue about our connections, working together, our experiences in thinking about the psychology of black and Asian peoples and working with white people as black therapists.

Having someone who shows understanding of the impact of race and culture in the process keeps the therapist/supervisee focused on the work with the client and assists them in not getting distracted by their own material (countertransference). Aware of possible collusion, we indicate to each other where we need to work in our own therapy, by interviewing each other and showing the challenges and rewards of being male and female black British therapists. Our own journeys through life and the education system have been key in shaping our perspectives.

Keywords

Supervision, racism, gender, training, identity, history, clients, Eurocentric, black, clients

Arike: What initially drew you to seeking a black supervisor?

Isha: I remember feeling as though there was no space for me to talk about the impact of my own identity in client work. I had group supervision on my training course, and work with black issues was absent. Accounting for the context of heritage and racism for black and Asian clients was marginalized and they were left at the bottom of the allocation file. Terms like borderline were assigned to those with African/Caribbean heritage and they were kept for what was deemed to be more experienced therapists. I experienced this conduct as racism, because they did not feel that my experience as a black counsellor was relevant or useful. This was partly because of the Eurocentric psychodynamic training that I received.

I had a white supervisor when I started to work independently and I remember after a few months of working together, I asked her why she went silent after I spoke about concerns that related to my experience as a black woman. I felt she did not have enough experience to help me work with these issues. My frustration led me to start teaching workshops on the context of racism in therapy training. I soon realized that I was a pioneer in the field, but not getting appropriate modelling to support these issues as a therapist. I joined the Association of Black Counsellors and I found other frustrated therapists seeking support.

Arike: In terms of your needs as a black female therapist, what do you get from current co-supervision?

Isha: There is trust in our relationship as peers, co-counsellors, supervisees and male and female working together. We each get the experience of supervising, knowing that the impact of racism, oppression and cultural diversity is part of our life experience and therefore entwined in our client work. I know that you know and understand that racism and sexism as well as other oppressions exist in our work. I have an expectation that you will value and support me with my concerns as a black woman and in my work with both black and white clients.

While being African heritage therapists may be taken for granted, we cannot take for granted our diversity as man and woman. Having worked through some of my distresses about men, I have arrived at a place where I can challenge you to reflect on your position as a black person and as a male therapist. In some of the therapeutic dynamics you don't equally challenge me, and this may be because I often raise this issue myself. The benefit of working across gender is twofold. I am challenged to be assertive in getting my needs met as a black female therapist. I am also challenged to articulate my awareness of male oppression and ways that you might repress your needs as a black male therapist.

Arike: How does this support your personal development?

Isha: Attention to personal challenges related to identity and culture in therapeutic exchange becomes much clearer and this gives me an opportunity to create safety to work through these areas. We seem to have an understanding that anything that makes it easier for us to challenge each other on what comes up may be useful to work through and this includes black issues. Our co-supervisee relationship is a work in progress and of course this means that as we continue to build our personal process and include reflection on our cultural identities and oppressions, we become more robust.

Arike: How does this support your client work?

Isha: It kind of goes with the territory, understanding and accepting that black and Asian individuals in the UK may be impacted by racism is part of our work with clients. Also, that all black and Asian people need to have access to anti-oppressive therapy, that celebrates their heritage. I am aware that my own ethnicity can impact on my work with clients and this in a way gives me permission to work directly with my clients on these issues if they are raised in the therapy. In this way, I am developing my approach so that I can think about the imposition of Eurocentric theory on my style and responses to clients. I can therefore take risks and challenge myself to think outside a Eurocentric framework when evaluating client work.

Isha: What initially drew you to seeking a black supervisor?

Arike: One of my early supervisors was a South Asian man. It was him as a South Asian man and me as an African heritage man. The question did not arise, in that the context of race, culture and ethnicity were contextualized in the supervision. In another job, I had group supervision. There were three of us: a white man and a white woman and me, and we had a white supervisor. I got by.

Isha: In terms of your needs as a black male therapist, what do you get from current co-supervision?

Arike: I can relax into it. I have had a long-term relationship with you as my current supervisor, who knows me both as friend and colleague. You see me. You know my struggles; you don't get confused and you are able to sensitively challenge me.

Isha: How does this support your personal development?

Arike: Supervision can be a place where in order to develop I have to allow myself to show where I am vulnerable and possibly not thinking clearly and making mistakes. I need to feel confident that I am seen and understood, in order to put myself in that place. Having you allows me to do just that, because of the trust and the understanding that we have around being black in the world, and a black professional. There is a layer that is taken off in working with you.

Isha: How does this support your client work?

Arike: I know that you as a fellow black professional will have experienced some of the dynamics that can arise and will probably understand better than a white supervisor some of the nuances that will be occurring in the therapeutic space. This gives the client the benefit of a more thorough exploration of what is happening. It's not just a generic client and therapist, it is very specific because you understand those nuances, so it gets addressed.

Training

Isha: I was trained in the psychodynamic approach. I found that the trainers were standoffish and interpreted individual behaviour in the teaching room based on psychoanalytical theory. This meant that if you did not understand the theory, you might feel lost as to the meaning of their comments. A distance between tutors and students was created by the one size approach to understanding humanness. There were standard theories about personality development and the influence of family attachment and separation issues. The theories were useful, but I felt lost as the only black student.

I felt marginalized as a black woman on the course because cultural background and racism were not attended to. Students were encouraged to select their therapist from the recommended list on the course. There were no black working-class therapists on the list and my therapeutic needs were not catered for. All the tutors were white middle class or owning class, so I did not experience them as role models for my learning.

I found the theories interesting and I was curious about how things worked relationally with clients, but I resisted the idea of applying white Eurocentric theory to all clients. I formed a bond with a white gay man, a couple of Jewish women and an Irish nun. It was like the minority group dividing off from the privileged students. We had our feelings about oppression in common, but I did not gain much confidence in how psychoanalytical theory could be applied to support interracial dynamics. I left the course feeling isolated in my learning and I was determined to try and change the way counselling training courses were run.

Arike: I began my counselling training in the mid-1980s. It was a course specifically set up for people who were using counselling skills as part of their everyday work practice. It was a means by which they could deepen their understanding of the processes that they were intuitively engaged in in order to approach work better armed to tackle what they might face. We were a diverse group of men, women, heterosexual, gay, black, white and mixed ethnic background from various professions.

Unless these were brought by the students, issues of race, culture and difference were not raised on the course. On the one hand, it was good to exercise autonomy over my learning and on the other, it would have been useful to have had some direction.

Gender

Isha: I feel as if we have arrived at quite a challenging question about our working with gender as black man and black woman. I think it's because I have only worked with a handful of men. My concern is about how we work or don't work with those issues in supervision. What it is like bringing them to supervision and do we bring them, or do we not bring them, or do we only bring them once in a while and is it something that we don't address that often? What goes on between us? I certainly don't feel that you ask me much about what it's like bringing those issues as a black woman.

Arike: It's an interesting question because I don't know if I assume that you are working mostly with black women. It has not occurred, and I don't know if I have asked you if the woman is black or white. That's something to look at, in future supervision. We need to make sure that we do address that. I think it is an assumption that mostly you work with black women.

Isha: That might happen because I act independently, and I raise it. I often say that this is a black woman that I am talking about and I will speak about my clients as black women or Asian women. And I would say that I sometimes bring it up for my clients, because most of them say that they come to me because they want to work with another black woman. They have women's concerns as well as being black, and they have experienced racism, and this creates intersectional oppression. It might be because I act independently and I bring it, so you don't raise it. We have stumbled on a gap that we have not really reviewed.

Sometimes I do ask you what something is like as a black man.

Arike: You do. You don't hesitate to raise that question.

Isha: This also reflects the way I work with that part of the women. I bring it up. If they are black and gay, I address homophobia and racism. I say those things to them and sometimes it's awkward, because they have actually come with it. I say to them I know you came to me because you wanted to work in these areas, and they remember that it is an area that provoked some of their distress.

We chose each other because we are a black man and a black woman working together and that gives us strength, but there may be ways that we have taken that for granted. I also feel that talking about the theme now brings some clarity to our supervisory dynamic.

In answer to your questions, this was fundamental to how I attract clients because there was a time in my life when I only went to women's groups and hung out with black people, and during that period, I closeted myself from an essential part of the world. It may be when I was doing my training that I began reflecting more on my identity as a black mixed heritage woman. And this gave me strength. It was roughly a year when I went through that phase and I seemed to mainly attract black women as clients.

This could have been a black feminist phase. I have worked with white women as well but not many. One group of women I particularly attracted was people who wanted to explore their identity as black women or mixed-race women. I believe this was because I had published a book with my sister. The book was about searching for part of my identity as a woman of black mixed heritage. That attracted people who wanted to explore their identities, and as women they wanted to explore things like sexuality as black women and sexual abuse as black women. That was a kind of attraction and demand on my services as a black woman.

One of the first questions I would ask them was, 'So what do you want from me as a black woman?' I would not ignore it. They specifically chose me as a black woman, so I wanted to know what they wanted from me. That would be an opening for them to talk about themselves as black women. From there all kinds of issues arose, like our different skin tones and some of the hurts they had experienced because of the hue of their skin. Things like racism and homophobia interact with each other and women were then able to recognize all kinds of areas that had been buried. It was not always easy, because sometimes there were women who took me for granted and expected things I couldn't give, like not paying anything. I also got venom from some women.

Some of those areas I never talked about in our supervision because of the shame. That is probably something important that I can bring up now. Some of the hidden stuff I didn't bring and there is an opportunity now to let you know what I was hiding. That's pretty scary because there is a depth of work that we may not have reached.

The fundamentals to how I attract black female clients were to do with my own process as a black woman and working through my own identity exploration. I never really made a decision that I was just going to attract women. After my training, I was working with a white gay man who I'd seen during my training and then he became a private client. Then several male clients came to me in my home and one of them was a white man who told me he had done something awful that he couldn't tell me about and the first thing I thought about was murder and I found him a bit scary. I then became aware that I did not want to see men in my home. I worked in a few agencies, where I saw men and I have also worked with heterosexual couples and gay couples. I realize that I do have the skills to work with men, I just did not attract a lot of them as clients. My clients had mainly come through word-of-mouth.

Arike: How does it feel to be thinking about that now?

Isha: Not easy because it's history and I never really thought much about who was coming to me and how I was working with different groups. I know that I have had a lot of black women who wanted to work on their sexuality as well as racism and a few of those were lesbian women. There were few black female therapists at the time who worked with sexuality and understood that as part of being black and female. I have had one or two white female clients. They have mainly come to me because they have seen me in the context of presenting some of my work at conferences or read my writing and seen the

Therapy in Colour

context of my transcultural work. They may have had a black partner and there was a link with being black that they wanted support with. It seems as though the demand has come because I'm a transcultural therapist.

I would say yes, there is a challenge in working with men per se. I have only worked with a couple of male supervisees. I feel as if the challenge of working with men has been a parallel with my own process of becoming more curious about men. As I gain more experience as a therapist, I have gained more experience of men. In my early childhood, I did not have a father or a male role model and I was bullied by white boys, so therefore organically I have not attracted men whom I have not been ready to work with.

As a mature woman and therapist, therefore my work with men is a work in progress. I am working on being more curious about men and being more open to understanding how men work and accepting that I don't really have a clue what it's like to be a man unless I listen to their story. If I base my work with men on my history of men I'm working from a place of hurt. This is something I bring to my supervisees. I feel that women don't generally challenge each other on the way we relate to men or how compassionate we can be to men because men are part of an oppressor group. Likewise, I have learned how compassionate I can be with white people as part of an oppressor group. It is an ongoing work in progress and the more I learn about men the better I can hold men in the therapeutic process.

Arike: In my profile, I talk about my particular interest in working with men, although I don't say I only work with men. I think it's quite clear that I'm not saying I only work with men, but I do work with men so that's there in my profile: However, I would say the majority of clients that I have seen have been female and they have come specifically because they wanted to work with a man. I think the issue of whether it's important that I am a black man has not always come up, but it's come up in some situations where people have said, 'You know I am a black woman and I have never worked with men', or, 'My image of black men is a negative one and I think it would be good to challenge myself to have a black counsellor, you know, to work with you as a black man'. So that's been there.

Isha: Well, my question sort of spins off from what I was saying about raising the issue of working in that area, because they had specifically chosen you. So, if a black woman comes to you and says, 'I am a black

154

Conversation About Co-Supervision with Two Senior African Heritage Therapists

woman and want to work with you as a man', clearly, they've chosen you as a black man too, so the question is about whether that gets addressed, whether you respond to it, so that there is some process around it.

Arike: Okay, I am trying to think of specific clients. There's one person I have worked with where most of the work that we do in session is about her relationship to black men. That's the backdrop, so your question is reminding me that it may be useful to go back into the work with her and keep reminding ourselves that she's there as a black woman working with me as a black man, rather than it being incidental, but for it to be a key bit of what I keep in the room.

Isha: I feel that this happens because during our training we were not really encouraged to work on that particular identity as part of the connection between us as therapist and client and yet we attract clients who come for that reason or they choose us because that's part of them making safety for themselves.

Arike: There's something about the way in which I talk and the way in which I am and the circles in which I move. The internalized racism is played out in such a way as to make me feel odd, as if I am an outsider and that other black people are more of a community and I am outside that community. I don't talk black. I don't talk 'street'. Have I sold out? Am I a coconut? In working with people, my history is in me, even though I have had sessions and worked on it. I have a good sense of myself as a black man, but I have that history about feeling I'm not black enough.

Isha: Yes, I do identify with that. In my early childhood, I was the only one, in primary school. Then in secondary school, a girls-only school, I got to know girls whose families had come across from the Caribbean.

Arike: You were there with more black people around you. In both my primary and secondary school, that wasn't the case. I was in a tiny minority and this continued at university, so my socialization with black people came much later, in my twenties and thirties. It is all that prior experience which makes a difference and that is interesting in itself.

Isha: Well, it is interesting. As a mature student, I found myself back in the situation where I was the only one and I didn't feel heard. I didn't really feel that there was a place for me. I didn't really feel intelligent. It was more about feeling outside the white group while being in it. The black group was outside my studies and outside the university, whereas

155

the white group was inside. I just made use of my black peer group and read black literature.

I think this part of the discussion is our emotional history about being black people and it's really key to how we have chosen to work.

Arike: Fifty years later, I ended up working in Broadmoor Hospital with black men. It's as if somewhere something registered for me as a black man about how we deal with the emotions. There's been something working unconsciously in me, so one answer to the question 'Why did you end up as a therapist?' is that unconscious forces were operating in me from childhood that are to do with loss of contact with my father at the age of four.

Isha: There is such low understanding of the cultural dimensions of distress for black people and you just reminded me that when I was working in Broadmoor with black men I went in there to work with Orville Blackwood, who subsequently died after rapid tranquilization, restraining and seclusion. I was also working with the families of other young black men who were in the mental health system while I was employed at the African-Caribbean Mental Health Association (ACMHA).

Going into ACMHA and some of the local mental hospitals to see our clients was, for me, a way of facing my fears about men, because to me, men were a bit scary. I internalized racist stereotypes about some of them being big and black, but it wasn't the fact that they were big and black it was the fact that I had experienced domestic violence and racist bullying as a child. I was raised in a way that ignored the fact that I became frightened of men.

I was challenged within the Re-evaluation Counselling (RC) community to work on this old material. It was a safe place that understood the oppression of women and the oppression of racism. This helped me overcome my fear of men, by getting to know men. It raises another question about how many of us women in particular face fears about men. I don't think a client has ever come to me and said that they are afraid of a man. However, it arises in the work over and over again and so the women have been afraid to release themselves from a relationship where they've been treading on eggshells.

Co-supervision
Arike: Working with someone who is black, a person with a lot of melanin in their skin, means that I need to be sensitive to particular ways

that people might want to approach me to get support. Therefore, I have to question myself about how I can appropriately work with the person who is in front of me. We have to develop a relationship in the work with the client that is specific to that client. Having a fellow African heritage co-supervisor means that I can feel relaxed about saying that I am doing this thing over here, that it feels like the right thing to do but it doesn't necessarily fit within the usual norm or framework.

Well, I don't know if it is true with everybody but I know it's true with you because it's you and me. Because of our longstanding relationship and the things we've been through together I know that I can share these things with you and feel confident that you are not going judge me. I can trust that you won't think I'm a bit wacky or off the wall or something. It is as much about you and me and about who we are, because I don't think it would be so for every other African heritage supervisor. Do you see what I'm saying? It's about our relationship as well as the fact that it is about you as a black woman, who I've known for years.

Co-supervision for me means co-operating with each other, co-supporting each other as two people rather than as a group. For us, there are those elements of being of African heritage which means, yes, we can take some things for granted because of our backgrounds and the fact that we know each other and that we know and understand how racism operates. We can't take each other for granted because we have separate lives and we grew differently and, also, we are different genders. So there are those contradictions but there's a comfort in knowing that even if it's difficult we can take for granted that we work with each other as black therapists and that there is a level of understanding about how racism impacts ourselves and our clients.

Isha: There is one other thing that came up in terms of the ethical context. Traditionally, I was taught in a psychodynamic approach which kind of suggests that the therapist is a blank slate, even with your supervisor. I'd had white supervisors who couldn't cope with me talking about my experience as a black woman, as being part of the therapeutic work and how that might impact on both me and clients. In those early days, objectivity was supposed to be the way we do it. You don't know the other person and they don't know you. You try to get to know them, but if they haven't been exposed to how racism impacts you are struggling all the time, which is what happened to me. It was a relief to come into co-supervision with someone who actually gets it and who struggles with me in that, as opposed to being outside it and saying well I don't know much about this, or I am sorry I don't have that training or experience.

For me, it was like, okay, this is another phase in the supervisory process and I don't feel that we are breaking any rules. I feel that we are challenged by the fact that we have a friendship as well as supervisory support. My work hasn't suffered as a result of it; in fact, it has probably developed because of it. This brings up this question of ethnic matching and whether it is appropriate or not and whether it works or not, whether by choice or not, which I believe all our clients should have.

Arike: There is more arising from what you said and I think it's about saying a little bit more about the strength of our relationship. We have got similar histories and our paths have crossed in different ways. For example, in terms of our identity as African heritage people we have travelled the same path together particularly around African spirituality. It's about recognizing that I am a British-born African heritage man who wants to actually know what that African heritage means and I have taken the particular path. It's also a path that you have walked and we've actually been companions on that path, which has been really great. Then there is the path of re-evaluation counselling, whereby there is a very particular understanding of how oppression works and its centrality in the way in which the world operates. Both these things have added to our understanding of the dynamics when people get together and what they bring to the situation. It is not like a shorthand but it's also that I know that you know about that history and so it makes what we have rich.

Conclusion

This chapter was written before Arike passed away in 2020. Living through the challenges of his loss, the pandemic and resurgence of Black Lives Matter has given me new insights into self-care and pathways that create a safe backup for the sudden departure of therapists, supervisors, colleagues and family members.

The clients and supervises that relied on our connection, thought processes and safety to share their stories are also bereft of the safe place that I experienced in co-supervision with Arike.

While we discussed how far we had come as co-supervisors, the conversation raised areas that we would have wanted to develop in terms of our gender, ethnicity and intersecting experiences of working in a

Eurocentric field influenced by institutional racism. Although there is a gap in Arike's contribution as a black man in the field of psychotherapy and counselling, his calm, wise and courageous presence remains with us. This chapter is dedicated to his memory.

Chapter 10

Sitting With Discomfort or Embodying Joy?

MORIAM GRILLO

Abstract

The chapter explores the impact of racial trauma and the learned helplessness we may experience in a dominant culture that appears to profit from our psychological distress.

I invite the reader to consider another way of being beyond the influences of a hostile environment which constantly leaves us in a state of homelessness.

Looking at the role of the therapist who has to achieve a sense of self-determination in order to support an *other*, I ask if we have worked enough towards healing our own racial trauma to begin this work with clients. I conclude that our healing must be sought through introspection and self-care. For the work to be done, with integrity, with clients, we must first heal ourselves. It is in this dynamic healing that we can begin to move from a state of discomfort to one of joy.

Keywords

Racism, trauma, body, unconscious, homelessness, Eurocentric, self-care, healing, consciousness, art-making

Introduction

In this chapter, I consider the impact racism has on the body and what this means for us as therapists, while reflecting on our sense of agency within the social construct of racism, and our choice to survive or thrive. In the context of the tragic murder of George Floyd, I discuss how my own stored feelings of helplessness and rage resurfaced in response to his death. Drawing on my own experiences during training and in practice as a newly qualified art psychotherapist, I reflect on the challenge of managing these feelings while negotiating white majority spaces. I question the absence of focus on Black identity in training, as well as our responsibility to develop this new learning to address these issues for ourselves and our clients. Lastly, I consider ways we can counter the heaviness of racism and trauma work through companionship and self-reflection as self-care.

What does it mean to live in a Black body? To feel more used to struggle than ease. To have your sense of self hijacked by the projections of others. To be the only Black body in a white space and deemed invisible. And far too often, to sit with discomfort. While we know that the converse is also true: we live rich lives, where we can experience joy, laughter, safety and belonging. We also know that we hold a unique position as Black people in continually having these positive feelings challenged by the impact of a racialized experience.

To clarify, throughout this chapter I use the term Black to collectively refer to Black, Brown and People of Colour as a means of solidarity, that acknowledges the political experience of being othered in the context of a white majority. The term Black does not intend to detract from the celebrated nuances and differences that exist in our shared and diverse cultures and heritages. Instead, it is used in singularity to serve as a unifier articulating a cultural mean and acknowledging an experiential mode.

> The body, not the thinking brain, is where we experience most of our pain, pleasure and joy, and where we process most of what happens to us. It is also where we do most of our healing, including our emotional and psychological healing. And it is where we experience resilience and a sense of flow. (Menakem, 2017, p.12)

Our bodies are containers, physical repositories for our thoughts, feelings, experiences and memories. What we feel, we absorb, what we absorb has a physical, emotional and psychological effect on our bodies. We may feel helpless in the onslaught of weathering from microaggressions and negative projections, but stand firm and resilient in the face of this adversity. How long can we do this without our containers overflowing with negative affect?

This chapter is an opportunity to explore the notion of belonging for those of us who live in Black bodies; to name personal and societal oppressions, and the effect ignoring these elements has on the very bodies and psyches they assault. It is important to state here that these ideas are based on the premise of surviving a system of monocultural universalism that is self-serving. A societal construct that places everything other than itself in the periphery – deeming it irrelevant, deficient, invisible. By taking a wider world view on these themes then focusing in, I hope this chapter will serve as a journey of change exploring new ideas and questions about ourselves. I invite the reader to be introspective and reflective in their process to complete this chapter in order for new ways of seeing, and being, to emerge.

The death of George Floyd caused a tumultuous ripple in the fabric of our society and brought about a conversation on race politics that is ongoing. For some, it has highlighted an understanding of the experiences of others. For those oft-regarded as other, it has confirmed a foreboding reality of the depths of systemic racism in our societies. How have these two camps been able to exist side by side? How can this perpetual discomfort be managed? And how can we, as therapists, support our Black clients through this malaise while protecting and caring for ourselves?

I graduated from my art psychotherapy training in 2018. As with other training in the field of psychology, it followed a Eurocentric approach to mental health and wellbeing, with literature that supported those ideas. I can remember sitting in lectures and seminars waiting to be included in the rhetoric and constantly asking, how does this relate to me and others like me? I felt as though I was in between two states, where my experience was simultaneously thought and denied. I found it challenging to manage the disappointment when I realized that the curriculum didn't relate to me and never would.

As in everyday life, I would have to learn to negotiate another space where I would be deemed insignificant based on a projective identity (Casement, 1985) that was not my own. As an act of resistance, my final submissions explored whether it was possible for a Black person to find safety and resolve in the therapeutic space; if the theories, notions of being and unconscious biases continually worked against them. The motivation to explore this topic was influenced by a discussion on diversity during an academic seminar. The resultant racially charged utterances by my peers left me feeling isolated and deeply hurt. This experience led me to reflect more deeply as to whether the field of art therapy could offer clients from diverse backgrounds opportunity for full acceptance – a safe space where notions of inequality, difference or otherness do not exist and where such a client can be perceived as person without prefix.

Macrocosm/Microcosm

While it would be deemed best practice to acknowledge and be accepting of cultural difference, this has remained unchecked and absent in my training. I felt so isolated in my experience and I was not aware these conversations were happening elsewhere. I had just become aware that something was broken. It was the same brokenness that existed in society at large but I had naively hoped would not exist here because this was deemed a safe space. The safe space I thought I would find within my training was not supporting me. How could that be? Was this to become another space where I could neither see myself nor be myself? A space where I felt isolated and would shrink myself in order to survive?

Needless to say, my experiences in training were traumatic. Conveying this in retrospect to my course tutor I was greeted with confusion. When explaining racial trauma to those in positions of power, their oblivion often vacillated between ignorance and arrogance. Post-training, there was a tremendous amount of healing to be done and a necessity to consolidate and recalibrate the learning to best serve my community. For those not living a racialized experience, this may not make sense. However, for those of us that do, it remains an unspoken reality that constantly threatens our wellbeing. A silent oppressor that leaves us in a state of isolation, particularly when we are in white spaces, but also internalized when we are alone with ourselves.

Black body politics

As a Black, Muslim woman I am preceded by the intersections of my identity before I enter the room. The judgements and perceptions of others are projected onto me before the 'I' that I perceive to be true is known. Deep reflection and inner work have enabled me to cope with the reflux of these dynamics, allowing my own relationship with racial trauma to become the basis of my 'learning'. Journeying beyond my own self-imposed mutism, dissociation and morphing has helped me to develop a keen understanding of the processes at play when our very being feels under threat. The learnings from these experiences have enabled me, through art therapy and creative expression, to support others encountering the same struggle. In effect, my formal training did not prepare me to serve my community but my experience during my training did. I was aware of the gaps in awareness of our needs and I was aware of what these needs looked like and how they played out in relation to the dominant culture.

Fast forward two years and the tragic murder of George Floyd compounded feelings of hurt and isolation that I had attempted to sublimate for years in order to survive. The rage that I felt made me aware of the now septic wounds of racial trauma that had remained open but had been ignored. It was difficult for me to suppress my rage. I knew that if I did not take action, this same rage would consume me. It was as though this anger and deep sadness would implode on my Black body and I would never recover. I would be inconsolable, defensive, dislocated and unable to work or function appropriately. But at least now I knew I was not the only one holding these agonizing feelings. I knew I was not the only one sitting with this discomfort of feeling imprisoned by my own body due to the introjection of not belonging. Because, as Fanon rightly said, 'in the white world the man of colour encounters difficulty elaborating from his body schema' (Fanon 1952, p.90).

A duty of care

Circa 2020, Covid-19 and the Black Lives Matter protests highlighted one of the greatest dilemmas of our time in this field: the lack of understanding in the medical and therapeutic industries to support individuals experiencing racial trauma. This led to a spate of online training which, for the most part, served to placate white therapists by taking a monocultural stance to exploring difference. Mainstream training still led from a supremacist vantage point using the inferiority model to maintain a racialized power dynamic within the therapy room. It was another experience that failed to offer a reprieve from the dominant culture politics of everyday life.

As Black therapists, our foremost intention in doing the work is to enrich the lives of our clients and to create change. While we are able to reflect a certain knowing to one another of our shared racialized experience, sometimes it is either too painful to address or deemed too dangerous to acknowledge. What does this mean in terms of our practice and in terms of the wellbeing of our clients whom we intend to support? If race is the elephant in the room in our own therapeutic relationships, we must question why that is. Particularly when dismantling the impact of racism will fulfil our initial intent of enriching lives?

As Black therapists, we understand that we need to name and negotiate these *dilemmas* with our clients. We understand that society at large does not prioritize the acquisition of a positive lifestyle and wellness for Black bodies, let alone the promotion of positive mental health, belonging or self-love. What appears to be the case is that something is working against us. The fact that we are more likely to live in deprivation, suffer mental illness, be arrested and imprisoned shows clearly that the systems in place neither serve nor support us. In some way, we are caught up in a dystopian chasm in which the psychological distress we experience appears to serve something or someone other than ourselves – a nebulous something that from before our birth until our demise is intent on eroding the very core of our being. This oppressive regime that stunts our progression is fuelled by systemic constructs rather than stemmed or stopped.

This is the deep conflict we are working with when we offer therapeutic support to another living in a Black body and having a racialized experience. Layers of unrecognized trauma often present as fear, denial, confusion and rage. Masks worn to survive in the hostile environments in which we work, study and live. It is our job to facilitate the diffusion of unspoken feelings and hurt; to encourage a shift from self-loathing to positive regard; to enable a paradigm shift and a conscious awareness of what we *allow* into our bodies. I say this knowing that sometimes we have no choice as to what enters, but then at least we can learn how to deal with the invasion.

Radical self-care

How often do we give pertinent time, and space, to begin to address these feelings of discomfort within ourselves? Are we able to help another if we have not begun to explore and unpack our own racialized experience? This is not something we are taught in our training, but, as with Socratic questioning, we are capable of the unearthing of an awareness that resides deep within us, along with the answers to initiate resolve. This change can happen whether we believe it is possible or not. I understand that not everyone will feel there is a problem that needs to be solved. Some therapists will feel best served to never move beyond the western frameworks of our training. Others will feel unaffected by racism and believe that their clients' experience is the same. And some will not be aware of what their bodies may be carrying, not recognizing that their physical aches and pains may have a somatic root. Regardless of where we stand, it is important to just start the process because 'it is vital that therapists become aware of the potential for Black clients to harbour these symptoms, whether they are explicit or not' (Mckenzie-Mavinga, 2016, p.142).

As much as we support others to address internal conflicts and resolve personal issues, we need to make space to do the same. We need to heal from the trauma of our training and the microaggressions in everyday life. We need to give ourselves permission to be at one with ourselves, to be free from the constraints of otherness and at peace. It was during training with Dr Isha Mckenzie-Mavinga that greater awareness of these issues was born. Reflection with others sharing my life experience enabled emotions and feelings that had lived internally in a state of gestation to be articulated and released. Needless to say, this training was a cathartic experience that lightened the burden of my experience, as did the copious hours of art-making that ensued.

Clinical psychologist and psychotherapist Dr Annielee Jones PhD (2020) describes this personal activism as a drawing out of one's own imagining of a sense of self (Jones, 2020) by redefining it on our own terms. In her talk 'White Gaze, Black Skin: Binaries of Seeing and Being Seen', Jones (2020) speaks of the need to use our mental, psychic and internal resources to safeguard ourselves from the toxicity of the white gaze. This utilization of our internal state enables a distinction between truth and falsehood; what is ours and must remain, and what is not and should be eradicated. This relocation of our sense of self, as distinct from a sense of that self being seen (Jones, 2020), allows for a freeing of our black bodies from the infiltration of the white gaze. An infiltration that places our minds, bodies and internal drives under siege by conflicting with our own notions of selfhood (Jones, 2020).

It is important to recognize the impact that management of our heightened awareness of being seen has on our being, and the impact the destructive nature of what is projected has on our psyche. The impact can be so great as to displace us from ourselves and render us homeless (Black, 2020). It can be a loss that can inevitably blind us from seeing who we truly are. Making the distinction between how we see ourselves, and how we are seen, is a saving grace in our constant navigation of our internal and external worlds.

Conscious awareness of this interplay enables us to exorcise introjected identities and replace them with a truer sense of ourselves, offering the opportunity to locate (Jones, 2020) ourselves within our bodies on our terms and in our own image. This is an image of self based on our heritage and cultural narratives, a self that exists in its true fullness, devoid of single stories and stereotypes. This can only be fostered if we have opportunity to connect to a deeper sense of self beyond the noise. By this, I mean moving beyond a cacophony of prejudices and projections that lead us to feelings of self-denial, guilt and deep sadness; beyond cognitive dissonance that is masking a deeper psychological distress. Managing an awareness of being seen through the veil of white supremacy is challenging in and of itself. It is exhausting and disheartening to be bombarded by projections that encourage us to introject and become dislocated from our own selves.

The question is, what measures do we have in place to support us in sitting more comfortably within ourselves? A great deal of effort has been used to sublimate us over time. In turn, a great effort will be needed to resolve and heal us. But at this point, it is important not to be disheartened by the immensity of the work at hand and remember that the macrocosm could not exist without the microcosm; nor the giant leap without the first step. That is to say, small changes based on big ideas can create lasting impact.

Dr Jones (personal communication, 12 February 2021) shared how she would spend her weekends in retreat from the world after the exhaustion of spending the whole week in white spaces. She said that actively creating this space enabled her to re-centre herself. Reading during this private time encouraged internal musings to conjure new thoughts and a truer sense of herself *for* herself. This form of self-care is fundamental, especially in our role as therapists; it is essential to uphold a consistent regimen of self-care to maintain resilience and wellbeing in ourselves, not only because of the constant care we give to others but in order to minimize the impact of racism on ourselves. Self-care is important to balance out what is taken from us. It is the action of giving something back to ourselves in order to feel whole. To this end, focused, considered self-care can be the means to begin to live, comfortably, inside our bodies, the means by which we migrate from discomfort and be able to embody joy.

We have not had the privilege of this experiential learning in training. But what our training has taught us is to manage uncertainty, sit with discomfort and seek out resolutions to our feelings of internal conflict. It has forced us to choose between some semblance of congruence and the visceral and somatic nature of our experience. We have emerged all the more resilient for it even though we would have preferred to have a *different* experience. There are parallels here with the potential narratives our clients will present – the oft-presented notion of sitting with the discomfort in order for understanding and growth to happen.

Destruct the construct

A recent group discussion on race as a social construct was met with a violent outburst by one of the participants, an elder Black woman, who found it unnerving to consider this fact. The idea that a notion which had played such an influential part in her life experience was being questioned was confusing. A strong attachment to these experiences had become so fused with her own sense of identity that the process of trying to dismantle this belief had caused deep anxiety and distress. Not only did this encounter highlight the extent to which racial trauma impacts our psyche, but it also showed how attached we can become to our trauma through living embodiment and enactment.

However, just as racism starts at a distance from ourselves and works its way into our being, our counter-response must start from deep within exorcising negative oppressive ideations of ourselves in order to create a safe space within; to give us space to encounter our true selves and to negotiate the inevitability of microaggressions and hostile environments with greater ease.

Dr Jones (2020) recognizes that as Black people we are often aware of ourselves being seen by others and subsequently influenced by these judgements and ideas. Jones warns of the danger of accepting this dynamic on its own terms and calls for us to seek out a truer, more indelible sense of ourselves as a countermeasure. When we do not see ourselves represented well outside our bodies, it can have a negative influence on our self-judgements, as does not having an outer world that fosters a true reflection of ourselves. But the real problem is how these experiences impact on our internal world and affect our own perception of ourselves.

Most of the experiences we embody happen on an unspoken and unconscious level. Our bodies however, do know and these experiences can manifest as anxiety, heightened vigilance, lowered self-esteem and mutism. On a conscious level, these feelings are often ignored – felt but not named, embodied and at the same time denied and renamed as an ailment that, on the surface, has nothing to do with racism. Although we feel it, we choose not to acknowledge it, because it is easier to align with the lie that lives with vigour outside our bodies than to fight it and increase the turmoil within.

Ultimately, it is submission to this unthought known (Bollas, 2018) that will save us from the epistemic homelessness (Black, 2020) we experience from the trauma of living in our Black bodies. It is the activism of carving out a safe space in our internal world that will help to drown out the oppressive noise that lives within and outside us – an active endeavour to exist in a truer image of ourselves, devoid of projective identities (Casement, 1985).

In part, this can be done by engaging in safe spaces of resistance in which we become the majority by the very nature of our collective presence. We are seen simply in seeing ourselves in each other, we share stories that recognize a commonality of themes and experiences, and we come to know that we are not alone even though we often feel isolated. These spaces become the tools that connect us to our deeper selves; these are tools that dismantle our sense of homelessness (Black, 2020) by eradicating the noise of systemic racism, societal projection and internalized oppression (Mckenzie-Mavinga, 2016).

It is necessary to focus inwards and begin to conjure new ideas about ourselves and our stories; to initiate deep healing in safe spaces where we can see ourselves and be protected from the interpretations of others; to connect with our inner child and the psychic wounds it holds, offering instead compassion and healing.

According to art psychotherapist and trauma therapist Marion Green (personal communication, 20 March 2017), trauma causes damage to the corpus callosum, the central tract that connects the two hemispheres of the brain. This latent physiological split is reflective of a psychological splitting that is more explicit and impactful in our daily lives. As an art therapist, I understand that this damage to the brain can be repaired through creative expression, be that poetry, art-making or play. This shift in how we engage with our bodies has a huge impact on our healing and how we feel. In other words, working towards releasing and healing trauma is inevitably attained through activities which will ultimately bring us joy. It is with this new location of our beingness that we can work towards embodying joy in the longer term.

Creating ripples

When we have done this work, perhaps it will be easier for our clients to do so as well, to recognize, through unconscious transmission, an origin story that can be born in their conscious self.

As therapists, we have begun to work on ourselves, consciously and unconsciously. It is in the nature of this inner work that the key to how we can best support our clients resides. We cannot rely on society to improve our situation and so we must *do for self*. In order to do that we must begin to live as our truest selves without fear of reprisal,

169

authentically and with integrity. Not only is increased self-care crucial in order to manage the immensity of this work, awareness that you are already doing the work is also a fundamental part. It is safer to bring the work into conscious awareness, to name the elephant rather than pretend it is not there and collude with clients in denial and shame. This must be done with sensitivity to ensure a sense of safety for the client and ourselves.

We must also remember that 'trauma is a wordless story' (Menakem, 2017, p.8) and processes that enable us to articulate and understand our experience should be put to use. Art-making in art therapy is an opportunity to express feelings when words are not easily available. Similar approaches can be utilized within our private or therapeutic spaces. These will serve as opportunities for us to begin to understand what lies beneath the surface of our experiences but is often played out unconsciously and often unbeknown to us.

Let us not forget ourselves as it would be far too easy to do so. It is easier to maintain our roles as caregivers and for our giving to always have an outward trajectory. In order to safeguard ourselves that giving needs to flow inward as well as out, to be centrifugal as well as centripetal, we also need to give space to the fragmented aspects of ourselves, and bringing this into conscious awareness will encourage wholeness to follow. As therapists, we will often leave ourselves outside the therapy room and although things may arise within us, we may never get to fully address them. It is easy to forget the importance of actively and consistently seeking out healing spaces aside from personal therapy. These must be in the world but also within ourselves. Balancing these will safeguard us from burnout and despondency. It is crucial for us to be actively resilience-building through self-care and recreation in order to survive the work we do.

After all, we want to move beyond survival and existence, ultimately thriving in the reality of our true selves. While this is a personal journey, we cannot survive alone so it is important to seek out healing spaces where we can see ourselves in those who share our experiences and stories, as 'it is not so much the verbal interaction, but the non-verbal interaction, the implicit expression of experience that gets met and responded to on a body-to-body level' (Ellis, 2020, p.199). This sheds light on the importance of not feeling isolated and alone but supported by being perceived, witnessed, acknowledged in our truest sense – a healing that redresses and affirms a true sense of ourselves and a wholesome sense of ourselves being seen (Jones, 2020).

My work as a therapist using a trauma-informed approach speaks to sharing our stories and seeing ourselves as whole people. All too often we are the therapist in one arena, and the parent, sibling or child in another. When we have the opportunity to share our whole selves, we feel better for it. Let us name the elephant by naming the trauma. This way we can begin nurturing our own realities of ourselves and in doing so release ourselves from a state of discomfort and make a shift towards a better horizon.

When we can give ourselves permission to be the authors of our own narratives by shifting our focus away from those created about us, we can delight in the stories we have chosen for ourselves and celebrate all the intersections of who we are without fear of judgement. This is the freedom of discovering the true nature of one's existence, no longer shackled by the white internalized gaze of our black racialized bodies. And it is with this freedom that we can manifest the true spirit of joy.

Conclusion

In his book, *My Grandmother's Hands*, Therapist Resmaa Menakem states 'Sometimes trauma and healing aren't just private experiences. Sometimes trauma is a collective experience, in which case our approaches for mending must be collective and communal as well.' (Menakem, 2017, p.13)

In conclusion, healing is a social responsibility and it is important for us to choose our society. In an age of globalization and virtual proximity we can create our own communities on- and offline, with access to them at our fingertips. So being creative with our support networks is vital, particularly in a time when leaving our homes can be life-threatening in more ways than one. Regular online discussion groups and forums that promote Black majority spaces will help to counter the challenges of racism, as will spaces where we can share our stories and experiences and be reminded we are not alone. To have a positive reinforcement of the validity of our life experience is crucial in beginning to rekindle a new image of ourselves devoid of destructive influences. Time alone will also support this new way of being and generate a new relationship with ourselves. So, when we are alone, we must dance, sing or scream if need be in order to release the tensions stored in our bodies and make space for new ideas of ourselves to be planted. It is important that this new way of being takes root in ourselves, that our bodies become grounded in a new identity, as though we are trees with feet connected to the earth, arms outstretched to the heavens in a state of transcendence. We are retreating from the everyday into ourselves – selves that have been cleansed of the taintedness of otherness and other, providing room for us to sit, stand or dance from within.

To end, it is a necessary part of our healing and wellbeing to recognize the negative impact that dominant culture politics has on our psyches. Taking measures to counter these experiences lies with us and we can do this best by creating a collective consciousness of healing and renewal. It is essential that we engage in this work, and it is our responsibility to first do the work on ourselves before attempting to support others.

References

Black, K. (2020, 10 October). The Plurality of Belonging & Homelessness. Online talk: Radical Therapist Network.

Bollas, C. (2018). *The Shadow of the Object*. Oxford: Routledge.

Casement, P. (1985). *On Learning from the Patient*. London: Routledge.

Ellis, E. (2020). *The Race Conversation*. London: Confer.

Fanon, F. (2021). *Black Skin, White Masks*. London: Penguin.

Jones, A. (2020, 27 September). Race, Imperialism and the Contradictory Clinic [video]. https://youtu.be/rpFmlocqDCM.

Mckenzie-Mavinga, I. (2016). *The Challenge of Racism in the Therapeutic Space*. London: Macmillan.

Menakem, R. (2017). *My Grandmother's Hands*. Las Vegas, NV: Central Recovery Press.

Chapter 11

Embodied Ancestors

Inter and Intra Psychic Reactivations of the Colonized Self in Psychotherapy and Supervision

ROSHMI S. LOVATT

Abstract

This chapter focuses on the affects, dynamics and behaviours which re-emerge through our bodies as ancestral memories provoked within psychotherapy and supervision training.

Drawing from the key areas of UK-based trainings, this chapter looks at how each area activates the colonizer/colonized dynamics of our ancestors. Vignettes focus primarily on how we re-member (i.e. through our bodies), and re-create (through artwork), these painful dynamics in the inter and intra psychic dimensions. I bring this to life by describing textures, nuances and sensory material from mine and others' experiences. In order to keep the vignettes anonymized and unidentifiable, I write about a collective experience, based on the experiences of a number of therapists of colour. Therefore, specific identities of people and context are protected. I then look at my experience of how these dynamics have been addressed or facilitated and the impact of these dynamics on therapy and supervision trainees and trainers. I posit the idea that it is these unnamed and unacknowledged processes which result in the lack of trainees of colour within the profession. With a view to encouraging potential trainees of colour to navigate these areas of their trainings, I offer my take on what supports me to continue to pursue my professional ambitions in the presence of my colonized self.

Keywords

Race, psychotherapy, colonized, curriculum, body, migration, ancestors, mutate, identity, intersectionality

Embodied ancestors: Inter and intra psychic reactivations of the colonized self in psychotherapy and supervision

In this chapter I present my experiences in the psychotherapy profession through the lens of intersectional diversities. I begin with a backdrop of how I came to training as a psychotherapist in the UK. I examine through the lens of my non-western, non-white identity, the various aspects of psychotherapy and supervision training, including theoretical taught models, groups, creative methods, skills practice, supervision and personal therapy. I draw on an amalgamation of experiences from a number of colleagues in order to provide generalized vignettes. In particular, my emphasis in this chapter is on my experience of migration from former British colonies, and the subsequent dynamics of colonizer and colonized that are present covertly and overtly in all my interactions within the profession. I examine how my race, ethnicity and skin colour, in relationship with a predominantly white profession, allow these dynamics to emerge in complex and nuanced ways, giving rise to deeply embedded emotions such as complex shame, guilt, fear and rage.

Migration – brown bodies in the UK

I had an active imagination growing up. I would lock myself in my bedroom for hours and 'play act', pretending that I had some superpowers and I could swoop in and save the day in the face of some baddies. My superpowers were mostly inspired by the *Bionic Man*, a 1970s TV show where a man's physical ability is enhanced by robotic technology. In all of my imaginings, the character I would take on would be moral, decent and devoted to fairness and justice. All pretty normal for a child, I think, but here's the thing. I always played a character who was a white, blonde, tall, blue-eyed boy. In real life, I was, and still am, a brown, short, dark-haired and dark-eyed, slightly plump girl. But alone in my bedroom from as early as I can remember, I wholly believed myself to be white and male. I mean, I literally felt it on my skin and inside my body, even in my genitals, as I played out scenarios where I was powerful and heroic. When I reflect on this now, I realize it was all about power. Even at this young age, for me power did not belong to the body I had. My body had to mutate and look very different in order to adopt poses or be capable of power. This idea of mutation, coupled with my migration story, has become an important aspect of my racial journey.

Born in Kenya of Indian Bengali parents, I spent my infancy in Nairobi, my toddlerhood in Kolkata (then Calcutta), and my early childhood in Singapore, before finally moving with my family to London at the age of 11. Migrating to a country where you become suddenly a minority, visible by the colour of your skin colour, has lasting and profound effects. During my childhood in Singapore I had grown up with very diverse friends and neighbours – Tamil, Malay, Chinese, Korean, Japanese, American, British, Dutch and more – all represented in my childhood social atom: 'The social atom is the smallest social unit, not the individual' (Moreno, 1947, p.75). As Kakar (1991, p.4) states, 'From the first birth cry to the last breath, an individual exists in his soma, his psyche and his polis; in other words, a person is simultaneously a body, a self and a social being.'

The influence of this on my young self was a kind of sensory richness of different colours, sounds, tastes, smells and skin sensations which blended to shape my internal world and a strong 'skin ego'. Stauffer (2010) asserts that 'the importance of the boundary between inside and outside cannot easily be overstated (p.108) and goes on to say that a 'good skin ego makes it possible to negotiate this boundary' (p.114).

It is also important to note in my migration story that all the countries of my childhood were British colonies in some form, and for my parents, a life in England was the ultimate, a sought-after aspiration which they had been waiting for. I now see the irony of how they must have leapt at the chance to come to the homeland of our long-idealized ancestral colonizers. My family's migration first from my parent's homeland of India, and second from my childhood home of Singapore set in motion a lifelong sense of displacement, a yearning to belong and a multiplicity of identities. We came from colonized lands to the homeland of the colonizers, bringing inevitably in our brown bodies the ancestral positions of superior and inferior, dominant and subjugated: 'for many Indians, the polis consists not only of living members of the family and the community, but also of ancestral spirits' (Kakar, 1991, p.4).

We arrived in north London in the late 1970s. It was a time when the UK's problems with racial tensions due to immigration were high. South Asian immigration to Britain had started seriously in the 1950s after the Second World War and the British Nationality Act of 1948. In 1972, the expulsion of Asians from Uganda by Idi Amin's military dictatorship brought further waves of brown-skinned people to the UK. Tensions between white and brown communities were palpable on the streets of London, Birmingham and other UK cities. The word 'Paki' was applied by white racists to identify all people with brown skin, a descriptor which was in itself a misidentification of people from the sub-continent and beyond. The word was, and still is, used not only as a racial slur, but as a reference point of danger in the context of beatings and lynchings which were a regular occurrence on the streets of the UK. In this respect, any identification with the word and what it represented was at the same time dangerous and wholly visible.

My multicultural (and perhaps 'colour blind') childhood had not prepared me to conceive of racism in the way that it presented itself – overtly and violently – in British society. As Frantz Fanon (2008) writes in *Black Skin, White Masks*, 'In the twentieth century the black man on his home territory is oblivious of the moment when his inferiority is determined by the Other' (p.90).

For the first time, at age 11, I began to be aware of segregation and separation of colours and cultures. I began the process of realizing my otherness from something that came to be known to me as the dominant group, the majority or the norm. This separation and otherness-in-relationship was in many ways a replaying of ancestral experiences, of my parents' and grandparents' experiences of racial trauma which travelled to me via the generations. The fact that race as a concept exists in the first place is due to a perceived necessity to other. To divide and rule.

My homeland of Bengal was split during the partition of India by the British in 1947. This splitting mechanism is ingrained and inherent in my process of socialization and racialization and creates within my nervous system a sense of ongoing racialized trauma as well as an increased sensitivity to being othered.

My first experience that I remember of overt racism was on my first day at school aged 11. I was standing in queue for lunch when I saw a group of white older girls approach me. The 'leader' of the group looked me in the face and said, 'Ugh, your face is dirty. You should go wash the colour off it.' I turned to the girl in the queue behind me and, touching my face, asked her, 'Oh, have I got something on my face?' You could say in that moment, my naivety around racism and skin colour difference meant that I took that girl's comment literally at face value. Yet even in my naivety, the ferocity and hostility with which her words were uttered stayed with me. I could feel something unfamiliar inside my body, like foreign matter which had penetrated the layers of my skin and was now inside me. This thing travelled through my pores, into my bloodstream and landed inside my belly where it created a feeling of nausea and unease. Reflecting now on this first remembered experience, I recognize that this was a racial projective identification – an experience one recognizes by the feeling that something has got 'under one's skin' and often comes from some aspect of a person's ego which has been split off and projected into another.

In race terms, the skin is literally the point of contact with racialized projections. The skin is the layer which is seen, judged, hated and projected into. The splitting mechanism, reminiscent of the divide and rule policy, serves the purpose of projecting out unwanted or undesired feelings or states, the 'badness', so that the ego of the projector remains good and powerful. The skin on my 11-year-old body received, absorbed and redistributed into my body this 'badness' and hostility. The fact of migrating into the colonizer's world, bringing with me a body which was prone to subjugation, contributed to my absorption of this projection. I did not consent to it, yet I had no way of knowing, let alone stopping the process. Even now, over 40 years later, there are still times when I am caught off guard, and my skin is penetrated without my consent. Today, it is not always in the form of words, but also with looks, atmospheres or body language.

> So whenever we feel that something or somebody has gotten under our skin, we respond with a sense of urgency to get rid of it. Violations of our boundaries, from everyday forms of disrespect to full-blown abuse, can easily be experienced as traumatic and leave us deeply shocked. (Stauffer, 2010, p.109)

In the late 1970s, as a newcomer to the UK, my acculturation strategy was to blend with white friends. My social atom, having changed overnight, now required me to mutate the whole of myself to fit with a new social norm, and one in which I was visible as 'other'. This migration of sorts, into a different self-state, earned me an 'honorary white person' status, and split me from my brown identity. This honorary whiteness persists in my current life. In racial identity terms, this creates both a conformity and a dissonance, the tension between the two fighting it out in my own body.

This incident at age 11 has stayed with me, and become the point which I go back to, to somehow retrace my steps in my racialization process. That first meeting with racism brought to me the first emergence of my 'colonized self' – the state that I have come to recognize as a deeply visceral and relational response to white others.

This was also the first time that I, a brown person, became aware of the colour of my skin. My skin is my largest organ and my interface or boundary with the world. My skin is where the world stops and I begin, or from the inside out, where I stop and the world begins. My skin is the place where I meet and touch the world. My skin is of me. My skin is of my ancestors. My experience in that moment when my colonized self first emerged was visceral, emotional and sensorial. The feeling contains heat, prickly damp heat, which rises through my body and dampens my skin. It wants to empty the contents of my bowels, throw up the nourishment in my body, and tighten my joints until there is no longer room for even a fine hair to pass between ball and socket. As it travels from my ancestry, through me, to my skin, it brings waves of shame, rage, and hatred. It silences my desire to scream and denies me the right to retaliate, to even exist. This internal state that I have come to recognize as my colonized self is located in racial trauma within my nervous system and brings the feelings of complex shame, rage and fear.

Psychotherapy and supervision training

My desire to train as a psychotherapist had at its core a feeling of not belonging, carried through from my history of migration. Salman Rushdie writes, in his essay *Imaginary Homelands*, that the moment one leaves one's home country one becomes a perpetual foreigner: 'Our identity is at once plural and partial' (Rushdie, 1992, p.15).

This foreignerhood, together with some early life losses and tragic bereavements, brought me first into psychotherapy and then into psychotherapy training.

I began my psychotherapy career with a foundation year in counselling in 1995, moving on to a longer psychotherapy training. My first tutor on the counselling foundation was a black woman, and in hindsight I can see the macroaggressions she endured every lecture from predominantly white students. 'Racial microaggressions are brief and commonplace daily verbal, behavioral, or environmental indignities, whether intentional or unintentional, that communicate hostile, derogatory, or negative racial slights and insults toward people of color' (Sue *et al.*, 2007).

I noticed this in the way she was spoken to, questioned as if she was not a 'real tutor' or that she was not someone who could be taken seriously. Other students would talk over her, or carry on a private conversation while she was trying to teach. One peer on the course said to me once that she was frustrated because the tutor 'couldn't control the class' and I agreed with her. Reflecting on this now, I realize there were so many racial dynamics being acted out in this process. We as a predominantly white student body could not tolerate a black woman in a position of authority. Reminiscent of my early mutation into a fantasy white male character, I too did not see power as belonging in the black body of my tutor. We all undermined her power and then accused her of being ineffective.

It is only now that I can name microaggressions as such, because it has a word which has filtered through to popular usage. Now, as a trainer and facilitator, I can feel this tutor's experience more deeply as I carry my authority in my brown body. My relationship with my own power and authority is a complex one which needs to continuously navigate the disempowering dynamics of microaggressions, internalized racism and the projections of white others.

In my subsequent four years of psychotherapy training, I was the only person of colour in my year group. To even open that up for exploration felt dangerous for me – dangerous because of the risk of activating racialized trauma. I had worked really hard, unconsciously over the years since my arrival in the UK, at developing something of a 'proxy self' (Thomas, 1995) which I used to be in relationship with the white dominant group. It was my survival strategy, and it served me well as I went about living a life that was not quite my own. This 'proxy self' mirrors also the fact of migration – coming from one system into another and needing to change the whole of oneself in order to fit and be accepted: 'Some black children employed a "proxy self" for psychological protection against racism in their dealings with white people and securing a sense of identity in a racist society' (Thomas, 1995).

Groups

In this section, I draw from a joint experience of psychotherapy and supervision training as experienced by trainees and professionals of colour. The group element of training has been by far the most difficult part to navigate for myself and other trainees of colour. The group is where the racial trauma and colonized self can emerge in impactful ways. For example, a common experience as a person of colour in a group is to not have your identity validated. Often, when there is one man in a group of women, the group can name that there is one man. However, when there is one person of colour in a group of white people, our experience is that this difference is never highlighted by the white people. When a trainee of colour has the courage to name this difference, the experience is that this is met with silence and avoidance – swept under the carpet. Over many years of being in training groups – lectures, workshops – I have come to know and understand this silence as part of the process of race being acknowledged in the room, an emergence of recognition trauma: 'This concept identifies the process that both black and white people go through when emerging from being silenced about racism. It describes the awakening of hurtful experiences, which sometimes evokes feelings of guilt, shame, hurt and anger' (Mckenzie-Mavinga, 2011).

Equally in supervision training, there is a similar experience of being unacknowledged. For example, when racial identity is named by a person of colour they are told that those are 'just labels', thus dismissing their lived experience. This brings the experience of the 'colonized self' which for me has been the prickly heat of shame in the moment and for many days afterwards. Many trainees report that any challenge will be met with bewilderment, defensiveness and even anger, linked to the white fragility. Moreover, when the ancestral baggage of the colonizer and colonized emerges in the moment, the body remembers the injury and subjugation of our ancestors, carried in the pores, the skin, the bones and the tissues. These scars are made raw again and the pain is intolerable. Sometimes there is little choice other than flight. In this respect, the familiar pattern of fight, flight and freeze (Levine, 2008) is at play to keep people of colour safe. How do we work within the profession to enable tutors and facilitators to recognize these processes and to offer time for the group to process these? It would be valuable and empowering if facilitators had the skill to call out microaggressions as they occur in the room.

Many trainees come to recognize that the group space is not a safe space to be with one's racial identity. In trauma response terms, the amygdala fires off warning signals which close down the body (Levine, 2008). The nervous system, dysregulated from this encounter, plays back the moments for many days after, like a stuck record, and the look on the white peers' faces returns as a flashback to that moment of trauma. In training groups, this requires a survival strategy on the part of the trainee of colour, often gained by shutting down or becoming an 'honorary white person'. Either way, there is a loss of self. For me, this links back to the idea of migration – I have to mutate myself in order to survive.

One of the questions which I continue to explore within the profession is whose responsibility is it to name race? On many trainings, it is evident that bringing the issues of race and colour is the responsibility of the trainee of colour. The misperception is that the issues only belong to the person of colour, and not to white peers. Perhaps there is not sufficient reflection on the fact that white people are also a race and that whiteness is linked to power, privilege and position. Perhaps naming race might mean that we have to acknowledge the historical and ancestral atrocities inflicted by white ancestors in colonized ancestral countries. This emergence of colonizer/colonized dynamics might be too hard to endure – perhaps too shaming. The avoidance of one's own feelings of shame and guilt is central to the survival of the ego.

For many trainees of colour, the discomfort of being often alone in naming racial difference creates the development of a strong proxy self which is able to navigate group interactions without activating shame and rage. The proxy self is not just about blending. It is about changing the whole of you to become someone else in order to be accepted. I had spent many years after my arrival in the UK blending into society in order to stay invisible, to not stand out. The proxy self which I had to acquire within my psychotherapy training was more profound and deeply changing – in itself a migration of sorts from one internal self-state to another. Added to this migration of myself, there is the question of how to position myself, and how I am perceived, not only in the here and now of the group, but in the stereotyped imaginings between white and brown people. There is a stereotype in the intersections of being brown and being a woman – subservient, subjugated, quiet, domesticized, holding positions of servitude. I carried this position in my body. The idea of 'stepping out of line' feels dangerous, perhaps even life-threatening. Having spent a lot of my career working with Indian and Bangladeshi women who have suffered domestic abuse, I have seen the danger which comes from stepping out of line. In the presence of an all-white group, the amplified white gaze activates in me the subjugation of my ancestors and the stereotypes held around brown women.

Shame is intrinsic to the experience of social subordination, as is the negative self-evaluation which comes with shame. This has the effect of silencing people of colour in groups. A common experience for many colleagues is that this silence often goes unacknowledged by tutors due to their own lack of awareness around race and power dynamics. Another experience is that the silence is misunderstood as being resistant to participation or a lack of engagement, rather than being understood through the lens of oppression:

> ...the use of space varies across culture, gender, age, and other social factors...high-status individuals are afforded greater personal space...

> [lower status individuals] not feeling allowed to take up space, resulting in an overall constriction of body movement: hunched posture, limbs held close to the body, and small gestures. (Johnson, Leighton & Caldwell, 2018, p.163)

This lack of insight and acknowledgement results in a high dropout rate for students of colour. In training organizations, it feels vital that tutors are aware of the difficult, nuanced balance of working with race and the complexity of racialized shame, which is deep, visceral and ancestral. Naming race in itself can be re-traumatizing for students of colour and risks the dangerous feeling of being either annihilated or put on display. Yet not naming it forges a sense of being erased. This feeling of erasure over and over again for many trainees of colour remains unchecked due to social conditioning. In this sense, many students of colour are unable to hold any power in the group and end up absorbing the white gaze into their brown and black bodies in ways that are profoundly shaming. In particular, in trainings which model intersubjective relationality and embodied processes, it seems vital to integrate experiences of societal and organizational injustice and oppression.

Other questions which I have debated over many years in the profession are: Do we become abuser and abused simply because of the colour of our skins? Does being white mean that you are automatically colluding with structural racism? What does that mean for white psychotherapy organizations? What does it mean for me as a person of colour? How do we name the movement that happens between positions of persecutor, victim and rescuer in the race triangle? (Karpman, 1968).

Theoretical models

Here I talk about the experiences of therapists of colour who have trained in a wide variety of modalities. Eurocentric models of psychotherapy taught on the courses add to feelings of alienation, for example with an emphasis on the individual versus group identity, or seeing individuation as the 'norm' and the 'ideal' outcome of therapy. An example of this is when trainees of colour speak about their lived experiences of migration and living between cultures and races. Often white peers take it on themselves to facilitate an 'integration' of the two worlds as if this is an 'ideal'. This can be felt as a kind of pressure to reach an 'integrated' position, an imperialist view of psychological integration rather than a collaborative understanding of a world view. As Kakar (1991) reflects:

'The aesthetic satisfaction of a Hindu myth resides in the full savouring of both the extremes rather than seeking a synthesis' (p.11).

Also, it is well known that many traditional schools of therapeutic thought recommend that socio-politics is left outside the therapy room. However, this recommendation means that entire lived experiences of people of colour are ignored.

Within the reading lists and taught components, there are often no books by black or brown writers. There are still few black or brown tutors, except for some external tutors who come in to take very specific sessions. I had to search and find texts which represented my experience of being in the world as a brown British Asian woman, texts which reflected and spoke to my culture, and texts which mirrored my inner world. I then had to find a way to thread these texts and learnings into the core models of my training – once again trying to make them 'fit' – a migration of another sort. I discovered the writing of Sudhir Kakar, an Indian psychoanalyst. In the days before Amazon, I vehemently tracked down a copy of his book *The Inner World*, a study of childhood and society in India, as well as his other wealth of writings on psychoanalysis and the Indian psyche. The works of black writers and therapists such as Frantz Fanon and Marie Battle Singer went unacknowledged. This modelled for me that psychotherapy training was representative of only white people – not a world in which black or brown people could be successful. Many practitioners of colour have had similar experiences – having to go outside their training to find material that mirrors their experiences, and then having to integrate these into their training.

Personal therapy and supervision

One of the difficulties present in the era in which I trained (late 1990s) was a lack of brown or black therapists and supervisors in the profession. As training organizations usually require the personal therapy part of the training to be with a therapist of compatible modality, this often leaves trainees of colour with little choice in locating a therapist or a supervisor. 'The issue of choice, or the lack of it, may still be an important issue to address in the early stages of a therapeutic and supervisory relationship, because it identifies some of the expectations influencing the power dynamic' (Dokter & Khasnavis, 2008).

With many white therapists, the issues of race and colour cannot be addressed by clients of colour. In line with the above segments of this chapter, there is a discomfort, silence and re-emergence of racial trauma, which prevent these issues from entering the room.

For me, there is also a nuance in recognizing my own internalized racism as a contribution to working with numerous white therapists during the course of my life. From this respect, the 'white' part of me has been able to engage enough to find therapy very beneficial, but again, the brown part is often not acknowledged. Often clients of colour are unable to work through the racial trauma which they carry in relationship with a white therapist. How do we address the profession so that therapists of all races are equipped to address issues of power, privilege and position with all clients?

It is still difficult to find a supervisor of colour. In the experiences of my colleagues, bringing intercultural and transracial material to a white supervisor who may not be equipped to work dynamically with this means that these issues are often left outside supervision. When the issues of race, and in particular of power, are not addressed effectively, there is again the experience of erasure, both of the supervisee and potentially also of the clients. There is a difference between working interculturally and working transracially. Culture can sometimes be glorified or exoticized, so that people are usually very comfortable to speak with me about my culture – food, clothes, music – as something they find rich, exotic and colourful. However, people are really uncomfortable to talk about race and skin colour. When we open up about race and skin colour, we open up the enormous ancestral wounding which has taken place in the history of humankind, a history in which white people are often the perpetrators of atrocities against people of other races. It is a kind of history of taboos – slavery, colonialism, apartheid – things which most white people do not want to associate themselves with. There's an uncomfortable truth which likes to remain silent and in being silenced becomes split off into the unspoken.

Increasingly over the past several years, and now as a senior practitioner, I am able to address power and privilege which come with race and skin colour and I hold enough of a sense of my own power to be able to call out racism or white fragility (DiAngelo, 2018) in my work. However, it is important to note that I continue to find biases in myself which are so deeply embedded as survival mechanisms from my past that I haven't realized that they are there. This note is important because part of what good supervision needs to offer is the lens through which these unconscious processes can be made visible in myself and other practitioners.

Skills facilitation practice

One of the common experiences of trainees of colour across several trainings is around the sort of words which are used to feed back from observed practice. Words such as 'shamanic' or 'spiritual' used to describe trainees of colour, while perhaps flattering for some, might feel like they have racist undertones. Words like these position trainees of colour in a religious/spiritual frame rather than a clinical one. When these words are projected onto brown and black bodies, they bring a perception of mysticism, a guru-like status rather than of a serious clinical practitioner who has agency.

Creative process

For many trainees of colour who trained in some form of arts therapy, a common experience is that their stories, artwork, movement and imagery are received by white peers as 'rich and exotic'. This becomes a kind of 'ghettoization' of creative process based on eastern cultural exoticism, and misses any exploration of what the artwork reveals and comments on around the race dynamics in the room. As the creative process enables us to go deeply into the unconscious, what emerges are stories, images, paintings from the collective psyche. However, for many trainees of colour, when met with the white gaze of peers, the images themselves begin to become what is 'expected' rather than what emerges organically for the creator. Again, the colonized self can emerge in this way through the art, speaking to a history of artefacts stolen from the colonies and exhibited in the West.

Training and workshop facilitation

In running trainings and workshops now as a senior practitioner, I am always aware of the risk I take of activating my racial trauma and in particular my colonized self. Ironically, in running trainings about racial trauma, what gets activated is racial trauma. If my colonized self is the part of me that emerges out of my racial trauma, it emerges not only carrying my lifetime's worth, but also the experiences of subjugation and denigration of my ancestors. It is an inheritance of racial trauma, being played out in the current field within a still predominantly white profession. Often after trainings or conversations around race, I'm left with what I've come to call a shame backlash. It takes the shape of a trauma response where I have 'stepped out of line' and owned my power and authority. This trauma response dysregulates my nervous system and gives me flashbacks to certain moments in the training, often moments when I have challenged white people. Within this trauma response, I'm sure, is also that person's fragility and projection of their own shame and guilt.

I have noticed in the most recent lockdown situation while I have been training on Zoom, that I miss the body-to-body resonances which happen when we are live in the room. There is something safe yet unsafe about the body-to-body contact which is missing from the online format. One of the repercussions of this is that I notice I have been used more as a 'bad object' than I have ever been before by groups and individuals. Somehow body-to-body in the room I can use my awareness of the nervous system and polyvagal theory (Porges, 2011) to create some sort of regulation, even in uncomfortable conversations. However, online, something about the body being inside an object somehow has amplified the use of my brown body as an object and taps into what happens around racialized splitting and projection in society.

I often come away from delivering trainings and workshops with more questions about how I have to continue to challenge myself to hold my authority in my brown body. What helps and what hinders that process? What gets silenced? How do I sit holding a group around racial processes, while also being racially re-traumatized? How do I take care of myself?

In offering trainings, I am also aware that there is again a 'ghettoization' of my expertise – I get called on to run diversity training, rather than for example training on self-harm or eating disorder. This is seen as my contribution as a brown person, and I also buy into this by making it my 'specialist' area of interest.

Conclusion

There are complexities and nuances to being brown in a white profession. The emergence of ancestral history, of colonization, imperialism and partition is inevitable when white and brown worlds meet in the context of the profession. The phenomenon of colonizer and colonized dynamics determines how individuals may behave consciously or unconsciously in trainings, therapeutic encounters and supervision. It is a collective responsibility to equip ourselves to honour and process these dynamics in order to see each other in our wholeness.

References

DiAngelo, R. (2018). *White Fragility: Why It's So Hard for White People to Talk About Racism.* London: Penguin, Random House.

Dokter, D. & Khasnavis, R. (2008). Intercultural Supervision. In P. Jones & D. Dokter (eds), *Supervision of Dramatherapy* (pp.111–129). Hove and New York, NY: Routledge.

Fanon, F. (2008). *Black Skin, White Masks.* New York, NY: Grove Press. (Original work published 1952).

Johnson, R., Leighton, L. & Caldwell, C. (2018). The embodied experience of microaggressions: Implications for clinical practice. *Journal of Multicultural Counseling and Development*, 46(3), 156–170.

Kakar, S. (1991). *Shamans, Mystics & Doctors.* Chicago, IL: University of Chicago Press.

Karpman. S. (1961). *Drama Triangle.* https://themindsjournal.com/karpman-drama-triangle.

Levine, P.A (2008). *Healing Trauma.* Boulder, CO: Sounds True.

Mckenzie-Mavinga, I. (2011). The concept of recognition trauma and emerging from the hurt of racism. www.baatn.org.uk/wp-content/uploads/The-concept-of-Recognition-Trauma-and-emerging-from-the-hurt-of-racim-Paper-1-1.pdf.

Moreno, J.L. (1947). The social atom and death. *Sociometry*, 10(1), 80–84.

Porges, S.W. (2011) *The Polyvagal Theory: Neurophysiological Foundations of Emotions, Attachment, Communication, and Self-Regulation.* New York, NY: W.W. Norton & Company.

Rushdie, S. (1992). *Imaginary Homelands.* London: Granta Books.

Stauffer, K.A. (2010). *Anatomy & Physiology for Psychotherapists.* New York, NY: W.W. Norton & Company.

Sue, D.W., Capodilupo, C.M., Torino, G.C, Bucceri, J.M. *et al.* (2007). Racial microaggressions in everyday life. *American Psychologist*, 62(4), 271–286.

Thomas, L.K. (1995). Attachment in African Caribbean families. www.conferonline.net/modules/intergenerational/pdf/lennox-thomas-paper-1.pdf.

Part IV

Therapeutic Needs and Psychological Wellbeing

In the Context of Identity, Culture and Belonging

Chapter 12

Transracial Adoption

Keeping Race on the Agenda

ANTHEA BENJAMIN

Abstract

On 25 May 2020, African American George Floyd was killed in America in a modern-day lynching by police officers. This violent act was captured on video and was circulated via social media, causing a worldwide outcry for justice. This event has highlighted once again the racism and inequality that exists here in the UK. The white majority were then confronted with the reality of people of colour's lived experiences of living within a structural and institutionalized racist society. This was further reflected within the growing evidence that the communities most impacted by Covid-19 and its devastating effects were people of colour. This has led to a response from most organizations to reflect on and reinvestigate how historical and racial bias within a social context built on imperialism and colonialism still informs all organizational cultures in Britain. It is this social context that continues to put people of colour at a disadvantage and often perpetuates oppressive practises. Rankine (2015) wrote about this in an article for *The New York Times*, stating:

> Though the white liberal imagination likes to feel temporarily bad about black suffering, there really is no mode of empathy that can replicate the daily strain of knowing that as a black person you can be killed for simply being black; no hands in your pocket, no playing music, no sudden movement, no driving your car, no walking at night, no walking in the day, no turning onto this street, no entering this building, no standing your ground, no standing there, no talking back, no playing with toy guns, no living while black.

This sentiment is particularly true within transracial and intercountry adoption. These issues are rarely addressed within therapy trainings, even though for the most part therapy is offered mostly to marginalized ethnic and racialized communities. I locate myself within this context as an integrative arts psychotherapist, who has worked within adoption for over 15 years, first, as a staff member within a child and family team in one of the UK's biggest post-adoption services and then as a freelancer in private practice. Throughout my training, I was never taught to address these important themes related to identity, but after my training I gained an interest in this area. In light of race becoming a central issue in society, how are these issues addressed within transracial and intercountry adoption?

Keywords

Transracial adoption, intercountry adoption, race, Black Lives Matter, adoptive parents, living while black, identity, racial identity

The current context

The term structural racism has become a household term leading to a 'consciousness awaking' across the UK. There is no biological truth in the idea of race (Banton, 1987; Smedley & Smedley 2005) in its functioning of categorizing people as a form of hierarchy. However, it has real significance and a devastating impact on people of colour. I have been wondering about the impact for transracially and intercountry adopted children and families. What does this mean within the current climate of racial politics?

We are led to believe that central to any loving secure relationship are trust, empathy, compassion and love (Bowlby, 1970). But what happens when the belief in a loving relationship has been destroyed and the capacity to trust has been killed off (Hughes, Golding & Hudson, 2019, p.26)? When this process includes losing your family, your culture and your country, this leads to multiple losses which cannot be named (Kalmanowitz & Lloyd, 2005, p.2). Many children who have had experiences of neglect and abuse have come to believe that they can only depend on themselves. The emotional task of adopting a child from these backgrounds is a formidable emotional undertaking. In many cases, it is a task that adopters often do not feel fully prepared for. There is a dilemma about how to fully prepare adopters for raising a young person who is likely to be traumatized from previous experience within their birth families and having to adapt to alien environments (Roy, 2020, p.58). Racial identity adds another layer of complexity and a lack of camouflage for children who already feel displaced. My interest in this work is in how best we can meet the needs of these families. This is especially relevant in the resurgence of racial awareness, the impact of racism and racial trauma.

Summary of history in UK

In the UK there has been an ongoing and controversial debate over the years about transracial and intercountry adoption, and the increase of white families adopting children from ethnic backgrounds. The debate has been a longstanding and difficult one. The government has also changed its position on policies, depending on the dominant discourse, more recently moving towards a position of prioritizing the need for children going to loving homes as quickly as possible (Sargent, 2015). The awakening to the reality of entrenched racism throughout the UK has implications for children placed outside their culture, and needs ongoing reflection. This means racial, ethnic and religious matching of children to ensure their connection to their cultural identity. For families far removed from their children's cultures of origin, we need to find creative adaptations to try to meet these significant cultural markers.

Transracial adoption started taking place in the UK around the 1960s to enable white parents to adopt children of colour from different communities, including children of mixed heritage. This was mostly due to the high number of white parents who were waiting to adopt and the lack of enough white children waiting to be adopted. At this time, British adoptions were set up to address the growing numbers of children of colour who were deemed 'hard to place' due to their ethnicity. In 1972, the National Association of Black Social Workers (NABSW) released a statement about its stance on transracial adoption, making it clear that the association strongly opposed black children being adopted by white families. In the opening paragraph, it voiced 'a vehement stand against the placement of Black children in White homes for any reason' (Bremner, 1974, n.p.). Members of the NABSW opposed transracial adoption for multiple reasons, including:

- Black children have different 'developmental needs' from White children to cope with a racist society.

- Only black families can provide nuanced ways of thinking, acting, and reacting to this society.

- White families are not interested in the wellbeing of black children or concerned with helping the black community by adopting black children.

- White families must be taught what to teach children about aspects of black culture.

Some of the reasons why the NABSW opposed transracial adoptions are still relevant in today's racial, ethnic and cultural climate. There are still challenges for children of colour, particularly black children, who must still make sense of living within a racist culture. There is no question about the need to tackle unnecessary delays that keep children in care for longer than they need to be. In 2014, the government decided that one of the key problems in this delay was down to 'politically correct attitudes' that have seen children from ethnic minority backgrounds disadvantaged because a perfectly matched family for life is difficult to find. To this end, legislation was passed that removed the requirement on adoption agencies to consider a child's racial and cultural background to increase transracial placements. Yet for many in the adoption world, a good cultural fit is still an important way of creating a sense of belonging for an adopted child as they grow up.

The paediatrician and psychoanalyst Winnicott (1971) talked about how being held in mind gives rise to a deep sense of security. However, children who have experienced neglect, deprivation and a profound sense of rarely being held in mind often struggle to trust in their relationships and this is known as developmental trauma (van der Kolk, 2009). One of the challenges when parenting these children is withstanding stirred-up feelings that young people cannot control or make sense of. In most cases, children need to expel these intense states that are too difficult to hold and push them out into the parent as a way of getting them to feel their feelings. This is often a painful and difficult process for parents and the focus for adoptive parents is on these attachment needs. But we also need to hold in mind the culture of the child as an important part of the process, acknowledging and integrating their whole identity (Hughes *et al.*, 2019, p.82). Winnicott's ideas of being held in mind are often facilitated through the parental gaze. In this process, the child takes in a reflection of themselves and internalizes this. When this gaze is of another culture, this becomes more internalized as the child cannot have their cultural self mirrored through this process. This can lead to a 'proxy self' Thomas (1992, p.150), a false self which black children can present to fit into predominantly white environments. This can lead to a rejection of their culture or disgust at their own skin colour, which often raises anxieties and leads to referrals to a therapist of colour to be a 'good cultural object' (Andreou, 1992, p.162). Families are an important part of this process in being able hold their children's intersubjective experiences around race as central.

Transracial adoption can have particularly good outcomes, but common issues that keep cropping up are about identity, feeling unsupported in navigating issues of racism and not feeling grounded in their own culture of origin. For anyone, being separated from their family is a painful loss that can be extremely difficult to manage. But considering that racism continues to operate in society, what are the professional responsibilities in addressing this? How can this be looked at in a robust way with adopters, to ensure that the mental health needs for children of colour are met?

Article 20 of the United Nations Convention on the Rights of the Child (1989) states that 'Children who cannot be looked after by their own family have a right to special care and must be looked after properly, by people who respect their ethnic group, religion, culture and language.' Most people who are fortunate to grow up within their own culture are surrounded by cultural references which become internalized over time. But once a child is removed and placed in a different cultural context, exposure to their culture can be as little as seasonal contact, which significantly reduces their sense of connection with their cultural identity. This can set children up to live in a limbo existence of not belonging anywhere. But why is this important? Black, Asian and mixed ethnicities children are disproportionately represented in the 'looked after' system and are among the most vulnerable and disadvantaged. In England, the government (Department for Education, 2012) is concerned about this group of children in care because of the following reasons:

- They often have low rates of adoption.
- There is a 'delay' in finding suitable families.
- The difficulty particularly in placing black boys.

All children in the care system are likely to experience 'delay', isolation, alienation and instability. For children of colour, the experience of racism means they are forced to confront the difficult issues of identity relating to their ethnicity, culture and language in a less than helpful, ignorant or hostile environment which can be especially problematic for those who have lost contact with their birth families and communities.

These experiences can lead to difficulties in forming safe and lasting relationships, in achieving at school and in taking up their full potential as citizens and parents in our society. CoramBAAF (British Association of Adoption and Fostering) believes, as a general principle, that children should be placed with families who can reflect their ethnic, cultural, religious and linguistic identities and promote these factors, as well as those who can help them navigate racial and other stereotypes. So, what is the current practice to support these adopters in addressing these racial needs?

Current practice

Social workers, as part of their assessment of adoptive parents, explore adopters' histories of trauma and their ability to offer a safe and stable home life. There is some exploration about what it would mean to adopt a child outside their culture, and some training to explore the issues this would raise for them as a family. My experience has been that most adopters have not considered fully the impact of culture and 'learn on the job' about the full ramifications of racism as these issues come up. This is a real stretch for most adopters, who for the most part have lived a privileged life in terms of experiencing or addressing racial issues. These issues are raised in the adoption training and parents are supported in levelling up their understanding of discrimination and racism. There is also input in considering the reality of children's feelings, being different and the impact of having no camouflage in not looking like their parents. It is important for parents to be able to keep holding this in mind as it is often easy for this to go underground and for the thinking to stop, particularly when the child or young person wants to avoid talking about these issues. Adopters need to be robust in helping children to make sense of their identity and deal with their uncomfortable feelings about these issues (Brodzinsky, 2005). The complexities of class, religion and ethnicity within 'white' adoption and fostering families have not been widely discussed throughout the UK. There is little known about the 'lived experience' of people of colour, adopters and foster carers who have cared for children of colour in the face of adversities such as racism. This seems a shame as these members would be a good resource for other adopters who are raising children outside of their culture of origin. Covid-19 highlighted the historical disparities in black communities. It is clear the difficulty placing children from black communities was a direct result of their experiences of disparity of privilege, protection and power, as well as access to resources. We know that social inequalities in housing, healthcare, employment and education shape every aspect of life from cradle to grave (Khan, 2020). These issues are still key factors in modern-day Britain and were significant throughout the debate about transracial adoption.

In 2010, seven years after the enactment of the 2002 Adoption and Children Act, Martin Narey, the then chairman of children's charity, Barnardo's, warned that adoption agencies were interpreting the legislation too literally and this was resulting in black and Asian children waiting on average three times longer than white children for adoptive families (Narey, 2011). In October 2015, the government asked Sir Martin Narey to conduct a comprehensive review of children's residential care. It was in response to his findings that the emphasis on racial matching in adoption became redundant and no further reflection on addressing cultural needs for children was promoted or highlighted in this transition. In many ways, this was in response to the idea of us living within a post-racial society. The death of George Floyd has unearthed the ongoing work needed to address anti-racist practice to address institutional racism.

Reni Eddo-Lodge writes in her book, *Why I Am No Longer Talking to White People About Race*:

> I'm no longer engaging with white people on the topic of race. Not all white people, just the vast majority who refuse to accept the legitimacy of structural racism and its symptoms. I can no longer engage with the gulf of an emotional disconnect that white people display when a person of colour articulates their experience. (2018, p.ix)

Her statement speaks to the need for wider institutional change. But what about the need for children and young people of colour being supported to understand covert and overt racism? One of the ongoing difficulties of transracial adoption is ensuring that white adopters understand and can learn to support children of colour to navigate the hurdles they face growing up in a world that upholds the belief that they are other. If we accept the fact that we live in a racist world that discriminates against people who are non-white, then children need to develop skills to be able to cope with this reality (Brodzinsky, 2005). If we are prioritizing a loving home for children of colour, do we not need to also prioritize the training of white adoptive parents, to ensure the coherent sense of identity and psychological wellbeing for children who are more likely to experience discrimination?

Therapeutic considerations

As a therapist often working with white adoptive parents, I am working on building resilience and understanding about the dynamics of race while raising children within a racialized society. I encourage parents to read a book like Reni Eddo-Lodge's to understand the British context about race and to help them to become more attuned to the racial undertones their child will likely face. Daniel Stern (1985) talks about attunement, empathy, rupture and repair as key aspects of raising any child. These take on particular significance when raising a child who has experienced intensive psychic injury. My role as a therapist is to offer the same attunement to adoptive parents to enable them to think in depth about meeting the cultural needs of their children. The model I find helpful is dyadic developmental psychotherapy (DDP) (Hughes, 2011). DDP's core ethos is staying with and responding to the child's intersubjective experience. Through use of the PACE (Playful, Acceptance, Curiosity and Empathy) model, the child's experience is met authentically. Although this model does not hold race as central, it has a helpful framework for parents to reflect on their own experiences, which may lead to resistance to thinking about these themes or staying with their child's pain in relation to race. The key areas of importance for adoptive parents cover a range of issues, including:

- being willing to learn about the role of race and culture

- addressing their own unconscious bias and white privilege

- redefining themselves as a multicultural family

- teaching their child about their racial and cultural history and taking pride in this

- building links with the children's culture of origin in a meaningful way – it takes a village to raise a child

- helping children to deal with racism and develop strategies to address this.

As a black therapist, I find that the challenge arises when parents are resistant to addressing these issues as they feel we live in a post-racist world. Sometimes parents can feel uncomfortable discussing this with me as a black woman and this can lead to an enactment of the power relations related to race. I can be told culture/race is not an issue and they can defer to the child needing to raise the issue for them to feel they need to respond. I explain that like their other attachment needs that they respond to without request, they need to be able to hold culture as central for children's sense of self. In worst-case scenarios, this can lead to complaints which I view as a form of white fragility (DiAngelo, 2018) and a form of silencing. For this work to be effective, the system needs to hold adopters accountable for meeting the cultural needs of their children. I find the best way to be alongside parents is to build the strong working alliance before working with children and making links with their own childhood. This makes an easier link to thinking about oppression, having engaged with their own vulnerabilities, which gives me a doorway to beginning to think about power relations and how this pertains to their children.

In the 1940s, psychologists Kenneth and Mamie Clark designed and conducted a series of experiments known as 'the doll tests'. The Clarks used four dolls, identical except for colour, to test children's racial perceptions. They worked with children aged between three and seven years old to identify the race of dolls they preferred. The outcome of the test was that most children preferred white dolls and assigned all positive qualities to the white dolls. This is particularly relevant for transracial and intercountry adoptive families in understanding the effects of racist microaggressions throughout society. In 2005, the TV series *Child of Our Time* presented by Professor Robert Winston commissioned new research to understand what four-year-olds understood about ethnicity and race. Over 200 children were interviewed across the UK. They showed the four-year-olds pictures of children's faces from a range of ethnic backgrounds and asked which characteristics they would put with which face – the suggested characteristics were kind, friendly, helpful, hard-working, smart, clever, mean, nasty, rude, lazy, stupid and slow. The findings were that almost all the white children associated the white child with positive characteristics while often associating other ethnic groups with negative ones. Over half the black four-year-olds interviewed made the same associations. This suggests that while most white children connect good characteristics with people like themselves, the same is not the case with black children. Dr Adam Rutland went on to say these findings are in line with previous research that suggests children are influenced by racial stereotypes at a noticeably young age. These experiments confirm the mechanism of internalized racism (Agoro, 2003, p.19) in individuals who begin to believe prejudiced ideas about themselves and others who share their race or ethnicity. The criticism of this test is that the person conducting the test can influence children, and children present a 'proxy self' to white facilitators. The shocking thing for me is this is rarely referred to in most child therapy trainings and most therapists are not trained to think interculturally to be able to work in depth with these cases. This poses a concern across trainings in skilling therapists up to work interculturally with both children and adults.

The concept of adverse childhood experiences (ACEs), developed in America by Dr Nadine Burke Harris (2018), has become a focus for people working with young people. ACEs are potentially traumatic events that occur in childhood, including:

- domestic violence

- parental abandonment through separation or divorce

- a parent with a mental health condition

- being the victim of abuse (physical, sexual and/or emotional)

- being the victim of neglect (physical and emotional)

- a member of the household being in prison

- growing up in a household in which there are adults experiencing alcohol and drug use problems.

Toxic stress from early ACEs changes brain development and affects how the body responds to stress. ACEs are linked to chronic health problems, mental illness and substance misuse in adulthood. ACEs are defined as exposure to severe and pervasive emotional and psychological difficulty. Race is not a current existing category but considering the impact of racism it is of particular concern for children placed outside their culture of origin. The charity Body and Soul has adapted this model to include racism which I find a helpful tool in illustrating the needs.

Banks (2001) states that children of colour have specific identity needs which require systematic input if a they are to develop psychological completeness. This thinking has influenced my work with adoptive families. This starts with the parents and the culture within the home environment.

When I begin to work with parents who are adopting transracially, I tend to explore in depth their adoption journey and what led them to adopt a child from another culture. Most parents do not see race as an issue and identify loving a child as the most important thing. Although this is important, the reality is that they are not just raising a child, but raising a child from a different culture. The need to explore raising a child to be culturally proud, and who will probably face experiences of racism and discrimination, is often a hard issue to get across. Most parents do not want to think about their children struggling and sometimes I can be seen as pushing 'the race issue', which can induce white fragility (DiAngelo, 2018). Depending on where parents are, I need to explore over time how we can lean into the discomfort of this conversation. This gives an indication of the parent's capacity to think in depth about race, and their robustness to talk through these difficult issues with their children. This ensures that when this comes up in therapy work, they have done enough work to respond appropriately.

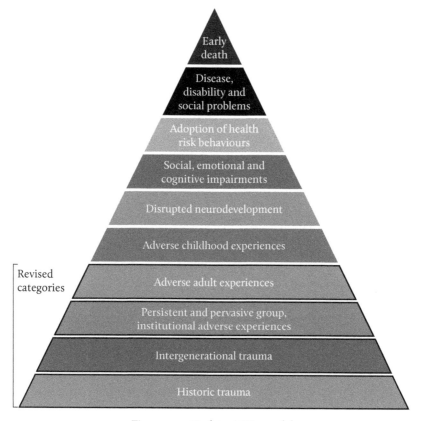

Figure 12.1: Update ACEs model

Transracially adopted children's difference is visible so they have an added sense of colour consciousness that white parents can often not see as they are raised not to see colour. Accepting that being different will not go away for their child or them can be a painful process as this links to their own history of loss of not having a biological child. The reality of institutional racism needs to be addressed, otherwise children and families are left without tools to address everyday racism. I am often identified as a therapist for children so I can become a metaphorical cultural good object (Andreou, 1992, p.162) for them in the therapy. This can set up a rivalrous dynamic with parents who want to be everything for their child but cannot bridge the cultural gap. It is important for me to work closely with parents in addressing this and ensuring that I am not holding all of this as the black therapist, so they can take this work forward, as I will not be in the child's life forever.

Working with parents and children

In my work with parents, I am often listening out to get a sense of their world view as a family. It is important to know what this means for both them and the child they have adopted, as they will no longer be a white family. Thinking about the network of support is important, as is empowering the parents to think about consistent positive racial representation. The need for positive images of cultural identity for children feeds into building a solid sense of their cultural identity. I often share Peggy McIntosh's (1990) paper on the invisible knapsack of privilege which explores privilege and the lack of privilege when you are not the majority culture. I sometimes engage in a process of creating knapsacks with different messages and experiences they have as parents. I ask the parents what might be in their children's bags that they will carry throughout life. This is often a shocking exercise where parents want to quickly flee into how it will be different for their child. Peggy talks about white privilege as an 'invisible package of unearned assets'. I explore this with parents and how this cannot always apply to their children although they can benefit somewhat from some of their apparent privileges.

Microaggressions are like paper cuts, seemingly little but each one painful (Cousins, 2019, p.54). It is important for white adoptive parents to be robust in being able to support children to make sense of their experience. Racism often leaves people feeling 'mad and bad' and the parents need to have tools to enable them not to dismiss their experience. Reni Eddo-Lodge (2018) refers to this in her experiences of not wanting to continue talking about race.

The Black Lives Matter movement was so much more than another paper cut; it was a deepening of an existing, open, infected wound. Many children I work with asked me 'Why do people want to hurt me because of the colour of my skin?' It has been hard to answer this other than to say, 'It's really hard to understand, it doesn't make sense and it isn't fair.' This leads to, 'Racism is a lie; many people believe that one race is better than another, but this is not true, unfortunately a lot of people still believe this so it's important to know how to deal with these hurtful experiences.' Making sense of the racism that many children of colour continue to experience needs to be believed, accepted and contextualized so they do not internalize any further sense of there being something wrong with them.

One of the practical pieces of work I do with children is to create a body map for the child. This is done with the parents in the room. The child is invited to lie down and the parent draws around them creating a life-size outline of their body. We then use skin colour paint to find the matching skin tone to paint their skin, eyes, hair and so on, to create a reflection of them. This work is helpful diagnostically, as children struggling with their identity want to paint themselves white like their parents or change the shape of their eyes to be western, or lighten their skin tone due to the negative message internalized about their skin. We take time to talk about this together and to think about different skin tones and what it is like to be in the skin/bodies we are in. This is a helpful model for parents in how to talk about race and I take time to debrief with them and contextualize the issues that come up.

In the aftermath of Black Lives Matter, I talked to all the children I worked with about this and it opened a range of conversations about race with children from many different races and ethnicities. I spent more time talking to children who had been transracially adopted. In some cases, the parents were quick to shut it down by saying it was not an issue for their child. This may have been true for some families but for others it was a form of avoidance and needed further thinking. The children who were given space and did artwork were able to express their deep pain about racism and the difficulties being in their skin. Talking to children about feelings of not wanting to be black/brown is a very painful and powerful process, which is particularly complex for children vulnerable to rejection. I take time to talk about this and wherever possible include parents in this process. Some parents think it is unhelpful to keep the focus on race, as this will make children internalize a negative self-image. The problem with this is that often children are thinking about it anyway. When we stay silent for these children, they do not develop tools in managing micro-aggressions and are left alone dealing with these difficult feelings. When a parent can hear their children's concerns about race, they can be too quick to ascribe a benign meaning behind the perceived microaggression and unintentionally dismiss the child's experience. Again, the damaging impact of this is that the child is left alone with their feelings and can only come to understand this as a communication that they are wrong. As therapists, we can bridge this and enable families to find healthy ways of thinking and talking about these important issues by building robustness and educating families about the importance of culture and race. It can be challenge for the therapist, particularly when there is resistance, which is why other professionals need to be on board ensuring this work takes place. Working with resistance is an art form and can be challenging when the therapist has their own history of racism, so, it is important to have culturally safe supervision to process these dynamics and feel empowered to do the work.

Conclusion

We need to create safe ways of openly talking about racism to support children adopted transracially and via intercountry processes to make sense of their experience. Being adopted is already a difficult experience that raises a range of difficulties connected to loss and separation. Race and ethnicity add another painful layer which needs to be addressed, considering we are not living in a post-racist society. Adopters need to be empowered and supported to develop tools to address this and work through their own unconscious bias so that they can be advocates for their children. With this much-needed support therapists can help adopters in enabling their children to grow up feeling proud of their heritage and able to navigate the world with skills in addressing racism.

References

Agoro, O. (2003). Anti-Racist Counselling Practice. In C. Lago & B. Smith (eds), *Anti-discriminatory Counselling Practice*, pp.16-32. London: Sage Publications.

Andreou, C. (1992). Inner and Outer Reality in Children and Adolescents. In J. Kareem & R. Littlewood (eds), *Intercultural Therapy: Themes, Interpretations and Practice*, pp.161-170. Oxford: Blackwell.

Banks, N. (2001). Assessing Children and Families Who Belong to Minority Ethnic Groups. In J. Howarth (ed.), *The Child's World – Assessing Children in Need*, 181–199. London: Jessica Kingsley Publishers.

Banton, N. (1987). *Racial Theories*. Cambridge: Cambridge University Press

Bowlby, J. (1970). *Attachment and Loss. Volume I Attachment*. New York, NY: Basic Books.

Bremner, R.H. (1974). *Children and Youth in America: A Documentary History, Vol. 3, Parts 1–4*. Cambridge, MA: Harvard University Press.

Brodzinsky, D.M. (2005). Reconceptualizing Openness in Adoption: Implications for Theory, Research and Practise. In D, Brodzinsky & J. Palacios (eds), *Psychological Issues in Adoption: Research and Practise* (pp.145–166). New York, NY: Greenwood.

Burke Harris, N. (2018). *The Deepest Well: Healing the Long-Term Effects of Childhood Adversity.* Monument, CO: Bluebird.

Cousins, S. (2019). *Overcoming Everyday Racism: Building Resilience and Wellbeing in the Face of Discrimination and Microaggressions.* London: Jessica Kingsley Publishers.

Department for Education (2012). *Statistical First Release, Children Looked After in England (Including Adoption and Care Leavers), year ending 31 March 2012.* London: DfE.

DiAngelo, R. (2018). *White Fragility: Why It's So Hard for White People to Talk About Racism.* Boston, MA: Beacon Press.

Eddo-Lodge, R. (2018). *Why I'm No Longer Talking to White People About Race.* London: Bloomsbury Publishing.

Hughes, D.A. (2011). *Attachment Focused Family Therapy Workbook.* New York, NY: W.W. Norton.

Hughes, D.A., Golding, K.S. & Hudson, J. (2019) *Healing Relational Trauma with Attachment Focused Interventions.* New York, NY: W.W. Norton.

Kalmanowitz, D. & Lloyd, B. (2005). *Art Therapy and Political Violence With Art, Without Illusion.* London: Routledge.

Khan, O. (2020, 20 April). Coronavirus exposes how riddled Britain is with racial inequality. *The Guardian.* www.theguardian.com/commentisfree/2020/apr/20/coronavirusracial-inequality-uk-housing-employmenthealth-bame-covid-19deprivation.

McIntosh, P. (1990). White privilege: Unpacking the invisible knapsack. *Independent School,* 49(2), 31–36.

Narey, M. (2011). The Narey Report: A blueprint for the nation's lost children. *The Times,* 5 July.

Rankine, C. (2015). The condition of black life is one of mourning. *The New York Times,* 22 June.

Roy, A. (2020). *A For Adoption: An Exploration of the Adoption Experience for Families and Professionals.* London: Routledge.

Sargent, S. (2015). Transracial adoption in England: A critical race and system theory analysis. *International Journal of Law in Context,* 11(4), 412–425.

Stern, D. (1985). *The Interpersonal World of the Infant: A View from Psychoanalysis and Developmental Psychology.* New York, NY: Taylor and Francis.

Smedley, A. & Smedley, B.D. (2005). Race as biology is fiction, racism as a social problem is real: Anthropological and historical perspectives on the social construction of race. *The American Psychologist,* 60, 16–26. doi:10.1037/0003-066X.60.1.16.

Thomas, L. (1992). Racism and Psychotherapy: Working with Racism in the Consulting Room – An Analytic View. In J. Kareem & R. Littlewood (eds), *Intercultural Therapy: Themes, Interpretations and Practice,* 146–160. Oxford: Blackwell.

United Nations Convention on the Rights of the Child. Article 20. https://www.unicef.org.uk/wp-content/uploads/2010/05/UNCRC_united_nations_convention_on_the_rights_of_the_child.pdf.

van der Kolk, B. (2009). A developmental approach to complex PTSD: Childhood and adult cumulative trauma as predictors of symptom complexity. *Journal of Traumatic Stress,* 22(5), 399–408.

Winnicott, D.W. (1971). *Playing and Reality.* London: Tavistock Publications.

Further Reading

Alvarez, A. (1992). *Live Company: Psychoanalytic Psychotherapy with Autistic, Borderline, Deprived and Abused Children.* London: Routledge.

Banks, N. (1992). Techniques for direct work with black children, adoption and fostering. BAAF. 16(3), 19–24.

Kendi, I. X. (2019). *How to be An Antiracist.* London: One World.

Chapter 13

The Power of a Name

UMAA THAMPU

Abstract
This chapter reflects on personal experience of being othered and working as a Gestalt therapist in London. I include issues related to my ancestral baggage, unfinished business and share insight from my therapeutic work. This chapter explores the nuances surrounding a name and theoretically illustrates this through Zinker's Cycle of Awareness, Dr Isha Mckenzie-Mavinga's concepts and the Johari Window. This highlights the evocative themes regarding the initial meeting between therapist and client that strike the transferential relationship and establish a pattern around power. I have used Jennifer Mackewn's Interruption to Contact table as a model to demonstrate the implications for therapists working with difference and how to heighten awareness around the initial meeting and ongoing working alliance. The chapter includes pop culture references to highlight English stereotypes that still add pressure to speak and present as English, and exposes the internalized racism and oppressive energy of living in two cultures or more.

Keywords
Racism, Cycle of awareness, Johari Window, ancestral baggage, Gestalt, patterns, code switching, internalized racism, assimilation, anglicize, recognition trauma, black empathetic approach, pre-transference

The power of a name
A multitude of traumatic events shocked and surged like a thunderous roar pulsating through every country in 2020. On 23 February, Ahmaud Arbery was shot by police while jogging in his local neighbourhood; on 13 March, Breonna Taylor was shot by police as she slept in her bed at night

and on 17 March, the UK and America went into lockdown as Covid-19 started to take hold of our lives. The international Black Lives Matter movement urged everyone to 'say their name'; this need for immediate action felt important and it was vital not to lose momentum in seeking justice. The name George Floyd has immense global power as this indicates a brutal moment in time. The quick succession of these episodes led therapists to be living in trauma alongside their clients in real time, and a sense of emergency grew into understanding racism in more depth. In this chapter, I share personal and client experience with the aim of making explicit the emotional conflict connected to a birth name. I will identify the need to anglicize birth names while living in the UK and then make recommendations of what I have found useful and not useful in assisting clients in the integration of their cultural identities.

As a Tamil, South Londoner, able-bodied, lighter-skinned, cisgender woman teaching and practising as a Gestalt therapist, I acknowledge my privilege and that I can unwittingly fall into the role of oppressor. This is a caveat in examining the complexity of working with intersectionality and struggling with the hurt that comes from the unconscious conditioned roles of the perpetrator or the oppressed. As human beings, we differentiate each other by our names; names have meanings and importance. Legally, we need a name and having a name enhances our humanness. Can you imagine what it would be like to not have a name? It would lead to a feeling of being unmoored or unrooted. Names give us grounding, make up our identity and tell us information about each other regarding religion, gender and heritage. When parents or caregivers pick a name, it can involve rituals like a naming ceremony or baptism. It is when the name is outside the home that a sense of otherness occurs. In exploring this theme, I will pick and mix ideas from Dr Isha Mckenzie-Mavinga's concepts and Zinker's Cycle of Awareness and Johari Window, and quote BIPOC (Black, Indigenous, People of Colour) writers who explore the evocative themes regarding the initial meeting between therapist and client that strike the transferential relationship and establish a pattern around power.

I am aware when a client initially books an appointment, the pre-transference begins as my biases set in about a client's heritage, gender, sexuality and culture. As Catherine Jackson (2018), who explores Andrew Curry's (1964) theory on pre-transference in her *Therapy Today* article, 'Why we need to talk about race', states, 'Pretransference describes the ideas, fantasies and values ascribed by the black client to their white therapist or the white client to their black therapist, long before they first meet in the consulting room.' When we see a client's name for the first time it brings up the stock images, prejudices and biases; a name that is unfamiliar will naturally lead to curiosity and we will ask the question, 'Where is that from?' This innocent common question begins the 'othering' and can feel intrusive as the therapist leads most of the assessment in the initial stages. I acknowledge that the therapist's intent is to be open and that this line of questioning can also clumsily fall into, 'Where are you really from?' These dialogical common niceties are striving for connection and, exacerbated by the anxiety of meeting a new person, they cover the awkwardness of sitting with a different name. Other interventions that are not so intrusive could be, 'Where does your name belong to? Or how do you feel about your name?' This allows the client to lead and expands the dialogue around difference and identity. As a therapist, I work alongside the core ideology of the Black, African and Asian Therapy Network (BAATN, 2021) and believe that no one is inherently racist; we are born into racism therefore need time to process these inherited biases in personal therapy, supervision or BAATN professional development workshops.

My name contains two syllables and four letters. I have noticed several interesting relational dynamics that are played out within the first few seconds of introducing myself or meeting a new client and exploring their birth name. I am used to spelling and re-iterating my name a few times. It is an onerous, frequent task, when meeting people for the first time, as is seeing my name misspelled on paperwork or WhatsApp messages from friends or, worse, my name being forgotten, and I am called by another BIPOC colleague's name. After attending 'The Challenge of Racism' workshop in June 2020, facilitated by Dr Mckenzie-Mavinga, I felt inspired to explore the importance of names. During the workshop, a colleague pronounced Isha's name as I-eesha and Dr Mckenzie-Mavinga simply stated, 'Can you say my name as it is.' It was a powerful intervention, and my recognition trauma set in as memories of my name being misspelled and mispronounced flashed through my mind and I became aware of themes in my client work where vibrations around power and identity were played out around a name.

Misspelling or completely forgetting a name is a well-known cultural faux pas, a Freudian slip, a sign of disrespect and incredibly exposing in the therapeutic relationship. My experience as a therapist and client has enabled me to notice patterns, including a set of trauma responses for individuals who do not have an English-sounding name in the didactic relationship. This internal conflict emerges when challenging or not

The Power of a Name

challenging the other person regarding the pronounciation of their name. Here is a sample from the range of replies I have received when correcting a person about my name:

'I know, but, oh, is it?'

'I thought it was spelt like this.'

'I am sure in the previous thread it was spelt like this?'

'Really?'

When someone demonstrates an inability to hear a person and then denies their reality, failing to pause, it allows these types of responses to exacerbate the feeling of otherness, anger and pure 'crazy-making'. I have been left with a feeling of shame and that I am a nuisance, the one with the problematic name. This feeling of shame provides an insight into why parents and clients feel the need to anglicize a name, as it makes it easier to navigate through the covert and explicit layers of discrimination. Growing up in south London, I recall my parents' fury at primary school teachers spelling my name incorrectly: 'Omar', 'Umar' or 'Una'. Simply taking out a syllable or adding a letter to my name configuration leads to a different gender, ethnicity, location and religion. Omar is an Arabic name for a boy; Una is often a girl with Irish heritage. Currently, as I write, I feel the need to stretch my neck as my left shoulder holds embedded knots and links to my ancestral fury. As a Gestalt therapist, I acknowledge that my body sensations connect to my family's unspoken trauma. It can be quick to erase someone's identity and in my case this would be reminiscent of the ongoing genocide of Tamils in Sri Lanka.

It is well known that people with curriculum vitaes showing non-English names tend to be offered fewer job interviews and this provides a rationale for the need to anglicize names. I have friends of Chinese or Ghanaian heritage, who have an English name but at home their Chinese or Ghanaian name is used, and their first language is spoken. This ties in with the theory of the Johari Window, where someone can present a different version of themselves depending on the context and how these parts emerge and are witnessed in the therapy space. The Johari Window, devised by psychologists Joseph Luft and Harrington Ingham in the 1950s, is a teaching tool to raise self-awareness. It is made of four windows: the open area, the blind spot, the hidden area and the unknown area. Looking at the open area, a client living with two cultures or more will present different parts in therapy, at home or in the workplace. As therapists, we

209

work with all four windows and usually the aim is to increase the open area to reduce the client's need to present fixed habitual ways of being and to live from a more authentic place. An intervention I recommend when the working alliance is good enough is to take time and space to ask how a client inherited their name or the meaning behind their name. Also, to think back to the first session and what it was like to meet me as a therapist and hear me say their name. When I have examined this, some clients have explained that I have not been saying their name correctly.

The Johari Window's hidden window or 'facade' (known by the self, but peers or others do not know it) links to how some clients have reported colluding with the therapist in the mispronunciation of their name as it was 'just easier'. We may be working with clients currently or have had clients leave without knowing how to say their name. This quote from Luan Baines-Ball's (2021) *Therapy Today* article, 'Why pronouns matter', explores similar feelings regarding gender diversity, and painfully says, 'an element of my struggle was that in being fully me, I risked shame, rejection and judgement'. This links back to the 'open window', that trying to get clients to be more authentic is risky as the waves of racism and discrimination are circling around and threaten a client's livelihood or physical safety. The therapy space may be the only safe space a client has regarding the exploration of their difference. When I have taken time to explore a client's ancestral lineage, country and circumstances around their name, this adds trust to the working alliance. I can see the growth in a client's warmth and a heightening of their self-awareness regarding identity. Focusing on a name can be a vehicle for understanding the impact of othering, familial introjects and how clients code switch due to living in two or more cultures.

Other recommendations include observing and assessing the diversity in your counselling practice, and exploring in supervision and with your colleagues the client that you are attracting. As therapists, notice how clients hide parts of their cultural identity and expression of sexuality to survive in families, relationships or the workplace.

Zinker's Cycle of Awareness helps to demonstrate the interruptions to contact in the client/therapist experience, and I do this by sharing that when I introduce myself. I need to state my name and be understood. I notice sensation in my body and utilize energy to mobilize facial muscles to say my name. The next phase is action; I scan the person's face to note if they smile but I can sense that they struggle to say my name. As times passes, I begin to feel self-conscious. I feel hot and there is tension around my mouth and their mouth. This leads to noticing another physical sensation: growing awkwardness as they avert their eyes from my gaze or I avoid eye contact and then I begin to feel hotter.

This moment illustrates various interruptions to contact as I notice and swallow introjects . Introjects are messages that have not been self-reflected on. My introjects can consist of "I am too much", "This is too difficult, I should make life easier for the other person", "I should not correct or I should not interrupt" .This exacerbates the feeling of shame as I feel the need to reassure, withdraw or give up as sitting in the discomfort is unbearable and I just want to move on. Introductions are brief moments in the therapy room and, as the therapist, we can slow these down, noticing how a name is pronounced in English or their first language, and asking where it comes from and how they were given it.

The next stage in the Cycle of Awareness is recognition and mean-ing-making. It is here that many possibilities arise, including uncon-sciously moving away from the distress of being othered and noting internalized racism and that it is painful to be different so the urge to merge with the dominant culture becomes figural. This need to merge is about survival and not feeling exposed or vulnerable to attack. One suggestion is to stay with the discomfort, to pause. Initially, clients have anxiety about coming to therapy and want to bring other things, and this enables the exploration of their name to retreat into the background (Mackewn, 1997, p.107).

The Interruptions to Contact is a flexible framework into which you can add your own concepts. This is a starting point to explore the multifaceted way in which names are a useful therapeutic tool for discovering a client's relationship to their sense of identity and what work the therapist needs to do regarding ongoing exploration of racism, sexuality and assumptions about gender.

Table 13.1: Interruptions to contact in the therapeutic relationship regarding a name

Confluence stage	During supervision and personal self-reflection, take time to explore if your client has a need to anglicize their name. This could be to fit in with the majority culture and it 'being easier'. Here, you could take time with the client to explore their name. Some clients will be confident in differentiation, will state their name clearly and make important connections to their heritage, race, culture and ethnicity. An example of confluence, through a heteronormative lens, is when traditionally a woman takes a man's surname in marriage, giving up their original surname. It could be worthwhile when working with couples to explore partners' names and nicknames.

cont.

Retroflection stage	Take time explore how a client anglicizes their name due to feelings of fear and shame around identity, to merge with the dominant culture. This can include moments when a therapist mispronounces the client's name or says an incorrect name. Feelings of shame are excruciatingly painful, but try to stay with your own discomfort and encourage the client to speak of their feelings when their name is not said correctly. This pattern of mispronunciation happens elsewhere. During the therapist–client relationship a new confidence could emerge after conflict with the therapist and lead to developing meaningful contact with client's feelings of frustration, irritation or anger.
Introjection stage	During the first few meetings in therapy, the client's name is relevant to how they present in therapy. It is important for therapists to notice if a client has rejected their birth name completely or has no link to the context of their name. This can be for many reasons, including family breakdown, rejection of their culture, heritage or expression of gender or sexuality.
Projection stage	By this stage, you will have assumed you have said the client's name correctly and the client submits, becomes confluent and agrees. This stage can go on for the duration of the therapy, completely without awareness. It can also be aided by the client's deflection as they smile throughout and appear agreeable and compliant. This emphasizes the power dynamic that therapists have and how important it is to welcome the client's feelings of anger towards the therapist as a vital piece of therapeutic work.
Desensitization stage	This is the stage to explore whether the client displays a numbing sensation with regard to their name, and has no interest or curiosity in their birth name. The name is a connection to their heritage, culture and identity, so you need to know where the client is in relation to this important aspect of themselves.

Table 13.1 gives an idea of potential scenarios and dilemmas when working with names that are non-English. When introducing myself, I see that clients often greet me with a smile. It is a polite nicety. A client's smile can hold many meanings and is a survival method when othered. A smile covers confusion and hurt and is a coping mechanism to get through various scenarios such as returning to the UK at border control, job interviews or in the therapy space where suddenly a BIPOC individual has felt othered and disempowered; as Zora Neale Hurston (1928) says, 'I feel most coloured when I am thrown against a sharp white background.' When a BIPOC individual arrives for therapy, their name, skin colour and gender disclose immediate differences or similarities.

The therapist needs to be aware of their pretransference, countertransference and projective material. This will be important in how they will utilise this important information whilst paying attention to the nuance regarding the client's and their own intersectionality.

As therapists, we acknowledge that everything is of equal importance, from how a client makes payment to what they wear and how they present in the room. One client I worked with had a European-sounding name. The client had parents from Italian and French backgrounds and within the initial few minutes of introductions they reassured me by saying I could pronounce their four-letter name the English way. I self-reflected that the nuances of colonialism were prevalent, as they would beat themselves up for not having confidence to speak during presentations at staff meetings. The client could see my skin colour and yet the need to merge with the dominant culture of being English was figural.

I emphasized that English was their second language and I utilized Dr Mckenzie-Mavinga's (2009) 'black empathetic approach' and encouraged them to speak in their first language. During the dialogic process, a few moments would pass, the client would lose their words and their inner critic would arrive to beat them for not knowing the English word. This is where I would intervene by saying, 'Do you know what the word is in your first language?' Although I did not understand their first language, the intention was to give their neural pathways a break and not have to try to find the correct English word. The therapeutic space is where we can nurture indigenous identity and invite these parts to feel welcome. There was no demand to code switch to the idea of being 'English'. Within the first few seconds of meeting me, my client wanted to make life easy for the person in authority. The person in authority, the therapist, can unwittingly collude with the client by not taking time to ask about the story behind a client's name, or quickly misspelling their name, or watching the client go blank and struggle for a few minutes for words when their first language is not English. The therapeutic space is a microcosm of external realities around power, and it is here we need to be sensitive and urgently grow into awareness of the racist power dynamics surrounding identity. As Dr Dwight Turner explained at the BME Voices, Black Trauma Conference in 2020:

> From the more conscious, where, for example, the removal of one's name is actually a form of dehumanisation and loss of identity; to the more subtle and psychological where the barely concealed subtlety of systemic microaggressions is actually a means of Supremacy maintaining its control and power over the objectified other.

In October 2020, a senator at a Republican rally deliberately mispronounced Democratic politician Kamala Harris's name a few times. Amber Ruffin (2021), an American, female, black comedian responded by using humour. She told white folks that the name Kamala played to their strengths as it is pronounced the same as Pamela. As the sketch progressed, Ruffin made links with slavery and how white people renamed enslaved black people and that black people took their power back by reclaiming their names. Ruffin said, 'We've created names that fill up your lungs, your chest and your whole mouth when you say them out loud! So, fix your mouth and say it right! We have beautiful, melodious names that tell the story of being black in America.' This example is a tactic used by white supremacists, a verbal missile launched from afar highlighting otherness, with the sole aim to dehumanize and ridicule a human being. As therapists, we need to be vigilant to what happens in the working alliance, so notice your anxiety and what you are transferring onto your client. What is happening in your mouth, jaw and chest? Words have power and the English language lexicon has so many possibilities, meaning and nuances. Dr Dwight Turner explained at BME Voices:

> X started therapy a month after the brutal killing of George Floyd. The traumatic impact of this viral video catalysed many people, including friends, family, clients to experience a rush of harrowing racist flashbacks during a worldwide pandemic. One weekday evening, X arrived and described herself as a woman of mixed heritage. I could sense she was tense from her clipped words when speaking to me. Initially keen to see me as part of a couple, she decided to come to see me for individual therapy. Unfortunately, due to UK government restrictions during the lockdown, we were unable to meet in person and the loss of the therapy room impacted our privacy, as there were interruptions from her children due to demands of home-schooling, and her husband could be heard nearby.
>
> X described challenging conversations with her husband and his parents about recent events. She had met her white British husband at university and described him as a hard-working, loving father. I acknowledged that time was needed to build the ground between us to establish trust. As sessions progressed, it became clearer that she was struggling with recognition trauma regarding racism. She described painful moments with her white in-laws about how to include her heritage with her children, as the in-laws seemed to forget or subtly dismiss her needs around her culture.

The Power of a Name

White people will use a variety of defences to avoid sitting in the pain of racism. In her book *Caste* (2020), Isabel Wilkerson examines, through historical events, white people taking selfies at lynchings and sending these photos as postcards to friends, and behaviours including taking a piece of flesh from the body as a souvenir. My mind holds images of African American men hanging from lynching trees in America's Bible Belt and, sat nearby white folks are eating lunch, smiling for their photo. This horrific image provides insight into the inherited inability of white people to feel empathy when the dialogue surrounding racism starts, and is part of the harrowing traumatic oppressive conditioning. It is a trauma response, desensitization includes apathy and denial and enables the racist drama triangle to be stuck. As James Baldwin (2021) asked passionately, 'How much time do *you* want for *your* progress?'

X explained that her daughter had two names, her English name and a personal name she had given to her that was related to her own father's African heritage. The English name was her first name and the African name her middle name. I asked her what her daughter's African name meant, and she said it meant a person full of joy and blessings. I suggested an experiment and asked her to say her daughter's English name out loud and take a moment to imagine who came into her mind's eye. She said she saw a white woman. We sat in silence and she said, 'but my daughter is brown and clearly of mixed heritage'. W.E. Dubois (2021) wrote about double consciousness and here I imagined that her child at the tender age of eight was already in a power struggle around identity. X was witnessing the slow, covert erasure of her daughter's African heritage. Her daughter's name had culture and depth and yet it was a middle name for no one to hear out loud. In sessions, I would often say her daughter's African name out loud, and I could see my client's eyes widen. I asked her how it was to hear her name and where she would be able to say her daughter's African name. Would it become shortened or used at home? During one of our sessions she said, 'I like her first name and I wonder if George Floyd hadn't happened, maybe we wouldn't be talking about this.' In hindsight, I could see this as a trauma response but at the time I felt an emotional kick and had to ground myself. I sensed the difficulty in exploring her white family dynamics and her loyalty she had to her husband and in-laws. I responded, 'Maybe not now, but your daughter will ask you questions when she is 14? Or 21?'

In looking at the complexity of raising a child with mixed heritage

I noted that my client was unconsciously repeating her trauma of living as a brown-skinned woman in the UK and passing down the introjected messages that in order to survive you assimilate by anglicizing your name, code switching by no longer speaking your first language, and no longer wearing ancestral clothing in order to weave into being English. As Reni Eddo-Lodge (2017, p.102) writes, 'White privilege is never more pronounced than in our intimate relationships, our close friendships and our families.' As sessions progressed, I suggested another experiment as we spoke about white privilege, and I emailed her Peggy McIntosh's (2019) 'White Privilege Checklist' and suggested she went through the checklist with her husband. She would often say to me that her in-laws were not 'bad people', and I recognized her need to 'split', a common response when working with the challenge of racism that 'racists are bad'. This deflection blocks the progress of self-awareness and I attempted to normalize that we are all born into racism; racism is a set-up, our education, political and government structures are incredibly classist and racist.

The anxiety surrounding the topic of white privilege led to a silent rupture. In the cycle of the therapy, I was unable to go further with my client as some weeks passed with many cancellations due to last-minute work meetings. The sessions became irregular, and this indicated to me that this work was too hard, too painful and confusing for the client. I had become 'the know-it-all therapist' by trying to educate my client, and my cerebral intervention was an avoidance of sitting in her wounding regarding racism. X had been hurt by her in-laws' lack of curiosity and respect towards her heritage and her daughter.

During my client practice, a range of well-known English stereotypes have arisen, from Harry Potter to Mr Darcy. As well as being unable to hide one's skin colour or name, having an accent is like typing in a sat nav postcode for identity, as it instantly tells the other person where you are from and what class you are. These stereotypes are the introjected, internalized gold standard of 'English-ness' (to be well spoken, polite and to have a proper English accent). It is often remarked at various counselling CPD gatherings, where I have experienced overt racism from fellow colleagues, that I speak very well. It is a poignant reminder in the here and now of the impact of colonialism and that being English is still revered as the epitome of being classy. I acknowledge that I speak well as another way for me to survive, as I just want to get through.

In 2016, an interview in *The Guardian* with BBC news presenter, Naga

Munchetty says, 'My mother started calling me Naga, because it means cobra and she dreamed of snakes when she was pregnant. I've always hated the name and for a while I thought about changing it to Nadia. In some ways, I wish I had' (Moorhead, 2016). A similar script with a birth name is written in Afua Hirsch's (2018) book *Brit-ish*, where she describes not being able to pronounce her name while growing up in a predominately white culture in Wimbledon. These uncomfortable vignettes show the complexity of living in the UK and highlight internalized racism. So, what does this mean when working therapeutically? The reflections from Naga Munchetty and Afua Hirsch, growing up as brown bodied and with a mixed heritage identity in the UK, highlight the sensitivity needed and a particularly valued skill set of how therapists attune to a client's unconscious or conscious internalized racism.

This will be difficult terrain, as the experience of internalized racism is a unique personal embodied knowledge felt in black and brown bodies and also passed down through transgenerational trauma. The impact of racism is evident through inner child work and clients speak of witnessing their own parents' experience of racism and how this can contribute to conflicting feelings related to their identity, culture, heritage and a desire to fit in.

Questions that assist in expanding the context of the multifaceted nature of internalized racism can include: 'Do they speak their first language. Does the client have opportunities to celebrate their ancestral clothing or have a chance to visit the home of their ancestors?'

Observing where the energy is when these questions are answered is difficult, traumatic and heartbreaking work.

Additionally, therapists who do not identify as white will need to take time to have explored these layers of internalized racism in their own personal therapy and supervision. For white therapists, it is crucial to explore the impact of their whiteness in their supervision and their own therapy.

When I type BIPOC names into a word document, a red line appears underneath indicating I need to spellcheck. It is subtle, but the word document repeatedly reminds me I have not spelt these names correctly, therefore they need amending. The effect of seeing these red lines dotted around and 'adding to the dictionary' perpetuates the binary idea that a non-English name is not correct. So a name, with its rich reference to culture, ancestors or geography, is often deleted, shortened or anglicized in order to fit into the majority culture.

Rizwan Ahmed (2020), British Pakistani actor and rapper, explores through metaphor in his Oscar-winning film *The Long Goodbye* and compares his relationship to Britain as a romantic relationship with an abuser. This struck a chord with me, as in 2018, I observed the trauma of those who had gone before me. The UK government targeted the Caribbean community with an immigration policy that was like ethnic cleansing. I read in the news that elders were being asked to show papers and suddenly deported or feeling the need to hide from a country which they had been invited into, where they had lived, raised families and placed roots. As a South Asian woman, I was alarmed and frightened in the aftermath of the Brexit vote and the rise of the Far Right in America, and I thought, who is next?

My அப்பா and அம்மா evoked a sense of pride in their British passports and they were told that the UK was the best place for education and opportunities. I was going through some of my அப்பா belongings and discovered a letter he had written to the bank in 1975.

> During my stay in the UK for the last nine years I found that friends, associates and officials with whom I have to communicate find it difficult to pronounce my Christian name. To make life easy I have decided to follow the British tradition of signing and being called by my surname. I hope you will appreciate the change.

I have read this part of the letter over many years and feel the heartache of racism that my அப்பா held in his body and psyche. His letter is a painful example of how hard my அப்பா and அம்மா tried over nine years, and then he felt the vibrations of oppression and needed to erase his identity to fit into the idea of the English stereotype. So, what does this mean for us in the therapy room? I invite us to make links to those who have gone before us, to explore the stories, themes behind names, surnames, nicknames and how are they celebrated or forgotten. Grandparents, significant caregivers, often children, are named after valued relatives. Certain cultures have name days to celebrate alongside a birthday, or other cultures may not name a child for a few days after the birth and there are important rituals around a name like baptism, confirmation or marriage.

I want these agonizing reflections to be shared to urgently improve understanding and increase the openness of how we work in the therapy room, as demonstrated by Faisal Mahmood (2021) at the BACP Ethics Hub talk: 'We will take the law concerning equality, diversity and inclusion into careful consideration and strive for a higher standard than the legal minimum' (Good Practice, point 23). We all have judgements and biases and need to be aware of how this affects us in the working alliance. There are many possibilities highlighted in Table 13.2 and as therapists we need to be in a place of wonder and humility. The fast pace requires therapists to keep up and seek support via BAATN workshops and therapy, supervision, peer support to make time to explore in depth themes regarding the dynamics around racism. I acknowledge this work is not for the faint-hearted and as we know from the Johari Window, if we have the courage to venture into the unknown we can bring a richness not just to our clients lives but to the quality of being human by celebrating the uniqueness of a name.

References

Ahmed, R. (2020). The Long Goodbye. www.youtube.com/watch?v=Lzz50xENH4g&t=5s.
BAATN (2021). Core ideology. www.baatn.org.uk/about.
Baines-Ball, L. (2021). Why pronouns matter. *Therapy Today*, 32(2), 30–33.
Baldwin, J. (2021). How much time do you want for your progress? www.youtube.com/watch?v=OCUlE5ldPvM 2021.
Curry, A. (1964). Myth, transference and the black psychotherapist. *International Review of Psychoanalysis*, 45, 89–120.
Dubois, W. (2021). *The Souls of Black Folk*. London: Penguin.
Eddo-Lodge, R. (2017). *Why I Am No Longer Speaking to White People About Race*. London: Bloomsbury.
Hirsch, A. (2018). *Brit-ish: On Race, Identity and Belonging*. London: Jonathan Cape.
Jackson, C. (2018). Why we need to talk about race. *Therapy Today*, 29(8), 8–13.
Johari Window (2021). Wikipedia. https://en.wikipedia.org/wiki/Johari_window.
Mackewn, J. (1997). *Developing Gestalt Counselling*. London: Sage Publications.
Mahmood, F. (2021). Political Correctness, repressed racism or contaminated imagination. Ethics in Action Video, BACP.
Mcintosh, P. (2019). *White Privilege: Unpacking the Invisible Knapsack*. http://codeofgoodpractice.com/wp-content/uploads/2019/05/Mcintosh-White-Privilege-Unpacking-the-Invisible-Knapsack.pdf.
Moorhead, J. (2016). Naga Munchetty: When I said I was studying English, my mum said, 'What are you going to do – become a poet?' *The Guardian*. www.theguardian.com/lifeandstyle/2016/jun/17/naga-munchetty-when-i-said-i-was-studying-english-my-mum-said-what-are-you-going-to-do-become-a-poet.
Mckenzie-Mavinga, I. (2009). *Black Issues in the Therapeutic Process*. London: Palgrave Macmillan.
Mckenzie-Mavinga, I. (2020). Challenge of Racism Workshop (20–21 June 2020).
Neale Hurston, Z. (1928, 2021). www.quotetab.com/zora-neale-hurston-quotes-about-white.
Ruffin, A. (2021). Kamala Harris' name isn't that hard to pronounce. www.youtube.com/watch?v=KXzVKmnukhA.
Turner, D. (2020). BME Voices Trauma Conference. www.bmevoices.co.uk/wp-content/uploads/2020/10/online-trauma-conference-2020.pdf.
Wilkerson, I. (2020). *Caste: The Lies That Divide Us*. London: Allen Lane.

Further Reading

Joyce, P. & Sills, C. (2018) *Skills in Gestalt Counselling and Psychotherapy*. London: Sage Publications.
Klein, M. (2021). Paranoid-schizoid position. Melanie Klein Trust. https://melanie-klein-trust.org.uk/theory/paranoid-schizoid-position.
Mckenzie-Mavinga, I. (2016). *The Challenge of Racism in Therapeutic Practice*. London: Palgrave Macmillan.

Chapter 14

Belonging: Who Decides?

KAREN MINIKIN

Abstract
This is a personal and reflective chapter that tracks the connections between personal life experience, intergenerational legacy and the longings and ruptures around a desire to belong and feel 'at home'. The chapter brings together the political and the personal, with links and connections made between the social culture and environment and the impact on the family. In considering racial identity, the author remembers and reflects on early childhood experiences that are both conscious and unconscious. She reveals the exposure she had to life in Nigeria during the 1960s and life in England during the 1960s and 1970s. These international life experiences reflect a post-colonial identity that she has struggled with, leaving a sense of ongoing labour in finding and retaining a sense of 'home'.

Keywords
Belonging, home, identity, racism, trauma, war, abuse, poverty, Brexit, alienation

Belonging: Who decides?
Definition of *belonging* – an affinity for a place or situation (Oxford Dictionaries, n.d.).

Introduction: Why belonging?
In the UK, the drama over Brexit continued for several years before our actual departure. The referendum was controversial, the fights were acrimonious, the fallout politically, economically, socially and culturally

was yet to be tested before the Covid-19 pandemic hit us in 2020. The Brexit issue raised a number of familiar questions for me: Who do I belong to? Is it just to myself or to others too? Like my country, when I face a group, I question, *am I in? Or am I out?* This question faced my country as it struggled to decide forced a critical review of who the UK is as a nation. It forced questions such as are 'we'? What does 'we' stand for? How do we use national power? How do we use authority? How shall we disagree? How shall we debate, collaborate and compromise? Whether gripped by those debates or fatigued by them, the British people were shaken out of political passivity and pushed hard to take note of the relevance of politics in our lives. For me, the nature of the discussions, debate and the unfurling consequences felt deeply personal.

The referendum in 2016, was a campaign based on lies for many, a terrible mistake for some, a body blow to others, a cry of protest as well and altogether an eruption of the terrible splits we have in our British society around class, race, ethnicity, sovereignty and democracy. The last few years have seen a shocking rise in hate, some of which unravelled over the murder of George Floyd and the ongoing institutionalized racism of the US police force. The protests around the world were passionate and focused and there was also the subsequent backlash in the UK, to diminish the right to protest via the Police Crime and Sentencing Bill in April 2021.[1]

During the Brexit debates, I felt psychologically bounced back to my adolescent years and the 1970s. I had felt provoked by the rise of the National Front and I joined the Anti-Nazi League and the Rock Against Racism movement, both of which opposed the rise of racism and also homophobia. As a younger child, I had spent six years living in Nigeria from the ages of four to ten. Nigeria was in its early days of post-colonial rule and at war within itself as the fight for Biafra was on. As a young child, I was faced with the brutality of war, alongside the aggression and violence of the post-Victorian schooling in Nigeria. My response was to escape from the outside, by withdrawing within. I became mute and did my best to accompany my silence by becoming invisible. To be ignored was to be safe, and within this bubble I created a nostalgic vision of my 'homeland', my mother country. I was missing home.

I longed for something I imagined I had known – comfort, calm and gentleness. In my silence, I dreamt of a soft summer, soft rain, a soft

---

1 www.gov.uk/government/publications/police-crime-sentencing-and-courts-bill-2021-factsheets/police-crime-sentencing-and-courts-bill-2021-protest-powers-fact-sheet.

home. When I was ten, I was happy to know I was returning to England with my mother and siblings. I was so excited and so unprepared for what I was going to encounter.

Instead of softness and comfort, I discovered the violence in the UK of the explicit racism of the early 1970s. We were not welcome. The verbal abuse for people like myself in the 1970s was 'Paki!' A word that was hurled and delivered to encompass the full force of hate, rejection and destruction. This demeaning of who we were alongside 'Go back to where you came from!' left me further traumatized and confused. I had thought England was my home, it was where I came from, I could claim it – and now my desire for home had been thwarted. Everything felt wrong – me, my family, my longings.

And, we were poor. My mother was now a single parent defending herself in the face of the prejudices about that, and I had lost my father. And so began a conscious time of facing my identity, figuring out how to survive this atmosphere, how to feel about the England I was so desperate to claim and which now seemed to be rejecting me. Who was I in the midst of such conflicts?

Legacy of colonialism: Indian sub-continent and Africa

A close colleague once said, 'Karen, you are a post-colonial child.' She was a woman of Indian heritage who had also lived in Africa and England. Although I already knew that, to hear it said by someone else – by someone who also knew these places – penetrated me and stayed. It was an offering of an identity and I can recall the exact occasion she said it. As I write this, I think about how we need others sometimes to tell us what we already know so we can hear it and receive it in new ways. We come to know ourselves through others too. To see how they see us and to take that all back inside – it matters a great deal. What we say is therefore of profound importance. We are social beings; what others say and do is meant to matter to us.

Without colonialism, my parents would never have met, we would never have gone to Nigeria. In my family, I am the first generation of a post-colonial era. My father lived through it, witnessing partition in the Punjab. He experienced his friends turning into enemies – the splits, the violence, the terrible ruptures are all there in his mind. He spoke nothing of it during my childhood. It is only in recent years when I asked him about it and he said, 'I got one of the last trains out of Delhi – before the butchering started.' Then, looking up, into the space ahead of him, he said as if still in shock, still in wonder, 'They were my friends – Sikh and Hindu boys – I went to their homes.' The horror and shock of having friends one day and enemies the next is just one of many awful stories of the Punjab during the 1940s. Friends, families, communities split apart violently. There is much to recover from the legacy of colonialism – a legacy that has spilled out into the next post-colonial generation. Specifically, it is the legacy of racism and exploitation.

In my childhood, I was accustomed to relating with ease in multi-racial and multicultural groups in both England and Nigeria. From our Nigerian friends and neighbours, I had absorbed some of the tensions in the early post-colonial era of West Africa. The legacy was complicated and the rising middle class in Nigeria were struggling to come to terms with both the introjected superiority of Englishness, as well as their resentment rising to understandable fury that this had been done to them and now there was a psychological, social, cultural, political and community mess to sort out. I took all this in – as a child does, accepting and absorbing the feelings of it all. I experienced the conflicts without intellectualizing the details or facts. I knew who I liked, who I loved, who liked me. I knew my father loved me and I knew our Nigerian 'baby nurse' Florence also loved my siblings and me. And I loved her. Watching close at hand her interactions with her own family, I saw and absorbed the subjugation of working women in Nigeria during the 1960s and I registered that their life was hard.

Children identify with those they love and Florence was no exception for me. Without realizing it at the time I was taking in the domination and submission (Benjamin, 2017) that was so apparent in the hierarchical cultures around me. The long, ancient, sophisticated and at times autocratic history of the Yoruba people had encountered the engulfment of colonialism by the time I arrived in Ibadan. So, there was a long and complicated relationship with power and I was watching the gender and race politics of the 1960s as Nigeria was being born into the new post-colonial era. I saw and was pained by Florence's subjugation (Shaw, 2014) and I was also heartened and enlivened when witnessing the love between her and her husband and their loving acceptance of me and my siblings. It has been decades since I lived with this family that had such a lasting influence on me. In recent years, I remembered Florence in my therapy – someone important in our lives, someone who had maternal love and compassion. She was a generous woman – without her, I fear I would have descended further into myself, retreated inevitably into my dreams to escape the splitting of the violence around me.

In my infancy and early childhood, I had been left with childminders in London as my mother had to go back to work immediately after my birth. I learned in adulthood that my white English childminders had neglected me and though I have no conscious memory of this, my father indicated that this had been about race. More recently, I learned that my family had suffered terrible racism during the early 1960s before we had left for Nigeria. During this time, I was spending a lot of time out and about with my father as a toddler, and these are the experiences I have only a dim recollection of.

In Nigeria, I harboured a somewhat distorted memory and vision of life in England. I felt a keen loss of what I had known. The introduction to a new place, a new people and a new life was a dramatic change for me. My father had already encountered the cultural change that came with needing to settle and live in new places and possibly took this in his stride. For my mother, it must have been a shock, though she was simultaneously excited to have the wider world brought to her. For me, the loss of homeland was immense. No wonder then that when I returned, aged ten, the rejection of overt racism hit me hard as it played into what inevitably I must have taken in through my body from the era and situation into which I had been born. So, all in all, belonging via place, another or my skin and body has been complex and full of alienating experiences (Steiner *et al.*, 1975; Minikin, 2018).

Roots and belonging

I never met my grandparents. Without conscious and concrete knowing, I wonder about the landscapes they lived in. From the coalmines of the midlands in England, to the rural Punjab, my grandfathers were men who worked directly with what the land could offer. My Indian grandmother died in childbirth when my father was four. My English grandmother was an orphan who married a miner, a man much older than her, then he too left, passing away when my mother was three. So, my parents encountered early losses. From different continents and different landscapes, they came together in London having witnessed the traumas of war and partition in the early post-colonial years.

As young adults, neither my mother nor my father had the presence of any family members around them – no siblings, no aunties, uncles, parents or grandparents. While this may have offered a sense of freedom, it also left them unsupported, uncontained and ungrounded. It is hard for me to know what the full meaning is of not knowing any of my grandparents. I can only imagine the sorts of lives they had and the sorts of people they were, from the little my mother tells me about her mother and the little my father has told me of his father. I know they were all poor.

Despite having enjoyed a middle-class life as an adult, I do not feel that this is intrinsically who I am or where I belong. My father fought long and hard to educate himself and as a result has forged a life very different from other members of his family. It means, though, that he is the odd one out – the one who didn't belong, the one who left Pakistan – and Islam. He has led an interesting life, one that has taken him to live in three different continents and many different countries. He clung to his acquired British passport, believing that it would allow him to be safe in the world – an ironic reminder of the old influence inside him of the British Raj. He had longed to read and learn and so he did. His education from India and Pakistan was not enough – he wanted to learn in England too. This was partly because he had registered that in India, the Brits had more and partly because he was destined to harness his independent mind in order to critique the oppression of colonialism and its ongoing effect on the world. He specialized in international relations and wrote about the subsequent mistakes, as he saw it, of India and Pakistan post-partition. This has had a huge impact on his identity and his sense of belonging. He retired from Nigeria and went to live in Berlin, Germany. It suits him there, but for me it feels bittersweet and I see him as a nomad. A rather resourceful one to be sure, but I struggle to see him truly belonging anywhere really.

No doubt my father's nomadic life has contributed to my longing to find a place, a situation, a landscape that I could call home, that felt like home, a place that might welcome me. As an adult, I settled in south-east England and taking up gardening seemed to offer me a connection and love of the land, of creating something from seed. Gardening offers me some satisfaction of the sort I have been searching for – 'to find affinity with a place, a situation'. However, after many years in therapy, I realized it was looking within that I needed most. I literally had to come to terms with my skin. I had to feel it was a skin that could protect me, that it was a good skin to belong to, one that could survive a degree of attack, and I had to learn to speak. Speak properly I mean. I had to learn to speak about what I knew, what I had learned, what I stood for, what hurt me, what angered me. Years of being mute as a child meant this was a long and arduous process.

Breaking the Silence: BAATN Conference, 2019

The BAATN Conference in 2019 was themed Breaking the Silence and invited all participants to reflect, speak and share who they were – and how had they come to be able to tell who they were. The video opened with snapshots – a range of moving personal anecdotes that described the wounds caused by cultural, social and interpersonal oppression. The keynote speaker offered a very moving account of her experiences as a child and young adult and the way she frames and understands that, making use of her main modality in psychotherapy – transactional analysis. It was a reminder about the adversities we have had to navigate and come to terms with in life. A reminder about how we carry our histories in our minds and bodies.

As I reflect on that, I find myself thinking about vulnerability and projection. We all come into this world vulnerable and available for contact. It is our unprotected vulnerability that leaves us capable of absorbing the undigested and unwanted processes in others. I found myself revisiting my thinking about oppression married with mystification (Steiner *et al.*, 1975), and the exploitation of vulnerability via the deception of mystification. The seduction of vulnerability goes something like this, *lean on me, trust me, I can be good for you, I can give you...* Through colonialism, a state of economic dependency gets created and that in turn becomes cultural, social and psychological. Vulnerability and trust get perverted and we lose a part of our self, our resources, to the other. I understand that this is not one-way traffic and this is not the whole story – but when it comes to breaking silence, there is an awakening, an opportunity to speak out, to cry, to register what has happened and what we have begun to do to ourselves.

When I returned to the UK full of hope and excitement about being back 'home', my vulnerability was open and so I did not know how to protect myself from racist projections. I took them in, identified with the white bullies who told me to go home and I believed that there was something fundamentally wrong with me. I did not belong, I was not wanted and whatever thought I had about my own Englishness was tainted and spoilt. At home, I had a white mother who was herself trying to survive her own vulnerability. We were poor, a single-parent family and my mother's strengths were in her capacity to 'get on with it'. She had not made her own sense of this mixed racial and cultural marriage. To her, my father was just a man – a rather selfish one in her view. She could not respect his academic ambitions and she had had enough of his destructive side. She reached a point where life was going to seem better without him than with him. Taken up with her own stresses and strains in her life, I felt as a child that we needed to keep our spaces small and untroubled so that she was not burdened with us. So between us, little space was made to wonder and explore our emotional world and our identities. Once, she considered emigrating to Australia and that was one time I heard her explicitly acknowledge our racial identity and her wish to protect us from racism. She had registered that Australia was not a place to take children of colour so she abandoned that idea without realizing that my siblings and I were already encountering aggressions.

As Jayakara Beverley Ellis, at the BAATN Conference 2019, described, the scripting we create within our families is interwoven with our social groups and the wider normative society. Our encounters with this as we grow are complicated and as we navigate the boundaries of these different groups, we absorb projections, we become colonized, we seek others who may be available to receive our unwanted processes and that in turn evokes further complications in the mire of the personal and social unconscious. Writing this stirs mixed emotions – loss at the missed opportunities in my family, as well as gratitude to the people who have helped. Along the way there have been several 'Florences', as well as dear friends, colleagues, supervisors and therapists, all of whom have helped me expand and deepen my personal, social and individual relationship with myself.

Current dilemmas over home

At the time of writing this, I was closing my practice, moving home and office from one part of England to another. I was half-way through saying goodbyes to friends, colleagues and long-term clients. I knew many of these for more than ten years, some for more than 20. They have been a part of my life, my social, professional, personal and psychological fabric. They and my edited manifestations of them have been in my thoughts, my dreams. They have mingled, consciously and subconsciously with my internal psychic landscape as well as my professional one. So, I am caught between places, I am held in transit before I can land in a new environment.

I have found it personally disturbing to have this experience of being between homes – to be out of reach of where I wish to be. I am reminded of childhood experiences of being uprooted, feeling homesick to the very core of my being. My first conscious heartbreak was to find myself, as a four-year-old child out of reach of all that had seemed safe and secure.

Now, as a woman of mature years, I remember those times. I go over and over the range of natural and human landscapes I have settled in. From the Biafran war in Nigeria, to London suburbs, inner-city Birmingham, bohemian seaside towns and rural England, questions arise. Where was I truly at home? What does it mean to be at home, to have a home? Who gets to decide and define home? What does it mean to belong?

I often struggle to be away from my house, my home. As I sit here, having written these few lines, Shamima Begum comes into my mind. I cannot stop asking myself – *where will she go?* What is to become of her now she is stripped of her citizenship? How can she belong nowhere?

Clinical practice

This has been a personal account – an autobiographical account in many ways. Several times, I have stopped myself, wondering if this is 'self-indulgent', these personal stories, about content and events – how can all this be relevant in a book about psychotherapy?

The relational and co-creative movements in the field have brought into focus the importance of the self of the practitioner in creating the therapeutic alliance and relationship. While this is essentially about the sort of mind and the psychodynamics of the therapist, that is co-created with our experiences. We are our history, and we are our present lives. I do believe we are permeable to the times that we live in and the experiences that our parents, grandparents and ancestors have endured. I think we must carry these experiences and their impact in our bodies. My grandmother was an orphan, raised in a Victorian orphanage, and my mother was sent to state boarding school at a shockingly young age. I know that in part these experiences influence my draw to belonging in organizations as well as some of the resistance I feel about belonging. I wonder whether this gives me some sort of unknown, unthought sensitivity to those who have been institutionalized? I may never know exactly what my clients are doing with my invisible histories. However, I do hope that the less invisible and unspeakable they are to me, the more they can serve as resources to open doors in our work.

Conclusion: Belonging, self, each other, community and place

This chapter explores questions of belonging, culture, community, self and place from personal, social, political and cultural perspectives. I have started with myself, as a person who has experienced and has come to identify with migration. I say identify with, as throughout my life there has been opportunity to experience new personal, professional environments and social landscapes and to recycle the questions around belonging. How do I engage with strangers? How do I include myself? How do I explain myself? How do I distinguish myself? How do I anticipate your reactions? How do I respond to your reception of me?

As the African proverb says:

No matter how far you are from your house, you will keep going until you get home.

References

African proverb: www.kalimaquotes.com/quotes/8089/no-matter-how-far-you.

Benjamin, J. (2017). *Beyond Doer and Done To: Recognition Theory, Intersubjectivity and the Third.* Abingdon, Oxfordshire: Routledge.

Ellis, J.B. (2019). Keynote speech, BAATN Conference.

Minikin, K. (2018). Radical relational psychiatry: Toward a democracy of mind and people. *Transactional Analysis Journal*, 48(2), 111–125. https://doi.org/10.1080/03621537.2018.1429287.

Oxford Dictionaries (n.d.). Definition of 'belonging'. https://en.oxforddictionaries.com/definition/belonging.

Shaw, D. (2014). *Traumatic Narcissism: Relational Systems of Subjugation.* London: Taylor and Francis.

Steiner, C., Wycoff, H., Goldstine, D., Lariviere, P., Schwebel, R. & Marcus, J. (1975). *Readings in Radical Psychiatry.* New York, NY: Grove Press.

Chapter 15

Embodied Experiencing – Relational Learning

CARMEN JOANNE ABLACK

Abstract
This chapter explores embodied-relational-emergent awareness through identity processing and phenomenological exploration, utilizing vignettes to highlight possibilities and insights arising. Drawing on more than 30 years' practice, I move between my own embodied-relational origins as ground and highlight different figures of interest in exploring experiences of heritage, race and identity in contexts of relational working.

Keywords
Active imagination, embodied-relational differentiation, diversity, figure-ground, identity-as-process, intercultural, movement-as-process, phenomenology

Introduction: Pushed to our limits
When pushed to our absolute limits, inability to continue functioning well occurs. We find huge reserves of resilience for a period and this eventually becomes a source of stress and distress. Hanks and Vetere (2016), discussing extreme abuse in families, groups and organizational situations, underline a 'slow process of impacting on the well-being' (p.66) of individuals and groups. They highlight 'creeping symptoms of malaise' as signs arising from 'prolonged repeated stress that causes long-term physical and emotional harm' (p.71).

For Black, African and Asian (BAA)/People of Colour (POC) practitioners, facilitating groups, working with couples and relationships,

Embodied Experiencing – Relational Learning

teaching, training people in organizations, similar harms can occur. Whether or not 'race and racism' are named, they are equally present for staff, clients, service users, trainees and supervisees identifying as BAA/POC.

Through my early life story and a couple of vignettes, I pay attention to processes of 'embodied intercultural' experiencing and existence of 'experience denial of the ground that is forming' (Ablack, 2019, p.128). I offer explorations of embodied-relational learning arising.

My embodied-relational ground

As a young child, I needed to move my body, to feel myself rising, falling, vibrating in space and time. I yearned to live in moving, pulsing worlds where expression, exploration and compassion were externalized. Through the glory of moving – smallest movements of hand, then limb, into large movements, bending and twirling, my whole body at one with the living world, dancing with winds, exulting in rhythms of rain on leaves and differentiated percussions from various sun-heated rooftops. Sitting in dirt watching insects, listening to flowers popping open, Julie mangoes ripening and plopping to earth in fragrant storms of immediate smells and heady lingering perfumes. Mingling with other smells and sounds of the Caribbean Garden over time, some welcome, some frightening, like the slithering of a boa constrictor in a tree after the remnants of a hurricane or spotting a tarantula out of the corner of my eye – me running back indoors, screaming 'like a banshee' on shaking little legs. This innocence remains evocative as olfactory, kinaesthetic, embodied memories to this day. I still can 'smell' the rain as it hits warmed earth.

I took part in a local 'kiddies' carnival and started dance classes having moved to Trinidad after experiencing my first two years in Hertfordshire, where I was born. At that point I was the youngest child of a Tobagonian mother and a Trinidadian father, technically British citizens as Trinidad and Tobago (T&T) was not yet an independent country.

Dad came to mainland UK before the Second World War to go to university on a scholarship; my mother came several years later, either before or during the war. They married and started having children after it was over. They loved music, she loved to dance, both were athletic. Mum played netball to a high standard, Dad played cricket and later commentated on cricket matches nationally and internationally before I was born. Ken Ablack (1919–2010) appeared for the West Indies XI in 1944 and in (Sir) Learie Constantine's XI in 1944–1945. Dad became a producer for BBC Overseas Service (the World Service) and he was a member of the first Test Match Special broadcast team from 1950 to 1962. He returned to T&T when independence seemed likely, wanting to be part of building his country of birth. He was a diplomat for T&T in the late 1960s. I spent most of my childhood moving around, experiencing different cultures and schools. I grew up hearing calypso, steel pan, jazz, blues and sitting with Dad as Mahalia Jackson brought me to tears with the soaring notes of 'Go Tell it on the Mountain', an African American spiritual first compiled by John Wesley Work Jr.

My mother, Barbara Theresa (Terry) Ablack née Carrington (1923–2002), deciphered and decoded during the war effort in the UK; she was always brilliant at cryptic crosswords. She read widely, retaining an interest in the world, in volunteering, and playing bridge for most of her life. Coming back to London, she took me to see Nureyev and Fonteyn dance together. These shared experiences allowed me to feel seen and understood by her. Later, I got to know about Janet Collins, the first Afro-American prima ballerina at the Metropolitan Opera, a 'trailblazer in the white world of classical ballet' (Lewin, 2011, back cover). I was devastated when told at ten years old I was too tall to be a ballet dancer. My understanding of the importance of both dance and movement in therapy is expressed by Chodorow, 'dance/movement as active imagination fosters the healing process' (1997, p.2). I knew something of this as a child.

'Moving' towards embodied relationality

Figure 14.1: Card with added design by Eugene Ellis (Credit: nuranvectorgirl. iStock ID 502623685)

Founders of BAATN, Eugene and Jayakara Ellis produce beautiful, inspiring cards for each new year. I opened this card, glanced at it, reading, 'Move your Body the Way it LOVES to Make you Move'. Then I saw the actual words on the card. I experience my 'reading' and the actual words like an embodied perceptual gestalt, moving rapidly between two perceptions, *both acknowledging our bodies are moved and move us.*

I discovered that the dance, if I let it, dances me. Getting out of my own way, I allow creative, embodied-relational expression to emerge, grounding me throughout many stages I have found myself in life. No matter how ugly, hard or despair-making situations and contexts are, my cultivating of a process of inviting, allowing and being with emergent moving, breathing and listening deeply to self and other has been a saving grace. Even when too ill to get out of bed at different points in my life, or so debilitated by something dysfunctional and unexplained in my body, I have welcomed dance in a prone position. Realigning myself and coming into relation with something more than my own awareness of me, I touch on something profoundly beyond myself.

I studied psychology and sociology, later training as an integrative and body psychotherapist and a Gestalt therapist. I was drawn to experiential learning relationships with indigenous teachers, where often deeply embodied, transpersonal processes took place. At first I was shaken, then accepting, finding imaginal 'practices' of childhood daydreaming, and 'teachings' from recurrent 'elder instruction' dreams as a girl child, emerging as actual lessons in my adult engaging with multicultural shamanic study. I found emerging ability, a stepping between worlds as I learned, explored, inhabited and engaged on multiple levels with many groups of different people, in the natural world. It was deeply challenging and occasionally frightening, and all that practice running away from spiders became an internalized attempt at 'escaping' what needed to be known.

I practise by revisiting, revising and letting go of my beliefs, understandings and thoughts in the face of profoundly experienced otherness in myself and others, including our natural world. I continue with experiencing as learning, fundamental to my existing and to my work. On a beach in Australia, feeling a deep, somewhat disturbing, pulse from the land, I needed to dance in the moment, allowing what was emerging from me. I was wild, sinuous, angry, staccato, elated, flowing and joyful. Days later walking into a Sydney show by Aboriginal artists, and on seeing an exhibit of heads and bodies in the sand, I lost the ability to stand, falling to earth, weeping there on the floor, writhing in pain and feeling waves of despair. Two women artists stood over me like healing sentries, allowing me to cry out my fill. It was a profound experience of sisterhood and understanding requiring no words. I had found a place where I felt total permission to simply be with my experiencing of that level of grief, of pain, and importantly, a releasing. I have come close to this feeling elsewhere, sensing total freedom to be with the fullness of my emotions and phenomenology – while teaching, being in and facilitating groups, on dance workshops and lately in gratitude and moving medicine work with Susannah and Ya'Acov Darling Khan.

This Aboriginal exhibition space experiencing remains an embodied memory of relational connecting, both haunting and informing. I recognized – as the two sister-girls recognized with me and in me – a shared, yet differentiated sense of historical pain, a rightness, an honouring in the outpouring of my tears and movements.

In Australia, undertaking personal research into ways in which a group of Aboriginal peoples were working with trauma in their communities, I was grateful to the elder men and women willing to sit with me and share their work, allowing me to briefly enter their world through their stories. Profound for me in terms of learning, in deepening understanding of myself, was their unquestioning acceptance that I was a sister-girl to them, they trusted me to get it, simply and deeply. As Ellis (2021) highlights, this non-verbal embodied process is prerequisite to moving into relational dialogues' challenging 'enduring relational themes' (Jacobs, 2011) that have a dependency on field conditions of relationships and allied power dynamics in play, especially when dealing with the constructs of race and racism. Moving from our fixed positioning into something more fluid and embodied.

I changed, and continue to change, evolving through this and other experiences across BAA/POC diasporas, experiencing profound meeting often requiring few words and much attuning to beyond what is immediately obvious or named. This is embodied-relational, deepened listening, requiring capacity to expand into what is offered by *availability to be affected* and being willing to affect. *This is being a psychotherapist for me.* I engage in embodied-relational meetings, shared experiencing and expanding capacity to share our differentiated understandings, therapeutically and in wider world work.

Self for me is an unfolding, differentiating event in constant relationship with something. Gestalt notions of selfing, where we are all evolving events in relational contexts, offer connection to profound awareness – relating deeply, attuning to fuller aliveness in a variety of ways, including voice use, movement and prosody. Speaking itself and embodied-relational processes are offering the ground of psychotherapeutic experiencing (Totton, 2015). By exploring and seeking deepened understanding in the context of issues arising for us as BAA/POC peoples – as clients, practitioners and communities – we are striving towards *proactive engagement with our own wider mental health and wellbeing.*

An early organizational lesson

In the early 1990s, I was invited to externally facilitate paid staff of a small mental health charity. The management group wanted 'staff' to resolve 'their' issues, with no mention of management's role in this. Alongside my experienced black colleague, I wanted us to engage *all* the organizational groups – staff and management – and consult with volunteers and service users, *before decisions were made about ways of going forward.*

Racial, class and educational differences and divides emerged, indicating potential differentiated impacts on the groups. The mainly white male management group all held university degrees, some qualified in more than one profession, some retired professionals from 'significant' careers. By contrast, the staff group was mostly women and BAA/POC identified, many less academically qualified, and many more experienced in mental health workplaces. After several consultation meetings, we convinced participants to work separately and then come together. The staff group was immediately on board. The management group agreed to being facilitated on diversity issues in the context of mental health working in the community it served, and members agreed to interact with other groups over time, making themselves available for the process. We worked with discrete groups, discovering individuals who were committed to undertaking the work. However, participants began indicating that levels of safety were not well enough established across the organization.

We fed this back to management, encouraging initial work on sufficient safety and trust to support 'the whole' to embrace development and change. Several management and senior staff resigned, went off sick, or became 'unavailable' after this. What was emerging was fear and seeming lack of capacity to flex into looking at their responses, reduced reflexivity, being pushed to their limits. Whole-group development could not be supported, staff and volunteers felt undermined by comings and goings at senior levels and were stuck with increasingly unmanageable workloads.

We facilitated the remaining groups to *discover proactive engagement*, encouraging different racial and class sub-groups to hear each other, find better connections, extend socio-cultural awareness in the context of shared pressures, and seek active awareness of each other's positions by reflecting understanding and appreciation. They really worked at knowing more about each other as individuals, groups and communities. This was rewarding in and of itself, for them and us. However, ongoing resistance from many management members meant we reluctantly stepped away, drained and dissatisfied. Yet we were learning an important lesson, ensuring that our mental wellbeing and stress levels were taken care of, recognizing when the system (and us as a temporary part of it) had absorbed as much as was useful and possible. We proactively disengaged.

'MICHAEL' – A VIGNETTE WITH COMMENTARY

'Michael' is a created vignette where I reflect my own thinking, exploring and experiencing. An Afro-Caribbean-descent black British man practising as a therapist for five years, Michael returned to his own therapy after a break of two years. He told me at our initial session that he was struggling with his relatively new supervisor. He wanted to talk to a senior psychotherapist of colour about what was happening for him, as his sessions as supervisee became harder to handle. In our early therapy sessions, I consciously chose not to ask Michael if he had raised his difficulties with his supervisor. I wanted him to tell me about the sequence and importance of events happening for him, in his own way and time.

Supervisees who are BAA, POC and/or LGBTQIA+ have related some similarities of experiences where supervisors are questioning or making statements with a tone of 'telling' or 'teaching' from the outset, *before understanding situation and context for the supervisee*. I have picked this up most often as a supervisor of white, cisgendered, straight practitioners, a kind of misplaced eagerness to help show the (right?) way. Such behaviour, masking racism, heteronormativity, transphobia and homophobia, is damaging to both the supervision relationship and supervisee and needs to be addressed by the supervisor in their own development.

Often out of awareness, an unowned assumption is made that supervisee (or client) is somehow needing (their) guidance or teaching. For these supervisees, the impact of such assumptions can be pernicious. Some supervisees, from one or more of the LGBTQIA+

communities, have shared that they can experience a sense of embodied shame in supervision; they experience what Ellis Johnson (2021) recently named 'feeling the gaze on me'. An aspect at play here is inability and unwillingness to tolerate critical evaluative questioning (as practitioners and more widely as a profession).

For some BAA/POC supervisees, a toxic mix of assumptions and projections happens, based on speaking with an 'accent' or in a way that is not part of the supervisor's 'normal' experiencing. Facing attempts at 'improving' their language skills, they also can experience the shaming gaze on them, seemingly more pronounced when issues of perceived or real class differences are also present. An intersectional layering dynamic is present, with a deteriorating impact on the supervisee, further risking the supervisory relationship.

Differentiated effects and affects are at play for individuals, groups and communities, and what seems common is a need for more honest, self-reflective and group collective interrogation into these different dynamics, allowing for deepened deconstructive and ongoing reconstructive processes to emerge. I know this is true for me and I imagine it is the case for us all.

Some white and/or heterosexual supervisors, in supervision with me, are challenging such habitual positioning in themselves, exploring what it means in terms of assumptions and biases of conferred power and authority. This is painful deconstructing of their own racism and involves recognition of contexts of bias against self-challenging, concomitant homophobia, able-bodism, classism, cisgendered heteronormativity, transphobia, to name some possible intersecting processes. By interrogating and developing understanding of how and why they can leave supervisees feeling wrong-footed and wounded by exploring how and what is communicated to supervisees about both supervisee and supervisor, they start to understand their 'collective delusion' in perpetuating the impacting of racism (Menakem, 2017, p.84). In his study of masculinity, sexuality, and culture, Kincel names a need for experimentation at boundaries of 'appropriateness' in counselling and psychotherapy, if we are to 'untangle the field that produces bodies that breathe in and out prejudices and repression of uncomfortable themes' (2021, p.58). I believe this is applicable across all genders and none, across other identity processes named earlier, and is sorely needed when it comes to unpacking what happens for BAA/POC clients and therapists.

In not assuming Michael had or had not raised his difficulties with his supervisor, I attempted to stay open to getting a felt sense (Gendlin, 1996) of his situation and context, as he experienced it. I stuck to his words, not rewording by saying, 'I understand you to mean...' or, 'I hear you saying...', and not substituting his words with my own. Replacing clients' words with our own, as therapists and supervisors, often does not convey understanding. It becomes an evocation of internalized processes of lack of self-worth, and an emphasis of 'mastery' by the practitioner over the client. An obliteration of BAA/POC meaning-making, in favour of therapist's or supervisor's, is an assault on equality and co-created relationality, as there is no 'learning together'.

I tried speaking at Michael's pace and rhythm, quoting his words back to him:

Carmen: 'You said, "She makes me feel little, you know smaller than she is (his pause/so my pause in reflecting back)...like I'm not really saying things right..."'

His jaw visibly tightened and his eyes lowered as I re-spoke his words. I waited for him to breathe, to see if he wanted to say more without me prompting, and after a moment he looked up.

Michael: 'It's hard to hear those words.'

Carmen: 'Your words...?'

Michael: 'Yeah...' He looked down again, staying silent for a couple of moments.

Carmen: ' I see you looking down now...'

Michael looked up and gripped his jaw, his breath obviously more shallow: 'I can't stand it... I can't stand the way she kind of...you know...tells me I'm not doing okay.'

The temptation, depending on the orientation of the supervisor, was to ask him how she did this or to speculate if she was reminding him of someone. Instead, I invited him to notice his experiencing.

Carmen: 'As you say "I can't stand the way she kind of" tells you, you are not okay... Do you notice what is happening for you...'

Michael: 'My temples are tense... I often come out of supervision with her with tension in my temples...'

He rubbed at his temples.

Carmen: 'You're rubbing your temples and feeling what now?'

Michael, with a change of voice tone: 'Um...I'm feeling...um, I guess, rejected...'

Carmen, matching his tone: 'Say more...'

Michael: 'Well...as if I really don't belong...as if she was telling me without saying it, "you're not good enough".'

Embodied Experiencing – Relational Learning

Carmen: 'As you say, "rejected", "don't belong" and "not good enough" – just let yourself notice me here, with you.'

I invited Michael to become more aware of his bodily experiencing and of being with me as he spoke. I moved away from reflecting whole sentences to picking up on words he stressed that seemed (as far as I could tell) to have more emphasis – this is not an exact science, but comes with practice, noticing my felt responses of breath, the sensations in my body and affect in response to his words, actions, tone of voice and pace of speaking – his phenomenology, including prosody.

Michael: 'That's hard...like, what will you be thinking about me... like...maybe you'll think I'm not good enough...' He glanced at me, looked away, then looked at me directly.

Carmen: 'Umm, you could check with me. Do you want to ask me directly?'

I deliberately drew more attention to him *and* me, inviting him to say what he needed to hear from me – this was done to support him, maybe to see if this was a safe enough space for him to ask for what he needed.

Michael: 'Well I assume you'll support me... Oh yeah, Carmen...I hope you get it and you'll understand cos...but I just realized, that's an assumption...maybe you won't get it?'

He took a big breath, looked at me again, with what appeared to be more 'light' behind his eyes. I noticed myself breathing more easily, feeling very present with him. I could sense my total presence and engagement as he spoke and moved.

Carmen: 'Yes, it is an assumption...and you notice you make an assumption about me "cos?"...'

Michael: 'Cos I assume something similar has happened to you... Maybe you felt judged by a white supervisor? Or left feeling not good enough...?'

Carmen: 'I'm going to answer your question in a moment... For now, what is your feeling or experience when you remember feeling judged, thought about as not good enough...as you talk with me?'

Michael, a small pause: 'I don't like the feelings it brings up... I think I feel shamed...yes, shamed...'

I took a breath and felt my skin flutter in response to his words. I took a risk with disclosure, answering his question.

Carmen: 'I can remember times when I experienced shame...in response to something a white supervisor or therapist has said to

239

me... I felt "othered" either as a client, a supervisee, a therapist, or a supervisor.'

I offered a few things here with my not-too-specific disclosure. I answered his question, building the working relationship at this point. I wanted him to know he was not alone as a BAA/POC therapist experiencing this or something similar. I wanted to offer another word, owning it as mine: 'othered', hoping it captured something of his experiencing, and so he could respond saying if it fitted or not for him. I was not attached to my 'word', I was interested in his. I included 'therapist' and 'client' in my response, making the ground safe for him to talk about his experience as a black male client, a black male therapist, as well as a supervisee. By offering a widened ground of possible exploration, I was allowing him to choose to look beyond his immediate presenting situation and to his wider context of experiencing. I was inviting his noticing of how phenomena arose for him in different contexts.

Michael: '"Othered"...um well, yes...I think I've been "othered" throughout being involved in therapy... My first therapist was really a closet racist. He would correct my pronunciation of some names of various authors I was reading... I said to him when he did, that I felt stupid...all he did was ask me if I had felt stupid in other situations... I wanted to shout in his face...but didn't want to confirm his picture...'

Carmen: 'His picture?'

Michael: 'Yeah...he was always subtly prodding me to get angry, kept telling me I was "repressing"... Looking back, I think he was trying somehow to put me in my place...you know, Carmen? Like, get me to be angry, then he would be proved *right* about who I was as black man... Something like that.'

Carmen: 'When you talk about this now, what connects, what happens for you? Sorry, I mean, what do you notice?'

Just one question would have been better here. I was caught up in my somatic resonance (Geuter, 2015), losing my sensing of Michael in the moment. I was attempting to stay with him, and I was experiencing an empathic blush of shamed anger crawl across my skin. I was aware that I had lost attunement momentarily, with my own bodily memories of being 'othered'. I had lost a sense of the wider field, including Michael (Kincel, 2021).

Michael: 'I feel really furious... Like I know I'm going to have to deal with this kind of "shit"... sorry...you know, Carmen... It's always gonna happen, isn't it? I guess I...'

He took a deep breath.

Carmen: 'So the "shit" is always "gonna happen"...and you take a deep breath...'

Michael: 'Yeah, I guess I am back to where I started...umm... I wanted a different word when you said "othered". I wanted to say I feel their "contempt"... That is what othering of me is...their contempt.'

Carmen: 'So shame and contempt... When you repeat those words Michael, I am aware of a sense of toxicity... I feel a bit nauseous.'

Michael: 'Yeah...yeah...I get that... I feel like I want to expel it all... it isn't *mine*... I want to let it go...to get it out of *me*...'

He pushed his arms out in a sharp movement away from his heart, and his breath was louder.

Carmen: 'See if you want to do more ...' (mirroring the movement)

Michael, standing up, made his movement over and over, breathing more loudly. I stood up, reflecting his movement, also breathing to be heard by him.

I was consciously reflecting his movements and joining in temporarily. I was allowing him to not feel on show, giving him a non-verbal invitation to stay with his experiencing and actions. He moved from leg to leg, I did similar for a couple of times, letting him see me, gently reflecting his movements.

Suddenly he yelled loudly, pumping his arms and stamping in rhythm through his legs.

Michael: 'ENOUGH... ENOUGH... ENOUGH ALREADY... I'm done with that...'

He then laughed loudly from his belly.

I smiled and laughed quietly, not wanting to interrupt him. He sat down and forward in his chair, smiling at me.

Michael: 'That was great. When I looked at you, Carmen, and saw you also moving...I felt like we were dancing out anger and pain... together...I felt your support.'

Carmen, nodding: 'And...?'

Michael: 'I think I am reclaiming something of me... I feel like I won't swallow their "shit" anymore. Like you were seeing me, real me... I felt my sense of "it's enough".'

Carmen: 'I saw you and I experienced you...'

I confirmed he had my support.

Michael: 'Like moving and using my voice was somehow healing it... You know I think like... I want to go home and dance with my daughter, to show her that I am okay, I am not ashamed of being me...to show her *we are* okay'.

Tears were in his eyes.

Final thoughts

Chodorow writes that contempt and shame 'force(s) us to grapple with... experience(s) of alienation', leading to developing abilities to 'evaluate' complex networks of human relationships (1997, p.91). Shared experiencing of movement, rhythm and history offers ground from which we can find our voice and our words and allows us to re-evaluate therapeutic and other relationships. *Language, movement* and *voice* are elements, at the client's choice, to visit in future.

They are also elements I draw on more in my organizational work. There is such a need for shaking up what is static, be it thoughts or embodied feelings of being missed, dismissed or overlooked. We need to develop capacities to tolerate ambiguities and instabilities arising from challenging certainties within us that tend towards defining others. This happens only if the profession is willing to interrogate what is being done.

Dynamics of toxicity, compassion fatigue and burnout when dealing with ongoing patterns of racialized engagement in different settings are real and can be soul-destroying. Over decades of running groups and organizational consultations, I have deepened my whole self-sensing of how fatigued I and colleagues from BAA/POC communities get after being with the ongoing toxicity of hidden/sub-textual racism in therapy rooms, training and mental health organizations and society.

Ellis (2021) reminds us of the necessity for stepping out of constraints of race-based constructing into more lived processes, embracing 'a non-verbal sense of "getting it"'. He invites deepened awareness of moving ideas, thinking and concepts into transpersonal embodied relating where we are embracing compassion, healthy humility and 'worthfulness' (p.142) as fundamental to understanding and expelling traumatized and traumatizing toxicity that is debilitating, requiring digging deeper, expanding further, focusing beyond individual processing, letting this healthier dance – reflecting collective responsibility, mutuality, and freedom – dance us...

References

Ablack, C.J. (2019). Embodied Intercultural Ground. In B. Ababio & R. Littlewood (eds), *Intercultural Therapy: Challenges, Insights and Developments* (pp.126–136). London and New York, NY: Routledge.

Chodorow, J. (1997). *Dance Therapy and Depth Psychology: The Moving Imagination*. London: Routledge.

Ellis, E. (2021). *The Race Conversation: An Essential Guide to Creating Life-Changing Dialogue*. London: Confer Books.

Gendlin, E.T. (1996). *Focusing-Oriented Psychotherapy: A Manual of the Experiential Method*. New York, NY and London: Guilford Press.

Geuter, U. (2015). The History and Scope of Body Psychotherapy. In G. Marlock, H. Weiss, C. Young & M. Soth (eds), *The Handbook of Body Psychotherapy & Somatic Psychology* (pp.22–39). Berkeley, CA: North Atlantic Books.

Hanks, H. & Vetere, A. (2016). Working at the Extremes: The Impact on us of Doing the Work. In A. Vetere & P. Stratton (eds), *Interacting Selves: Systemic Solutions for Personal and Professional Development in Counselling and Psychotherapy* (pp.65–84). London and New York, NY: Routledge.

Jacobs, L. (2011). Critiquing Projection: Supporting Dialogue in a Post-Cartesian World. In T. Bar-Yoseph Levine (ed.), *Gestalt Therapy: Advances in Theory and Practice* (pp.59–70). Hove: Routledge.

Johnson, E. (2021). *Intersectional Relational: Inquiring into Gender Beyond the Binary*. TRS online training workshop, speaker (personal communication, 4 July 2021).

'Ken Ablack.' In Wikipedia. https://en.wikipedia.org/wiki/Ken_Ablack.

Kincel, A. (2021). *Exploring Masculinity, Sexuality, and Culture in Gestalt Therapy: An Autoethnography*. London: Routledge (Instituto di Gestalt: The Gestalt Therapy Book Series).

Lewin, Y.T. (2011). *Night's Dancer: The Life of Janet Collins. With Her Unfinished Autobiography*. Middletown, CT: Wesleyan University Press.

Menakem, R. (2017). *My Grandmother's Hands: Racialized Trauma and the Pathway to Mending Our Hearts and Bodies*. Las Vegas, NV: Central Recovery Press.

Totton, N. (2015). *Embodied Relating: The Ground of Psychotherapy*. London: Karnac Books.

Test Match Special. In Wikipedia. https://en.wikipedia.org/wiki/Test_Match_Special.

Chapter 16

The Impact of Racism and Culture on Identity

A Psychoanalytic Intercultural Approach

GITA PATEL

Abstract

This chapter will explore several concepts within the Nafsiyat Intercultural Therapy model. The concept of the self is assumed in the western world to be a universal concept, meaning that most therapeutic interventions are based around this idea of the self. The 'category fallacy' (Kleinman, 1988; Littlewood, 1990) argues that all models of healing are embedded in the culture in which they are practised and helps us to see that the concept of identity only really exists in its own cultural framework.

Living in a minority culture and experiencing racism will inevitably affect the internal world and identity. Negotiating identities while living between two or more cultures can lead to an internalization of the cultural norms which identify a dominant and subdominant identity (Littlewood & Ababio, 2019), and lead to emotional distress, including depression, guilt and anxiety.

I will explore how I have used my own personal and professional experiences to further develop the Nafsiyat Intercultural model. I will be addressing issues of identity, race, racism and culture and the internalized assumptions around that. I will explore how the Intercultural model can support therapists and organizations to deliver a more accessible and inclusive model.

Keywords

Nafsiyat Intercultural Therapy Centre, Nafsiyat Intercultural Psychoanalytic Psychotherapy model, concept of self, category fallacy, identity, racism, dominant and subdominant identity, cultural self, culture, internalized racism

Introduction

As a child of parents who migrated from India to the UK in the 1950s, I have found the concept of the self a constant part of my own identity and of many others who end up living in the UK. I was made aware of my difference as far back as I can remember; it forms an integral part of my development as a child, my personality as an adult, as well as my professional development as a psychotherapist. Being aware of my difference was not a choice but due to the reactions from others towards me and my parents, leaving us with the task of how to manage and negotiate issues of racism and cultural difference.

My counselling course led to me to see how my experiences and the experiences of others like me were absent in my training. I struggled to understand how I could integrate who I am with the training that I was receiving. Coming from a working-class background and having years of experience in community work helped me to see how the training was contributing to making counselling and psychotherapy inaccessible to large sections of the population who did not share the white, middle-class values that permeate most trainings.

I went on to train as an intercultural psychotherapist with Nafsiyat and University College London. This training provided a space to explore the theories of psychoanalytic psychotherapy with different perspectives. Our own cultures and identities were an important part of the thinking rather than us feeling that we had to put aside our race and our experiences to engage in the training. The Nafisyat Intercultural model combines aspects of anthropology, psychiatry and psychotherapy to explore how identity and culture can be understood in relation to psychotherapy.

This chapter explores the concept of the self, and the 'category fallacy', which is the simple transportation of a healing model into another culture. It then looks at the ideas of a 'subdominant identity' (Littlewood & Ababio, 2019), which can be created in response to racism and discrimination. I use two vignettes to demonstrate clinical work, but note that the clients' names have been changed to respect confidentiality.

The category fallacy

Psychiatry and psychoanalysis have previously considered cultural and social phenomena to be the external layers of a universal core of the self and a universal model of the mind (Kraepelin, 1904), but how universal is this self? From a global perspective there are many views on the self and many models of the mind, Kleinman (1988) says that the simple transportation of western models of thinking into another culture is a category fallacy. He believes that all models of health and healing only exist in the context of the society in which they are practised.

Psychotherapy is a model of healing and its practice and development is embedded in the western culture. Most models are simply transporting the western model to patients from a different culture and this is akin to Kleinman's category fallacy. This simple transportation can affect the efficacy and outcome of treatments. Studies in transcultural psychiatry assert that culture is fundamental to the causes and course of psychopathology and also to the effectiveness of systems of healing (Kirmayer & Minas, 2000).

Many therapists and psychotherapy institutions are adopting this category fallacy by offering training and services based on the western concept of self, and specifically a white, middle-class, heteronormative identity and all that that involves. This leads to professionals struggling to work with issues of race, culture and discrimination, expressing that they are unprepared to work with these issues in the consulting room, as they were not addressed in their training.

I have worked in many different organizations, some racially diverse teams and some all-white teams, offering psychotherapy to clients from very diverse backgrounds. I have observed how the rare mention of race and culture will often focus on matters of fact. These include family structure, food, clothes and religion, but these are the conscious and known ideas. The deeper explorations of how culture, race and racism have fundamentally affected the formation of the psyche and identity at an unconscious level are often missed. This is striking in organizations that believe they are offering a rigorous psychoanalytic model of therapy and yet cannot think about the unconscious factors in race dynamics. The most complex aspect for therapists is exploring race in the transference, which requires an exploration of their own race, assumptions, prejudices, power and privilege and how this can be enacted in the consulting room. There can be a category fallacy for organizations that believe that their models are neutral or a blank sheet and therefore can apply to all clients. This comes with an expectation that the client will have a conscious awareness of how cultural factors have affected them. In the Nafsiyat Intercultural model, we are dealing with the unconscious processes in addition to the conscious, and the effects of the social and cultural factors on the internal world, the internal objects and the developmental formation of the self. The client themselves cannot be expected to do all the work without a therapist who can analyse the unconscious processes at play and have an understanding of race in the transference. Race issues will rarely be absent in the consulting room, even when therapist and client share a cultural and ethnic identity (Littlewood, 1992). As a therapist and supervisor, I have found that the idea of category fallacy has informed much of my work, as I explore how treatment models are embedded in the western concept of the self. Services and trainings start with a set of beliefs and ideals that are based on a cultural assumption of the western ideas of the self and the expectations and prejudices that accompany that.

Kareem (1992) says inter and intra psychic events profoundly affect the individuals psyche and develop as part of their unconscious life. He goes on to say that exploring identity within a cultural context can enhance the practice of psychotherapy to develop a more intercultural psychoanalytic approach. The Nafsiyat Intercultural model believes that the external structures are internalized in the psyche and clear divisions between the internal world and the external world are a barrier to delivering effective therapeutic interventions.

Institutional policies addressing culture

Culture is a dynamic and changing process, rather than a clearly defined set of ideas. In the UK, policies have been developed in relation to race and culture. In the 1960s and 1970s, the polices of assimilation were prevalent, where there was an expectation for everyone to be the same and any difference should be suppressed or eliminated.

> TONY
>
> Tony reported his experiences of schooling during the 1970s. He felt as a Jamaican boy that he had two choices: either be labelled as the 'bad' or naughty one, like so many of his Black friends, or work hard and try to assimilate as much as he could. His parents were very keen for Tony to study hard and achieve a professional career, and this led him to follow his teachers and parents wishes, believing that this was his best chance of a future. As an adult, in therapy, he began to discuss the cost of this decision to him. He felt that he had had to adopt the persona of a white person whom the teachers would praise

and in doing so he had lost many of his Black friends and a sense of himself and his identity. He was told to ignore the issues of racism in school by his parents and teachers to the point where over years of repression he began to believe that he had not experienced any racism at all during his childhood. The overt racist remarks he had experienced had been explained away as just isolated incidents, and the perpetrators designated as exceptions who were not important to him. As an adult, Tony became depressed and anxious following problems at work and so he started therapy. During this time, he struggled to begin to acknowledge himself as a Black man. It was a very frightening idea for him and something he had avoided for most of his life by working and living in an almost all-white environment. He has so many negative associations with being Black, feeling that acknowledging his identity would land him back into the group of so-called 'naughty Black boys' that he had worked so hard to escape. He had tried to assimilate like the 'good' boy he was. Once he was able to begin this exploration, he began to remember the trauma of the racism he had experienced. He felt it was painful to realize he had suppressed his feelings and reactions in order to cope with his conflicting sense of self. He felt he had eliminated and erased a part of himself in order to fit in and he began to feel the loss and grief of that, leading him to begin to adapt his identity to incorporate his heritage.

The experiences of Tony will be familiar to many children of immigrants. Assimilation was then equated with success; however, 50 years later the successful assimilation has not stopped casual racism, institutionalized racism or discrimination in the workplace. The use of the category fallacy and intercultural therapy to understand this is critical to working with clients such as Tony. To begin to acknowledge trauma loss and grief as it relates to race and racism was important for this client. Talking about racism in therapy can trigger past traumas and evoke painful memories that could make the client feel very vulnerable. For therapists, there has to be an active acknowledgment of racism in the UK to be able to create a space for a client to be this vulnerable. At Nafsiyat, many clients had previously seen white therapists, but reported that they had never mentioned their traumatic experiences of racism (Kareem, 1992) as these spaces did not feel safe. Only when they arrived at Nafsiyat where race and culture were openly acknowledged could they begin to talk about racism and the trauma they experienced.

The 1980s introduced the concept of multiculturalism, which promoted the acceptance of differences, but also created the idea of the exotic other. The 1990s brought us the recognition of institutional racism through the Macpherson report (1999), leading to an exploration of racism as a social and cultural phenomenon. Racism was the less attractive sibling of multiculturalism, and mostly avoided in the debate around diversity, as it provoked such intense emotions. Exploration of racism demands the examination of relationships, prejudices, violence, history and oppression and locates the problem in the hands of the perpetrators. Instead of focusing on the exotic other it asks professionals and institutions to examine their own prejudices, privilege and assumptions. Recently, with the rise of Black Lives Matter and debates around structural racism, we are entering another aspect of discussions about race and culture in the UK. It is important to understand the complex intersections between social and institutional processes behind identity formation (Krause, 2019), as they will have an effect on psychotherapy.

The dominant and subdominant identity

The experience of living in the UK as a minority culture has many effects on the concept of the self. There are historical factors such as colonization and slavery which may exist in the consulting room through inter-generational trauma (Thomas, 2019). There may be an internalization of difference which in itself is not necessarily problematic, but in a racist environment it is accompanied by a clear message that the western model of the self is always superior to the 'other'. Fanon (1967) describes this as 'self-division' as a result of colonial subjugation. It leaves the 'other' to try to negotiate the splits that are created, and these conflicts can have a profound impact on the sense of self and the development of the psyche. This idea has been explored by several writers who have used different terms to describe the processes, such as internalized colonial objects (Ababio, 2019), internalized oppression (Agoro, 2019), inferiorization (Sigalas, 2019), recognition trauma (Mckenzie-Mavinga, 2019) and internalized racism (Rose, 1997; Speight, 2007). They refer to a process whereby there is an unconscious taking in of prejudiced and racist assumptions resulting in a subdominant identity (Littlewood & Ababio, 2019). An individual internalizes the idea that within a white western context they are subdominant, inferior or less than. Often the extent of this self-deprecation or even self-hatred can be unconscious and individuals may struggle to see or articulate this concept to others or to themselves. As a therapist working interculturally, I find that there is an ongoing assessment of how much these ideas are embedded in our clients' lives and in our own professional thinking. It can be hard for white therapists to see themselves as the dominant culture in order to begin to address the idea of dominant and subdominant. One white, middle-class, heterosexual male therapist once asked me, 'Do you really think that you have had fewer opportunities than me in the UK?' This comment alerted me to the enormous task of intercultural work in even beginning to address this way of thinking, which seemed to be prevalent in the psychotherapy profession, and the number of clients who were receiving substandard treatment due to these perceptions.

The cultural self

Western psychoanalytic theories focus on the development of a separate self, formed from birth. Psychoanalysis has at its centre the development of a strong and separate ego and assumes a goal of western individualism for all our patients, encouraging a strong ego that can remain the same through the experiences of everyday life. In contrast, the communal self aims to be able to suppress individual desires for the communal or family values and develops a strong sense of self through the reputation and status of the extended family and the community. A harmonious and successful family will increase its status, and the status of the community.

Many cultures have the notion of a familial communal self where all the roles are clearly defined. In my own upbringing as an Indian female the idea was embedded from birth that we exist to meet the needs of others. The concept of a separate self or strong ego was seen as dangerous and detrimental and was actively discouraged; passivity was the desired state. The idea of the familial self for all genders leaves little space for individual needs and tastes; these can be acknowledged but are not important in the everyday way of life within the family (Roland, 1989). The western model of a nuclear family may not be relevant to many cultures. In extended families, the concept of brother and sister is merged with cousins and other relatives, and can have more significant importance. The self is seen as merged with others and even the use of the word 'I' to describe oneself can be a process in itself. Gungor (2019) talks about a Turkish client who for the first time used 'I' instead of 'we' and noticed that she did not feel guilty about it.

The cultural self may be passed on from parents and grandparents, and the experiences of racism in the UK can be integrated into the formation of the self and can lead to an internalization of racism (Rose, 1997) and a denigration of heritage and culture. It can be seen as a coping mechanism or a defence against racism, one of the ways to cope with the violence and trauma of living in a racist society. This then has to be negotiated and integrated with the cultural self to navigate daily life; often these two or more ideas of self can raise conflicts. Racism in the UK against Black and Asian people who are immediately identified as minorities due to skin colour gives a particular cultural context that then becomes the cultural context in which an identity is formed from childhood.

The case study below illustrates how the cultural self was brought into therapy and the issues it raised.

LATA

Lata, an 18-year-old Sri Lankan woman, sought therapy as she was feeling depressed and finding it hard to motivate herself. She came to the UK at the age of 14; her elder sister was successful in her studies and planning to go to university. Lata described that throughout her life she had felt that she was not separate from her sister or her family, and that all her sister's achievements actually belonged to Lata. At some stage, around the age of 15, she started to realize that she was indeed separate from her sister. The communal cultural self was being questioned and this led to her becoming depressed and seeking therapy. Lata was very angry about having to think for herself; part of her wanted to be independent and be what she described as 'westernised'. We began to see how her thoughts and ideas were very much embedded in her cultural traditions. She wanted to be educated and follow a career, yet she also felt guilt that she should be a 'good girl' staying at home and cooking and cleaning for her family.

In the transference, Lata would often see me as part of the British society. She would regularly denigrate her community and was surprised when I challenged her on these comments. Her talking about her community in a derogatory way seemed to be a defence against what she imagined I and the rest of 'westernized' society thought of her and her family. This was a reflection of how she had internalized the racism she had experienced since coming to the UK. She had a very low self-esteem and part of the task was for her to accept all the parts of her, including her cultural background. Lata saw her future as two extremes, either being Sri Lankan, which in her mind meant, ignorant oppressed and with no future but staying in the midst of her family, or being 'westernized' and intelligent and so far removed from her family that she would be isolated and lonely. Lata had problems with her studies although she was capable of getting good marks, and it was as though she could not be successful at her studies as it would not fit in with her self-image of a Sri Lankan woman/girl. When Lata came close to an examination or an essay, she would not work, or would go into an exam and not write anything, even though she knew some of the material. It seemed that part of the function of her ego was to keep her regressed, which she associated with her culture.

Lata struggled with her feelings about growing into an adult and tried to keep a merged state; for her, the process of separation was compounded by her cultural values. It was a new idea for her that she could embrace her two ideas of self, communal and individual, embedded in two different cultures. Lata had two very split systems in her mind constituting her Sri Lankan and British identity. Some of the splits are shown below:

Sri Lankan	English
Child	Adult
Girl	Woman
Ignorance	Intelligence
Housegirl/wife	Psychotherapist/film-maker
Sex object	Sexless
Midst of family	Loneliness
Depression	Freedom
Feeds others	Feeds herself
Wife/doormat	Intellectual partner

The greatest achievement for Lata in the therapy was to introduce a middle ground of ambivalence and for her to explore that space in her search for herself as separate from her family but still connected to her community.

Lata initially tried to make her therapy her British world, inviting me to collude with the idea of her Sri Lankan subdominant self. I began to gently challenge this and encourage her to explore her culture and her identity within that. Through this process, we could see how negative her view of her culture and therefore herself had become. The therapy reflected her search for her identity, from when she realized that she was not merged with her sister to beginning to accept that she was responsible for who she was. If culture was not integrated into her therapy then most of her associations would not have arisen as they were so integrally linked, and her psyche would have remained split into western and Sri Lankan worlds.

Her system of splitting her western self and cultural self was having an effect on her mental health and contributing to her depression. The process of exploring and understanding her systems was a gradual one and in time she was able begin to explore an identity that was autonomous, but also embedded in her culture and community.

In this case assuming a western model of the self through the category fallacy would have negated the communal self and prioritized the development of a separate self as the only goal, and in doing so confirmed the Sri Lankan identity as subdominant. Addressing both concepts of the self supported the integration of the whole rather than encouraging or consolidating the split self. It demonstrates the need for practitioners to address race and racism explicitly in their work (Thomas, 1995).

This therapy allowed an exploration of identity within a cultural framework. For children and adolescents this is particularly important as they may be used to splitting at school and in other settings. They can simply transport this adaptive self to therapy and unless therapists are alert to addressing the cultural self it can lead to us working with the proxy self (Thomas, 1995) and losing the opportunity to work with the whole of the client's experiences. From a young age, Black and Asian young people can integrate the idea that their culture is subdominant to white western culture and try to hide these aspects of themselves for protection.

Conclusion

My journey in developing intercultural therapy, supervision and training has necessitated the incorporation of my own exploration of identity into my work. The category fallacy informs my thinking that our personal and professional experiences of our cultural self and of racism and discrimination rather than being an obstacle, as is often presented, can actually be used as a skill that can improve the quality and efficacy of our work. This applies to all therapists from dominant and subdominant communities. Working interculturally in the consulting room also requires technical skills, and training and is not simply a case of providing space for the client to inform or educate the therapist. As therapists, it is important that we equip ourselves with these skills, personally, through exploring our own culture and heritage and through analysis, and professionally, through supervision and training to consider issues of power, privilege and the category fallacy. Networking in groups such as BAATN and Nafsiyat, where therapists can come together to think through issues of race and culture in psychotherapy, has also been a valuable experience that has enhanced my intercultural practice. These skills go far beyond the scope of traditional psychoanalytic theories. Recognizing the limits of current theories can help us to explore different models such as the Intercultural model, which includes an understanding of our interaction with the changing socio-cultural world around us.

The concepts in the Nafsiyat Intercultural model which primarily address race can inform the development of a paradigm that helps us to understand and work with issues of intersectionality. The model puts cultural phenomena, prejudice and discrimination at the core of identity and the concept of the self. Through examining power and privilege in relation to all sections of our communities and exploring differences in the conscious and unconscious processes in the consulting room, we can address the issues of intersectionality openly with clients. A model of therapy that does not consider culture and the socio-cultural environment is not just lacking but is less effective and can affect the outcome and quality of psychotherapy. If we seek to develop more intercultural models of therapy in our increasingly diverse settings, the concept of the self and identity formation from a cultural perspective can help clinicians to be more vigilant in seeing the hidden assumptions of a universal self and their use of the category fallacy. This can support the development of an intercultural model of working.

References

Ababio, B. (2019). Not Yet at Home: An Exploration of Aural and Verbal Passing Amongst African Migrants in Britain. In R. Littlewood & B. Ababio (eds), *Intercultural Therapy Challenges, Insights and Developments* (pp.40–60). London: Routledge.

Agora, O. (2019). Who's being assessed? Postmodern Intercultural Therapy Assessments: A Synergistic Process. In R. Littlewood & B. Ababio (eds), *Intercultural Therapy Challenges, Insights and Developments* (pp.24–39). London: Routledge.

Fanon, F. (1967) *Black Skin White Masks*. New York, NY: Grove Press.

Gungor, D. (2019). Group Psychotherapy with Turkish Speaking Women at Nafsiyat: Migration, Gender and Ethnic Difference as Catalysts to Growth in the Psychodynamic Group in Intercultural Therapy and New Liberalism. In R. Littlewood & B. Ababio (eds), *Intercultural Therapy Challenges, Insights and Developments* (pp.60–70). London: Routledge.

Kareem, J. (1992). The Nafsiyat Intercultural Therapy Centre: Ideas and Experience in Intercultural Therapy. In J. Kareem & R. Littlewood (eds), *Intercultural Therapy: Themes, Interpretations and Practice* (pp.14–38). Oxford: Blackwell.

Kirmayer, L.J., & Minas, H. (2000). The future of cultural psychiatry: An international *perspective. The Canadian Journal of Psychiatry*, 45(5), 438–446. https://doi.org/10.1177/070674370004500503.

Kleinman, A. (1988). *Rethinking Psychiatry: From Cultural Category to Personal Experience.* New York, NY: Free Press.

Kraepelin, E. (1904). Comparative psychiatry. *Central Journal for Neurology and Psychiatry*, 11(2), 108–112.

Krause, I. (2019). Intercultural Therapy and New Liberalism. In R. Littlewood & B. Ababio (eds), *Intercultural Therapy Challenges, Insights and Developments* (pp.10–23). London: Routledge.

Littlewood R. (1990), From categories to contexts: A decade of the 'new cross-cultural psychiatry'. *British Journal of Psychiatry*, 156, 308–327.

Littlewood, R. (1992). Towards and Intercultural Therapy in Intercultural Therapy. In J. Kareem & R. Littlewood (eds), *Intercultural Therapy: Themes, Interpretations and Practice* (pp.3–13). Oxford: Blackwell.

Littlewood, R. & Ababio, B. (2019). Introduction: Process and Development in Intercultural Psychotherapy. In R. Littlewood & B. Ababio (eds), *Intercultural Therapy Challenges, Insights and Developments* (pp.1–9). London: Routledge.

Mckenzie-Mavinga, I. (2019). The Challenge of Racism in Clinical Supervision. In Littlewood R. & Ababio B. (eds), *Intercultural Therapy Challenges, Insights and Developments* (pp.167–177). London: Routledge.

Macpherson, W. (1999). *The Stephen Lawrence Inquiry.* (Cm 4262-I). London: The Stationary Office.

Roland, A. (1989). *In Search of Self in India and Japan*, second edition. Princeton, NJ: Princeton University Press.

Rose, E. (1997). Daring to work with internalised racism. *Journal of British Association of Counselling*, 8(2), 92–94.

Sigalas, A. (2019). Inferiorisation: Approaching a Stigmatising Reality in Therapy. In R. Littlewood & B. Ababio (eds), *Intercultural Therapy Challenges, Insights and Developments* (pp.111–118). London: Routledge.

Speight, S.L. (2007). Internalized racism: One more piece of the puzzle. *The Counselling Psychologist*, 35(1), 126–134. https://doi.org/10.1177/0011000006295119.

Thomas L.K. (1995). Psychotherapy in the Context of Race and Culture: An inter-Cultural Therapeutic Approach In S. Fernando (ed.), *Mental Health in a Multi-Ethnic Society* (pp.172–179). London: Routledge.

Thomas L.K. (2019) Intercultural Psychoanalytic Psychotherapy and Generationally Transmitted Trauma. In R. Littlewood & B. Ababio (eds), *Intercultural Therapy Challenges, Insights and Developments* (pp.137–152). London: Routledge.

Further Reading

Levine, R.A., Dixon, S., Levine, S., Richman, A., *et al.* (1994). *Childcare and Culture: Lessons from Africa.* Cambridge: Cambridge University Press.

Chapter 17

Character Work

SHIRANI SITUNAYAKE

Abstract

Character work can help facilitate reclamation of the parts of us that have been shut down, buried or forgotten. Through creating images of the dominating characters, we can begin to see and understand their origins and honour how some may have protected us.

Keywords

Re-engaging with our authenticity, character work, creativity, fighting against conditioning, discovering our core self, transcultural, intersectional

Introduction

My chapter explores the use of character work in the therapeutic process, which uses the theory that our world is often dominated by certain characters, who may be born out of conditioning or degrees of trauma.

The term 'character work' refers loosely to a myriad of applications – including, but not exclusively, shamanism, archetypes, dramatherapy, performing arts, parables and stories. The way I embrace it includes elements of some of these approaches.

These characters may obscure many aspects of our identity and often distort and limit our self-expression, communication and relationships, both with others and ourselves.

This is particularly destructive if we belong to a Black or minoritized group, or groups, reinforcing the belief or experience that only certain parts of us or our behaviours are acceptable or belong. Where an intersection of identities that are maligned determine our footsteps in the world, this can be an annihilating experience, creating an existence that denies us the place to live in flow or connection.

Character work can help facilitate reclamation of the parts of us that have been shut down, buried or even forgotten. Through creating images of the characters that dominate our lives we can begin to see and understand their origins and honour their use in perhaps protecting us. Inching our way through this crowd we can discover the other characters that might represent a more essential, unique part of us. Then they can move forward to populate our world

Some clients have drawn them, others described them in words – all of them have been given names. The process involves an intimate connection with the characters – what they look like, how they behave and what their motives or impulses are. They become three-dimensional and in conclusion, once our other characters emerge, the work seems very much about owning all of who we are and not shutting that down.

In the UK at this particular time, being our selves can be a painful, rage-filled and endlessly frustrating experience for Black and minoritized people.

I write below what may be perceived as a rambling story, without titles, headings or external academic references. This a deliberate honouring of my own culture, particular knowledge and experience. A refusal to refer to, or engage with, a validation outside of this way of being with clients or myself – potentially dead white men who still sit at the top of therapy towers, determining how we work. I reject a further injury to my authentic self and those of my clients by doing this.

INVISIBILITY

Brush strokes of whitewash are painted over
the undesirable and different aspects of me.
At birth began the orchestrated amputation.
I am invisible, unseen, not there,
Without presence or substance.
But childhood memories and sensations
nurtured and long guarded,
push through the debris of this deliberate suffocation.
I cannot be dismantled or demolished,
for I am more than memory.
I am spirit,
An essence,
A sound,

A smell,
All things in the realm of senses
which cannot be dulled or bashed in.
In my mind lives the brown child,
Innocent of doubt or duality.
This energy sustains my longings and desires,
spinning me out of bright white shadows
weaving a web of inclinations.
And if I am exiled
it is only in the eyes of others,
who seek to draw margins around their existence.
I am the colour of their indiscretion and defiance,
the mirror of their illusion.
I am the invisible witness of their convergence.
I am forever my own memory,
the gatekeeper to my own story.

By Shirani Situnayake, 1982

My extensive work with women clients, who sit at the edges of this society, and/or whose sense of self has been fractured and diminished by trauma, is in part described by the poems referenced above.

The necessities of a thick skin or frozen state that clients wear to protect themselves, so often end up imprisoning them, shutting down or away their essential selves. The selves are no longer recognizable, lost in the various armouring they wear – often expressed through anxiety, anger, depression, addiction, self-harm, dissociation, numbness, to name some of the survival tactics.

Within my therapeutic work, I try to facilitate a client's self-empowerment and authorship, listen to their stories, as witness and ally – helping them rediscover and name themselves – 'claiming the identity they have been taught to despise' (Cliff, 1980). It is often a consequence of domestic and sexual abuse, child abuse, sexual abuse, racism, anti-lesbianism and misogyny.

Building a bridge of trust and encouraging them to enter into engagement through the medium of art – meeting and establishing a three-dimensional aspect of the characters who have populated their world – can be a powerful, immediate and safe way to explore what was once too terrifying. Without exception, every client who has embarked on this encounter with their characters/masks/faces/shadows/aspects/identities has made immediate connections.

I worked with one client for almost a year, intermittently, meeting and fleshing out her characters, honouring their roles and purpose in navigating and surviving a difficult and traumatic life/beginning, recognizing how these characters now limited and constrained her. We invited these characters to step aside, enabling the entry of previously hidden or obscured aspects of her to take centre stage. Where they had been the interface of her, as a brown, queer woman, surviving and navigating the world, they had become shadows she lived behind, one-dimensional and suffocating.

Initially, the idea of creating a character/s of the main player/s has often been met with embarrassment, unease and stumbling entries, yet I have been unfailingly awed and humbled again and again by my clients' resilience and determination. The spirit of each client, the face that has almost been erased, that fights to find themselves, to recover what was lost, hidden or suppressed – this seems sewn into their imagination and creativity, and it is the road back to their essential self/selves. It is a connection, a pathway that has refused to be killed off. I am always honoured to be trusted and enriched by the characters that come forth into the light, liberated in my clients' world.

My own journey involved two main characters – Shit Head and Ratarang Baba (Sinhala for golden child). Initially, I thought Shit Head was responsible for all the trouble in my life: loud, angry, provocative and often destructive – yet I also loved this part of me, that somehow represented the outspoken and bold aspect of me that is Sri Lankan, but was in trouble so often in what felt like a moderated British environment.

Figure 17.1: Colombo, Sri Lanka 1959, photographer unknown

It transpired that Shit Head was protecting Ratarang Baba, from her child sexual abuse and all the vulnerability and pain she tucked away with her. But the blonde-haired, blue-eyed, light-skinned mixed-race baby seemed responsible for her own traumas – and when she emerged, I initially hated her. And so began more work of reclamation, of the sweet, loving, joyful, innocent aspect in the heart of me, to assimilate my exiled self.

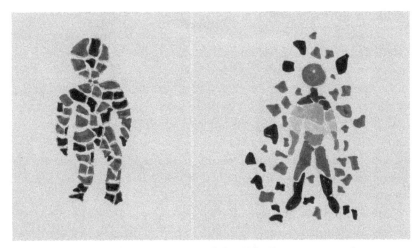

Figure 17.2: Immobilization to Breakthrough. Shirani Situnayake, 2011

Where are we reflected back, how does that distort our sense of self, aspects of us? The characters that populate our world are clues to these breeches and distortions.

Superficially, Ratarang Baba, in a colonial 'Ceylon' was a representation of a tenuous ideal, an anomaly in a brown-skinned world. But if you scratched beneath the scabbed surface there lay envy, disdain, anger and even hatred. Any wonder I developed an unconscious rage towards this child – subjected to child sexual abuse, the ultimate weapon of war.

None of this was apparent until much later on, after my family's exodus to England, and ironically after Sri Lanka's independence. I was slammed into the frozen greyness of February in the Midlands and the confines of my maternal grandparents' house and regime.

The untrammelled child in knickers, running around in the hot spaces of the tropics, when forced into clothes, quiet, alien landscapes and sounds, with a hostile grandmother, quickly turned to anger, seething, boiling and eventually derailed and was swallowed whole.

Here is one of the interfaces, where worlds meet and characters are birthed: like a ferocious, flowing stream whose course is altered by obstacles, damming, gradients and landscapes, forced to erode its own banks or shoved underground.

This porous, expansive and fluid child, in its bid for survival, adapts and morphs into something else, or other and begins its journey, dispossessed and already repositioned, re-aligned. From this skewed misalignment, we grow around ourselves, forgetting who we really are in entirety, or confining these unacceptable parts to hidden corners.

The 'main players' in our world, those who helped us survive our beginnings, reinforcing the idea that this is all of who we are, take centre stage. However, within us may lie an emptiness, a discord, an aggressive clashing, a yearning for something lost, or more, a feeling of limitation. Imprisoned in an idea of ourselves that was sculpted by others, we feel our deep unhappiness, frustration and erasure.

At times, we may find ourselves meeting those exiles in moments or outbursts – creativity, movement, relationships, activism, encounters with nature. Through dance, poetry, sport, cooking, connection, music, we may find a new voice and tone, a joy previously unknown.

At its worst, our encounters may be funnelled into self-destructive outlets – alcohol, drugs, self-harm, risk and dysfunctional relationships. Our initial experiencing of these feelings is embedded in these actions. There is an absence of safe expression, nurturing or unconditional positive regard determining that any encounter with these feelings may be unsafe, shameful, bad, wrong and totally unacceptable.

Encounters with our characters are one way of repositioning ourselves – recentring us in the essential core of who we are. Engaging with these main characters releases them and begins a dialogue, and often clients experience a deep compassion for these sometimes dominating and terrifying parts of themselves – Characters that can and have shut them down, cornered and immobilized them and railed against them with negative, painful, limiting and destructive commentary.

In recognizing where these parts originated and how they may have protected them, clients might choose to keep them close. Alternatively, some recognize that they belong to others, or are indeed others – the voice of an abusive parent, the chorus of bullying peers, the tyranny of a racist teacher. However, the objective never seems to be about annihilation, more the face-to-face meeting, a process of understanding, acceptance and sometimes empathy – at its heart, empathy for ourselves.

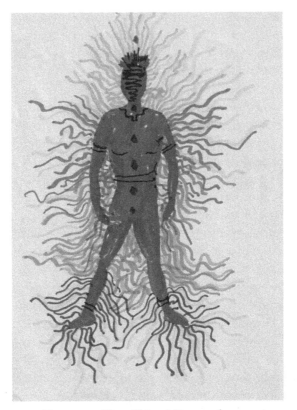

Figure 17.3: Flow. Shirani Situnayake 2011

Some characters have been 'retired', sent to rest, go on holiday or are banished. And as they step aside, we can see who was hidden or smothered by this character and begin the process of meeting them. Within the boundaried witnessing of a therapeutic space, this experience can be profoundly transformative.

Within this there is the potential to set free parts of ourselves, to become whole and fluid in our expression and responses to the world – from a place of authenticity, there is possibility to embrace all of whom we are and to recognize our selves in entirety, without apology, shame, guilt, fear or uncertainty.

Into this space step the ghosts, whom we can reclaim. By accepting and absorbing Ratarang Baba, I gave myself permission to be soft, vulnerable, honest, playful and free. I no longer needed Shit Head to stand guard, spitting fire at perceived threats, fixing me always at the edge, outside, waiting to be 'othered' – the mixed heritage Sri Lankan immigrant lesbian, bristling with expectation, poised for battle.

Shit Head has become the trusted guardian of the outer edges of awareness – names the unnameable, speaks the unspeakable – rummaging through the shadowland for truths and clearing a pathway for Ratarang Baba to emerge. Shit Head is the hot-headed chilli eater, the intense, immoderate, blunt firecracker, whom I now openly honour and love.

There lies in these two a strong reflected duality – though as an adult no longer blonde, Ratarang Baba may be the mixed heritage individual who is often disowned as brown, made invisible, marginalized and often unseen. Shit Head is the Sri Lankan persona – noisy, garrulous, loud, emotional and excitable, and very visible.

In all cultures, characters are celebrated and popularized – as archetypes, myths, fables and stories. Their broad sweep can help us understand our humanness, yet within us we have a particular world of our own stories, reflecting where we have come from and what has shaped us. For Black and minoritized people the reclamation of our stories, our own characters, is a vital liberation from the possible tyranny of our families and that of the dominant and inherently racist culture we find ourselves in. It may be a road map back to ourselves.

Perhaps characters are all a result of a degree of trauma, or injury to the self. Incumbent on us then, as therapists, is the capacity to sit with another's trauma, really pay attention, regard the symbols or portrayals without judgement but with openness, curiosity and a deep regard.

Conclusion

We may not share the same cultural reference points, but we may, in a connected relationship with our client, resonate with their feelings by stepping onto a bridge with them. As therapists, our capacity to know ourselves, our own wounding and an awareness of the characters, scripts and storylines that populate our lives is what may open our hearts to others. To understand our own dislocation and disassociation and the damage done to us, to know from where we came and who our ancestors are, places us astride our clients in this heightened capacity.

Entrenched within this exploration sits the brutal acknowledgement of where we sit across the room from our clients, who we are in the world and how this potential dynamic could play out between us. In knowing ourselves, no longer exiled, we can sit face to face with others and really see them.

Our stories may not be the same and the language of their telling differ, but if we listen astutely we will hear what our clients are telling us.

Therapy in Colour

ANCESTRAL HIJACK
Memories nibbled
into shredded paper effigies
shriek in the hot breeze.
Skin stripped to bone
uncovers grooves scoured during beginnings.
What is left of the tattered recall
but an idea or dream.

Reconfigured I stagger out directionless
until my feet hit the ground
and I tug at the heartlines that lie beneath me,
making contact with my familiars and ghosts.
Paper kites jerk in the beach skies and wind,
sucking waves threaten to drag me in
and spit me out far away.
Once again polishing me down to bone.
In this different, alien place what am I,
Wild sprawling laburnham
Or chaotic yellow flowered poison?

By Shirani Situnayake 2019

References
Cliff, Michelle (1980). Claiming an Identity They Taught Me to Despise. Persephone Press.

Part V

Celebrating Our Intersectionality

Ancestral Constellations – African Healing Contexts, Traditions and Origins

Chapter 18

A Queer Love Letter:

The Severing and Redeeming Power of Eros in Psychotherapy

JOEL SIMPSON

Abstract

This queer love letter contemplates the redeeming power and connectivity of Eros to mutually heal, re-awaken, stimulate and inspire psychotherapists, counsellors and trainees' practice and queer African diasporan people's therapeutic experiences. My lived experience as an African diasporan client, working with a white Italian psychoanalyst, is included. Through a focus on ancestral lineage, intersecting identities, grief, fathers, and therapeutic relationships, an integrative approach is drawn on to examine how Eros may be severed in psychotherapy. Contrasting experiences of working with an African diasporan psychoanalyst consider how Eros may redeem 'kinship libido' owing to loss and transgenerational grief suffered from the African Holocaust's colonial legacies. Client vignettes, where both client and psychotherapist are queer and of African diasporan heritage, explore a wounded healer archetype and Eros as a messenger. Acknowledging discourse around ethical boundaries, love's potential as a conduit to promote the psychological wellbeing of African diasporan queer people who have been displaced and disconnected because of colonialism is foregrounded.

Keywords

African Holocaust, colonial, Eros, father, grief, intersecting identities, kinship, queer

Joel Simpson
London, England
February 14th, 2023

Dear fellow psychotherapists, counsellors and trainees,

My name is Joel. I'm a psychotherapist, who is a queer person of African diasporan heritage. These identities inform my practice, experience of the world and un/conscious reasons for writing this queer love letter to you. Love will be central to our discourse because of its capacity to heal and transform. I've spent my life relinquishing shackles of heteronormativity to live in my African-centred queerness. As part of my liberation, I'm affirmed by Beam's (1986, p.189) offering that 'Black men loving Black men is the revolutionary act.' Inspired by this revolution, as an often-marginalized research area, I foreground homoerotic love in psychotherapeutic relationships with people of African diasporan heritage.

The African Holocaust systematically forbade freedom to love, read, write and enjoy sexuality without forced reproduction by a colonial power. My engagement with you through letter writing was once outlawed. I'm reclaiming what was severed. I honour the African diasporan liberationists who have enabled this opportunity to write freely to you. As you read, we might mutually re/awaken, stimulate and redeem our therapeutic practice. There may be healing potential available to us and our clients when we practise working more relationally and intimately.

Like any act of love, this letter necessitates openness and vulnerability to enable meaningful connection. Eros acts as a conduit to 'open up a way of seeing' (Haule, 1996, p.9) into the unconscious erotic lives of therapeutic couples. I use love and Eros interchangeably to contemplate ancenstral lineage, as it intersects with gender, sexuality and relationship diversity. I consider unworked silence where the subjective and collective unconscious intersect (Robertson, 2018, p.50) because the 'personal is political' (Burch, 2012, p.139) *and often needs to made voiced and worked with consciously.* Although maternal and paternal transference dynamics imbue therapeutic relationships, I focus on paternal transference and countertransference dynamics, given the specific legacies of the loss of the father during the African Holocaust. I consider the impact of severing Eros in psychotherapeutic relationships and contemplate what may be redeemed from this transgenerational and intergenerational trauma when Eros is considered.

Queer means many things to many people. For me, queer/queerness invites ever-expanding, non-definitive, non-normative opportunities to look again at a uniqueness of self, where what has been severed and assigned to shadow may be redeemed from imposed dishonour to honour. Queerness, within this letter, thrives beyond binary, reductive, monolithic colonial impositions. I draw on my writing elsewhere (Simpson, 2023) to foreground African-centred queerness that predates imperialistic proclivities. Such colonially-infused dogma often underpins religious and cultural sanctions and is used to dictate and reinforce queerphobic discourse within, and beyond, African diasporan communities. Yet still, African-centred queerness may be understood as an embodiment of resilience, power, wholeness, emancipation, pride, and survival in the face of oppressive regimes, where ancestral lineage, gender, sexuality, and relationship diversity intersect. In true queer spirit, I write without definitiveness; my offerings may be replete with contradictions and I resist proposing therapeutic techniques. Instead, my invitation to you is to contemplate ways of being in practice, through this intentionally 'relationally conscious' letter (Adams, Holman Jones & Ellis, 2015, p.35). May this extended meditation offer us opportunities to reflect on past and current knowledge and practice, whilst transforming and deconstructing unfolding dynamics (Frank, 1995) within therapeutic relationships.

Through composites of real experiences, I begin by focusing on the impact of severing Eros through personal and racial layers of experience between myself and Filippo, a fictional, white, Italian, male psycho-therapist. Through amalgamated lived experiences, I offer fictional client vignettes with Chuka and Leroy to amplify considerations about working with Eros in practice. Finally, I consider the redeeming power of Eros as a client when working with Glenford, a fictional analyst of African diasporan heritage.

Working with Filippo

I was once a client in the throes of a seven-year, thrice-weekly analysis with Filippo, a white, Italian, 50-something-year-old, analyst. I felt unsettled, with an ambivalent attachment between us. Oftentimes, our relationship felt fraught with anger-evoking, constipated silence. This felt punishing and confusing. When I shared experiences of oppression at the inter-section of my identities, he seemed unresponsive. Momentarily, Filippo appeared tender and attentive, such as when I suffered long-term mobility issues from a car crash en route to his practice. As I lay on his couch, he beckoned me to cover myself with his blanket. I felt discombobulated in following sessions when warmth seemed severed. Appearing detached, he never mentioned the accident. I felt shame and self-compassion for my yearning for his consistency. Despite Filippo's oscillation, the regularity of our meetings provided reliability and some security in vulnerable times.

Unnameable feelings associated with the severing of paternal care may have constellated in the silent, unworked, transference between me and Filippo. Smith (2011) considers that African diasporan children may be affected by cycles of unconscious and violent splits imbued in their father's and forefather's psyches. Colonial laws stripped African fathers of rights to parent their children. Their children became the property of masters of enslaved people. Perhaps this was part of my struggle to find a secure internalized attachment, where it felt safe enough to love and hate the paternal object (Klein, 2002). Instead of hating the therapeutic father, perhaps I unconsciously hated myself: staying in an ambivalent, often-hostile, relationship, where Filippo seemed silent about my explorations of queerness, age and class dynamics between us, and my mobility issues owing to my accident. I yearned to be loved and seen by him, while imbued with transgenerational cycles of loss and archetypal grief (Brewster, 2019). I showed up hungry, somewhat displaced and disconnected, grasping in a futile way after a parental object – unable to know who or what had been lost through the severing in the African Holocaust.

While I was delighted to be fed by Filippo, on occasion, the disparateness evoked a vacuous hole in my psyche too agonizing for words to capture (Bly, 1990; Hollis, 1994). The analysis offered limited scope to attend to this transgenerational wounding and maintained an emotional indefinite detachment (Bowlby, 1973, 1980). A mediating system between me and Filippo, which could have activated and maintained attachment through feelings, behaviours and thoughts, seemed deactivated. I had to bear 'father hunger': an unyielding 'ripe chronic unresolved grief reaction' (Erikson, 1993, p.259). A transference projection on to Filippo as the distant father (Samuels, 1985, p.41) continued. I was caught in an unrelenting primitive agony (Winnicott, 1974), which lingered between us like 'as a gravitational field, pulling us downward toward anxiety and dread' (Weller, 2015, p. 39). There seemed to be missed opportunities to attend to the dread as part of an unconscious erotic fantasy related to mourning and melancholia (Freud, 1917) of the loss and absence of the African father. I was desperately seeking a sense of aliveness (Eros) in unbearable deadness. I sought to mobilize the persistent anxiety and dread: 'Filippo, I hate feeling like the subordinate queer black man on his knees, begging you like you're the white colonial master; unsure if you'll respond.' Continually unresponsive to the explicit lived and ancestral despair, Filippo regarded me as violent and attacking. He hypothesized that I was setting him up to fail and seek revenge. Despite my attempt to engage with the plausibility of this pertinent unconscious, revenge fantasy, he seemed collapsed and annoyingly defended in our explorations. His red-faced exasperation shielded his fragility as he dismissed the collective racist, queerphobic histories that sat between us. I felt sorrowful and unmet. He'd positioned me as the aggressor and overlooked my vulnerability and sensitivity.

Perhaps we were relating to each other as colonial objects (Lowe, 2008), which Filippo seemed unable to see or consider with me. Healing and transformation within our relating necessitated working with transferential colonial dynamics to feel into the potential of moving beyond part object-relating to whole object-relating. Yet, we seemed perpetually caught in an unconscious grip of an 'activated racial complex' (Brewster, 2019), which can be understood as an aspect of the psyche that was/is fragmented and underpinned by trauma. This trauma was part of both of our ancestral stories, yet remained unanalysed. One of the central features of a racial complex is that it evokes dissociation. Perhaps dissociation between the two of us went unacknowledged and unprocessed, which led to my feeling of disconnection and erotic severance in our encounter.

Filippo seemed to bypass these unconscious complexes to communicate with me through humour and playfulness, such as when I forgot my mobile phone in his room. I returned to retrieve it. He pretended it wasn't there, momentarily. I felt pushed into a cruel game of hide and seek, which seemed to baffle him. How could I play? Without attending to the colonial object relations between us, the climate wasn't safe enough to play (Winnicott, 1971, p.137). Invitations to play lacked mutually co-created grooves to make non-verbal interaction safe (Benjamin, 2018, p.31; p.75). At a personal level, Filippo seemed competent when attending to my perpetual life-long sorrow and transferential dynamics between us related to my actual absent, dead father. However, at a racial, archetypal and intersectional level, we were at an impasse. It seemed impossible to experience a 'good enough facilitating environment' (Klein, 2002). After seven years, my experience of this ongoing 'luminous absence' (Mathers, 2001, p.5) became too much to bear. We terminated working together – sad, but necessary for my healing potential as a queer, paternally orphaned person of African diasporan heritage.

Love's potential

In a letter to Jung, Freud suggested that psychotherapy's 'cure is effected by love' (McGuire, 1974, p. 12). (McGuire, 1974, p.12). Freud's 1915 paper considered how notions of love and Eros in psychotherapy can distort one's perception and be considered as unreal and a resistance to psychotherapeutic processes (Mann, 1999, p.8). Yet, Kavaler-Adler (1992), in their work on mourning, offer a helpful nuance: Eros as a resistance more aptly describes when it 'fails to be a conduit for conscious desires' (p.527). Eros as resistance and its failure to act as a conduit for both conscious and unconscious desires seemed to reflect my work with Filippo. We might consider Eros as a conduit, when it 'allows the chance for [desires] to be understood, thereby reducing all forms of resistance' (Mann, 1999, p.257).

As such, fellow psychotherapists, counsellors and trainees, this queer love letter offers an invitation to you to deepen understanding by feeling into what Eros's desires might communicate, rather than reducing our discourse to a focus on resistance. In the process of being confused, overwhelmed and aroused, our craft necessitates bearing 'the heat without fanning the flames' (Wrye & Welles, 1994, p.87).

Premature conclusions reduce Eros to limited considerations around ethics, prohibitions and violations. Eros must be explored in all its complexities: 'sexual, spiritual, incestuous, sublimated, related, "kinship libido" connected, "heart-centred"' (Sedgwick, 1994, p.36). Eros, as a connecting entity, isn't inherently dangerous. Perhaps Eros is a messenger inviting us to make meaning of the call for union. This call, powerful, seductive and disorienting as it might be, invites us to slow down, observe and make meaning. While psychotherapeutic connection might cultivate 'you' and 'I' meeting to become a 'we', this doesn't necessitate dissolving individual capacity to hold boundary and difference (Haule, 1996, p.138). What presents as dangerous might be reframed as clients' unconscious articulation through erotic communications. Severing Eros' potential limits our capacity to work at depth with clients and ourselves. Eros invites potential to redeem what has been cast into shadow.

Drawing on composites of real experiences, I now offer two fictionalized vignettes to highlight Eros' potential through work with Chuka and Leroy. These case examples will exemplify the concepts and reflections explored so far and support your own considerations.

CHUKA

Imagine Chuka: a 50-something, ebony-skinned, Nigerian, non-binary dancer. Chuka is in a polyamorous relationship; their secondary partner pressures them for anal sex. Chuka feels fatigued, which disables their libido. Our sessions sometimes leave us feeling drained of energy. You might resonate with a sense of dread that creeps in when the field feels sleepy. The field may be understood as the integrated, mutually constellated, conscious and unconscious processes that are evoked and intersect when we meet with our clients (Schwartz-Salant, 1984, p.29). Despite Chuka's seemingly defensive claims that 'I don't do anger and rage, Joel. It's not productive', I experience them as seething. They speak through clipped sentences which arrest me in the midst of lethargy. We share mutual bodily responses of shallow breaths, tight chests, raised heartbeats and muted sexual arousal.

Eros necessitates paying attention to countertransferential bodily responses and Chuka's fantasies that 'We could both do with a good old lay down, together.' Eros is a conduit for connection. I'm reminded of Freshwater and Robertson's (2002) proposition that 'the desire for eroticism does not belong solely to the client, but is a longing felt by us all, including the therapist' (p.70). I connect with my longings for queer connection and stay curious about symbolic union, suppressed rage and suffocating sleep. Chuka demands, 'Fix me, Joel! Won't you?' Not knowing what to do with their desperate plea, I feel into the feelings present between us to embody qualities of the wounded healer archetype. This evokes a strange sense of incompetence, which puzzles me and I surrender to it. I resist having answers – an important part of our craft as psychotherapists, counsellors and trainees. Instead, the intuitive call is to deepen into the presenting despair at not having an egoic resolve, which evokes Chuka's confessions about humiliation from their partner around sexual inexperience. By recognizing I don't know what to do, we drop into an erotic, deeply empathic and attuned meeting place and encounter what ails for Chuka: their lived experience of loneliness, existential aloneness and shame.

Redeeming Eros necessitates openness that doesn't cast sexual arousal between us, or feelings of incompetence, into the shadow as shameful. Rather than sanitize fantasies, Orbach (1999) highlights how psychotherapists, counsellors and trainees might think about and make meaning of their erotic feelings towards their clients – and what these mean. Rather than quash or reject daydreams, I allow my spontaneous aroused imaginings of our lips drinking from the same part of a cup. We enjoy steaming black coffee, on a summer's day, and are strangely cuddled outside a well-known London gay bathhouse that merges into a tropical setting. I remain curious about the meaning and associations of each part of the fantasy – particularly as I don't like coffee. The craft of our work as psychotherapists necessitates conscious mastication of erotic fantasies as unconscious communications. Doing so symbolically, without censorship, may limit potential for literal enactment. As our work deepens, Chuka shares kinship fantasies of becoming my friend; they fear I'll reject them when I discover the real them, whom they hate. After a lifetime of performing on stages and wearing a facade to mask the loneliness, Chuka expresses meta needs for union with 'truth, beauty, goodness, love, honesty, innocence, growth, authenticity, peacefulness and so on' (Maslow, 1967, p.101). Chuka sees these qualities as idealized in me, yet feels disconnected from them personally. They brushed against them briefly through a relationship with someone else – a barista they met on tour in Brazil. Perhaps this accounts for the bitter-sweet sexual arousal in the countertransference, and the coffee fantasy. The barista encounter was shaming and enlivening for them; it happened as a result of an affair in a previous monogamous relationship. It was one time in their life when they felt truthful, beautiful and accepting of themselves. Rather than reduce my panic at sexual arousal to prohibition, Eros, becomes a helpful messenger. Through experience of betrayal, our relationship (a type of kinship), and the parts of me that they long for, which are hidden parts of them, Eros highlights and redeems Chuka's shadow qualities, through experiences of betrayal, our relationship (a type of kinship), and the parts of me that they long for, which are hidden parts of them. We connect to their core wounding beliefs: 'I am inherently unlovable, untrustworthy and vile.' There's something redemptive about re-visioning the meaning of erotic desires as transpersonal yearnings for what is divine, rather than solely literalizing and policing desires without thought and context – this incapacitates meaning-making. Working with Eros, in this way, invites giving 'up the kind of control which the ego demands' (Rowan, 1993, p.60), so that we might be available to hear and see our clients rather than control and order Eros' messengers.

LEROY

Fellow psychotherapists, counsellors and trainees, through this queer love letter of homoerotic therapeutic encounters, let's continue to consider Eros as a messenger through my work with Leroy. Picture an almond-skinned, proud afro-wearing, 35-year-old, single, Antiguan academic, trans man, who uses a wheelchair after an accident damaged his spine. Enamoured by what he deems as my large book collection, Leroy declares, 'Ooh, I need you to penetrate my mind...intellectually.' Sizing me up, head to toe, he wishes we'd met outside the boundaries of psychotherapy: 'Bwoy, Sah! I'm not gonna lie; you're my type, Joel. Mi madda wudda love yu, yu si! Lawd! Yu pretty, eeh? Don't it?'. Leroy laments a deceased father, who rejected him aged ten when he began using the wheelchair. Leroy's bright smile and flirtatiousness seem to construct a persona that hides a fragile self-construct: 'People will reject me when they see the real me.' I experience sorrow and self-hatred palpably in my gut, which summons my curiosity. Leroy struggles to recall anything positive from a childhood of radicalized-based violence. Having grown up middle class between Antigua and Jamaica, he's renegotiating the complexities of clear social class translations in the UK. It is challenging to find language and community to articulate this confusion and difference; our therapy becomes a healing container for this wound.

Roazen (1976, p.367) highlighted Freud's position that 'one could effect far more with one's patients if one gave them enough of the love which they had longed for as children'. For Leroy, receiving this longed-for love evokes tender work: we share fairy tales and queer-centred ideas for comic magazines he'd like to create. Creatively, we deepen into a realm of connection where Eros provides safe territories to explore vivid night dreams. Twice weekly sessions of 50 minutes feel timeless. Peering into our consulting room, you might witness the kinship of two, youngish, queer African diasporan beings relishing the joy of aliveness – together. This queer love letter highlights that when working with clients like Leroy, good practice necessitates thinking about the symbolism of transferences, countertransferences and fantasies, in the same way that we work with dreams – moving beyond, and including, the literal.

Leroy's father only allowed him to read academic books, and his older brother died in adolescence. Eros's aliveness presents through my interest in Leroy's imagination, which stimulates grief at paternal and sibling loss. The desire to be penetrated by me seems to stem

Therapy in Colour

from a primitive need to feel wanted (Covington, 1996, p.347) and a longing for long-lost kinship. Eros makes 'it safe enough for him to begin to express his love, grief and hatred' (Mann, 1999, p.12). One session, when words seem unavailable, the rhythm of Snooky Young (1989) playing the trumpet on Count Basie's classic orchestration, 'Lil' Darlin'', floats through my imagination. Spontaneous, synchronous humming from him leads to my invitation to play it. Lying on the couch, he weeps. Through a tear-stained face and grief-choked voice, Leroy recalls the only men that he ever felt loved by: his great-grandfather, brother – now me. Through a tear-stained face and grief-choked voice, Leroy recalls the only men that he ever felt loved by: his great-grandfather, brother – now me. He feels inspired to share a long-held secret wish: to play in a band, one day. His father had scoffed and disapproved at his childhood dream and he'd abandoned it. Eros invites us to look backwards to Leroy's infantile origins and ancestral roots, while simultaneously looking forward to as a sense of developmental progression. It's as if Leroy and I enter into a union, where there is healing, redeeming potential for us both – an intimate, soulful meeting place. Beautiful as they may be, moments like these don't only feel great. My work is to also remain curious about my simultaneous resistance to feeling so close, and intimate, at these times. Perhaps it is because I am simultaneously in touch with feelings of loss, grief and tension, which has been shielded by the protective veneer of his flirtatiousness. This craft of meaning making through the healing potential of our therapeutic relationship highlights the necessity of de-conflating the sexual and the erotic and reducing our encounters to a reductive non-meaning making, literal focus on fear – dressed up as ethical consideration and so-called professionalism. Whilst the interpersonal field between the two of us might be understood as love, it seems to reveal a connection rooted in our shared orphanhood at the loss of the severed African father.

Working with Glenford

Years later, I became a client of Glenford, an African diasporan analyst who is heterosexual, older than me, and from a similar class background. Sobbing through my first session, Glenford seemed caring and attentive as I recounted where, alongside moments of celebration, pride, and affirmation, I'd sometimes felt displaced at the intersection of ancestral lineage, class, culture, gender and sexuality. Rather than responding to me like a suspicious 'other', being worked out across the room, Eros seemed to redeem and awaken a sense of kinship libido and mutual connection that felt transformational. While difficult to capture through words, as a queer person of the African diaspora, there's something profound about having another African diasporan man mirror me through deep listening, meaning-making alongside me, being playful, bearing wordlessness and being open and curious to talk about our encounters. Glenford could hear the cultural complexities of my familial life, without pathologizing or hearing me through his missattuned theoretical lens – devoid of cultural interest/context, understanding, nuance and respect. Eros highlighted an unconscious search (Haule, 1996, p.62) for a connection with the African father that can't be fully known and articulated, but was somehow felt when we sat together. This queer love letter beckons psychotherapists, counsellors and trainees to cultivate culturally attuned personalized styles to redeem something of that which has been severed for queer African Diasporan clients who've faced the bitter edge of oppression and marginalization. Our queer ancestors endured colonial, patriarchal, queerphobic rule; some were murdered; some continue to have our civil rights contested; some of us have internalized hatred. We may not have language to articulate this. Lots of us need a safe, sensitive, attuned space to consider how our bodies have held those traumas and how we might articulate and reclaim our voices through individual and collective histories of voicelessness. Eros wasn't only present when the work felt connected with Glenford, it seemed effective when the energy between us felt stale, or when we seemed unable to find our way through misunderstandings and hopelessness. Missing Glenford momentarily during the holidays made a place for Eros's aliveness and immediacy. Filippo, my previous analyst, seemed to chide me as 'defensive' when his holiday announcement evoked my glee that I'd save money. What he sought to pathologize could be reconsidered as further and necessary manifestation of an 'indefinite detachment' (Bowlby, 1973, 1980).

Eros, through my relationship with Glenford, awakened me to 'wholeness, a containment, and a future so foreign to my impoverished past' (Haule, 1996, p.62) with Filippo. I enjoyed my growing kinship with Glenford. Being understood through cultural anecdotes, humour and speaking in patois felt soulful. I didn't have to keep explaining. I could just be, somehow. Good practice necessitates queer African diasporan clients feeling freedom to include their cultural nuances, pertaining to gender, sexuality, sex, and relationship diversity, without explanation

– so that they can just be. This is healing. Eros is often severed through cognitive endeavours to translate cultural idiosyncrasies. Where there are intersecting differences, practitioners might draw on soulful embodied practices that utilize countertransference, gestures, images, metaphor, story, energy in words and dreams. These can be useful erotic portals that enable meaning-making, giving clients space to enlarge transformative union (Haule, 1996, p.68). Our work provided scope for me to make contact with how Sufis regard communion with the Beloved: a sense of sacred love and depth where the essence of life reverberated with my wholeness.

Severing and redeeming Eros

Love isn't a prerequisite for effective therapy. I want to advance a more nuanced position: love is critical for psychological health (Haule, 1996, p.85). Yet, contrastingly, what this queer love letter emphasizes is how silence, an unwillingness to engage with colonial object relations and the transgenerational impact of the African Holocaust, the severing of Eros and dismissing considerations around intersecting identities, impact psychological health. Love surpasses being nice and having good intentions. Love invites a deep sense of honouring and valuing clients, with sincerity, while we sojourn the heights and depths of inner worlds, creatively making meaning of the intersubjective transferential dynamics that constellate between us. While Eros is explicated throughout this letter, its appearance may not always be obvious and its presence may be taken for granted. Yet, its redeeming potential in your own practice is one that you might join me in considering and working with.

Unspoken love letters linger at this conclusion. For the African father, severed from his kin, there's a wordless lament, accompanied by a sense of resilient pride, that something of our shared horror can be articulated through this queer love letter to transform the way that therapeutic relationships are attended to. For Filippo and me, though I remain forever grateful for the tough times that he held me in, there's sadness that we seemed caught in a racial complex that couldn't be analysed and worked with appropriately.

For Chuka and Leroy, Eros afforded a creative path of kinship where 'potential space' (Winnicott, 1960) is cultivated and we might 'experience ourselves as alive and as the authors of our bodily sensations, thoughts, feelings, and perceptions' (Ogden, 1989, p.200). Eros may be understood as that aliveness which invites working with 'that unknown component which makes meaning possible, turns events into experiences, [and] is communicated in love' (Hillman, 1992, p.xvi). For Glenford, there is respect and gratitude that within spaces of rupture and repair, there were opportunities to consider Eros and its power to redeem what has been denied. There is literal and symbolic transformation possible in being seen and mirrored through kinship with another man of the African diaspora. Our connection offered potential to heal something of that which was so violently severed through the African Holocaust.

Fellow psychotherapists, counsellors and trainees, a psychotherapeutic relationship that is redeeming Eros through what has been severed, and wants space to be alive, seems fortuitous in soulful, healing practices. Perhaps my work with Chuka, Leroy and Glenford tell part of Psyche's unfinished story of redemption, where we are invited to come home to ourselves in the fullness of our African-centred queer potential.

As we come to the climax of our discourse, savour this letter's juice. You might breathe with me for a moment and reflect on where you connected, disconnected, felt resistant and were nourished. How is love severed and how might it be redeemed within your own practice? How might you attend and respond to Eros's messages? Through Eros and this queer love letter, meet me behind the smoky bike shed of contemplations, where we might refine the craft of soulful psychotherapeutic practice. Together, we might cultivate psychotherapy where there is deepening potential to redeem our queer birth right of exquisite aliveness, vitality and freedom.

With love and unbridled queerness,
Joel

References

Adams, T., Holman Jones, S. & Ellis, C. (2015). *Autoethnography: Understanding Qualitative Research*. New York, NY: Oxford University Press.

Beam, J. (1986). *In the Life: A Black Gay Anthology*. Washington, DC: Redbone Press.

Benjamin, J. (2018). *Beyond Doer and Done to: Recognition Theory, Intersubjectivity and the Third*. Abingdon, Oxfordshire: Routledge.

Bly, R. (1990). *Iron John: Men and Masculinity*. New York, NY: Addison-Wesley Publishing.

Bowlby, J. (1973). *Attachment and Loss, Vol 2, Separation: Anxiety and Anger*. London: Hogarth Press.

Bowlby, J. (1980). *Attachment and Loss, Vol 3, Loss: Sadness and Depression*. London: Hogarth Press.

Brewster, F. (2019). *The Racial Complex: A Jungian Perspective on Culture and Race*. London: Routledge.

Burch, K.T. (2012). *Democratic Transformations: Eight Conflicts in the Negotiation of American Identity*. London: Continuum.

Covington, C. (1996). Purposive aspects of the erotic transference. *Journal of Analytical Psychology*, 41(3), 339–352.

Erikson, B. (1993). *Helping Men Change: The Role of the Female Therapist*. London: Sage Publications.

Frank, A. (1995). *The Wounded Storyteller*. Chicago, IL: University of Chicago Press.

Freshwater, D. & Robertson, C. (2002). *Emotions and Needs*. Maidenhead, Berkshire: Open University Press.

Freud, S. (1915). *Observations on Transference Love, Standard Edition, 12*. London: Hogarth Press.

Freud, S. (1917). *Mourning and Melancholia. Standard Edition 14 (1914–1916): On the History of the Psycho-Analytic Movement, Papers on Metapsychology and Other Works* (pp.237–258). London: Hogarth Press.

Haule, J.R. (1996). *The Love Cure: Therapy Erotic and Sexual*. Woodstock, CT: Spring Publications.

Hillman, J. (1992). *Re-Visioning Psychology*. New York, NY: Harper Perennial.

Hollis, J. (1994). *Under Saturn's Shadow: The Wounding and Healing of Men*. Toronto, Canada: Inner City Books.

Kavaler-Adler, S. (1992). Mourning and erotic transference. *International Journal of Psychoanalysis*, 73(3), 527–539.

Klein, M. (2002). *Love, Guilt and Reparation: And Other Works, 1921–1945 (Vol 1)*. New York, NY: Simon and Schuster.

Lowe, F. (2008). Colonial object relations: Going underground, black–white relationships. *British Journal of Psychotherapy*, 24(1), 20–33.

Mann, D. (1999). *Erotic Transference and Countertransference: Clinical Practice in Psychotherapy*. London: Routledge.

Maslow, A.H. (1967). A theory of metamotivation: The biological rooting of the value-life. *Journal of Humanistic Psychology*, 7(2), 93–127.

Mathers, D. (2001). *An Introduction to Meaning and Purpose in Analytical Psychology*. Hove, East Sussex and Philadelphia, PA: Brunner Routledge.

McGuire, W. (1974). *The Freud/Jung Letters*. Princeton, NJ: Princeton University Press.

Ogden, T.H. (1989). *The Primitive Edge of Experience*. Northvale, NJ: Jason Aronson.

Orbach, S. (1999). *The Impossibility of Sex*. London: Karnac Books.

Roazen, P. (1976). *Freud and His Followers*. New York, NY: Knopf.

Robertson, E. (2018). The Third Body. In C. Robertson & S. Van Gogh, *Transformation in Troubled Times: Re-Vision's Soulful Approach to Therapeutic Work*, 48–66. Glasgow: TransPersonal Press.

Rowan, J. (1993). *The Transpersonal: Psychotherapy and Counselling*. London and New York, NY: Routledge.

Samuels, A. (1985). *The Father: Contemporary Jungian Perspectives*. London: Free Association Press.

Schwartz-Salant, N. (1984). Archetypal Factors Underlying Sexual Acting Out in the Transference/Countertransference Process. In N. Schwartz-Salent & M. Stein (eds), *Transference Countertransference* (pp.1–30). Willmette, IL: Chiron.

Sedgwick, D. (1994). *The Wounded Healer: Countertransference from a Jungian Perspective*. London: Routledge.

Simpson, J. (2023). 'Sanfoka's Quest: Cultivating Queer, African-centred, homecomings through intersectionality in therapy.' In Neves, S. and Davies, D. (eds), *Relationally Queer, A Pink Therapy Guide for Practitioners* (Chapter 7), Routledge, Abingdon.

Smith, F. (2011). *Transcending the Legacies of Slavery: A Psychoanalytic View*. London: Karnac Books.

Winnicott, D. (1960). *The Maturational Processes and the Facilitating Environment*. New York, NY: International Universities Press.

Winnicott, D. (1971). *Playing and Reality*. London: Tavistock Publications.

Winnicott, D. (1974). Fear of breakdown. *International Review of Psychoanalysis*, 1, 103–107.

Weller, F. (2015). *The Wild Edge of Sorrow: Rituals of Renewal and the Sacred Work of Grief*. Berkeley, CA: North Atlantic Books.

Wrye, H.K. & Welles, J.K. (1994). *The Narration of Desire: Erotic Transferences and Countertransferences*. Hillsdale, NJ: Analytic Press.

Young, S. (1989). *Lil' Darlin*. www.youtube.com/watch?v=RlXob-AJWz4.

Chapter 19

Ancestral Constellations

African Healing Ritual with a Therapeutic Edge

SONYA WELCH-MORING

Abstract

Ancestral constellations are short-term therapeutic interventions, that can be regarded as a form of brief therapy. They integrate western systemic thinking and African ancestral family traditions. They are a visual, embodied 'storying' process that explores unresolved past transgenerational relationships. I am interested in how these transgenerational patterns reappear in the current generation, impacting the psychological wellbeing of Black family life.

The constellations process can help to surface these repeating, often hidden family patterns. When they are revealed, steps can be taken to resolve the conflicts in relationships or find healing solutions for other family dilemmas. In my therapeutic practice, I am researching how this approach can be used as a support and resource to strengthen Black family relationships.

My systemic practice has highlighted the connection between a historical legacy of enslavement and colonialism and collective ancestral trauma. The impact of this resulted in social inequality and family fragmentation that has recycled down the generational line. The killing of George Floyd and rise of the Black Lives Matters movement has reinforced this inequality. Together with the Covid-19 pandemic, societal conversations around inequality and race are becoming more mainstream.

In contributing to this book, I want to initiate a social justice conversation around Black transgenerational lives. Ancestral constellations as a therapeutic intervention includes and foregrounds the 'African ancestral' embedded in the constellation's method, something that is often missing in therapy conversations. There is little focus in western counselling and therapy approaches on the ancestral aspects of family life from an indigenous African perspective. In researching the 'ancestral' in therapeutic systemic practice, I am exploring how to integrate a more African-centred process into my work, in the hope that it can be utilized as a strength and resource for Black clients and their families.

I am speaking to therapeutic practitioners from all backgrounds, who are interested in Black psychological wellbeing. And I am speaking specifically, to those of African and Asian heritage who share ancestral family traditions that acknowledge the role of elders and ancestors and who want to bring more of this way of thinking into their practice.

Keywords
Family constellations, systemic practice, ancestral research, Black psychology transgenerational trauma, African-centred therapy, ancestry, mental health, Black family, healing ritual

Introduction
Founded in 2016, ancestral constellations are short-term interventions that explore intergenerational and transgenerational relationships, family dynamics and community legacies. The method is often used in a workshop setting using 'human representatives' who take the place of family members in the process. But it is equally applicable for one-to-one consultations, couple sessions or workplace environments.

Figure 19.1: The Ancestor in the Constellation
© SWMGraphics 2022 Sonya Welch-Moring

Take a moment to imagine your family system. Where is there tension or conflict? Who is involved in the situation or relationship dynamic? Now visualize yourself sitting in a circle of 10 or 12 people. Imagine yourself choosing another participant to 'represent' your father, mother, sibling and other family members.

Then stand and take each of these representatives in turn by the shoulders. Slowly place them in the circle as you 'see them in your mind's eye'. Now add a representative for yourself. Sit back down and observe. Who is close and who is far away? Who is looking forward and who is looking back? Where are you positioned and who is next to you? Which members of the family are standing and who is sitting or lying down?

This is the start of the process of setting up a family constellation. In a workshop setting, a participant explores a personal family issue. This can take a variety of different forms, perhaps a mother–daughter relationship, a sibling conflict or another relationship dynamic that remains unresolved. The other group members are then chosen by the client to 'represent' different family members. This may be parents, grandparents, siblings or other family members.

Bert Hellinger (1925–2019) is known as the developer of the constellations approach, in Europe. He spent many years in Africa as a Catholic priest and missionary, also heading a number of schools in Natal province, South Africa. He observed African Zulu family traditions and when he returned to Europe he became a psychotherapist, author and group facilitator.

He adapted several different psychological traditions to create what became known as a family constellations approach, and integrated some of his South African experiences into this. Although Hellinger acknowledged that his 17 years spent in South Africa left its impact on him, he spoke little about his experiences there after he returned to Europe.

Within my therapeutic practice I draw heavily on the African influence found within the systemic constellations process and I am developing my own healing processes drawing on my experience working with African indigenous spiritual practitioners. I have found that this approach serves the communities that I work with.

I will share some of my learnings from my practice and include parts of my therapy journey. I will also describe my ancestral constellations practice and its impact on my personal ancestral journey. Constellations have helped me to explore themes of identity and belonging. I hope that my personal and professional journey will be of interest to others who want to find out more about their ancestors and cultural traditions.

The therapeutic search for ancestral roots

Up until the global economic crash of 2008, I had a thriving independent practice as a workforce development consultant and professional coach, but I had been ignoring the effects of the stress and toil on my mental health. I had always had an interest in the emotional wellbeing of Black, African Diaspora and Asian people through an earlier career in the therapy and counselling field. I decided that I wanted to transition into a therapeutic career and made the unusual choice to undertake a graduate mental health nursing programme in lieu of a more formal counsellor training.

With many decades of experience working with people, I already had a post-graduate diploma in systemic management, and training in different psychological methods. My first family constellations workshop in 2011 acted as both as an 'ancestral call' to find out more about my family ancestry and a therapeutic approach that I knew could extend and deepen my professional practice.

Before I 'found' family constellations I spent many years 'searching therapy', for what I did not know. I couldn't quite fathom why there was this heavy weight that I seemed to carry on behalf of my family. It was a legacy of anger and rage that has followed me throughout my life as I stepped from childhood into youth and then adulthood. It followed me into my marriage and into my relationships with others – an anger that was not inflicted onto others but an internal rage that felt self-limiting and anxiety provoking. It made me an extremely effective mediator of conflict resolution in the workplace.

I had a long history of therapeutic interventions to support my psychological wellbeing as an African heritage woman of South American Caribbean descent. Like many others, my family moved outside London and away from their 'community' to a predominantly white English community when I was seven. I remember my father's best friend asking my father, 'Why have you brought the girls here?'

For me, my sunny life became grey and bleak! Racism, sometimes subtle, sometimes overt, became a feature of my life. And with it my anger grew! As soon as I could leave home I did, at 17. Back to London, back to a 'community' that I had re-imagined in my mind, but I later realized didn't really exist. I took with me some of the issues that I was to grapple with in therapeutic encounters over many years: low self-esteem, internalized racism (Mckenzie-Mavinga, 2009) and deep and abiding rage!

I first looked for therapeutic help when I was in my late teens. I was drinking too much alcohol and felt an anger that threatened to overwhelm me. I began the therapy journey with six months with one therapist, followed by a range of different personal and spiritual approaches, followed by another six months with a different therapist. It took me until my fifties to find a therapist that I felt, 'okay' with. By then I was on the first step of an ancestral journey that has led me to my current work as a transgenerational facilitator and ancestral researcher.

I mention my therapy history because I have come to believe that a short-term, brief therapy like systemic constellations can offer something to those people not ready to step into longer-term therapy. I believe that many people from African and Asian communities are ready for a form of therapy, but not necessarily a long-term therapeutic relationship.

After I began my family constellations training I realized that the 'weight' that I was carrying, the anger, frustration and shame, was not just mine. I was holding it on behalf of my ancestral line. This is one dimension of the repeating pattern over generations. What has been left over from an earlier relationship can enter a different generation and be carried unknowingly by another family member.

Making sense of relationship entanglements

The ancestral constellations approach seeks to make sense of 'relationship dynamics' in a family or community. The constellations method explores these dynamics by re-including those family members who have for different reasons become excluded from the ancestral line. These people are the missing in the family, the dead, the forgotten and the unknown.

They are Aunt Sally, who nobody speaks of, or Grandfather Edward, who died young and in mysterious circumstances. If they are excluded they cannot belong, and the balance of the family line is disrupted. When everyone is returned to their rightful place within the family system and included, healing can be supported. Then the 'vibrational energy' is restored down the generations, bringing ease and more peace to current and future generations.

During a family constellation, a person who wishes to explore a family dynamic creates an 'embodied visual map' of their family system, past and present. As explained earlier, this is done with the help of other group members, who act as 'representatives' for family members. During this embodied process, the facilitator is responsible for 'holding the space' and other observers in the group who are not chosen as 'representatives' are positioned as 'witnesses' and support for the client doing their 'personal work'.

There is a structured process for clients to 'set up' the representatives from within the group. The person who is exploring their family issue chooses the representatives, based on their intuition or 'strong felt feelings'. They will place a 'representative for a family member' in the constellation space and that person will start to sense the feelings and movement of the family member.

The 'representatives' move in relationship to each other and unremembered or unknown hidden family dynamics emerge. It is the facilitator's task to explore the communication that emerges from the constellation. They may ask questions of the 'representatives'. For example, why they are standing in a particular position or how they are feeling. They use this information to guide the constellation. Others representing family members move, speak and articulate their feelings and emotions. You can see how people, stand, sit and move in relation to each other.

Participants that are representing family members often appear to know how the person feels and are able to express this even though they may not know them. This arises from an intuitive felt sense of the other person, an inner knowing, a deep connection with the person that they are representing. Their verbal feedback and body posture can help to examine some of the core issues within the family. This allows the issues to be explored between those setting up the constellation and the facilitator who is guiding the process.

This may seem unusual, but we often have connections with unknown people. We may walk into a room and suddenly feel sad or angry and realize that we are connecting to the feelings of others. Or we may meet someone who reminds us of a family member or friend. They feel familiar even though we do not know them. Often it is about the way that the person looks, at other times it is a gesture, a way of walking or talking.

How can this be explained to a rational western mind? Often not easily because this sense of knowing has been lost in many western cultures. Yet it is something that many indigenous communities around the world accept and know instinctively. When I have done workshops in the Caribbean, America or with people of African heritage in the UK, there is an understanding of this knowing. It is deep in our bones and psyche, and it is part of the African ancestral traditions that were lost or suppressed during the transatlantic slave trade.

Constellations are a powerful method to aid transformation, reconciliation and healing. As you witness the process unfolding, you gain insight and greater clarity on difficult and complex issues by literally being able to 'see' family and community patterns emerge. The method can help to clarify personal experience and supports clients in becoming more conscious and aware of the dynamics of their own family system.

A step onto the ancestral path

Ancestral constellations from my perspective is a step onto the ancestral path. The ancestral path can be defined as a search for roots, looking back down the ancestral line to explore gaps in knowledge or reconnect to lost or missing cultural traditions. It is a psycho-social approach that lends itself to exploring the intergenerational and transgenerational healing of families, communities and individuals. It is a therapeutic approach that sees us all in relationship with each other: the individual, the community, society, nature and ancestors, a world that integrates the living and the dead.

Ancestral constellations can be viewed as a type of applied genealogy or 'embodied' ancestral family tree. There is growing interest in exploring transgenerational lives from an African Diaspora perspective and this approach can support the search for identity. Black people want to find out more about their ancestors, cultural lineage and collective histories. They are seeking DNA tests and exploring ancestry websites, while others are taking courses in genealogy, hoping to find out more about their family traditions.

Slavery, genocide, wars and colonialism result in migration, immigration, social injustice, poor health and economic inequality. Even though slavery ended two centuries ago, societal influences remain that lead to discriminatory practices. These systemic oppressions remain in the psyche and DNA of many family histories, resulting in patterns of behaviours and ways of thinking that can be passed from one generation to another.

All these issues contribute to the breakdown of the African Diasporan family system. And they all impact the psychological wellbeing of Black transgenerational lives. When I am working with Black clients facilitating their constellation, I can clearly see the connection between a historical legacy of enslavement, colonialism and ancestral trauma handed down the family over generations. Today we see the influence of these historical traumas in parenting relationships, split and dispersed families and second-, third-, fourth-generation questions about identity and belonging.

Ancestral constellations can give clients an opportunity to explore these unresolved intergenerational and transgenerational patterns. In my practice with communities of colour, there is no clear distinction between individual family dynamics and community trauma. Social and political considerations are always in the background, if not always actively addressed.

Dynamics of African ancestral practice

In many African cultures, ancestors are regarded as part of the living family after death. They have a place in the family system and are remembered and honoured. When I first saw a family constellation, it felt very familiar! I recognized some of the constellation's process as a healing ritual drawing on African traditions, and I wanted to find out more about the 'ancestral' in the constellation, a metaphor that I use to describe the search for 'other ways of knowing'.

Ancestral constellations are African healing rituals with a therapeutic edge. A way to begin to 're-member' what has been forgotten and a 'rite-of-passage' ceremony. Many Diaspora communities through the process of colonialism and slavery have lost connection with the healing power of African ritual. Malidoma Some, a Dagara Elder who I have worked with and who has extensive experience of both family constellations and indigenous African wisdom, says this about family constellations and ritual:

> I do not know where the term Family Constellation comes from and my knowledge of the historicity of it is, at best spotty. However, I have had ample exposure to and involvement with the process to know that Family Constellations is one of the many faces of ritual. We define ritual as the involvement with spirit in sacred space for our healing. (E-Village News, 2010)

The aim in developing ancestral constellations has been to create a process, that is more 'African-centred'. By incorporating ancestral family research, can we give a voice to what has been forgotten or lost? By connecting to ancestral memories, can indigenous 'other ways of knowing' be used as a resource to support psychological wellbeing?

These questions guide my workshops in which memories of ancestral trauma often surface. In a presentation, given to the Confer

Conference on Post-Slavery Syndrome, 22–23 March 2019, Dr Aileen Alleyne described the difference between intergenerational and transgenerational trauma. Intergenerational trauma crosses generations, for example through secrets, lies, shame and guilt. It impacts relationships within and between family members. Transgenerational trauma, on the other hand, explores the psychological legacies of multiple generations of families and communities over centuries. There is usually a historical dimension.

Problematic family patterns and relationships also often bring participants to constellations work who are angry. Isha Mckenzie-Mavinga (2009) speaks eloquently about Black rage and the need to give space to it in the individual therapeutic relationship. I consider this to also be true within my ancestral constellations practice.

Behind the stories that emerge in my work, I can see that rage, hidden, controlled and very present. It is retold in the constellation that reveals the split family and children left behind while their parents go in search of work; the constellation that reveals the pain of losing a brother to gang violence; the constellation that reveals the heartache and burden of poor mental health in a family system.

While these issues are not the preserve of those of African heritage, anger, shame and guilt are all regularly featured in family constellations workshops. A traumatized ancestral legacy of slavery, colonialism and racism also appears and reveals 'that which has not disappeared': racism and discrimination recycling in family patterns. Unexplored issues of identity and belonging are also often present as themes in families and community life.

Time after time I would start to facilitate a client constellation and realize that the impact of the environment, the community and the family history was much larger in the constellation than the presenting 'personal issue'. Additionally, the dislocation, distance and fragmentation of many family structures as a result of community traumas, war, slavery, mass migration makes the community experience an integral part of the family experience.

As we explore together in 'constellations space' each other's family stories, it is possible to share something deep, a present-day struggle or family turmoil. It is as though there is a wider sense of knowing, that goes beyond family and includes an unacknowledged past collective trauma history. Alongside this as the constellation develops, participants begin to understand more the interrelatedness of family and community, within which is the ancestral call to repair and heal our family heritage.

The ancestral constellations approach

Ancestral constellations honour both our ancestral line and family research that can support personal exploration of identity and belonging. In developing an ancestral constellation, three key features of African indigenous wisdom are highlighted:

1. The creation of a sacred space through an explicit acknowledgement of ancestors.

2. The exploration of ritual as a form of family and community healing of trauma.

3. The foregrounding of the indigenous African wisdom that is embedded in the method.

The notion of 'sacred space' is created before participants enter the room, through the use of a ritual and an invocation. There is a mini ancestral shrine with flowers, water, incense and representatives for the elders in the form of 'diaspora dollies' sourced from South Africa. This represents those from the past that are connected to us in the present.

The ceremony is not elaborate and does not have to be named within the group; the ancestral shrine just sits behind the group as we do the work. Before we start an individual constellation, there is acknowledgement of the family system and ancestors from the past to help guide us in the present.

During the workshop, there are also parts of the process that are rituals of connection and sometimes forgiveness in relationships; for example, ways of forming healing sentences through 'call and repeat' patterns or communication spoken between family members that help ease painful situations. Bowing to those we seek to honour is also another constellations practice.

Several examples of African indigenous wisdom can be found within the constellations process, in relation to levels of authority, rules of respect and the different orders within the relationship system. These include:

1. A clearly defined order to how family members stand in relation to each other.

2. Rituals like 'bowing' to elders and acknowledging authority and precedence.

3. Call and repeat patterns with clarifying or healing sentences.

Ancestral Constellations

4. Ancestors being welcomed into the process as a part of the family.

5. Elders are given a place of respect and precedence.

6. Acknowledgement of the role of nature in community and family life.

A personal case study

A constellation is an oral story about family legacy and ancestral inheritance. One of the main principles of constellations work is to include the excluded. This is done by the facilitator asking questions about family history. The excluded often show up as silence in the family system. They may be the alcoholic grandparent that no one talks about or the aunt who was never diagnosed, but everyone knew had a severe mental health problem.

Family members often do not want to think or remember these painful periods in family history. Other ways of excluding people are by not talking about miscarriages or abortions, because they are painful and sometimes taboo subjects, as is the loss of young lives in childhood.

In one personal family constellation I explored my father's generational line. I knew that he had an elder brother and a younger half-sister and brother. I had met them once when we returned to Guyana for a visit when I was a teenager. The facilitator of this particular constellation was very experienced and from the movements of the representatives, she hypothesized that there may be a sibling missing in the family system. 'Did your father have another sibling?' the facilitator asked. I was puzzled, as my father had never spoken about another sibling. 'I don't think so', I replied.

However, undeterred she put an extra 'representative' into the constellation for a possible unknown brother or sister. Determined to find out the truth I went home and asked my father. Sure enough, he revealed a family secret, my uncle who had been born between my father's younger sister and brother. It turned out that my aunt had accidentally either stood or sat on the child, who had subsequently died. It was never spoken about in the family again.

This incident showed me not only the power of the constellation's method, but the necessity for me to carry out my own family research. Over the next few years, I learned a lot more about my ancestral lineage. Over time, my father opened up and we deepened our relationship. I started to travel to Guyana and reconnect with members of my family

291

on both sides. And when my father died in 2018 I felt at peace. I had done as much as I could to bring a fragmented family system back into 'vibrational balance' and relationship harmony.

Conclusion: Re-membering as support for Black psychological wellbeing

Emerging questions from my practice include: 'How can constellations support the recovery of family memories? And in what way does that impact on the psychological wellbeing of individuals and families from African Diaspora communities?

A well-anchored connection to one's identity and belonging supports psychological wellbeing. For many people in African Diaspora communities, the search for identity and belonging is steeped in difficulty. There can be a loss of strong identity, or a deep knowledge of 'who I am' and 'where I belong' when migration and immigration has been part of the family story. A collective community past is often viewed through the filter of western European versions of history. These do not tell the full picture or often do not take a Black transgenerational perspective into account.

People often come to family constellations seeking answers to questions like, 'What is a homeland?' and 'Where are my ancestral roots?' Individual research into family ancestry, asking questions of parents, grandparents and other family members is an option. One problem with this is that often these family members do not want to remember the past or give information to later generations. DNA testing is another form of research, and revisiting parental homelands and ancestral hinterlands is also becoming more common.

Collective ancestral trauma, acknowledged and unacknowledged often resides in the body (Menakem, 2017) as memories. The embodied process of ancestral constellations can help 'liberate' these ancestral memories and reconnect us to a different time and place. By surfacing these memories, we can also reclaim our ancestors and cultural inheritance.

The Covid-19 pandemic has forced us to find other ways to bring this work to the world. I am using the creative tools of small figurines, Diaspora dollies, as I have named them. They are created by South African women and bring to the work a touch of 'African energy' to support the process. Going forward, I will continue to develop the process as an African-centred ritual healing process, with roots strongly in ancestral wisdom traditions. And there will be opportunities for you to learn and train in the approach. You can find out more on my website at www.ancestralconstellations.com.

References

Confer Conference 22–23 March 2019. Post-Slavery Syndrome: Exploring the Clinical Impact of the Trans-Atlantic Slave Trade. A recording of the conference can be found at www.confer.uk.com/module/module-slavery.html.

E-Village News (2010) pdf, p.6 https://eastcoastvillage.org/

Mckenzie-Mavinga, I. (2009). *Black Issues in the Therapeutic Process*. London: Palgrave Macmillan.

Menakem, R. (2017). *My Grandmother's Hands*. Las Vegas, NV: Central Recovery Press.

Chapter 20

A Journey in Decolonizing Therapy

OYE AGORO

Abstract

This chapter explores my personal experience of delivering therapy as a female therapist of Yoruba ancestry, drawing on my background in sociology and anthropology and over 30 years' experience of working in community therapy and mental health services as a therapist, supervisor, and manager.

The chapter outlines a model of social justice allied therapy based on a multi-dimensional liberation framework that promotes wellbeing and healing within a context of decolonization.

The chapter outlines an approach to therapeutic work which incorporates a critical analysis of the following and their significance to decolonizing therapy:

- The impact of neoliberal hegemony on wellbeing

- Intersectionality

- Trauma legacies

- Internalized oppression

- The problem of talking therapies and cultural imperialism

- What is decolonized therapy?

Keywords

Decolonization, intersectionality, cultural-competency, multi-dimensional, social trauma, internalized oppression, anti-oppressive

Introduction

When spider webs unite, they can tie up a lion.

This is an Ethiopian African proverb meaning: When we stand together, we can become bigger than ourselves.

As a cis woman of Yoruba ancestry, born in London during the 1960s due to the complex colonial history of Nigeria and Britain, I am aware that the way that I see and understand the world has been impacted by my social location and my lived experiences in the global north. My identity, along with an academic background in sociology and social anthropology, has greatly influenced the way that I choose to practice as a therapist. This chapter outlines my journey through decolonizing therapy.

Over my 30-year career as a therapist and supervisor, I have been increasingly drawn to the world views and understanding provided by intersectionality (Crenshaw, 2016), the liberation psychologists (Martin-Baro, 1994), anti-oppressive therapy (Dominelli, 2002), intercultural therapy (Kareem & Littlewood, 1999), feminist therapy (Eichenbaum & Orbach, 2013) and African-centred psychology (Akbar, 1996). These frames of reference have helped me to understand my emotional and psychological experiences of the world, and helped to make sense of the significant number of clients I have seen, who have displayed overt and sometimes less obvious expressions of distress related to experiences of institutional and/or intersectional inequalities and violence.

Neoliberalism

The consequences of living within the myth of white supremacist, patriarchal neoliberal economies are multifaceted. Neoliberal values have colonized the planet and now form the fabric of all our lives, imbedded and internalized in the ways that we see and treat ourselves, those around us and the planet. Neoliberalism has been characterized as glorifying aggressive competition, with the most important value being placed on the smooth operation of free markets, globalization, and the ruthless drive to maximize profits. Alongside this there has been a disregard for inequalities and the consequences of economic poverty, rapid depletion of resources, extreme and irreversible damage to the environment, and the erosion and destruction of cultures (Hervey, 2005; Sugarman, 2015; Brown, 2003).

Increasingly, the values underlying neoliberalism are being seen has having huge implications for our psychology and the assumptions that we hold about ourselves. Health, wellbeing, and human progress are often uncritically associated with embracing materialism, commodification, the importance of humans controlling nature, and people being seen as flexible units of production and responsible for their own success within the myth of neoliberal meritocracy. This is all underpinned by the championing of abstract individualism rooted in ableist, masculinist patriarchal, heteronormative belief systems, which can be seen as promoting narcissistic personality development.

The neoliberal vision represented by international corporations has been identified as being psychopathic (Achbar & Abbot, 2004; Abbot & Bakan, 2021) as outlined by criteria in the *Diagnostic and Statistical Manual of Mental Disorders* (American Psychiatric Association, 2017).

I believe that the cultural legacy of neoliberalism can be seen in the following realities in the world:

- The world's 22 richest men have more combined wealth than all 325 million women in Africa (Oxfam 2020). With 689 million people living on less than $1.90 a day, the world's richest 1 per cent owns twice as much as the bottom 90 per cent (PND, 2020). The Covid-19 pandemic is estimated to have pushed an additional 97 million people into extreme poverty in 2021 (World Bank, 2021).

- Globally 264 million suffer from depression (World Health Organization, 2017) and close to 800,000 people die due to suicide every year. Suicide is the second leading cause of death in 15–19-year-olds. Depression is the leading cause of disability worldwide. In addition WHO state that 264 million people suffer from anxiety. While an estimated 75 per cent of people with mental health disorders remain untreated in the global south.

Racism: A historical context

As a black diasporic woman, I know that the ethnic diversity in Britain today is the legacy of an imperialist history. This history included the emergence of capitalism from the transatlantic trade in enslaved peoples and the colonization of North America, along with the economic plunder, exploitation and genocide of peoples from Australasia, Africa, Asia and the Americas. It is being increasingly understood that any analysis of racism needs to be historic.

Racism has been defined as: 'An ideology which identifies a social group according to a particular biological characteristic and uses this to draw negative assumptions regarding that group's nature or capabilities' (Karlsen & Nazrro, 2007).

Skin colour has been the rationale and justification for racialized social hierarchies – white racism, rooted in the myth of white supremacy, has become historically enmeshed and fused with the development and expansion of capitalism and neoliberalism. Ruth Wilson Gilmore, the well-known geographer, describes this as racial capitalism (2020).

Skin colour hierarchies have been, and still are, an integral part of the histories of the global north and the global south, with racialized capitalism/neoliberalism observable today in the exploitation of peoples and the environment, especially in the global south. This is seen through: the destruction of rainforests and communities in South America; the widespread pollution and effects of the oil industry in the delta regions in Nigeria; the effects of the extraction and mining of Coltan for electronic devices in Democratic Republic of Congo; the deforestation and destruction of communities caused by palm oil plantations in Indonesia to meet the demand for palm oil in products.

Historically and currently, lighter and darker skin tones are coded based on ideas of the myth of white supremacy, where lighter skin tones are widely still admired and converted – consciously or unconsciously – because they symbolize the colour of colonial rulers. Within the myth of white supremacist ideology, white skin tones are seen as more beautiful and embodying superior traits such as: purity, intelligence and civilization. In comparison, darker skin tones are seen as being negative, inferior, a marker of being primitive, dirty, uncivilized and sexually provocative.

Western psychotherapy, psychology and psychiatry have had little to say about racism. At best, there has been an absence of an analysis. At worst, racism and colonization practices of the global north have been actively supported through the influence of some aspects of European science, namely eugenics, which has had a close association with ideas of white supremacy. The Encyclopaedia Britannica of the 1950s and 1960s (the modern equivalent of which is Wikipedia) printed, as scientific fact, that black people had smaller brains than white people, proclaiming that black people were less intelligent.

An important starting place in decolonizing therapy is the moral and ethical responsibility of accepting and acknowledging the history of racism and its relationship to neoliberalism and capitalism, and how it affects the wellbeing of us all. Without this analysis we run the risk denying racism, which can cause additional psychological and emotional damage to Black, Asian and Minority Ethnic (BAME) clients, and basically means that we are doing harm despite our best intentions.

Intersectionality: A starting point

Intersectionality has been defined as: 'Ways of understanding how aspects of a person's social and political identity combine to create different modes of discrimination and privilege' (Runyan, (2018).

The term was first introduced by Kimberlé Crenshaw (2016), and can be seen as drawing on the work of Audrey Lorde (1984, 2017) Angela Davis (2016) and Patricia Hill Collins (2002). Basically, it promotes an understanding and analysis of oppression that recognizes that racism, gender, class, religious and other forms of discrimination are not stand-alone inequalities but are often intertwined, interconnected and fused together in complex ways. For example, in thinking about Covid-19 infections and deaths, taking an intersectional framework we can hypothesis that the higher death rates in BAME communities may be a combination of race/racism, class, gender, housing and occupation, and working patterns.

Intersectionality is increasingly being seen as a valuable framework for understanding therapeutic work (Turner, 2021). When using an intersectional framework, an important starting point is for all of us to be aware of our social locations. Our personal and family histories, and our ever-changing identities affect what we see, what we are unable to see, and how we hear and interpret the narratives of clients we listen to.

Using an intersectional framework as a therapist can help us to be more self-aware in understanding our own social location in relation to privilege, discrimination, inequalities, and oppressions related to class, race/racism, gender, ethnicity, education, ability, sexuality, age, immigration status, religion and whether somebody's first or second or third language is English (see Figure 20.1).

Most of us experience positions of privilege and discrimination and being aware of this can help us to be mindful of power dynamics in operation, and how the social location of therapists and clients may impact on the therapeutic process. Our visible markers of privilege and discrimination such as our gender, skin colour, the way we present ourselves in our bodies, our names, and the ways we use language are all likely to impact on the therapeutic relationship we have with clients.

A Journey in Decolonizing Therapy

Having conscious awareness of this enables us to make conscious choices as therapists, which might mean that we just hold this awareness in mind, or this awareness may be an important area of exploration in the therapeutic work.

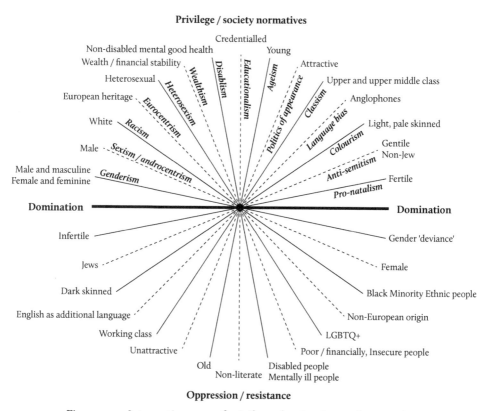

Figure 20.1: Intersecting axes of privilege, domination and oppression. Adapted from Natalya Dell (2014). Adapted from Pauly Morgan (1996)

When working as a therapist within an intersectional framework, I'm suggesting that a critical starting place is having an understanding and awareness of our social location and lived experiences (Dee Watts-Jones, 2010). Our social locations and identities will also impact what we are unable to hear or acknowledge in client narratives. I think this point is well illustrated in *Carl Rogers Counsels an Individual on Anger* (Rogers, 1974), where the white therapist Rogers, despite his pioneering work in developing person-centred therapies, struggles to hear and attend to the black male client's experience of racism and the pain it generates, and the power dynamics operating in the space between them. Isha

Mckenzie-Mavinga (2009) talks about the importance of the black empathic approach to address these issues.

Social trauma

Racism, discrimination and other forms of intersectional violence are increasingly being seen as a trauma. Racism is now being understood as producing a chronic stress response resulting in trauma and in some cases intergenerational trauma (Mckenzie-Mavinga, 2009). Oppression trauma is a 'social trauma' that deeply impacts on the psyche of the individual and affects the wellbeing of whole communities.

Recent developments in the field of epigenetics have established that trauma can be transmitted through parental genes over generations (DeGruy, 2017). The fact that this analysis has been pioneered and emerged from trying to understand the experiences of the children of Jewish Holocaust survivors is important to note in thinking about the histories and changing patterns of colonization and racism around the world.

Eduardo Duran, a liberation psychologist in the US, has developed innovative therapeutic practices around identifying culturally appropriate ways of working with First Nations and Indigenous communities, and the effects of social traumas such as genocide, land loss and the devaluation of culture. Indigenous and First Nations communities recognize these issues to be historical traumas going back over seven generations. From their ancestral knowledge, they see these past traumas as alive in current generations. Duran's therapeutic work provides a powerful and inspiring way of working therapeutically within the value and belief systems of Indigenous and First Nations peoples. He chooses to describe his work as healing cultural soul wounds (2021).

Essentially, the current understanding of oppression and intersectional violence indicates that many people are continuously living in a high stress response state, which for many individuals becomes post-traumatic stress disorder and complex post-traumatic syndrome that can be transmitted over generations affecting whole communities (Holmes, Facemire & DaFonseca, 2016).

As therapists, when we identify and become aware that a client may have experienced 'social trauma' it opens the possibility to name and explore the client's experience and narrative around the experience. Promoting the possibility of this exploration allows for the naming of historical and current survival strategies and resilience. It also allows for the opportunity to collaboratively explore the strengths and disadvantages of different strategies and resilience practices and the possibility of identifying different ones.

These interventions are likely to promote safety, resilience, and wellbeing, which are important protective factors in coping with, and resisting, oppression and structural inequalities, central to working within a decolonizing and intersectional framework. Without conscious awareness of social trauma, the opportunity for consideration and exploration of this area in therapy can be easily missed.

Internalized/Injected oppression

From my experience of working as a therapist and supervisor, I have concluded that no understanding of inequalities and oppression from a therapeutic perspective can be complete without and understanding of internalized oppression, or injected oppression – a term used by Wekesa Madzimoyo (2021).

Internalized or injected oppression is the process where we internalize and act out the negative stereotypes and myths about social groups that are often promoted by dominant cultural groups. Gramsci describes this as ruling class hegemony (1999). Franz Fanon clearly describes the effects of internalized racism in his book *Black Skin, White Masks* (1982).

This internalization process can result in feelings of self-hatred, shame, low self-esteem and conscious and subconscious feelings of not being good enough, potentially leading to false negative stereotypes becoming self-fulfilling prophecy.

The ways we consciously and subconsciously act out dominant discourses around ableism, ageism, class, gender, heteronormality, patriarchy and racism are complex and diverse.

Below are some examples of internalized/injected oppression.

Shadism/colourism – the acceptance and acting out of skin colour hierarchies in BAME communities, where lighter skin tones are admired and desired because they consciously or unconsciously symbolize the colour of white colonial rulers. One of the manifestations of shadism and colourism throughout the world can be seen in the use of skin-whitening products. Seventy-seven per cent of Nigerian women, 59 per cent in Togo, 50 per cent in the Philippines and 45 per cent in Hong Kong use skin whitening products (Mercury Policy Project, 2010). The World Health Organization has linked skin-whitening products to skin scarring, skin rashes, kidney failure, anxiety and depression (David, 2014). Skin-bleaching products are also on sale in many black beauty shops across the UK.

Uncritical acceptance of capitalism (internalized capitalism) – being enslaved to consumerism, the accumulation of money and material goods being seen as the primary marker of self-worth. The internalization and glorification of capitalist/western values can be seen in the embracing of rugged individualism, objectification and commodification. The material wealth of the capitalist economies of the global north is directly related to the profits obtained from the transatlantic trade in enslaved peoples, and colonization and appropriation of natural resources and ongoing exploitation of black and brown peoples from the global south.

Overworking – marginalized/oppressed group members overworking to be better or to gain acceptance from the dominant group. Overworking being the major driving force in one's life due to conscious or subconscious feelings of not being good enough and needing white/male approval to feel validated. This can be seen as the internalization of historical colonial and plantation-type dynamics.

Hyper-sexualization of black people – the internalization of white supremacist stereotypes of black sexuality, with black men and women typically being portrayed as sexually uninhibited and provocative, which is often reflected in the number of portrayals of black women on screen as 'whores' or 'prostitutes'. The sexualization of black women within white supremacy can be seen as justifying the systemic perpetration of sexual violence against black women during colonization and the transatlantic trade in enslaved peoples, alongside black men historically being seen as a threat to white femininity (hooks, 1996).

Passive acquiescence – being passive in response to inequality, living lives of unrealized potential (Watermeyer & Görgens, 2014). This reflects the subjugation and disempowerment that can occur under oppression, a form of learned helpless.

'Strong black women' trope – promotes the stereotype of black women as caregivers, servicing others with a smile, being there for everybody, creating the expectation that black women can cope with everything (Wallace, 1979). The strong black women trope can be seen as a form of dehumanization that assumes that black women do not have emotions and have a superhuman ability to deal with everything (Ira, 2020). Internalization of this stereotype can lead to self-sacrificing behaviours and difficulties in showing vulnerability or seeking help, along with an extreme drive to succeed, despite limited resources. The internalization and acting out of this stereotype can have significant consequences for black women's physical, emotional and spiritual health (Woods-Giscombe *et al.*, 2019).

Internalization and acting out of violence

In the UK, black men are twice as likely to be the victims of violent crime in cities, with police identifying that most of the crime in cities is being committed by black men. The high death rates of young black men from homicide in the UK and US have been linked to the internalization and glorification of black male stereotypes, often characterized as criminal, violent, aggressive and masculinist. As a result of peer group members being seen as inferior, anger and rage are directed horizontally at other group members rather than upwards at the dominant group.

As practitioners, we must be aware that there are critical issues around how rage and anger associated with intersectional violence and oppression can be expressed which can have enormous ramifications. Historically and currently, there are significant sanctions against some individuals/groups showing anger, especially black men, and women (hooks, 1996; Keating, 2002), who are more likely to be sectioned under the Mental Health Act than gain access to therapy.

If, as therapists we choose to position ourselves within a decolonizing and anti-oppressive framework, the therapy that we offer will have at its root a moral commitment to eradicating racism and delivering interventions that actively promote anti-racism. I'm therefore suggesting that an important function of therapy is to provide a space where patterns of internalized racism/oppression can be explored and dismantled in a safe, non-judgemental and compassionate environment. I believe that a safe and compassionate environment can be created by being aware of the ways that we are all in positions of privilege and discrimination. We all, at some point, act out internalized oppression dynamics as a way of surviving in environments which are hostile to the bodies that we inhabit.

Bringing an understanding of oppression and internalized or injected oppression into our therapeutic work can have a significant impact on the way we conceptualize a client's narrative and experiences of distress. Many presentations of distress, such as depression and self-harming within marginalized populations, can be viewed as an unambiguous expression of oppression.

Racism and other oppressions are often seen as only impacting and affecting the group directly experiencing racism – members of BAME communities. But racism and other oppressions can also be seen as affecting those in positions of power and dominance. By being complicit in oppression within our positions of privilege, we not only dehumanize those being oppressed but also dehumanize ourselves as perpetuators of oppression and intersectional violence. Diminishing our humanity has real emotional, psychological and spiritual consequences.

The interconnected nature of oppression, discrimination and intersectional violence can result in most of us unconsciously or consciously moving in and out of re-enacting positions of internalized domination and oppression in dynamic and complex ways.

As therapists, being aware of internalized or injected racism provides an important lens for considering and analysing the therapeutic alliances we form with clients. A compassionate and non-judgemental awareness of these dynamics can enable us to provide emotionally safe spaces for clients to unpack and deconstruct these narratives. This may help to ensure that clients are likely to bring more of themselves into the therapeutic space, rather than feeling the need to self-censor to avoid further social trauma from the therapeutic relationship.

Cultural competence

Cultural competence has been identified as a key issue in anti-racist and anti-oppressive practice and an essential skill when working cross-culturally, interculturally or transculturally (Nichols, 1997; Sue, 2002; Duran, 2021).

Our values, beliefs and identities as practitioners can have a significant impact on how we understand client narratives. An awareness of dominant western cultural values within psychotherapy and wider society is essential to ensure that these values are not imposed on our clients without conscious awareness, negotiation or agreement with our clients. Otherwise, we will be in danger of practising cultural imperialism, which has been referenced as a critical issue when working interculturally, cross-culturally or transculturally (Gilbert, 2006).

The values of western culture and western science are often obscured by the myth that western philosophy, culture and science are described as being natural and without bias. There is an unspoken assumption that other belief systems are deficient – an outlook described by Sebene Selassie as epistemicide (2020).

To think about the issues that cultural differences raise and how these differences can be played out in therapeutic relationships, I've drawn on the pioneering work of Edwin Nichols in his axiology paradigm (see Figure. 20.2), which highlights the importance of recognizing the axiology or values of differing world views.

Edwin Nichols: Cultural values and world views

Edwin Nichols suggests that there are four main axiologies, with each world view having a 'cultural essence':

- European, Euro-American

- African, Arab and Latinx

- Asian/Polynesian

- Native American/Indigenous.

However, given the ideological influence of white supremacist stereotypes, I believe it is important to be mindful about not reinforcing negative stereotypes or making generalizations about whole communities.

Member (relating/relationships)

Nichols identifies that in western culture, relationships and relating have a focus on the object or the acquisition of the object. I suggest that this can be linked to the values and belief systems underlying capitalism and neoliberalism. People are seen as production units, where individualism, commodification and materialism are actively valued and pursued. In comparison, in Asian cultures the highest value in relationships and relating is seen as being in the cohesion of the group. The highest value in African cultures is relationships and relating is seen as lying in the relationship between people. In Indigenous cultures, the highest value is seen as being in the relationship with the great spirit and togetherness with the great spirit.

Epistemology – Applied (knowing)

Nichols suggests that Indigenous peoples/Native Americans know through reflection and spiritual receptivity, such as purification rites. With African cultures, there is knowing through symbolic imagery, rhythm and intuition, or the ability to understand something immediately without the need for conscious reasoning. However, in western culture, knowing is achieved through counting and measuring with a focus on cognition. In Asian cultures, knowing is seen as coming from transcendental striving – conation.

Epistemology – Pedagogy (knowledge)

Knowledge systems in Asian cultural beliefs are characterized by the whole and parts being seen simultaneously. I feel this is expressed in Daoist knowledge systems and the idea of yin and yang and the emphasis on balance between the two. In comparison, in Indigenous knowledge systems the whole is seen in cyclic movement and seasons – the Medicine Wheel. African knowledge systems are viewed as more holistic, with a focus on the whole big picture. However, western knowledge systems go from parts to the whole, taking an atomistic view. In western medicine, psychiatry and talking therapies, this can be seen in the focus on symptoms to make a diagnosis.

Epistemology – Methodology (thinking process)

In Indigenous/Native American culture the methodology or thinking process is seen as environmentally experiential reflection, for example rites of passage. In western culture, the thinking process is linear and sequential, perhaps best illustrated by the assembly line in industrial neoliberal settings. In Asian cultures, the methodology can be seen as cyclical and repetitive, whereas in African, Latinx and Arab cultures Nichols describes the thinking process as critical path analysis – cutting to the chase (being direct or to the point).

Logic

In African, Latinx and Arab cultures, logic can be seen as diunital, a unison of opposites, a kind of duality which Nichols compares to Quantum Theory. On the other hand, in Asian cultures the objective world is independent of mind and thought – Nyaya – comparable to Chaos Theory. Within Native American cultures, Nichols describes logic as being the Great Mystery, with a set of four and a set of three forming the whole – like Super String Theory. Lastly, western logic is characterized as being dicrotous or binary – either/or – comparable to Newtonian Theory.

EPISTEMOLOGY

ETHNIC GROUPS WHO CAME TO THE US AND GROUPS WHO SHARE AN ETHNIC WORLD VIEW	AXIOLOGY	EPISTEMOLOGY		Methodology	LOGIC
		Applied	**Pedagogy**		
European Euro-American	Member-Object *The highest value lies in the object and acquisition of said objects*	One knows through counting and measuring	Parts to whole Atomistic – inductive Thinking	Linear and Sequential *Step 1 leads to Step 2 leads to Step 3; etc.*	Dichotomous *Either/or and no in between*
African African American Latino/a Arab	Member-member *The highest value lies in the relationships between persons*	One knows through symbolic imagery and rhythm	Whole Holistic – deductive Thinking *The big picture*	Critical path analysis *Cut to the chase*	Diunital *Union of opposites*
Asian Asian American Polynesian	Member-Group *The highest value lies in the cohesiveness of the group*	One knows through transcendental striving	Whole and parts are seen simultaneously	Critical and repetitive	Nyaya *The objective world is conceived independent of thought and mind*
Native American	Member-Great Spirit *The highest value lies in oneness with the great spirit*	One knows through reflection and spiritual receptivity	Whole is seen in cyclic movement *Seasons* *Medicine Wheel*	Environmentally Experiential reflection *Rites of passage*	Great Mysteries Disrasismo – union of opposites *A set of 4 and a set of 3 form the whole*

Nichols, 2008

Figure 20.2: Cultural competency paradigm – the philosophical aspects of cultural difference, developed by Nichols (2008)

In thinking about these essences within cultures, it becomes easier to identify the western values that are present in western therapy practice that actively promote neoliberalism:

- Emphasis on mind and cognition of the individual, which can promote a disconnection from our bodies and interpersonal relationships within communities.

- Importance on counting and measuring, which can be seen in the importance placed on randomized trials to identify effectiveness of therapies/interventions. Great value is placed on biomedical interventions.

- Seeing individuals as separate units – rather than the individual being seen as part of a wider community.

- Emphasis on time and deadlines. Nichols outlines how the focus and preoccupation with time and deadlines in the global north is related to historical geographical conditions and the significance and legacy of narrow growing seasons in the northern hemisphere.

- Importance being placed on doing and action orientation, with a tendency to pathologize being.

- A progress and future orientation, which can negate the value of being in the moment.

- Value being placed on dichotomous, binary, either/or and hierarchal thinking, which can be seen as prompting structural inequalities such as racism and sexism (Nichols, 1997).

- Value being placed on commodification and materialism and achieving success within neoliberal meritocracy, through taking individual responsibility and exhibiting self-discipline and striving for continual personal development and material wealth.

Having a conscious awareness of dominant white cultural values and neoliberal values as therapists can help us to ensure these values are not automatically being transmitted into our therapeutic practice.

Conclusion

To conclude, when providing therapy within a context of decolonization and intersectionality, I've outlined how this positioning is multifaceted and complex, and that the following important elements need to be incorporated into the therapy framework:

- An understanding of intersectionality and intersectional violence.

- A historical analysis of racism and awareness of the racialization of capitalism and neoliberalism.

- A high level of self-awareness and the ability to understand our own social location and the social locations of clients, along with an awareness of how these social locations may impact on the therapeutic alliance.

- An understanding of social trauma and oppression trauma legacies, for clients within a wider context of communities and intergenerational trauma.

- A critical awareness of western cultural values and commitment to not promoting epistemicide.

- Cultural competence, and an ability to think about interventions that take into consideration a client's culture and beliefs.

- Externalization of social inequalities – mindfully and proactively moving away from therapeutic interventions that blame clients for their experiences of racism and other oppressions and intersectional violence.

It can be said that much of African philosophy and cultural values are held within the meaning of proverbs which are passed from generation to generation. As an older woman of the African Diaspora, I find that the following Congolese proverb aptly reflects my challenges around attempting to offer therapy within the context of decolonization and intersectionality:

No matter how long the night, the day is sure to come.

References

Akbar, N. (1996). *Breaking the Chains of Psychological Slavery*. Tallahassee, FL: Mind.
Abbot, J. & Bakan, J. (2021). *The New Corporation: The Unfortunately Necessary Sequel* [film]. Vancouver: Grant Street Productions.

Achbar, M. & Abbot, J. (2004). *The Corporation: A Documentary* [film]. Vancouver: Big Picture Media Corporation.

American Psychiatric Association. (2017) *Diagnostic and Statistical Manual of Mental Disorders*, fifth edition. DSM-5.Cbs Publishing, American Psychiatric Association Publishing, Washington DC.

Martin-Baro, I. (1996) *Writings for a Liberation Psychology*. Harvard University Press, Cambridge, Massachusetts.

Brown, W . (2003). Neoliberalism and the end of liberal democracy. *Theory & Event*, 7, 37–59.

Butler, P. (2020). Nearly half of BAME UK households are living in Poverty. *The Guardian* (Online) www.theguardian.com/society/2020/jul/01/nearly-half-of-bame-uk-households -are-living-in-poverty.

Crenshaw, K. (2016). *The Urgency of Intersectionality* [video]. www.ted.com/talks/kimberle_crenshaw_the_urgency_of_intersectionality.

David, E. (2014). *Internalized Oppression: The Psychology of Marginalized Groups*. New York, NY: Springer Publishing.

Davids, F. (2011). *Internal Racism: A Psychoanalytic Approach to Race and Difference*. London: Red Globe Press.

Dell, N. (2014). *Intersecting Axes of Privilege, Domination, And Oppression*. https://sites.google.com/site/natalyadell/home/intersectionality.

Dee Watts-Jones, T. (2010) Location of Self: Opening the Door to Dialogue on Intersectionality in the Therapy Process. www.ackerman.org/wp-content/uploads/2015/12/Watts-Jones-Dee-Location_of_Self.pdf

DeGruy, J.A. (2017). *Post Traumatic Slave Syndrome, Revised Edition: America's Legacy of Enduring Injury and Healing*. Portland, OR: Joy DeGruy Publications.

Dominelli, L. (2002). *Anti-Oppressive Social Work Theory and Practice*. London: Palgrave Macmillan.

Duran, E. (2019). *Healing the Soul Wound: Trauma Informed Counselling for Indigenous Communities* (Multicultural Foundations of Psychology & Counselling Series). NY: Teachers College Press.

Eichenbaum, L., Orbach S. (2003). *Understanding Women*. CentreSpace Independent Publishing Platform, Scotts Valley, California.

Fanon, F. (1982). *Black Skin, White Masks*. New York, NY: Grove Press.

Gilbert, J. (2006). Cultural imperialism revisited: Counselling and globalisation. *International Journal of Critical Psychology*, 17, 10–28.

Gramsci, A. (1999). *Prison Notebooks*. Edited and translated by Quentin Hoare and Geoffrey Nowell Smith. London: Elecbook.

Hervey, D.W. (2005). *A Brief History of Neoliberalism*. Oxford University Press.

Hill Collins, P. (2002). *Black Feminist Thought: Knowledge, Consciousness, and the Politics of Empowerment*. New York, NY: Taylor & Francis.

Holmes, C., Facemire, V.C. & DaFonseca, A.M.D. (2016). Expanding criteria for posttraumatic stress disorder: Considering the deleterious impact of oppression. *Traumatology*, 22(4), 314–321. http://dx.doi.org/10.1037/trm0000104.

hooks, b. (1996). *Killing Rage: Ending Racism*. London: Penguin.

Ira, P. (2020). Why We Need to Stop The 'Strong Black Woman' Trope, It Is Not a Compliment. https://medium.com/equality-includes-you/why-we-need-to-stop-the-strong-black-woman-trope-it-is-not-a-compliment-c0b57a052c05.

Kareem, J. & Littlewood, R. (1999). *Intercultural Therapy: Themes, Interpretations and Practice*. Blackwell Science. Oxford, England

Keating, F. (2002). *Breaking the Cycles of Fear*. The Sainsbury Centre for Mental Health, London.

Karlsen, S. & Nazrro, J.Y. In Karslen, S. (2007). *Better Health Briefing 3 - Ethnic inequalities in health: the impact of racism*. [online] Race Equality Foundation. http://raceequality-foundation.org.uk/wp-content/uploads/2018/03/health-brief3.pdf

Lorde, A. (1984). *Sister Outsider: Essays and Speeches*. Trumansburg, NY: Crossing Press.

Lorde, A. (2017). *Your Silence Will Not Protect You*. London: Silver Press.

W, Madzimoyo (2021) WHB. Warriors, Healers and Builders HYPERLINK "http://www.ayaed.com" www.ayaed.com

Mckenzie-Mavinga, I. (2009). *Black Issues in the Therapeutic Process*. London: Palgrave Macmillan.

Mercury Policy Project (2010). Factsheet: Mercury in skin lightening cosmetics. Montpelier, VT: Author.

Nichols, E.J. (2008). Philosophical Aspects of Cultural Difference Connecting the past to the Present to the Future. In Jones, B. A. & Nichols, E. J. (2013). *Cultural Competence in America's Schools: Leadership, Engagement and Understanding*, 31–64. Charlotte, NC: Information Age Publishing.

Oxfam (2020) *Time to Change: Unpaid and Underpaid Care Work and the Global Inequality Crisis.*

Pauly Morgan, K. (1996). Describing the Emperor's New Clothes: Three Myths of Educational (In)-Equity. In A. Miller *et al.* (eds), *The Gender Question in Education: Theory, Pedagogy and Politics*. Boulder, CO: Westview.

PND (2020). Philanthropy News Digest. January 22, 2020. https://philanthropynewsdigest.org

Selassie, S. (2020). *You Belong: A Call for Connection*. San Francisco, CA: HarperOne.

Sugarman, J. (2015). Neoliberalism and psychological ethics. *Journal of Theoretical and Philosophical Psychology*, 35(2), 103–116.

Rogers, C. (1974). Carl *Rogers Counsels an Individual on Anger* [video]. Available at: https://youtu.be/uRCD3anKsao.

Runyan, A.S. (2018). What is Intersectionality and Why is it Important? *Academe*, 104(6).

Turner, D. (2021). *Intersections of Privilege and Otherness in Counselling and Psychotherapy*. London and New York, NY: Routledge.

Wallace, M. (1979). *Black Macho and the Myth of Superwomen*. New York, NY: Dial.

Watermeyer, B. & Görgens, T. (2014). Disability and Internalized Oppression. In E.J.R. David (ed.), *Internalized Oppression: The Psychology of Marginalized Groups* (pp.253–280). New York, NY: Springer Publishing.

Wilson Gilmore, R. (2020). *A Moment of True Decolonization #31* [podcast]. The Funambulist Podcast https://thefunambulist.net/podcast/daily-podcast-31-ruth-wilson-gilmore-the-beginning-of-a-perfect-decolonial-moment.

Woods-Giscombe, C.L., Allen, A.M., Black, A.R., Steed, T., Li, Y. & Lackey, C. (2019). The Giscombe Superwoman Schema Questionnaire: Psychometric properties and associations with mental health and health behaviours in African American women. *Issues in Mental Health Nursing*, 40(8), 672–681. doi: 10.1080/01612840.2019.1584654.

World Bank Blogs (2021). 11 January 2021. https://blogs.worldbank.org

WHO (2017) *Depression and Other Common Mental Disorders*. World Health Organisation, Geneva, Switzerland.

Further Reading

Owomoyela, O. (2005). *Yoruba Proverbs*. Lincoln, NE: University of Nebraska Press.

Chapter 21

Effective Anti-Racist Practice in Counselling and Therapy Training

TONIA MIHILL

Abstract

The chapter begins by framing the context within which the need for anti-racist practice sits. After this, it situates me as the author in the landscape of racial identity, describing my heritage and formative experiences. It goes on to survey issues of race and racism generally and the specific recent responses from professional therapy bodies, before putting forward ten practical, 'easy' ways that training courses can incorporate anti-racist practice. At the end of each of these ten sections, there are personal reflection and discussion points to actively engage the reader in examining and auditing their own thinking and experiences and to encourage them to extend and share this enquiry with others. In conclusion, the chapter places the work of anti-racist practice on the age-old and continuing path of advancing justice and enhancing the quality of human existence, with a call to see this as a task that requires and generates inspiration and visioning.

Keywords

Practical, reflective, opinion, dialogical, visioning, straightforward, instructive, checklist, guide, manifesto

Where we are

In the pursuit of justice and human development, dismantling any institutionalized oppressive force can be invigorating, inspiring but also an exhausting and dispiriting task and it is one that spans generations. In that context, I find it helpful to frame our efforts in ways that enable us to maximize our contribution to the ongoing struggle rather than measuring our inevitably limited power to effect change against the grand scale of the motivating vision – a world free of racism in all its incarnations. As African American tennis icon, activist and writer Arthur Ashe put it simply, 'Start where you are, use what you have, do what you can!' So, where are we in terms of race in counselling and therapy training? At the last published census, 85 per cent of the UK population was recorded as white (Office for National Statistics, 2011) and this group is overrepresented in the therapeutic professions. Black trainees and clients frequently find themselves with white tutors, supervisors, peers and therapists, while being required, for the success of the enterprise, to be open and in that sense vulnerable. At the same time, racism remains a force to be reckoned with and spaces that purport to be safe and facilitative of healing and growth can be at best inadequate and at worst re-traumatizing. This is the context and seriousness of the need for effective anti-racist practice in counselling and therapy training.

I am a black woman of mixed heritage – Northern Ugandan and East Anglian British. I grew up with my white family in a market town in Suffolk in the 1960s and 1970s with overt and subtle racism a feature of my childhood and a driving force in my decision to study in London, aged 18. I stayed there for another 15 years before returning to live in Norwich.

I feel comfortable with the strikingly similar wisdom and values in each strand of my family heritage. My white British grandad and my, more recently found, black Ugandan great uncle, both passed now, reminded me of each other, even down to their appearance – slight and dapper – and both were kind, generous and community-minded. In studying the person-centred approach developed by Carl Rogers, a white American, I found that its theories and practice sat well with me. I noticed and valued too that, as he moved through his professional life, Rogers was increasingly drawn to offering his skills in highly charged conflicts – race in the segregated US States and apartheid in South Africa, religion in sectarian Northern Ireland (Rogers,1977). Rogers' foundation in the observational discipline of science seems to me key here. He focused on what he observed worked and did not hesitate to test that in the fires of diverse realities.

For me, as well as within mainstream science, race as a way of dividing human beings into distinct genetic groups with indelible characteristics and inherent differences is not credible. However, racism as a socio-political construct remains a potent, toxic force that continues to poison our view of ourselves and each other and maintain and generate grotesque global and local inequity and violence. In my counselling training (2003–2007), I experienced racism in depressingly similar ways to those being discussed now, more than a decade on.

Having said that, anti-racist struggle over centuries has been charged by especially catalytic periods and I am writing in one of those. From 2020, in the wake of a resurgent Black Lives Matter moment sparked by the videoed police murder of George Floyd in the US but with global resonance, there has been coverage and soul searching to an extent not seen for many years. All the psychological therapy professional bodies made statements and published articles and letters on this subject. The British Association for Counselling and Psychotherapy (BACP) devoted the 20 September edition of its journal *Therapy Today* to the theme of 'We need to talk about race: but how? And what is stopping us?' and followed up in October with 'Listening to learn; Shifting institutionalized racism'. The testimonies present a disturbing picture of a profession which specializes in reflection, awareness, humility and empathy yet remains unable to consistently adhere to these qualities in relation to race:

> 'Counselling as a profession has not done the work it needs to do to address its own racism, at both individual and collective levels,' says child and adolescent psychotherapist Kemi Omijeh. 'Only last week another therapist said to me, "I don't see you as black". My answer to that is: "If you don't see me as black, then I don't exist for you".' (*Therapy Today*, September 2020)

In the 'Reactions' section of the next month's journal (*Therapy Today*, October 2020) a letter, that I assume represented a strand of responses, questioned the need to talk about race, with a call to common humanity, as if anti-racist practice somehow denies rather than strives for this. While I do not imagine this was the writer's intention, to me the letter read as a confident dismissal of the voices of very many black people, including the President of BACP, and of the requirements of the ethical framework its author has subscribed to as a member. This reflects the kind of division shown in a June 2020 CNN poll which found that 69 per cent of black Britons believed BAME people have less opportunity to succeed professionally compared to 29 per cent of white respondents (Allen-Green, 2020).

Though conscious of this moment, I am also drawing on a longer view – my experience of offering anti-racist training in Norfolk for over 25 years – and a consistent aim to chart and take my place on the (already) long and winding road to a non-racial future. For the last six years, I have co-created and delivered 'Race and Culture in the Therapeutic Relationship' workshop days for the Person-centred Diploma course at the Norwich Centre. I have been a Black, African, and Asian Therapy Network (BAATN) mentor since 2016. As a trainer, in that position of authority, I have very rarely encountered malicious adherence to racist beliefs, but I have routinely found that being required to actively engage with race can be daunting – both for those who are well versed in the issues but have had negative experiences of discussing them in group settings and those who have previously given race and racism little thought. Resistance can be present in various forms, including advancing stories of black success, diverting the conversation to others, forms of discrimination that the individual has experienced themselves or an insistence that they do not see race and treat everyone the same. Too often course coverage of racism is confined to days or weekends and focused on the need to educate white students, with black students treated as unpaid experts or, conversely, ignored. I have also observed the positive outcomes when tutors take responsibility for promoting anti-oppressive practice and consistently apply an equalities lens. I would summarize these as acceptance of the challenges, commitment to both individual and collective endeavour to change the unjust status quo and openness to continuous learning about how best to do that.

What we have

Racism is an arena of strong emotion, deep divisions and generational trauma. It is abuse on a grand, systemic scale. Facilitating dialogue in this context is not for the faint-hearted; however, this must not stop the task in its tracks. BACP's ethical framework directs us to be brave if we choose to take up a therapeutic profession: 'Key personal qualities to which members and registrants are strongly encouraged to aspire include...Courage: the capacity to act in spite of known fears, risks and uncertainty' (BACP, 2018).

I understand as another force of racism the suggestion that it is somehow more difficult to tackle than any other challenge we face, in such a way that ultimately leads to its too frequent avoidance or a skirting around edges with tick-box exercises. After all, we are no strangers to pain, discomfort, wounds, struggle and swirling internal and external dynamics. I have no doubt that, with the will and persistence we are conversant with wielding, courses can equip trainees with the level of proficiency required, in the multifaceted psycho/social/political terrains of race and racism, to provide consistently helpful and increasingly skilled educational and therapeutic services for black students and clients and, of course, therefore, for all.

From here on, I will not be further exploring the nature of racism or its ubiquitous reality. Rather, I will suggest steps to create anti-racist change within therapy courses, for all who are interested and wish to play a positive role in this undertaking. I am addressing multiple black and white audiences. Consciously united in our problematic and unequal diversity, concerted, collective action for a non-racial future can be a powerful counter to the intentionally fragmenting frameworks and distracting, delusion-inducing narratives that uphold racism.

I invite your active participation as the foundational requirement of anti-racist practice and suggest personal reflection and discussion points to assist with this. Enquiring within and without, knowing ourselves and our contexts, identifying and talking together about observable and subterranean destructive forces, working to combat these are all basic tenets and tools of our trade. We can choose to employ them to tackle racism, which as well as being a generator of persistent material inequality, operates pathologically within our individual and collective spirit and psyche to the detriment of us all.

So yes, depending on where you currently find yourself, this could be a guide, a checklist, a stimulus...or perhaps a manifesto.

What we can do

Ten easily achievable ways of incorporating effective anti-racist practice into training courses:

1. Establish from the outset that racism exists.

2. Explicitly state and demonstrate a commitment to anti-racist practice.

3. Enable all trainees to understand the impact of their racial identity.

4. Engage with the racial composition of each group.

5. Evaluate how best to integrate black experiences and expertise.

6. Ensure a basic knowledge of the histories of black people.

7. Expect trainees to show understanding of race and racism in their work.

8. Evidence the coverage of anti-racist practice and its impact.

9. Enter and commit to a continuous process of learning and development.

10. Enjoy and validate explorations of race and racism.

1. Establish from the outset that racism exists

Debates about the existence of racism, when this is convincingly evidenced, and the need for pervasive action to combat it, when laws and professional bodies require this, are disingenuous. Of course, as therapists we work with where people are, but, as educators, we must be crystal clear about the standards students need to reach in order to be professionally competent. A citizen is entitled to do nothing at all to understand racism. A trainee therapist has signed up for this task. The UK Council for Psychotherapy (UKCP) Code of Ethics and Professional Practice states:

> The psychotherapist undertakes to actively consider issues of diversity and equalities as these affect all aspects of their work. The psychotherapist accepts no one is immune from the experience of prejudice and acknowledges the need for a continuing process of self-enquiry and professional development. (UKCP, 2019)

In accrediting courses, BACP requires providers to show how students demonstrate 'awareness' of the nature of 'prejudice and oppression' and 'issues of difference and equality' (BACP, 2019).

Other initiatives are more explicit. In 'All In: Regularising Ethnic Presence in the Curriculum', a collaborative project between the University of Nottingham and the University of Birmingham in 2019/20 (Chauhan, 2020), the first key principle is 'acknowledging' the role of 'conscious and unconscious bias, racism in curricula'.

And then there is the bottom line. In addition to activities that raise awareness and encourage discussion, I always ensure that workshop participants know that racial discrimination is illegal. I outline the main points of the Equalities Act 2010 and make clear that abiding by this is essential.

> For personal reflection: How much do you know about racial discrimination in employment, housing, health, the criminal justice system and so on in the UK?
>
> For discussion: Do you know where racism originates? Why do you think it still exists?

2. Explicitly state and demonstrate a commitment to anti-racist practice

Course details and first sessions that state a commitment to anti-racist practice show clear intent and allow students to expect and, in that sense, prepare for this content and hold course leaders accountable for effective delivery. To be role models, tutors do not need to feel that they can answer every question, but they do need to show that they are seeking ways to equip themselves for the ongoing constructive conversation required. In *Race and Racism in English Secondary Schools* (Joseph-Salisbury, 2020), Dr Remi Joseph-Salisbury talks about 'racial literacy' and defines this as, 'The capacity of teachers to understand the ways in which race and racisms work in society... It also involves having the language, skills and confidence to utilize that knowledge in teacher practice.' On the journey towards this, it is helpful for tutors to present their limits as well as their current understanding. After all, it is part of the workings of racism to create those limits. Demonstrating comfort with this discomforting reality and commitment to progressive change is the essential rather than a comprehensive knowledge base, though this should be sought.

> For personal reflection: How confident do you feel in speaking about racism with a) friends and family b) colleagues c) strangers, and why?
>
> For discussion: Have you had teachers or tutors who you consider have demonstrated effective anti-racist practice? If so, describe what you learned from them; if not, what do you think this absence means to you?

3. Enable all trainees to understand the impact of their racial identity

Locating ourselves on the spectrum of racialized disadvantage and privilege is key to the awareness of our role in the ensuing power dynamics and the part they play in therapeutic relationships, as well as in creating specific mental health challenges. Although, frequently, black students will have had to engage with this, it remains vital that no assumption is made that, by virtue of being black, they are necessarily 'ahead of the game'. Racism works to put blinkers on us all and intersects with other societal forces – such as class and gender – in ways that can obscure its operation. As African American academic, author and activist bell hooks (1992, p.1) notes:

> Opening a magazine or book, turning on the television set, watching a film or looking at photographs in a public space, we are most likely to see images of black people that reinforce or reinscribe white supremacy. Those images may be constructed by white people who have not divested of racism or by people of colour/black people who may see the world through the lens of white supremacy – internalized racism.

> For personal reflection: Can you name your racial identity and describe how it has affected your life and perspective?
>
> For discussion: How often, if ever, do you have conversations about race and racism? Can you remember and share a recent or significant one?

4. Engage with the racial composition of each group

The apparent absence of black people does not signal an absence of racism or racial dynamics. As well, beyond the skin surface, people who appear white may identify as mixed heritage and white people may be deeply engaged in relationship with the black experience and black people as partners, children, extended family members or friends. And, of course, any trainee may have a black client. Black realities and racism need particular attention in every group, and it is essential that black trainees do not have to take responsibility for raising or leading on this. Tutors can ask themselves questions that explore the lie of the group's land; for example, do the black students feel able to share their viewpoints, do they offer regular contributions or is the space dominated by white students? Do all white groups discuss race/racism or is the subject of diversity tackled through other areas more known to the students – gender or sexual orientation perhaps? What is the level of knowledge about and experience of racism within the group? Is it a new subject or one that some have been negotiating for a lifetime? The earlier these differences are known the better.

> For personal reflection: How often do you notice race? What effect does noticing have on you?
>
> For discussion: Have you been in a situation where you are a racial minority? If so, what did/does it feel like? If not, why do you think this is, and how have either or both experiences affected your understanding of race and racism?

5. Evaluate how best to integrate black experiences and expertise

The internet, with its bulging 'library' of resources of all kinds, offers us a plethora of potential sources, aside from black students being required to tell their stories. Though this may sometimes be appropriate, exploration should not rely on that or stop there. There is a multiplicity of black experiences to reveal and the diversity of these to be actively demonstrated. Reading lists and source material should regularly feature black thinkers and writers, ideally from a spectrum of viewpoints.

There is an opportunity here for students and the tutor team to work collaboratively to create a programme of learning, and a generous rather than a punitive culture will increase the likelihood of productive engagement. 'Telling people they're racist, sexist, and xenophobic is going to get you exactly nowhere', said Alana Conner, executive director of Stanford University's Social Psychological Answers to Real-World Questions Center (Lopez, 2019). 'It's such a threatening message. One of the things we know from social psychology is when people feel threatened, they can't change, they can't listen.'

> For personal reflection: How do black cultures feature in your life?
>
> For discussion: When was the last time you studied the work of a black academic? Who was it and what did they say?

6. Ensure a basic knowledge of the histories of black people

Racism works to erase and deny the contributions of black people to human development and inflate and promote those of white people. A good grasp of the extent of this is vital to developing sensitivity to its profound impact on self and society. Fortunately, there are plenty of websites, documentaries and books, such as *Black and British: A Forgotten History* by David Olusoga and *Why I'm No Longer Talking to White People About Race* by Reni Eddo-Lodge, that provide accessible insight and information to combat the consequences of the omissions within the mainstream education system. Curating these into succinct, digestible resource lists that target areas within which the group has divergent levels of knowledge, and that all trainees are expected to be conversant with, will not only help with individual learning but also facilitate collective discussion.

> For personal reflection: What do you know about the pre-20th-century history of black people in Britain?
>
> For discussion: Were you taught any black history at school? If so, what is your memory of that?

7. Expect trainees to show understanding of race and racism in their work

Trainees could be asked to include this in a minimum number of assignments. In addition, or alternatively, specific tasks could be set. For example, a journal for observations of our society's racialized culture and the trainee's understanding and relationship to this or an assessment of the effectiveness of equalities policies and practice, related to race, in their placement organizations. The inclusion of assessed work on race and racism signals clearly that this is a key element in their professional competence and makes it unavoidable.

> For personal reflection: When was the last time you observed racism in action?
>
> For discussion: How confident do you feel in challenging racism and why?

8. Evidence the coverage of anti-racist practice and its impact

In the first instance, this can be as simple as detailing sessions and assignments that focus on this area; a baseline measurement of knowledge and understanding through self-assessment made at the beginning and revisited at the end of the course; and an evaluation by trainees of the effectiveness of the course coverage of these topics for them. Evaluating and evidencing is a way that courses can chart progress, or otherwise, be accountable and identify areas for development. There is also a variety of audit tools available that can assist with examining curricula and departmental structures to establish baselines and set clear targets as well as achievable steps towards meeting them.

> For personal reflection: How much training about and reflection on race and racism have you undertaken?
>
> For discussion: Share experiences of anti-racist training.

9. Enter and commit to a continuous process of learning and development

As with all cultural forces, race and racism are always evolving and transmuting. The facts that we no longer have signs telling us that landlords will not accept Irish, blacks or dogs and there are black government ministers clearly does not mean that all is now well. We need to be alert to the present and prepare for the coming incarnations of racism and avoid the temptation to prematurely announce the dawn of a post-racial world. Racism has through its ages co-opted black people to police and support its colonizing, white supremacist mission and shared a certain amount of power and wealth with those who accept this dubious honour.

Cultural studies pioneer Stuart Hall (1990, p.225) notes, 'Cultural identities come from somewhere, have histories. But like everything else which is historical they undergo constant transformation.' I do not give trainees lists of words and terms that are the ones they should use, though these are frequently requested. As race and racial identity are dynamic concepts, any such list will quickly become out of date and can never be absolute. A more useful focus is on raising awareness of racial terms and how they change, and an approach that is open to the inventive, creative, individual ways that each person may define themselves. These are often precious and meaningful expressions of their unique journeys to self-definition and empowerment.

> For personal reflection: What knowledge or experience do you think *you* need to enhance your ability to understand and work with race and racism?
>
> For discussion: How do you think that issues of race and racism might change over the next ten years? What evidence do you have for your views?

10. Enjoy and validate explorations of race and racism

None of this will be sustainable or effective if it is all felt as a dispiriting trudge through suffering and shame. Instead, though some of the landscape may feel treacherous, we can reframe this (another skill we have!) as an epic journey into constructive engagement with our times.

As Carl Rogers observed (Rogers, 1961, p.246), in education as in therapy, '...significant learning occurs more readily in relation to situations perceived a problems'.

We can relish the opportunity to play our role in progressing the restorative and liberating forces that therapists in training are frequently motivated and attracted by on a societal as well as an individual level.

...we are, more or less,
The makers of the future.
We create what time will frame.
And a beautiful dream, shaped
And realized by a beautiful mind,
Is one of the greatest gifts
We can make to our fellow beings

Ben Okri (1999)

Throughout this chapter, I use black in its political sense to refer to all non-white peoples whatever their cultural and ethnic origins. Both black and white groupings are as heterogenous as each other. Our membership of one or the other is determined by the legacies of colonialism and the presence of racism. I have been reflecting on the way black has proliferated into a multiplicity of terms – BME, BAME, BIPOC, 'black and brown', 'Black, African and Asian' – while white, a grouping that is also culturally, ethnically and in every other way diverse, stays as white. I have a sense that this might mirror the divide and rule power dynamics and racial hierarchies of racism. For all these reasons, I made a conscious decision to use the balder, reductive terms that I think lie at the heart of racism, in this chapter about anti-racism. I am very aware that other choices are equally valid. As bell hooks (1991) writes, 'Language is also a place of struggle.' The divide that seems to me increasingly crucial to the viability of a non-racial future is not so much black and white but whether we are perpetuating racism or practising anti-racism.

> For personal reflection: How can you contribute to the creation of a non-racial future – today, this year and over the next decade?
>
> For discussion: Imagine you are transported 200 years into the future to a time when race and racism are subjects studied in history rather than active forces; how will you know this is the case as you observe this future world?

References

Allen-Green, R. (2020). Britain's big race divide: CNN poll shows what Black Britons have long known – from policing to politics, their country has failed them. CNN, 22 June.

BACP. (2018). Ethical Framework for the Counselling Professions. www.bacp.co.uk/events-and-resources/ethics-and-standards/ethical-framework-for-the-counselling-professions.

BACP. (2019). Course Accreditation Scheme British Association for Counselling and Psychotherapy. www.bacp.co.uk/membership/accreditation.

Chauhan, C. (2020). Top Tips: Decolonising the Curriculum. From 'All in: Regularising ethnic presence in the curriculum', a collaborative project between the University of Nottingham and the University of Birmingham, September 2019 to August 2020.

Hall, S. (1990). Cultural Identity and Diaspora. In J. Rutherford (ed.), *Identity: Community, Culture, Difference* (pp.222–227). London: Lawrence & Wishart.

hooks, b. (1991). *Yearning: Race, Gender and Cultural Politics.* London: Turnaround.

hooks, b. (1992). *Black Looks: Race and Representation.* London: Turnaround.

Joseph-Salisbury, R. (2020). *Race and Racism in English Secondary Schools.* London: The Runnymede Trust.

Lopez, G. (2019). The challenge for anti-racists looking for solutions in Trump's America. www.vox.com/identities/2016/11/15/13595508/racism-research-study-trump.

Office for National Statistics. (2011). Census for England and Wales.

Okri, B. (1999). *Mental Fight: An Anti-Spell for the 21st Century.* London: Phoenix.

Rogers, C. (1961). *On Becoming a Person: A Therapist's View of Psychotherapy.* Boston, MA: Houghton Mifflin.

Rogers, C. (1977). *On Personal Power: Inner Strength and Its Revolutionary Impact.* New York, NY: Delacorte Press.

Therapy Today. (2020, September). The Big Issue: We need to talk about race so what's stopping us. Volume 31, Issue 7

Therapy Today. (2020, October). Reactions. Volume 31, Issue 8.

UKCP. (2019). Code of Ethics and Professional Practice UK Council for Psychotherapy. www.psychotherapy.org.uk/media/bkjdm33f/ukcp-code-of-ethics-and-professional-practice-2019.pdf.

Epilogue

Selah

KRIS BLACK

(pronounced sēlə sĕlə)

Selah is defined as a Hebrew word that has been found at the ending of verses in the Book of Psalms and has been interpreted as an instruction calling for a break in the singing of the psalm, or it may mean forever or pause or end or look back and reflect on. It is a word mired in controversy as to its true meaning.

'Selah' is also the title of an Emile Sande song that I was listening to today while writing up this part of the book. According to Spotify, Kanye West and Lauryn Hill also have a track entitled 'Selah', but Emile's is my favourite. I preferred using it instead of 'epilogue'. I enjoyed finding a word by chance or synchronicity, that although appearing over 70 times in the Book of Psalms, is shrouded in debate and controversy over its meaning.

The word *intersectionality* appears many times in this book and has also at times been shrouded in many meanings. It is also shrouded in the controversy implicit in the growing right-wing call for cancellation of critical race theory and trainings. Sometimes the central and core meanings of intersectional theory are stripped away so that it is interpreted simply as a theory of identity, and therefore not at all applicable or taking up its rightful place within the field of psychotherapy and counselling. I have tried to be instrumental where possible, to ensure that intersectionality becomes *more than* emergent, as a means of understanding different forms of oppression – structural, systemic and otherwise – that impact the therapeutic relationship, in all its forms. In reading *Therapy in Colour*, you have joined the growing awareness on a global level that calls for intersectional theory to take its rightful place as central to our understanding of each other as human beings.

If this book arose out of the psychotherapy and counselling field in the US instead of the UK, I might have been writing a different epilogue (selah). Intersectionality remains misunderstood in the UK within the psy-professions. Small wonder that a theory arising out of the black feminist movement in the US and UK, with its roots in a working-class movement's understanding of its importance and applicability, might have been covered by a shroud of invisibility and obfuscation. We have Kimberlé Crenshaw, Audre Lorde, bell hooks and the Combahee River Collective, all US women of African descent, to thank for intersectional theory taking root here in the UK from the early 1980s onwards within UK black feminist and activist circles. The work of understanding intersectionality, however, remains iterative, with different generations adopting and defending an understanding of its crucial theoretical importance.

What *Therapy in Colour* does is centre the voices of those impacted by intersectional discrimination, rather than focus on academic definitions, which negate its importance as central to theories of liberation. This book re-centres our understanding of how some aspects of intersectional discrimination manifest within the psy-professions.

As a human being and as an intersectional feminist, I have spent many years of my life teaching and promoting a theory that has equality and equity and spreads an understanding of structural discrimination. Intersectional theory has strong links to liberatory practice at its heart. Yet intersectionality remains shrouded in many mistruths and mysteries. The *aha* of its importance is often sidelined as a marginalized discourse with no importance, efficacy or relevance to psychotherapy and counselling. Yet here, within these pages, are many truths about why it is wholly important, and as a collectively marginalized discourse is given air.

This book has taken longer than many publications to see the light of day *precisely* because of structural discrimination and its impact on the psy-professions and the communities that BAATN serves and draws together under the shelter of its membership umbrella.

I hope that now you have found this book, some of the mystery of intersectionality has been revealed to you, and that by the time you are reading these words, you also hear the following as a call to action, as a *forever prayer* for the generations of therapists that may follow.

I hope that regardless of who you are, you take the opportunity to use your privilege to spread awareness about the words herein as a gift to others who are seekers of understanding about the field and applicability of intersectionality. Now that you have undertaken this journey with the authors, you understand its place as relevant to therapeutic praxis. The authors have been open enough and brave enough to write – I hope that you do not simply close this page and the cover of the book and just place it on a bookshelf to gather dust.

I hope that you choose to take an *activist* position in changing the world around you. Even a miniscule action can create change in the world – don't we know that as therapy practitioners? Therefore, I ask you to join us by making this book's contents known to all whom you encounter, that you spread its liberatory message far and wide, that you work with us to spread awareness of the wisdoms herein and its core *intersectional* message.

Many hours of labour have gone into the making of *Therapy in Colour,* and my prayer is that you, who are changed by its contents and the wisdom herein, take this into your practice as a therapist, into your lecture halls, into your training courses, and ultimately take intersectional *awareness* out into the world.

If you are a client reading this book, I hope that you take away the message that understanding your experience does not mean you have to leave your intersectional identity or struggles at the door of the therapy room in order to walk through it.

I hope that if you are a psychotherapist, counsellor or psychologist practitioner-expert reading this book, you have come to understand that intersectionality is central to understanding how some of the trauma of discrimination works and how trauma can be overcome within the therapy and counselling room by embracing an *intersectional understanding* of the life and trials and traumas of your clients. If you are impacted by discrimination in any form, I hope that it helps you embrace a better understanding of yourself.

This book is not the *end* of your understanding about intersectionality, however. It has an important place in the world of psychotherapy and counselling. It is part of the *beginning* of a continuous *journey* of understanding and reflexivity. I would invite those of you who are still mystified by intersectionality to see it as simply one piece of a larger unfolding puzzle about power, privilege and discrimination. This is important if you are to understand human existence, the trauma of discrimination and how to work effectively with clients who experience it's many-faceted impacts. This book focuses on and centres the traumas of racism and being a racialized other at the intersections of gender, colourism, racism and sexuality.

What you do with the knowledge that you now have in your hands, the result of over six years of hard labour, is ultimately up to you. My prayer for this book, which has emerged from within a movement for liberation and equality with hope and love at its core, is that its themes of intersectional identity and discrimination are no longer shrouded in secrecy, nor suppressed. It is our collective hope that *Therapy in Colour* takes its rightful place within the psy-professions as a core text, at least for those of us who can access it from the relative privilege implicit in our location as professionals in the global north.

As a child of the 1960s, and someone who has fully embraced the concept that black, brown and other people of colour are connected worldwide as a *global majority*, I share the hope that one day we might live in a world where the colour of a person's skin or eyes, or the texture of their hair, or their gender, or sexuality, or class or economic status or disability, may not be a barrier to their practising the art, science and profession of counselling and psychotherapy, or from participating in the liberatory act of healing from trauma as a client.

I hope this book will live a long life. It has outlived at least two of its contributors – Arike and Lennox – and it very nearly outlived me as an editor as I grappled with and overcame serious health issues. It has come at a time when we are gripped by a global pandemic that has meant death for many millions of humans of colour who constitute the global majority. These deaths are due in part to human resources being mismanaged and mis-allocated under the twisted rein of capitalism, when we live on a planet that has resources enough for all, and priorities appear focused on amassing wealth as individuals, rather than sharing our global inheritance as a human collective. Colonialism and patriarchy continue to hold hands as twin tools of power and repression.

This book has been waiting to be exposed to the bright light of day, and it is part of a long march for freedom from racialized discrimination that its contributors can all relate to. In conclusion, I can only hope that the labour it has taken to produce *Therapy in Colour* means that it lives long within the memory, bones and hearts of our psy-professionals. There is no better time for it to play a part in our collective, long-drawn-out, and often unheeded call for a truly *intersectionally informed* world.

Long may it play its part, and long may its lessons resonate. I remain grateful for having started and completed this journey with you, dear reader, and with the colleagues from BAATN herein who took the risk to write. I am also grateful for being able to have the final word – Selah.

About the Co-Editors

Dr Isha Mckenzie-Mavinga has 33 years' experience as a transcultural psychotherapist, supervisor, lecturer, writer and Reiki master. As a published writer and poet, she is the author of *Black Issues in the Therapeutic Process* (2009) and *The Challenge of Racism in Therapeutic Practice* (2016). She also co-authored an autobiography and contributed papers and poetry to several anthologies, including *The Handbook of Transcultural Counselling and Psychotherapy* (2011: edited by Colin Lago), *Making Research Matter* (2015: edited by Stephen Goss & Christine Stevens), *Intercultural Therapy* (2019: edited by Baffour Ababio & Roland Littlewood), *What is Normal?* (2020: edited by Roz Carroll & Jane Ryan) and *The International Handbook of Black Community Mental Health* (2020: edited by Richard Majors, Karen Carberry & Theodore Ransaw). She has a presentation on the Confer online module 'Women on the Couch' (2020) and has shared her work on various podcasts and conference videos, including the BME Voices Trauma Conference 2020. Isha initiated therapeutic services at the African Caribbean Mental Health Association in Brixton, and at the Women's Trust, working with women impacted by violence in relationships, and she was a student counsellor at London Metropolitan University. She has created Black Issues workshops, based on concepts created during her doctoral research (www.ishamckenziemavinga.com writeandheal@btinternet.com). Isha is a previous member of the BAATN leadership team and is now in the process of retirement and transitioning from professional practice to creative writing and art.

Kris Black (they/them) IAP, UKCP, MBACP, ISN, LLB (Hons) is a longstanding intersectional feminist, activist and trainer. Kris's social locations are that they are a non-binary trans queer, working-class, mixed racial heritage, disabled human. A committed community psychotherapist located within the UK QTIBPOC and the wider LGBTQ+ community, Kris served on the BAATN leadership team for seven years.

Professionally, Kris is a UKCP, BACP-registered integrative arts psychotherapist, an advanced accredited gender, sex and relationship diversities therapist, child and adolescent counsellor and clinical supervisor. As a therapist-activist, Kris founded Radical Dialogues, an intersectional training and education foundation, has served as a visiting lecturer for several psychotherapy institutions and has published papers in various journals. Kris is a senior clinical associate and member of the teaching faculty of Pink Therapy. Kris runs groups and intersectional training courses for BAATN members and also assisted with the launch and development of BAATN's pioneering Each One Teach One Mentorship Programme. Kris is active within the Psychotherapy and Counselling Union as the convenor for the BIPOC Members Forum and has served on the Executive Committee. Kris is an active member of Psychotherapists and Counsellors for Social Responsibility, having served on their Executive, organized their TABOO Conference, and been an invited keynote speaker on intersectionality. Kris is a committee member of the Coalition Against Conversion Therapy. Kris works as an independent clinical supervisor and consultant with several charitable organizations within the UK serving the education, housing, legal and LGBTQIA+ and mental health sectors. Kris is founder of the QTIBPOC Therapy Network UK and a member of the Free Psychotherapy Network.

Since the early 1980s, Kris has served on the editorial and management boards of a number of grassroots campaigning organizations and charities furthering the liberation of racialized and marginalized gender, sexual and relationship diversity communities. Kris has also worked extensively therapeutically with children and young people from racialized and working-class minorities. Kris has contributed to the collective production of grassroots radical community publications such as *Lysistrata*, *Mothertongue*, and *We Are Here* magazines, as well as *The London Rape Crisis Violence Against Women Handbook*.

Contact Kris at: www.arctherapy.co.uk and arctherapy@protonmail.com.

Karen Carberry MSc is a family and systemic psychotherapist and consultant family therapist for Orri, a specialist day treatment for eating disorders; Executive Director, Trustee and Acting Chair of the Association for Family Therapy and Systemic Practice; and Board Director and Consultant Clinical Supervisor for Hope Bereavement Support, an organization specializing in therapeutic work with Black and minority clients experiencing bereavement, child loss and trauma. Karen is an

Association of Family Therapy Accredited Systemic Supervisor; a Fellow of the Asian Academy of Family Therapy; and a former columnist for the British Association for Counselling and Psychotherapy *Workplace* journal. Karen gained her master's degree from the Institute of Family Therapy, and Birkbeck College, University of London. In addition to her former roles as a mentor on the BAATN, Each One Teach One Mentorship Programme, and family therapy in clinical inpatient and outpatient work in Child and Adolescent Mental Health Services and adult psychiatry, Karen is an associate lecturer and supervisor on the Systemic Supervision Course at the University of Exeter. She is also a visiting lecturer on the Doctoral Programme for Clinical Psychology at Oxford University, the Great Ormond Street Hospital family therapy programme, and the Institute of Family Therapy. As a practitioner-scholar, she is involved in a variety of academic activities internationally. Karen is also co-editor of *The International Handbook of Black Community Mental Health* published in 2020 by Emerald Publishing Limited.

Eugene Ellis is Director and Founder of the Black, African and Asian Therapy Network (BAATN), Honorary Fellow of the United Kingdom Council for Psychotherapy (UKCP) and Editorial Board Member of the journal *Psychotherapy and Politics International*. His parents moved to the UK from Jamaica in the 1960s, leaving their two children to later follow. Eugene was the first of five siblings to be born in the UK. Eugene grew up in a multicultural environment in North London with the cultural narrative of a colonized people just a few generations past. As a young man in the late 1980s early 1990s, he found success working in the music industry as a sound engineer during the so-called 'British Soul Explosion'. In the late 1990s, Eugene began training as an integrative arts psychotherapist. He then worked for many years with severely traumatized children and their families in the field of adoption and fostering, where he developed his interest in body-orientated therapies. Eugene facilitates dialogue around the intersections of race and other oppressions through talks, workshops, articles and podcasts. He is the author of *The Race Conversation: An Essential Guide to Creating Life-Changing Dialogue* (2021), which explores how the distress of intergenerational trauma, post-chattel slavery and colonialism lives on, not just in our minds but also in our bodies.

About the Authors

Oye Agoro is cisgender women of Yoruba ancestry and practises as a BACP senior accredited social justice allied integrative intercultural therapist and supervisor, with over 30 years' experience of working as a therapist and supervisor in a range of community, NHS and social care services. Alongside her clinical role, Oye has managed nine therapy services in London and been the Chief Executive Officer (CEO) of the Lorrimore, a charity based in Southwark providing therapy and social support to people with mental health difficulties. She was also the CEO of the African Family Mediation Service, a charity providing a range of support services to people in Lambeth, including a child contact centre, school and family mediation services, and black men's therapy service. Oye co-founded the Multi-Ethnic Counselling Service (MECS) in south London and previously worked as a social action psychotherapist at The Forward Project, a black mental health resource based in west London. Oye currently has her own therapy practice – www.waddonpondstherapy.com.

Carmen Joanne Ablack, body psychotherapist, Gestalt psychotherapist and supervisor, is also member of the BAATN leadership group, is accredited by UKCP and is an Honorary Fellow. Carmen is also accredited by the European Association for Body Psychotherapy (EABP) and currently serves its President. She teaches in the UK and Europe. A psychotherapy faculty member at the Gestalt Centre in London, Carmen holds a master's in Leading and Managing Health and Social Care (Advanced Professional Practice) from the University of Westminster. She has worked with groups, couples and relationships, individuals and organizations on equalities, diversity, inclusion, intersectionality, mental health and wellbeing since the late 1980s. She has written several articles and book chapters on these themes. Her most recent chapter appears in *Black Therapies + White Identities: Race, Respect + Diversity* (2021: edited by Divine Charura and Colin Lago).

Anthea Benjamin is a UKCP and BACP registered integrative arts psychotherapist, play therapist, dyadic developmental psychotherapy practitioner, group analyst and supervisor. Anthea has worked extensively with children, adolescents, adults, families, couples, and groups for over 15 years in various settings including schools, community projects and within the NHS. She works as a therapist delivering training and consultancy in a range of professional and educational contexts. Anthea also offers therapeutic services such as self-reflective groups and team supervision both in organizations and within her private practice in south London. Anthea has a special interest in racial trauma, particularly working with racial trauma in the body.

Ann Boxill completed an MA in Art Psychotherapy in Practice at The Northern Programme in Sheffield following a varied career in teaching. Ann has always been fascinated with the communication and connections between people, particularly how meaning is negotiated between verbal and nonverbal modes of interaction, including images, music and dance. Ann is motivated by the concept of service to others and seeks to support the communities she works with creatively and collaboratively. As she strengthens and deepens her practice as an art psychotherapist and public sector clinician, she continues to work for acceptance and social parity for minoritized and othered groups.

Patmarie Coleman has an MSc in Contemporary Person-Centred Psychotherapy, an MA in the Management of Teaching and Learning, a PGCE, Diploma in Humanistic counselling, and is a UKCP registered psychotherapist. She has taught for more than 22 years on person-centred courses. Patmarie is a senior counsellor at the University of Kent and has a private supervision practice. Her particular professional interests include working with transcultural issues; she is a member BAATN.

Paulette Gibson has a BA (Hons) in Counselling, a Diploma in Counselling, a Diploma in Person Centered Art Therapy Skills, a Diploma in Supervision and is a BACP accredited counsellor. She has been a counsellor in private practice for 22 years, has a supervision practice and has been a counselling trainer for 15 years on person-centred courses. She is currently employed as a senior counsellor and a clinical supervisor at the Royal Academy of Dramatic Arts (RADA). She has an interest in working with artists from Black and ethic diverse groups.

About the Authors

Arike Grant, a psychotherapist and educator, was a talented musician and artist, spiritually refined with integrity, calm and wisdom. May the heart that helped heal other hearts rest in peace. Arike practised as a counsellor from 1986 to 2020. He was a trainer, coach and supervisor, with extensive and diverse experience of supporting people to empower themselves, and he had a special interest in supporting black men. He worked at the African Caribbean Mental Health Association in Brixton, at Broadmoor Hospital and at Tudor Views, Birmingham, a rehabilitation hostel for ex-offenders. He was also a youth worker, teacher, college tutor, group facilitator, trainer, coach and supervisor. He taught at City University, London Metropolitan University and Lewisham College with Student Support Services staff. Arike was a member of BAATN's leadership group.

Moriam Grillo BA (Hons) MA HPCP is an accredited clinical supervisor, lecturer and art psychotherapist working in the community with a special focus on trauma-informed support for vulnerable women. Moriam is also Founding Director of the Butterfly Project, an arts and health organization offering art therapy and arts engagement to promote positive mental health and wellbeing. She is interested in collaborative and inclusive practices which offer greater access to the arts for all. Her anti-racism work includes 'Sitting With Discomfort', a series of online talks exploring race, racism and racialized experience.

Dr Narendra Keval is a psychoanalyst, psychoanalytic psychotherapist and consultant clinical psychologist in private practice. He is a visiting lecturer at the Tavistock Clinic, London, and was a visiting speaker in Cape Town, South Africa, Washington and New York. He is a member of the British Psychoanalytic Society, the Tavistock Society of Psychotherapists, and an Associate Fellow of the British Psychological Society. His book, *Racist States of Mind*, was published by Karnac Books in 2016.

Kiren Khosla is a counsellor in private practice and a single, disabled mum of three boys. She has worked with trauma and critical incidents within the workplace with black, brown, white and mixed race clients, and students with mental and physical health issues since she qualified in 2010. Kiren is an accredited postgraduate person-centred counsellor and is a mentor and the peer mentor contact for the Each One Teach One Mentoring Programme.

Roshmi S. Lovatt is a UKCP registered integrative arts psychotherapist. Since qualifying in 2001, she has worked in a number of settings including MIND (Brent), Asian Women's Counselling Service (Hounslow), Foster Care Associates (Milton Keynes) and NHS (Northampton), as well as in private practice. Roshmi currently runs a group practice which offers counselling, psychotherapy and creative therapies to the local community. Her organization, as well as her practice, model a strong sense of social justice. She is also a tutor, course leader and external assessor for the Minster Centre as well as being an independent trainer and group facilitator offering trainings that specialize in using creative and embodied methods to explore themes such as race, diversity, power and difference. Previous trainings Roshmi has delivered have included the ECArTE Conference, Krakow, in September 2017, the PCSR Conference, York, in May 2018, and ADMP/UKCP training, London, in March 2019 and November 2020. During her original training at the Institute for Arts in Therapy and Education, she became involved in a black and Asian trainees' group in order to support her learning as a student of colour. Since that time, issues of power and diversity have been central to her research and practice and to her ongoing process as a developing practitioner.

Tonia Mihill works as Head of Therapeutic Services at MAP, a youth charity, and as a freelance anti-racist educator and consultant. She is a qualified secondary school history teacher (since 1991) and in 2017 completed a Postgraduate Certificate in Service Leadership and Management at University College London. Tonia's therapeutic qualification is person-centred – a Diploma of Higher Education in Counselling and Therapeutic Care from Anglia Ruskin University in 2007. She is an accredited member of BACP and a member of BAATN, with whom she has been a mentor since 2016. Tonia became an anti-racist trainer in the mid-1990s when she returned to East Anglia after 15 years of living in London, keen to make a positive difference, and joined an anti-racist education project – All Different All Equal. In 2003, Tonia initiated and co-ordinated the first countywide Black History Month celebrations in Norfolk. Most recently (2020–2021), Tonia has been working with two local theatres on Rewriting Rural Racism, a project that has produced a film and an online play as well as anti-racist workshops for young people, theatre staff and other arts professionals.

About the Authors

Karen Minikin (she/her) has a BA (Hons) in Counselling, MSc Psychotherapy, a Diploma in Supervision (Psychodynamic), and is a UKCP registered teaching and supervising transactional analyst. She is a member of the leadership team at BAATN. She co-facilitates the Mosaic gathering, a regular meeting for therapists of bi/multi heritage. Working with intersectional dynamics around race, gender, class and sexuality is important to her and she positions this within her philosophy, theory and practice on alienation. Karen has a clinical and supervision practice in Wellington, West Somerset. She teaches transactional analysis psychotherapy at the Iron Mill, as well as visiting other teaching venues. She has served for a range of committees with her national organization and is currently a co-editor for the *Transactional Analysis Journal*, as well as associate editor for *Psychotherapy and Politics International*. She specializes in radical and relational approaches in psychotherapy and supervision.

Gita Patel has a BSc in Biological Sciences, a Diploma in Counselling and an MSc in Psychoanalytic Intercultural Psychotherapy from University College London. She is a registered adult and child psychotherapist with UKCP. She started her career as a community worker in London before training as a counsellor and then going on to train as a psychotherapist. Gita was born in the UK to parents who migrated from India in the 1950s. This background has given her a personal perspective on identity and its relationships to race, culture and racism. In 1995, she started working at Nafsiyat Intercultural Therapy Centre as a counsellor, where she was excited and stimulated by the conversations and thinking taking place around race and psychotherapy and the development of new and fresh ideas in the world of intercultural therapy. She was considering further training as a psychotherapist but when she looked at various mainstream training courses, she found them lacking in an understanding of race and culture. Fortunately, she was able to apply for an MSc in Intercultural Psychoanalytic Psychotherapy run by Nafsiyat and UCL, which continued her professional journey towards understanding and developing an intercultural practice.

Lydia Puricelli-Culverwell is a trainee integrative transpersonal psychotherapist, anti-racism consultant, coach, writer, speaker and trainer. She is co-chair of the Students of Colour and Allies network at the Centre for Counselling and Psychotherapy Education.

Wanderley M. Santos is qualified as an intercultural psychodynamic psychotherapist and holds a master's degree in Psychodynamic Psychotherapy from the Tavistock and Portman NHS Foundation Trust, London. He has dedicated more than 20 years to researching how structured racism affects communities and people's wellbeing. He has worked as a psychotherapist in the public sector and has extensive experience in private practice. He has been working as a counsellor at the Student Welfare and Support Service at the University of Oxford. He is a visiting lecturer on race, racism, mental health, transgenerational trauma and subjects relating to diversity at Goldsmiths, University of London. He is a facilitator on the race and wellbeing workshop at Black Learning Achievement and Mental Health UK (BLAM UK). Also, he is a facilitator of the 'In-space', a supportive collective thinking space for students at the Dutch Art Institute Roaming Academy, Arnhem, in the Netherlands. He works as a volunteer in the Casa do Brasil, a Brazilian charity that gives legal, educational and emotional support to Brazilian citizens. He was a co-convener of the course 'To Make a Work-Molecular Revolutions in Brazil' for the Dutch Art Institute Roaming Academy in 2015. Back in Brazil, his home country, Wanderley holds a degree in Psychology and a master's degree in Clinical Psychology (Treatment and Prevention) at the Pontifícia Universidade Católica de São Paulo. The Ford Foundation International Fellowships Program Alumni supported the master's degree. There, he had worked for more than ten years supporting communities in deprived areas to help them to find solutions for the challenges they were facing.

Joel Simpson is a UKCP registered psychotherapist, working in private practice, and an interpersonal group facilitator and trainer. He co-facilitates BAATN's Heart Hub for queer practitioners. With a background in education and non-profit sectors, and a master's degree in Curriculum, Pedagogy and Assessment, Joel has worked in diverse settings in Malawi and across London. Joel maintains interests in how human experiences, and individual and collective healing, may be shaped through shifting, converging identities, histories, power and politics. As a trained civil celebrant, Joel cultivates deepening meaning-making around rites of passage, transitions and celebrations. He crafts love-centred ceremonies for end-of-life thresholds, alongside naming and couples' rituals. Joel's professional commitments sit within a personal heart-centred intention to cultivate a reclaimed voice through listening, leading, writing, teaching and speaking.

About the Authors

Shirani Situnayake is a mixed heritage dual national lesbian, born in Sri Lanka. She has worked for over 20 years as a person-centred counsellor, supervisor, trainer, and equine facilitated psychotherapist (nine years). She is an accredited professional with the National Counselling Society and works in private practice. Shirani's female clients have consistently been predominantly black women and women of colour, both clients and supervisees, and many are survivors of trauma. She is passionate about engaging with diversity and facilitating women to find and amplify their voices. She has developed a robust sense of who she is as a Sri Lankan, her experiences as an immigrant and lesbian often positioning her at the margins of society – a place she has learned to occupy with defiance, that has left her with a stronger sense of herself. Shirani's deep connection with issues of displacement, silencing and self-definition drives the urgency to encourage clients to stand in their truth, be accountable to themselves and to find or recover their own authenticity. Raging at personal and political injustices impels Shirani to fight against this with clients. She believes creativity can be a vital reference to our own cultural imprints and sensibilities as black women and women of colour.

Symone Stephens-Morgan was born in Manchester and embarked on her journey in London from her adolescent years. Having completed a BA (Hons) degree in Printed Textiles and Surface Decoration in 2009, she went on to study the MA Art Psychotherapy course between 2014 and 2017. During her training, she recognized how this medium not only came to support her own and others' wellbeing, but was a particularly important communicative tool surrounding identity and culture. To date, Symone has worked in a range of organizations and has piloted art/creative therapies within the NHS as part of a recovery day programme for adults and with young people identifying as black or other ethnic minorities within a mainstream school setting. This has helped encourage her thinking about the endless benefits that creativity can have for recovery and healing. Symone currently practises privately and in a variety of settings, working with children, young people, families and adults. She identifies as black female and was born in the UK with Afro-Caribbean heritage.

Umaa Thampu Dip Couns. MBACP (Accred) has been working in a diverse mix of professional settings for over ten years. Her background is in social housing and youth charities. She began her path into counselling after being inspired by clients and their counsellors while volunteering at Twenty10, an LGBTIQA charity in Sydney. Her interests are in cross-cultural themes, shamanic, indigenous practices and working creatively to connect the body with nature and awareness. Umaa's passion is enhancing people's wellbeing and helping to cultivate meaning. She values the Gestalt approach as it enables clients to connect to their internal wisdom, amplifying mind–body connection. Umaa is currently in private practice and is a faculty member at the Gestalt Centre of London Counselling Department.

Lennox K. Thomas MA, CQSW, BPC, AFT, UKCP (Fellow) was the first senior probation officer of African Caribbean origin in the UK. He then trained in child development, clinical social work, child and family psychotherapy and psychoanalytic psychotherapy. He was Clinical Director of Nafsiyat Intercultural Therapy Centre and Co-Director of the University College London MSc in Intercultural Psychotherapy. He was also the co-founder and consultant psychotherapist at the Refugee Therapy Centre. Influenced by his work with children and parents in hospitals and probation, he had an interest in attachment and transgenerational family trauma. His teachings in the field of psychotherapy and counselling embraced the consequences and benefits of Eurocentric psychoanalytic psychotherapy and trauma. He advocated for the transformation of the discipline to account for racism, the impact of colonization, war, ethnic cleansing, immigration and assimilation on families and individuals.

Sonya Welch-Mooring is a systemic practitioner and transgenerational therapist. Her early career as a substance misuse counsellor and HIV trainer gave her insight and work experience in a therapeutic environment. She then built a career as an independent trainer, group facilitator and coach in the social and healthcare sector. After completing a Postgraduate Diploma in Systemic Management, she began training in systemic constellations in 2011. She founded Ancestral Constellations in 2016 and has built a therapeutic practice, integrating western systemic thinking and African ancestral traditions. Her work examines the deep scars of transgenerational trauma that remain in many Diaspora communities as a legacy of slavery and colonialism. Sonya has travelled extensively within the Caribbean and Africa on a personal ancestral journey that has contributed to her professional practice. She offers personal consultations and workshops, dividing her time between the UK and Barbados. Currently, she is working on her first commissioned book focused on African ancestral traditions and healing ritual.

Subject Index

Acharyya, Sourangshu 39
adaptations in therapy 46–8
adoption see transracial adoption
adverse childhood experiences
  (ACEs) 200–1
African-centred queerness
  268, 269, 279
'All In: Regularising Ethnic Presence
  in the Curriculum' project 317
Alleyne, Aileen 289
allyship 131
ancestral constellations 281–93
anti-racist practice in training
  black experiences in 320–1
  commitment to 318
  continual learning and
    development 322–3
  current position 312–15
  existence of racism 317–18
  and racial identity 319–20
  trainee understanding 321–2
  validations of race and racism 323–4
Arbery, Ahmaud 206
art therapy
  and BME patients 137, 139–43
  and BME therapists 137–8, 185
  engagement with 139
  'ghettoization' in 185
  and young people 140–1

belonging
  and Breaking the Silence
    conference 226–7

and colonialism 222–4
dilemmas over 227–8
impact of Brexit debate on 220–2
and roots 224–5
of therapists 228
Black, African and Asian Therapy
  Network (BAATN) 11–12, 46,
  66, 115, 120–1, 122, 137, 226
Black bodies
  duty of care 164–5
  living in 161–2
  living true selves 169–71
  macrocosm/microcosm of 63
  politics of 163–4
  and race as social construct 168–9
  self-care of BME therapists 165–7
Black and British: A Forgotten
  History (Olusoga) 321
black empathetic approach 213
Black History Month 67
Black Lives Matter (BLM) 122,
  123, 202, 207, 281, 314
Black Skins White Masks
  (Fanon) 42, 176, 301
Black Therapy Matters 121, 122, 133
BME Voices, Black Trauma
  Conference 213–16
BME therapists
  and art therapy 137–8
  and co-supervision 147–59
  duty of care 164–5
  and embodied-relational-
    emergent awareness 230–1

341

BME therapists *cont.*
and gender 151–6
reaction to 44–6
self-care of 165–7
as supervisors 183–4
training experiences 84–104,
107–18, 119–33, 178–87
with white patients 75–82
Bolle, Namalee 126–7
Breaking the Silence conference 226–7
Brit-ish (Hirsch) 217
Burke, Aggrey 39

Cameron, Gloria 40
cannabis-induced psychosis 39
Carl Rogers Counsels an Individual
on Anger (Rogers) 299
Caste (Wilkerson) 216
category fallacy 245–7
Centre for Counselling and
Psychotherapy Education
(CCPE) 123, 124
character work 256–64
Child of Our Time (TV series) 199
Clark, Kenneth & Mamie 199
collectivist culture 91–2
colour blindness 132–3
community counselling 40
Confer Conference on Post-
Slavery Syndrome 288–9
co-supervision 147–59
cultural competence 304–8
cultural self 250–3
culture
and cultural competence 304–8
and cultural self 250–3
dominant and subdominant 249–50
and institutional policies 247–9

Decolonizing Methodologies. Research
and Indigenous Peoples (Smith) 15
decolonizing therapy
and cultural competence 304–8
and history of racism 296–8
influences on 295

and internalized/injected
oppression 301–4
and intersectionality 295, 298–300
and neoliberalism 295–6
and social trauma 300–1
denials of racism 70–2
Diagnostic and Statistical Manual of
Mental Disorders (DSM) 39, 296
doll tests 47–8, 199
Drama Triangle 98–9
Drapetomania 38, 39, 127
dyadic developmental
psychotherapy (DDP) 198

elders 14
Ellis, Eugene 233
Ellis, Jayakara 233
embodied-relational-emergent
awareness 230–42
envy 42–6
Eros in psychotherapy 267–79

Floyd, George 72, 122, 160, 162, 164,
191, 197, 207, 215, 221, 281, 314

gender 151–6
grief 89–91
groups in training 179–82

Harris, Kamala 214
Hellinger, Bert 283
Helms model 94–5

Imaginary Homelands (Rushdie) 178
individualist culture 91–2
Ingham, Harrington 209
Inner World, The (Kakar) 183
Internal Racism: A Psychoanalytic
Approach to Race and
Difference (Fakhry Davids) 68
internalized/injected oppression 301–4
Interruptions to Contact
framework 211–13
intersectionality 295, 298–300

Johari Window 67–8, 207, 209–10

Kareem, Jafar 39
knowledge process development 14–15

Littlewood, Roland 39
Lipsedge, Maurice 39
Luft, Joseph 209

Mckenzie-Mavinga, Isha 120–1,
166, 207, 208, 213, 289
Mental Health Act (1983) 39, 141, 303
mental health issues
in BME people 38
white Eurocentric view of 14
Munchetty, Naga 216–17
My Grandmother's Hands
(Menakem) 171

Nafsiyat Intercultural Therapy
Centre 38, 40, 41, 46–7, 48
Nafsiyat Intercultural Therapy
model 244, 246–7, 254
names
importance of in therapy 213–19
and Interruptions to Contact
framework 211–13
and Johari Window 209–10
misspelling or forgetting 208–9
and Zinker's Cycle of
Awareness 210–11
Nichols, Edwin 305–7

othering 63–4, 207–8

PACE (Playful, Acceptance, Curiosity
and Empathy) model 198
Post-Traumatic Slave Syndrome 47–8
power within therapy 92–4
prejudice 66–7
pretransference 207–8
projective identification 65–6,
68–9, 76–8, 176–7
proxy self 41, 45, 179, 181,
194–5, 199–200, 253
psychotherapy
Eros in 267–79

Eurocentric models of 182–3
as liberatory force 47
suspicion of 38
training in 178–82

queerness 267–79

Race and Racism in English Secondary
Schools (Joseph-Salisbury) 318
racism
and decolonizing therapy 296–8
definition of 66
denials of 70–2
in mental health services 16–17
and othering 63–4
and prejudice 66–7
psychological trauma of 51–61
reasons for 64
shame felt 65–6
in training 84–104, 122–5, 178–87
as two-way process 62–3
recognition trauma 71–2
resistance to therapy use
and envy 42–6
general reasons for 38–40
reaction to Black therapists 44–6
reluctance to speak 40–2
and shame 42–6
Rutland, Adam 199

self-advocacy 16–17
self-care for BME therapists 165–7
self-disclosure 15–16
self-sabotaging cycle 100–1
shame
and names 209
and racism 65–6
and resistance to therapy use 42–6
Sitting with Discomfort 121, 133
social trauma 300–1
Students of Colour and Allies
(SOCA) network 128
supervision training 178–80, 183–4
symbolic thinking 58–9

Taylor, Breonna 206–7
therapists
  and belonging 228
  reaction to BME therapists 44–6
  self-disclosure 15–16
  training for 41–2 see also
    BME therapists
therapy
  adaptations for BME people 46–8
  decolonizing 294–309
  and Johari Window 67–8
  names in 206–19
  power within 92–4
  racism in 16–17, 37
  and transracial adoption 198–204
  use of by BME people 38
Therapy Today (journal) 207, 210, 314
training for therapists
  anti-racist practice in 312–24
  BME therapist experiences
    107–18, 119–33
  connecting with other BME
    students 120–2, 125–33
  and co-supervision 147–59
  in groups 179–82
  need for 41–2
  racism in 84–104, 122–5, 178–87
  supervision training 178–80, 183–4
transpersonal model 124

transracial adoption
  current practice 196–7
  history of 193–6
  impact of George Floyd killing 191–2
  and racial identity 192–3
  therapeutic considerations 198–204
Turner, Dwight 121, 128
two-way process in racism 62–3

'White Gaze, Black Skin: Binaries of
  Seeing and Being Seen' (Jones) 166
Why I Am No Longer Talking to
  White People About Race
  (Eddo-Lodge) 197, 321
'Why pronouns matter'
  (Baines-Ball) 210
'Why we need to talk about
  race' (Jackson) 207
Winston, Robert 199

'You're a white therapist: have
  you noticed?' (Lago) 43

Zengeni, Florence 14
Zinker's Cycle of Awareness 207, 210–11

Author Index

Ababio, B. 244, 245, 249
Abbot, J. 296
Ablack, C.J. 231
Achbar, M. 296
Adams, T. 269
Agoro, O. 199, 249
Ahmed, R. 217
Akbar, N. 295
Allen–Green, R. 314
Alleyne, A. 39, 91
Allport, G. 77
Altman, N. 47, 77
American Psychiatric Association
    (AMA) 39, 296
Andreou, C. 195, 202
Archidong, U. 63
Arnold, E. 15

Baines-Ball, L. 210
Bakan, J. 296
Baldwin, J. 215
Banks, N. 200
Banton, N. 192
Barber, V. 137, 142
Barrett Lennard, G.T. 96
Beam, J. 268
Benjamin, J. 223, 271
Bhugra, D. 42
Bhui, K. 42
Bion, W.R. 77
Black, African and Asian Therapy
    Network 115, 208
Black, K. 166, 168

Bly, R. 270
Bollas, C. 168
Bowlby, J. 192, 270, 277
Boyd-Franklin, N. 15, 16, 47
Bremner, R.H. 193
Brenman, E. 79
Brewster, F. 121, 270, 271
British Association of Adoption
    and Fostering 196
British Association for Counselling and
    Psychotherapy (BACP) 314, 315, 317
Brittain, A. 66
Britton, R. 80
Brodzinsky, D.M. 196, 197
Brooks, F. 109
Brown, W. 295
Burch, K.T. 268
Butler, P.
Burke Harris, N. 200

Caldwell, C. 182
Campbell, J. 72, 137, 142
Carberry, K. 14, 16, 17
Carter, R.T. 38, 45
Cartwright, S.A. 38
Case, C. 65–6
Casement, P. 162
Chauhan, C. 317
Chodorow, J. 232, 242
Cixous, H. 63, 64
Clark, K.B. 47
Clark, M.P. 47
Clarke, S. 77

Clement, C. 63, 64
Cliff, M. 258
Coard, B. 17, 42
Collins, P.H. 298
Cousins, S. 202
Covington, C. 275
Crawley, J. 69
Crenshaw, K. 91, 295, 298

DaFonseca, A.M.D. 300
Dalal, F. 66
Daneshpour, M. 14, 15
Darr, A. 63
David, E. 302
Davids, F. 77
Davis, A. 298
DeGruy, J. 47, 300
Dell, N. 299
Department for Education 195
DiAngelo, R. 116, 184, 199, 201
Dokter, D. 183
Dominelli, L. 295
Dubois, W.E. 215
Duran, E. 300, 304

E-Village News 288
Eddo-Lodge, R. 111, 197, 198, 202
Eichenbaum, L. 295
Ellis, C. 269
Ellis, E. 170, 234, 242
Ellis, J. B. 227
Erikson, B. 270

Facemire, V.C. 300
Fakhry Davids, M. 63, 68–9
Fanon, F. 42, 62–3, 65, 164, 176, 249, 301
Fletchman-Smith, B. 43
Frank, A. 269
Freshwater, D. 273
Freud, S. 64, 79, 271

Garland, C. 58
Gendlin, E.T. 238
Geuter, U. 240
Gilbert, J. 304

Golding, K.S. 192
Görgens, T. 302
Gramsci, A. 301
Grant, J. 69
Green, M. 169
Gungor, D. 250
Guzder, J. 38, 40
Guzzetti, J. 14

Hall, S. 322
Hanks, H. 230
Harrison, G. 43
Haugh, S. 113
Haule, J.R. 268, 272, 277, 278
Hermes, P. 100
Hervey, D.W. 295
Hickling, F. 43
Higginbottom, L. 47
Hillman, J. 278
Hinshelwood, R. 79
Hirsch, A. 217
Hollis, J. 270
Holman Jones, S. 269
Holmes, C. 300
hooks, b. 302, 303, 319, 324
Hopper, E. 55
Hopson, D. 48
Hopson, D. 48
Hudson, J. 192
Hughes, D.A. 192, 194, 198

Imber-Black, E. 15
Ira, P. 303

Jackson, C. 207
Jacobs, L. 234
Johnson, E. 237
Johnson, R. 182
Jones, A. 166, 167, 168, 170
Joseph-Salisbury, R. 318
Josephs, L. 79

Kafka, F. 53
Kakar, S. 48, 175, 182–3
Kalmanowitz, D. 192

Author Index

Kareem, J. 44, 46, 247, 248, 295
Karlsen, S. 297
Karpman, S. 98
Kavaler-Adler, S. 272
Keating, F. 303
Keval, N. 56, 60, 77
Khalid, S. 43
Khan, O. 197
Khasnavis, R. 183
Kincel, A. 237, 240
Kirmayer, L.J. 246
Klein, M. 68, 76, 77, 270, 271
Kleinman, A. 244, 246
Kraepelin, E. 246
Krause, I. 249
Krishna, M. 38, 40

Lago, C. 43, 92, 115, 117, 121
Leighton, L. 182
Levine, P.A. 180
Lewin, Y.T. 232
Littlewood, R. 44, 46, 244,
    245, 247, 249, 295
Lloyd, B. 192
Lopez, G. 320
Lorde, A. 111, 298
Lowe, F. 40, 271
Luft, J. 67

Mackewn, J. 211
Macpherson, W. 249
Madzimoyo, W. 301
Mahmood, F. 218
Majors, R. 14, 16
Mann, D. 272, 275
Martin-Baro, I. 295
Maslow, A.H. 274
Mathers, D. 271
Maynard, M. 66
McGuire, W. 271
McIntosh, P. 115, 202
McKenzie, K. 39, 43
Mckenzie-Mavinga, I. 41–2, 71–2, 89,
    97, 108, 110, 115, 116, 117, 121, 165,
    169, 180, 249, 284, 289, 299–300

McLeod, J. 109, 117
Mearns, D. 109, 115, 116
Menakem, R. 161, 170, 171, 237, 292
Mental Health Foundation 141
Mercury Policy Project 301
Miller, A. 79
Mimms, S. 47
Minas, H. 246
Moorhead, J. 217
Moorhouse, S. 46
Moreland-Capuia, A. 15
Moreno, J.L. 175
Morgan, H. 43
Morris, N. 136

Narey, M. 197
National Association of Black
    Social Workers 193
Nazrro, J.Y. 297
Neale Hurston, Z. 212
New Oxford Dictionary of English 66
Newnes, C. 14
Nichols, E.J. 304

Office for National Statistics 313
Ogden, T.H. 278
Okri, B. 323
Open University 89
Orbach, S. 273, 295
Oxfam 296

Patel, R. 14
Paul, S. 113
Pauly Morgan, K. 299
PND 296
Porges, S.W. 186

Race Relations Act (1976) 66
Rankine, C. 191
Ransaw, T. 14
Reid, O.G. 47
Ridley, C.R. 67, 68
Roach, F. 37
Roazen, P. 275
Robertson, E. 268, 273

Rogers, C. 86, 92, 96, 115, 116, 299, 313, 323
Roland, A. 250
Rose, E. 41, 249, 251
Rosner, S. 100
Rowan, J. 274
Roy, A. 192
Ruffin, A. 214
Runyan, A.S. 298
Rushdie, S. 178
Russman, T. 15
Ryde, J. 121

Sampson, E.E. 63, 64, 71
Samuels, A. 270
Sargent, S. 193
Sartre, J.P. 65
Sawyerr, A. 41
Schaverien, J. 69, 70
Schwartz-Salant, N. 273
Sedgwick, D. 272
Selassie, S. 304
Shaw, D. 223
Sigalas, A. 249
Sigodo, M. 14
Simpson, J. 269
Smedley, A. 192
Smedley, B.D. 192
Smith, F. 270
Smith, L.T. 15
Smith, B. 115
Speight, S.L. 249
Stauffer, K.A. 175, 177
Steiner, C. 226
Stern, D. 198
Sue, D.W. 178, 304
Sugarman, J. 295

Tan, R. 77
Tatum, B. 94, 95
Thomas, L.K. 41, 43, 44, 179, 194, 249, 253

Thomas, T. 16
Thorne, B. 109
Thompson, J. 92, 117
Totton, N. 235
Turner, D. 213, 214, 298
Tudor, L.E. 108

UK Council for Psychotherapy (UKCP) 317
United Nations Convention on the Rights of the Child 195
Uwahemu, A. 41

van der Kolk, B. 194
Vetere, A. 230

Wallace, M. 302
Watermeyer, B. 302
Watson, V. 117
Watts-Jones, D. 299
Weller, F. 270
Welles, J.K. 272
Wilderson III, F. 77
Wilkerson, I. 215
Wilson, A.N. 48
Wilson Gilmore, R. 297
Winnicott, D.W. 76, 194, 270, 271, 278
Woods-Giscombe, R. 303
Woollsey, S. 14
World Bank 296
World Health Organization 296
Wrye, H.K. 272

Yi, Y. 79
Young, S. 276